SHOTGUN DIGEST

By Robert Stack

Edited by Jack Lewis

Digest Books, Inc., Northfield, Illinois

EDITORIAL DIRECTOR
BOB SPRINGER

RESEARCH EDITOR
DEAN A. GRENNELL

ART DIRECTOR
ANDY GRENNELL

STAFF ARTISTS
PAT HOPPER
AL MORA
MICHELE BARBER
DIANE DEROSBY

PRODUCTION COORDINATOR
JUDY K. RADER

PRODUCTION ASSISTANT
WENDY LEE WISEHART

QUALITY CONTROL
DONNA SUE STORY

ASSOCIATE PUBLISHER
SHELDON FACTOR

Produced by

Charger Productions

CONTENTS

Dedication

SEVERAL YEARS AGO, while we were filming a segment of The American Sportsman in Africa, I was sitting in our camp one evening cleaning a shotgun after a day of grouse shooting. For no particular reason, the memory of Clark Gable popped into my head and acute nostalgia set in. Gable had always planned to make a safari to the so-called Dark Continent, but it was one of those wants — one of the few, in his case — that he never got around to fulfilling before his untimely death.

When I was just a kid, we shot a number of times on the skeet range at the old Los Angeles-Santa Monica Gun Club. That was back in the days when Harry Fleischman was trying to teach me to shoot the game. It was new to this country, sort of like a new adventure, and most of the top men in the movie colony were hooked on skeet.

Clark Gable probably led the fullest life of anyone I know. By the time he was forty, he had done just about anything and everything he wanted to do. He was a better than average wildfowl shot, as I found out while hunting with him, but there was another quality about him that I admire. He wasn't a do-or-die competitor. In short, he didn't have to prove he was a man; he was one and everyone knew it. Probably the best way of explaining his attitude toward shooting was the fact that he had the ability to go out with a few friends, to enjoy shooting and to savor the fun and the companionship. This was much more important to him than the number of ducks he shot. He could miss a shot and laugh about it rather than break the gun over his knee in a rage.

I was spending a summer at Lake Tahoe in Northern California, when I was introduced to Carole Lombard, the future Mrs. Gable. Until then, she had been pretty much the glamour girl, always being called upon to pose in slinky gowns and portray the ultra-feminine type. But she also realized that Gable was an outdoorsman and that if she wasn't going to be left sitting at home, she was going to have to shoot.

We had a portable trap which I would set up on the edge of the lake, the area being much less heavily populated then than now. It was with this that I taught her to shoot, although I was only about twelve at the time. After her marriage to Gable, she had little trouble in keeping pace with him in that department. Not only did she learn to shoot well, but it was a sport she found she enjoyed almost as much as did her husband.

But to give some idea of Gable's attitude toward shooting, Carole often whipped him on bird hunts. In fact, I received a telegram from her after one of their early shoots telling me that she had downed more birds than he.

Instead of resenting this fact, as might be the case with many a husband, Gable thought it was humorous. In fact, he would often brag to his fellow hunters about his wife's deadeye abilities.

It's tough to say whether Clark Gable ever could have developed into a championship skeet or trap shooter had he really worked at it and trained for such competition, and it's one of those questions that will probably always have to go unanswered.

Actually, I feel that the question is unimportant. What is paramount is the fact that shooting was a sport he thoroughly enjoyed. At one time, he, Barron Hilton and Ray Holmes, a Los Angeles contractor who was the actor's constant shooting companion, started their own duck club at Venice Island in the Stockton River in Northern California. I can't think of any place in the country where one could find the number of ducks that populated that particular area in those days, and even today, it's probably the greatest shooting spot on the North American continent.

It was there that one could find Gable whenever he wasn't working. In fact, he arranged his film schedules so that there would be no interference with his duck hunting. He's the only actor I know who had a clause written into his contract allowing him duck season free. He and that old Parker double of his were a team and when they were together in a duck blind, the rest of the world didn't really matter to him.

As a matter of interest, the duck club is still there and in a glass case is a partially full bottle of twenty-one-year-old Scotch and an empty glass. It was from this bottle and glass that Clark Gable had his last drink at the place shortly before his death.

There was a humility about the man, too, that one seldom finds. For example, we were in Colusa, California, one day, buying some rubber boots before heading for the duck ponds at my place. Gable was immediately recognized and surrounded by autograph seekers. He quietly signed the autographs as requested, joked with his fans for a few moments, then rejoined us where we were waiting at the car. The first thing he did was to apologize to the rest of us for holding us up in getting started with the shooting.

Gable's love of shooting and hunting, I feel, is one of the things that made him great. His joy at being able to join others in a duck blind, expecting no favors and following the unwritten rules governing gunmanship in the field, only added to my belief that he had a feeling of real humility which one finds in the true sportsman.

And that night, as I sat beside a campfire in the African wilds, staring down at the glint on the metal of the gun I had been cleaning, I thought of the great shooting we had experienced that day.

I couldn't help feeling a little sad that here was the one thing Gable had always wanted to do but had never accomplished before his death.

Then, as I sat staring into the dying embers of the fire, I had another thought, less sad. Wasn't it possible that he really was there with Joe Foss, myself and the others making up the safari?

I'd like to think so.

Bel Aire, California

Robert Stack

The Author

ROBERT STACK is internationally known as an actor, having won television's top award, the Emmy, for his portrayal of Elliott Ness in "The Untouchables." He also has been nominated for the highly prized Academy Award for theatrical motion pictures. His occasional stage performances also have brought better than respectable reviews.

However, the same Robert Stack was considered something of a boy wonder in shotgunning circles of the mid-Thirties. According to Jimmy Robinson, longtime sage of claybird shooting, it was young Bob Stack, a 16-year-old polo player turned shotgunner, who was one of the standouts of the first National Skeet Championships held in Cleveland, Ohio, in August, 1935. There were 167 shooters from twenty-six states. Stack ended up in second place in Junior competition that year behind 16-year-old Max Marcum, after a shoot-off with Billy Clayton, Stack powdering 24 of his 25 birds. The following year, Stack won the 20-gauge title at St. Louis.

When Jimmy Robinson picked his first All-American Skeet Team in 1935, Stack was listed as a member. He also was on the 1936 and 1937 All-American teams and several years ago was named to the National Skeet Shooting Association's Hall of Fame.

Over the years, Stack has put his claybird expertise to practice in the field and is considered an outstanding waterfowl shot. During World War II, largely because of his shotgunning experience and prowess, he was commissioned in the United States Navy and assigned to a marksmanship training unit, teaching shotgunning and machine gunnery to Naval aviators.

In spite of his busy schedule in films and television, Robert Stack has continued to compete in shotgun events on the West Coast, helping to fill his already overladen den with additional trophies.

Chapter 1

IN THE BEGINNING . . .

American Shotgun Development Is
A Reflection Of Need In Given Situations

ONE DOESN'T HAVE to know how the shotgun was invented to be able to shoot it, but this being the era of nostalgia or in the hope that anyone who picks up this book might be as interested in the background as I, it becomes rather difficult to talk about shotguns without at least giving some of the background.

The shotgun would appear to be almost as old as gunpowder, itself, so to keep from repeating great segments of history that experts already have committed to paper, I prefer to consider the shotgun in America, how it originated and under what circumstances.

As seems obvious, in the early days of settlement on the North American continent, the colonists were dependent upon their mother countries in Europe for firearms of all kinds. While the Europeans at home were able to obtain fine shotguns such as the double-barrel Miquelet, the colonists seemed to have been given the leftovers from the firearms industry, many of the guns used in this country being concocted from parts that were shipped here, then matched and assembled.

One must keep in mind that even the arms with which the colonists killed their game usually were smoothbore flintlocks and that they could fire a single ball, buckshot, smaller shot or a combination of all of these. During the Revolutionary War, for example, it became the fashion to load several buckshot behind the main ball in the muzzleloader. Thus, should the shooter miss the enemy in battle, or his deer in the hunting fields, he still had an opportunity to score with the smaller but nonetheless lethal shot.

In the development of firearms, inventors — and shoot-ers — went through a series of growths and improvements starting with the matchlock, which utilized a piece of rope-like material termed the match. This often was kept burning and, when the trigger was pulled and this smouldering match dropped into the powder, there was the required explosion. The wheellock came along to rotate a grooved wheel against a lump of iron pyrites, thus creating a shower of sparks to ignite the priming powder. The greatest problem with such firearms was the lack of speed in which they could be fired successively.

The next step in evolution of the gunlock was the snap-haunce, which slammed a flint down upon a striker to create the sparks and ignite the powder. Then came the earlier mentioned Miquelet lock which was invented in Spain and used on early shotguns, most of them in double-barrel configuration. This innovation has a large spring mounted outside of the lock plate, whereas earlier types had the spring mounted inside.

In that early era, steels left a great deal to be desired and the spring on the Miquelet was so large that it would have required cutting away much of the stock of the wood, weakening it, to incorporate it inside the gun. It was successful enough that this particular type of lock was in use for a couple of hundred years.

The next step in development of the shotgun — or any other gun, for that matter — involved the flintlock. One Marin LeBourgeoys, who operated a gunshop — also making crossbows and flutes — in France is credited with this invention.

The flintlock, like many inventions, actually was an

Though we tend to think of the pioneer long-guns in terms of the Kentucky rifle — usually made in Pennsylvania — many were smoothbores, or muskets. These offered considerable versatility, since they could fire a single large ball, of about bore diameter, or a quantity of smaller balls, shot pellets and like. A favorite load was "buck and ball," one large ball, plus a quantity of smaller round projectiles.

R. O. Ackerman

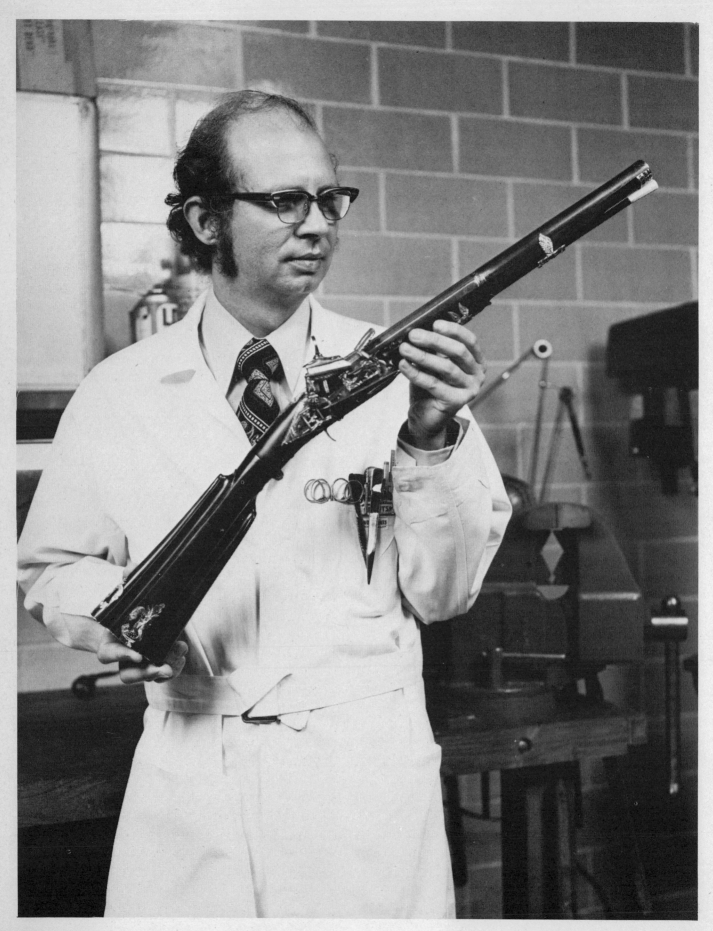

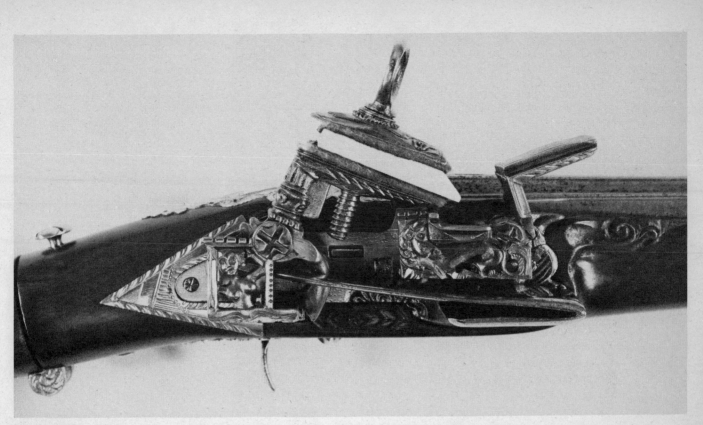

Opposite page, Keith Strawn, curator of the North Carolina Museum of History, holds a rare, one-of-a-kind Seventeenth Century Miquelet fowling piece, recently added to the museum's collection. Its single barrel is about the inner diameter of the modern 10 gauge. Photo above gives a closer look at the action. Stock is cherry wood, inlays of ivory and 8-k gold.

improvement on older systems. It combined the frizzen and one-piece hand cover of the Miquelet with the inside mainspring utilized on the earlier snaphance. A new sear system operated on the tumbler. Most of the early flintlocks were incorporated in military arms, moving to the civilian market later.

Various parts, such as the frizzen and hammer, were hand-forged, requiring more sophistication than many of the colonial blacksmith shops had at hand; therefore, it was easier to import them from Europe than to make them in the backwoods smithies of this country. This also explains why many valued collector pieces have American-made showing in their design and most of the materials, but the lock mechanism is European.

Through the Revolutionary War, most of the arms used by the colonials were of European manufacture. In fact, after the defeat of the British and their withdrawal, it was a French flintlock — a design more than twenty years old — that the tiny United States of America put into production as its first American-made military rifle. Made at Springfield, Massachusetts, it became known as the Springfield U.S. Model 1795.

Derived from this and other designs, including some by Eliphalet Remington, founder of the Remington Arms Company, American gunmakers ultimately moved into the shotgun field, building flintlock fowling pieces.

These guns were cumbersome, inefficient and often taller than their shooters! While today's shotguns are considered lengthy and good only for goose-getting, if they have thirty-inch tubes, some of these monsters had fifty-inch barrels.

As these guns had cylinder barrels with no choke, the theory among shooters of the day was that a longer barrel would give a tighter shot pattern, as well as more velocity. In the language of the day, they were supposed to "shoot harder." Tests have shown, however, that the excessive length made the guns heavy, hard to handle and almost impossible to use in serious wing shooting.

In keeping with the theory, however, there were some plus factors. The black powder made in the United States in that day usually was of poor quality. Even today, if one overloads a black powder muzzleloader of almost any kind and fires over a blanket of snow, he will find unburned powder spread out in a fan-shaped pattern in front of the muzzle of his gun, blackening the white surface. A longer barrel tends to allow more time in which the powder can be ignited and burned properly. At the other extreme, shot of the period also was less than uniform. As it battered its way down the long barrel tube, the shot tended to become badly deformed, which often resulted in poor shot patterns.

Double-barrel flintlocks first appeared, so far as we know, on the Continent and were considered sporting arms, whereas shotguns on the American shore were a tool of survival. It was the custom of the wealthy of the time to take their doubles afield with several servants to act as loaders and beaters, making a day of it on preserves that were carefully managed.

One of the great problems with guns of that time had to do with the delay between pulling the trigger, lighting of the primer powder and explosion of the actual powder load, not to mention the time it took for the shot to travel the length of the long barrel, becoming more deformed with each inch it ricocheted its way down that tube. As a result, wing shooting was considered something of a novelty. In time, all of this led to improved gun designs and, in the end, better shooting and better shots.

Most of the flintlock doubles that appeared in America were of European make — primarily English. One explanation for this is that, by the time American gunmakers had mastered the art of making such guns, they already were being replaced by percussion guns.

While over/under shotguns of the modern day are generally credited to the genius of John M. Browning, there were flintlock models that carried superimposed barrels. A number of these are being reproduced today and have found favor with black powder enthusiasts both as shotguns and as rifles. Black powder shooting by modern hunters and marksmen will be discussed at some length in a following chapter.

Throughout the Eighteenth Century and well into the next century, shotguns — especially double guns — were expensive. Making shotgun barrels, with their thin shell of metal, was an expensive proposition. With double guns, the problem was even more difficult, because it was necessary to join the two barrels together and, even when great care was taken, the heat and other facets of workmanship could cause one of the barrels to bend slightly, altering its accuracy potential. Also, in an effort to keep down the weight, the bores usually were small, which in turn didn't offer much in the way of shot load or patterning.

Some twenty years prior to the Civil War, gun inventors were experimenting with percussion arms, even investigating the possibilities of breechloaders. There is a theory that most important developments in medicine, technology — and arms — are made in time of war and it would appear that this was the case, to some degree, at least, insofar as the so-called War Between the States is concerned.

But in the period before the introduction of the repeating rifle actions such as the Spencer and Henry, using metallic ammunition, the percussion cap became a way of life for soldier and civilian alike. The flintlock continued as a tool for years on the frontier, however, where powder and ball could be made, but percussion caps could be difficult to obtain.

An Englishman, Joshua Shaw, probably should be given credit for having invented the percussion cap in about 1816. He came to the United States in 1817 and, because of technicalities in the law, did not obtain a patent until 1822. Even then, it appears, the patent was incomplete, because he failed to supply required models and working drawings.

The legendary blunderbuss gets its name from the Dutch "donderbus," meaning thunder box. The flaring muzzle was intended to aid in pouring in the projectiles, which could be almost anything that would smart when it hit. Accuracy with the large, unrifled bore, was quite sketchy, and this, in turn, made it desirable to use multiple missiles.

Wheellock carries a date of 1704. This example is in amazingly good condition, except that the key for winding the clockwork-like mainspring is missing. Note the elaborate hunting scene.

Here's a closer look at the flintlock firing mechanism of the English blunderbuss shown on the previous page. Dated 1815 on the side of the lock plate, it carries a price tag of $900 in the showroom of Elz-Fargo, a Santa Ana, California, firm dealing in antique firearms.

In 1818, a French patent on a similar device was registered, but the noted English gunmaker, Joseph Manton, is credited with being the first to introduce a percussion shotgun. He worked with Colonel Hawker, a writer of the day who concentrated on sport shooting. Between the two of them, they developed the gun mechanism, which created a good deal of dispute and even problems.

All that was necessary in the Manton design was to weld a heavy boss to the barrel with a horizontal touchhole, then a vertical hole was drilled and tapped to hold the nipple. The theory — still followed in modern reproductions — was that the nipples should have a double conical hole something like an hourglass, but less defined. This would concentrate the flame so that there would be rapid ignition. The problem lay in the fact that, while there was supposed to be less gas leakage than with the flintlock, some manufacturers made their caps too thin. The shattering of the copper re-

A flintlock shotgun, of the single-barrel pattern, with a chip of flint held in the cocking piece by means of a strip of leather. Charge of priming powder is in the pan, protected by the closed frizzen cover, ready for firing.

As the trigger is pulled, the cocking piece snaps forward, scraping the flint downward against the steel frizzen to produce a shower of sparks. At the same time, the pan is being uncovered, directing the sparks into the powder.

Third and final stage of the flintlock firing cycle shows frizzen knocked forward. The touch hole, through which the flame of burning powder goes into the main charge, can be seen here. Note the striated appearance of the Damascus barrel, typical of the era.

sulted in some serious eye injuries. Actually, the cap was supposed to expand under pressure of the explosion, falling off the nipple as the hammer was cocked again.

The percussion cap first was of pewter, but it soon was found that copper was a better material. It is a small cup with a slightly flanged rim. In its construction, detonating powder — usually fulminate of mercury — is placed in the bottom of the cup, being held in place by a small disk of paper covered with a thin coating of shellac. With the shellac acting as a seal, this ended the problems of wet detonating powder that had plagued shooters of flintlocks and earlier arms for several centuries.

The cap was placed over the nipple, then pinched on at the flanged rim to hold it in place. Then, when the hammer fell, the fulminate exploded, driving flame through the

Awesome dimensions of the gaping maw of the blunderbuss shown three pages previously can be judged in comparison to the dime in this view.

And — speaking of awesome — speculate upon the fun of firing this monster! Often termed a "punt-gun," the pin above the trigger was inserted in a socket in the gunwale of a skiff to help soak up the recoil. Favored by the early market-hunters, these often were taller than the shooter.

15

Spencer, above, was one of the earliest examples of the repeating pump shotgun. Left, traditional "rabbit-ear" hammer on an early double-barrel, percussion shotgun.

nipple hole and into the chamber where the main powder load lay.

The first percussion double barrels in America probably were of English manufacture. By this time, the barrelmaking technique for shotguns also had been simplified with the so-called Damascus barrel. With the technique used, steel rods were heated and twisted and forge-welded in a spiral formation, literally wrapping the rods to form a hollow tube. After this first step, the inner walls of the bore had to be reamed out, then the outside finished as well. The theory was that by finishing both inner and outer surfaces, one ended up with a thin-walled tube that helped to hold down the weight of the overall shotgun.

Such barrels were more than adequate for black powder and there still are many such guns available — mostly as

A close look at the name stamped on the barrel of the gun on the opposite page shows typical Damascus pattern.

An early breechloader, with the under-barrel locking lever and the usual exposed, rabbit-ear dual hammers.

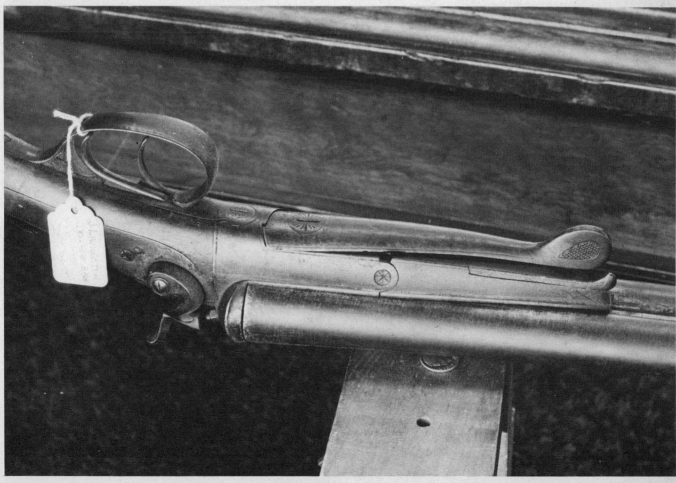

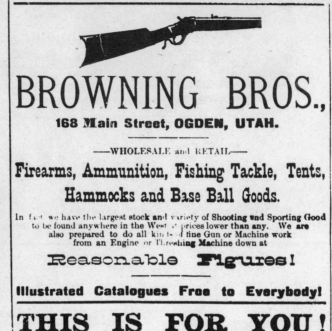
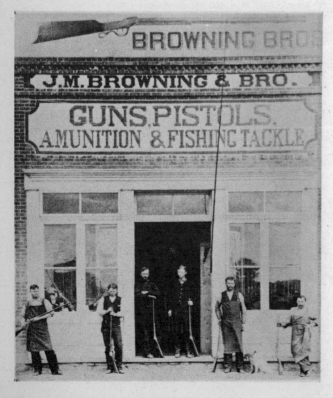

In 1887, Browning ad appeared prominently on the front page of the newspaper, flanked by entries indicating the importance of firearms in those turbulent frontier days. Left, the staff of the Browning shop take time out to pose and display the firm's wares. From left, Sam Browning, George Browning, John M. Browning, Matthew S. Browning, Ed Browning and Frank Rushton. Taken about 1882 in Utah.

collector items — today. But one should be cautioned against firing anything but black powder in them. In fact, in view of the age of such arms, it would be wise to have any gun with Damascus barrels checked by a good gunsmith for the safety factors before even taking up charcoal shooting with it. The barrels, incidentally, invariably are marked as being of Damascus steel. If not, hold the gun in the light and you usually can see the spiral-like pattern of the metal, where the rods originally were welded together. Treat such guns with care, as they usually are worth more on the collector market than as a modern shotgun!

18

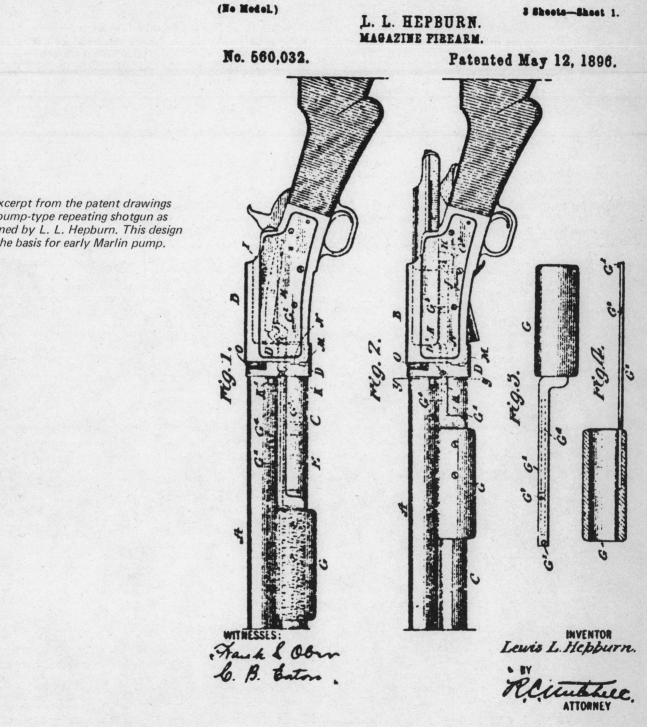

(No Model.)

L. L. HEPBURN.
MAGAZINE FIREARM.

No. 560,032.

3 Sheets—Sheet 1.

Patented May 12, 1896.

An excerpt from the patent drawings of a pump-type repeating shotgun as designed by L. L. Hepburn. This design was the basis for early Marlin pump.

Fig.1.

Fig.2.

Fig.3.

Fig.4.

WITNESSES:

Frank S Ober

C. B. Eaton.

INVENTOR
Lewis L. Hepburn.

BY
R. C. Mitchell
ATTORNEY

Remington Arms was among the first to come up with a native-made percussion double gun, manufacturing the same model for about forty years, until 1880. The same manufacture began making combination guns, featuring a smoothbore shotgun barrel beneath a .45 rifled barrel. Included for obvious reasons was a front sight and a rear peep sight. Considering the fact that the gun was designed for the frontier, it gave its owner a hunting capability that covered almost every game specie at that time.

As mentioned earlier, however, the Civil War brought about development of the breechloading arm. Lever-action rifles were the first repeaters and it was natural that the lever-action shotgun should follow. It was the Spencer rifle that introduced this area and this firm built more than 100,000 lever-action carbines and rifles starting in 1862, to become the most successful rifle of the Civil War. Oddly, Winchester, still a maker of lever-action rifles, was the first to try the action on a shotgun, which never proved especially popular. At the same time, Spencer was taking another step forward by coming up with the first slide-action or pump shotgun. Built in the mid-1880s, the Spencer slide-action introduced another dimension to American shotgun making.

During the latter half of the last century, many firms —

The "Four B" trap squad won considerable renown at live bird shooting in the early days of the Utah Territory. Here, from left, G. L. Becker, holding a Winchester Model 1887 lever-action shotgun; John M. Browning, with a Model 1897 Winchester pump; A. P. Bigelow, with a side-by-side double and Matthew S. Browning (John's brother) with M'97. Both of the two patterns of Winchester repeating shotguns in this photograph were designed for Winchester by Browning.

some of them still in existence — began to make shotguns, as this had become a way of life for Americans to put meat on the family table. Every farm family had a shotgun of one kind or another behind the kitchen door.

As early as 1865, the Parker Brothers began making a breechloading hammer gun that had an under-lever to control the action. They came up with their first double-barrel hammerless gun in 1889. At least one of the classic Parker designs still is being manufactured by Marlin, which now owns the rights and the company name.

The Ithaca Gun Company, now a part of an outdoors-oriented conglomerate, was founded in 1873, beginning to make double-barrel, hammer-type shotguns a few years later. There were dozens of others, many of them since absorbed by companies that still use the original names such as Fox, Stevens and others on some of their models.

The freedom of money for development in time of war has much to do with all sorts of advancements and the development of the so-called automatic shotgun can be credited to the fact that, with Hiram Maxim's invention of the fully automatic machine gun in 1885, the need for similar design spread to other facets of the gun industry.

By the mid-1880s, what then was the Winchester Repeating Arms Company was probably in the best financial

The third and final prototype of Browning's autoloading shotgun, dating from 1901. This design, hailed as one of his greatest triumphs, severed his relationship with the Winchester factory. At first, it was produced for Browning in Belgium. Later, Remington was licensed to make it in the USA, in which form it was called their Model 11.

Designed by Browning in 1885, this lever-action design was sold to Winchester, being introduced as their Model 1887. Made in 12 and 10 gauges, it carried four shells in the magazine plus a fifth in chamber.

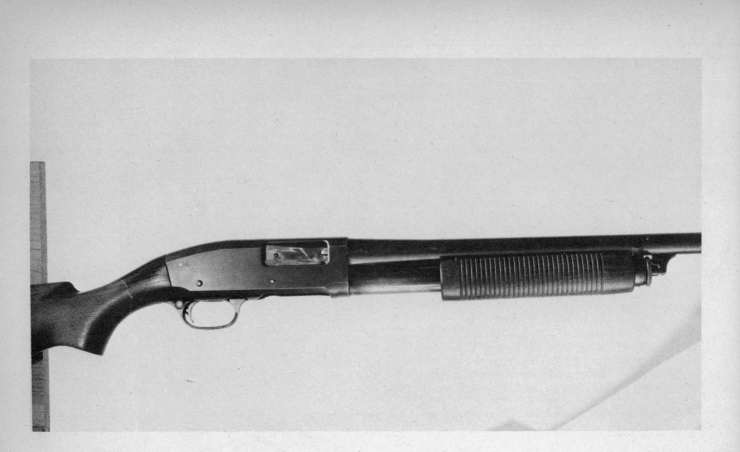

The beloved old Remington Model 31 "Cornsheller," a legend in its own time and down to the present. Famed for its smooth action and tough durability, the M31 was not put back into production after WW-II, being replaced by Remington's Model 870 pump design.

position of any and, at that time, even owned a part of the Remington firm. Winchester had an agreement with the earlier mentioned John M. Browning to purchase all of his shotgun and rifle designs. Browning, a true design genius, had new designs each year and the Connecticut firm purchased them all outright, whether they intended to place them into production or not.

It was in the 1890s that Browning came out with his first autoloading shotgun design for Winchester. At that time, he was dealing with a difficult problem, as the black powder used in shotshells fouled the action after only a few shots. Also, shotshells were dreadfully underpowered in comparision with center-fire rifle cartridges.

Browning decided on what he called a long-recoil action,

with the bolt locked to the barrel extension and barrel with a vertically sliding lock. A barrel ring encircled the magazine tube to drive a friction brake rearward against the return spring. Gas pressure drove the shot and wads forward at about 1100 fps, while the barrel, barrel extension and bolt assembly were sent rearward. After rebounding off the rear wall of the receiver, the barrel and the barrel extension moved forward, while the bolt remained in the rear position, having been unlocked from the barrel extension. With the shell ejected, movement of a new shell being fed in from the complicated magazine system released the bolt, which was driven forward by another spring installed in the buttstock.

This is a greatly simplified explanation of what required

endless hours of thought and experimentation by John Browning and became the pattern for most recoil-operated autoloading shotguns for the next sixty years or so.

This concept was patented in 1899 and immediately ran into difficulties, as there seemed to be some infringement on a patent of 1896 held by another noted gun designer, Hugo Borchardt. However, Browning went back to his drawing board and came up with a new system of linkages that circumvented the Borchardt patent.

Many other designs of autoloading shotguns have appeared since those early days. They can be subdivided into two categories: gas-operated and recoil-operated and the latter, in turn, breaks down into short-recoil and long-recoil systems. The gas-operated principle has come to be somewhat more popular, since it will handle almost any load without need for adjusting the friction bands, as on the recoil designs. In point of fact, the basic principles of harnessing both recoil and gas pressure to operate the mechanism of a repeating firearm were conceived by Sir Hiram Stevens Maxim for use in the machine gun and were adapted for use in shotguns by contemporary inventors such as John M. Browning.

Two early pump shotguns from Marlin; the Model 17 (top) is unusual in having a straight stock while the Model 30 has the pistol grip that is the overwhelming choice of U.S. shotgunners.

CHOOSING A SHOTGUN

With Numerous Styles And Capabilities, One Must Know His Type Of Shooting!

Chapter 2

SUGGESTING TO ANY shooter the type of shotgun he should use is a bit like telling him what type of girl he should marry. It is a matter of individual selection that is better left to the sportsman.

I've been through this myself on too many occasions, falling in love with a particular shotgun for the sake of appearance, then discovering that neither beauty nor price makes it shoot all that much better for my particular style.

A prime example is a rather valuable Purdey side-by-side that my father left me. It is a beautiful piece of shooting machinery, but I never have made it perform to the built-in capabilities I know it possesses. It was one of my Dad's favorite guns during his lifetime and performed wonderfully in his hands. When I found that I couldn't handle it with any great success, I had it restocked with the idea that it would fit me better and I should be able to shoot it. After that, I installed a Hydrocoil, had a Miller single trigger put into it, then shocked the purists by having a rib installed on this old classic.

But that was not the cure: if I did shoot a bit better, the improvement was a long way from score-shaking. There may have been some psychological factor involved, but it was a good deal less involved to shoot a gun that I could handle than to go through psychiatric analysis to determine why I couldn't shoot this one.

But in this day, there should be a shotgun to suit just about every need that the individual is likely to have. For instance, in the live pigeon shoots I have seen in Europe, the real pros — the money shooters who thrive and even live on such stiff competition where $1000 can rest on one bird — invariably seem old-fashioned, if you judge them by their armament. Most seem to favor the older models with side-by-side barrels and some with hammers that must be cocked individually.

This, however, is simply a safeguard when the chips are down for big money. When those hammers are back, they know that each barrel is ready to fire. Since they invariably fire guns with twin triggers, if one barrel has been shot, they know which one remains loaded simply by the fact that the second hammer still is in the cocked position. A minor point, perhaps, but again one of those psychological factors that can be so important in competition.

And while there may not be anything approaching the really true all-around shotgun, this doesn't seem important: while there may not be a shotgun to fit every man, there certainly seems to be a shotgun to fit every need. For example, among competitors who think in terms of fast action, perhaps getting off a second shot in a hurry, or even in the game fields after upland birds where one could get a chance for a double or a triple, no one gives much thought to bolt action shotguns. Yet, Marlin, with its Model 55 goose gun, sells this bolt action in consistent numbers year after year in those areas, where hunters are after a honker for the table, have the time to wait out a second shot to fill a sparse limit and don't want to get involved in spending a lot of money for a shotgun that has a truly specialized purpose.

In this same vein, George Hawes tells of his arrangements to take over distributorship in this country of the current AyA line of shotguns. To complete this contract, he had to agree to take on a certain number of 10-gauge shotguns that already were in the works in this Spanish gun factory.

"I didn't know what I was going to do with all those 10 gauges," Hawes admits, "but in some specific parts of the country — in duck and goose hunting areas — there seems to be more interest in the 10 than in the other more conventional gauges my sales force is handling."

A few years back, Browning — holding the patents — was the only firm making an over/under shotgun. Since those patents have become public domain, nearly every firm in the shotgun business has come up with an over/under design, including Roy Weatherby, the magnum rifle king. Now Bill Ruger, who made his name originally in handguns, then accuracy-inspired rifles, admits he has an over/under model on the drawing boards. It will be only a matter of time before these new Ruger-built shotguns begin coming out of his plant in Southport, Connecticut, or his new installation in Newport, New Hampshire.

Interestingly, though, it was not until the introduction of the Remington Model 3200, late in 1972, that shotgunners were offered an over/under manufactured in the USA.

In claybird shooting, Robert Stack usually favors an automatic shotgun, but finds Mossberg slide action is positive for duck, goose hunting.

25

This represents an updated version of the same firm's Model 32, introduced in 1932 and produced through the early days of WW II. For a long time, it was felt that it would be impossible to recreate the Model 32 in terms of the American wage scales. The factor that tipped the balance was development of numerically controlled machine tools, capable of high precision and uniformity of output.

In the meantime, other well-known brand names had explored alternate routes with considerable success. Winchester started the trend by having their Model 101 over/unders made in Japan, soon to be joined by Charles Daly, Ithaca and others. Brownings, traditionally made in Liege, Belgium, began having certain models produced in Japan, as well.

The popularity of the over/under in recent years has led other firms to have models made to their specifications in Spain and Italy, while some firearms' importers have simply been happy to import a shotgun that has the over/under look and mechanism and haven't worried too much about quality control.

Again, I feel, we have psychological factors involved in the popularity of the over/under. Because of its conformation, the superimposed models lend themselves more to Space Age thinking and have found most of their popularity with the younger shooters — those under 30, I would judge — although plenty of the older heads have fallen in line, influenced by the clean, graceful lines.

At the other extreme, simply because it has been around for a couple of hundred years or so, in one style or another, the double barrel side-by-side is considered old-fashioned by many; they point out that it is bunglesome and lacks the handling qualities of the over/under.

In my own experience, that is simply a matter of mind over gun. Plenty of the more experienced shooters favor the side-by-side, because it was the gun with which they were brought up; which first brought them success. It becomes a case of what you know best.

I feel this kind of thinking is best illustrated in the military. I have friends, for example who have served in some of the past three wars. Go back to the pre-World War II rifleman and he will swear by the Springfield .30/06 and he can't understand why they ever changed, even when the matter of firepower is explained.

Later, when younger servicemen began training with the M-1 Garand, they couldn't understand how anyone could possibly have tolerated that old-fashioned bolt action

In the game fields today, one will see a broad variety of firearms. One of the greatest problems, the author has discovered, is the fact that some don't understand capabilities.

Waterfowling guns for taking birds such as this flight of ducks in Illinois skies have special requirements, having to do with barrel length and choke of the barrels.

Springfield. Still later, between the Korean and Vietnamese wars, when troops were being issued the M-14, they failed to understand why the old-timers of late World War II and Korea could find anything loveable in the M-1. They felt the M-14 had it all over anything produced to date, and perhaps it did.

I made a trip to Vietnam and had an opportunity to talk with troops there. The M-16 rifle then was being introduced. Those young servicemen who had trained with nothing else thought it was the greatest invention since water, while those who had cut their best scores with M-1 and M-14 rifles could see nothing good about this lightweight, small caliber combat rifle.

With the sudden popularity of the over/under, everyone in the gun marketing field had to have one and the guns all began to look alike. The inner mechanisms may have differed a trifle, but the telling thing invariably was the engraving. If it was a Japanese shotgun, one could tell from the basic engraving patterns that had been used. They differed little from one firm's shotgun to the next. The same was true of the Italian-made shotguns, with their own particular engraving designs. With the Spanish, no matter for whom the shotgun was being made, the engraving seemed more or less standard in pattern.

This has changed in more recent years. Ithaca, for example, contracted with Japanese armsmakers for a shotgun — their SKB — that was somewhat different from the others. Another of the newer offerings, of notable elegance, is the Shadow, currently distributed in different grades by High Standard. At first glance, it appears to be a complete departure from other over/under models and it is just that. A lot of original thinking went into this shotgun.

Generally speaking, shotgun designs are rather basic. In the various configurations from single-shot through the autoloader, once the pattern has been set, there hasn't been a great deal of change over the years; there have only been additions or subtractions from the basic designs for improvement. But these improvements have added up in the end to make life more pleasant for the shooter. In the autoloader field, for instance, Remington apparently has come to agree with me that it doesn't take any rehearsal to be miserable. As a result, the firm has continued to engineer for reduced recoil. I would say their Model 1100 is one of the most pleasant shotguns to shoot that there is these days.

One of the best shooting guns I have — and again I'm certain this has a psychological basis to some degree — is a Model 58 Remington which I had equipped with a Hydrocoil backed by a big, thick recoil pad. I know when I put it to my shoulder that I'm not going to be pounded into the ground by a combination of recoil and weight of the gun.

There are those shotgunners who swear by the pump action. One is Lee Marvin, the actor. At one time, he seemed to lean toward autoloaders, but there was the occasion when he was in a thicket somewhere in Latin America, facing an angry jaguar. The autoloader, carrying buckshot loads, jammed twice. He still managed to get the big cat, but when it was over, as he tells the story, he wrapped the barrel around a tree. For anything other than upland game birds, on which he favors a double, he has been a pump action man ever since.

High Standard and Mossberg had done a good deal in the pump action line over the years, aiming at a specific market. The latter firm, in particular, has a going thing in what some of us refer to as behind-the-door guns. These are shotguns of rugged characteristics that may not be the most artistically conceived in the world, yet are there to function when needed, at a relative price.

The term mentioned is from the salesman's idea that farmers throughout the Midwest and South always keep such a shotgun behind the kitchen door, ready for varmints in the hen house, hawks that threaten the chicken crop or for that flight of ducks that may land on the pond in the Fall.

There is little doubt that there are many guns sold still for just such purposes and High Standard has learned of this marketing area, since it seems that the firm is aiming much of its sales pitch in that direction.

Any qualms as to the phasing-out of pump shotguns have been solidly allayed in the last few years. Now the shopper has a choice of many names, including several who built their reputation on rifles or handguns. Weatherby offers their Patrician pump, as well as their Centurion auto. Smith & Wesson lists their Model 916 pump and Model 1000 autoloader. High Standard has their Flite-King pumps and Supermatic autos. Harrington & Richardson has their Model 440 pump, counterparted by the Mossberg Model 500 pump, all clamoring for attention against other pumps such as Savage's Model 30 and Marlin's Model 120.

Winchester, having heard the call and read the writing on the wall, brought back their legendary Model 12 pump as a custom-production number, along with their even more legendary Model 21 side-by-side double. If your memory harks back to the Thirties, when you could buy a Model 12 for somewhere around forty bucks, you'd best brace yourself before checking the quotes on a 1974 version of the same gun.

One cannot mention pump guns without noting that the Ithaca Model 37 Featherlight remains alive and doing nicely. Remington's beloved old Model 31 "cornsheller" has departed long since, having been replaced by their Model 870. The latter has won considerable legendary status on its own and probably is represented by a larger number of units produced than any other pump shotgun ever designed.

However, in the matter of the Marlin pump action, I'm happy to report that we're back to steel construction at a reasonable price.

In spite of my comments that shotgun designs still remain basic, that does not mean that the shotguns have not improved over the years. They have. This is reflected in the scores being piled up in our U.S. trap and skeet competitions and it also is the reason why we are going to have to make the games tougher.

The shooters are better, too, than they used to be, I think. Some of this may be psychological adjustment wherein a man is more difficult to rattle or throw off his pace in shooting than he was in my day. In addition, there can be no doubt that the ammunition is better. The ammo firms have spent millions on research to improve their product and it has paid off in the game fields as well as on the range.

One of my favorite duck loads is the 2¾ Winchester HD magnum 4 load. With the lower half of the shot packed in polyethylene sawdust, this offers a much better cone and gives better kills, I've found.

Especially in magnum loads, the powder is pushing the

Even the double barrel shotguns of the current era are complete with such handy contrivances as automatic ejectors. Many will handle standard, magnum shotshells.

Many shooters prefer automatic shotguns for fast-flushing pheasants in areas such as this eastern South Dakota field, although two shots usually are adequate.

Stack feels that skeet gunners favor the 28-inch barrel on double guns and over/unders. On automatics, 26-inch barrels, plus the chamber length, add up to 28-inch-plus length.

Shotshells, as well as guns and their shooters, have improved in recent years. This makes competition increasingly more demanding for those in claybirding.

shot charge with such force that the front half is being pushed by the pellets in the rear under terrific pressure. This means that the bottom third of the shot column can be badly deformed. But the use of this polyethylene cushion is much like wrapping a Christmas tree ornament before packing it away with the others.

I sort of stumbled across the secret of this shell and used it in duck blinds with friends, not telling them about the ammo. I was stoning big ducks at fifty-five yards, which they couldn't understand. This shell tends to kill them deader, higher, from my experience, although I attempt not to shoot at any greater ranges than I normally do. It always is the tendency of any shooter to fire at the extreme limits of his magnum loads and it's a tough habit not to follow.

In this matter of ammo, Winchester-Western introduced in their Double A type what they call the Handicap Trap load. It has the compression-formed plastic hull with which most of us are familiar, but if you can believe publicity — it has "components especially designed to produce consistently denser patterns at longer ranges." They say it is "an ideal load for the second shot in trap doubles events." It has a new wad that is engineered to have something called shock-absorbing posts to provide precisely controlled cushioning of the shot during ignition, thus guarding against pellet distortion.

The shot is polished and extra-hard, then it is protected in the barrel by a special cup that eliminates the conventional base wad, providing a gas chamber seal to insure against irregular or patchy shot strings. This particular shell is available in 12 gauge, with three-dram equivalent, 1-1/8 load in choice of 7½ or 8 shot.

Not to be outdone, Remington, Federal and other ammunition makers have been taking advantage of technological breakthroughs to improve shotshells.

As mentioned earlier, this has made it tougher to be a winner on the American claybird scene...simply because the shooters are better and the ammunition has been improved. Since nothing is more perfect than perfect, we find more and more serious shotgunners who are coming up with perfect scores in competition, then most go into a near unending series of shootoffs.

This is not true, of course, of International trap and skeet, where the birds are going faster, there are variables in timing and the gun is not mounted on the shoulder before calling for the bird. In spite of the improvement in arms, ammo and shooters, the unknowns here still make it difficult and unpredictable...and my feeling is that more and more Americans are seeking ways of finding such a challenge.

When I was a youngster, one of the best drills in shooting the variables and unknowns was using a handtrap. The thrower would stand out of our line of vision and would hurl the birds at all sorts of speeds, angles and heights. It was great training in meeting the unknown and helped develop reflexes.

The claybird games were developed as off-season training for upland game bird hunting, but over the years, the variables have been deleted, therefore the original purposes have been aborted.

Instead, were one to be serious about shooting International claybird events, he undoubtedly would find the game fields, where the variables tend to fly up in front of one, better training than anything else available.

No Matter What The Shooter's Need Or Want, There Is A Shotgun Designed For Purpose And Cost Considerations!

A MATTER OF CHOICE

BEFORE GETTING INTO discussion of the different types of guns, I'd like to mention my personal philosophy regarding shotguns and their uses: Match the gun to the game bird.

For example, it would do little good for the occasional bobwhite quail shooter to procure a 12-gauge autoloader which digests three-inch magnum shotshells, with a thirty-two-inch, full-choke barrel. As bobwhites have the heart-stopping habit of exploding right at the hunter's feet, a great majority of short-range shots would be missed because of the full choking. And even if such shots connected, the amount of game bird which could be collected for quail on toast would be negligible: perhaps a toe, the beak and a pile of feathers at best, none of which excite my palate!

An upland gun, generally light of weight with short barrels and open borings, is used when quail, pheasants and grouse are the sought quarry. In my younger days, it was rare to see any of my older hunting companions using anything more powerful than a 16 gauge, more commonly a 20 or 28 gauge. Purdeys, Holland & Holland and other English-made side-by-side doubles took their share of ringnecks or fast-flying quail in the hands of these sportsmen.

But this meant a hunter who also chased the Canadian honker or snow goose had to own another gun, usually a 12 gauge which could handle three-inch loads. This was fine for those who could afford it — but a big percentage of the American hunting populace either couldn't afford or didn't want two guns.

Consequently, American armsmakers began introducing side-by-side doubles in 12 gauge chambered either for the 2¾ or three-inch shells. Examples of note, at reasonable price, are Browning's B-SS and Ithaca's SKB 100, both available either in 12 or 20 gauge. Interestingly, and doubtless caused by the less expensive handwork available abroad, foreign armsmakers' offerings outnumbered those of domestic companies nearly three to one.

Light autoloaders have been seen with increasing frequency in the hunting fields and seem to have captured a dedicated following. Remington's Model 1100 Small Gauge and 1100 20-gauge Lightweight seem to have been designed especially for this type of gunning. The Small Gauge is available in .410 bore and 28 gauge, with a twenty-five-inch tube choked either full, modified or improved cylinder. The M-1100 Lightweight tips the scales at 6½ pounds, with a choice of twenty-eight-inch full or modified-choked barrel or twenty-six-inch improved cylinder. Ventilated ribs are optional.

The second category of sporting shotgun could be termed the waterfowl gun, used primarily for the taking of ducks and geese. Because of the hard-flying abilities of the birds — and the longer ranges at which they generally are shot — bigger gauges, beefier chamberings, longer barrels, tighter chokings and repeating actions have become the standard fare.

By far the most popular gun found in the marshes and blinds is the 12-gauge pump, with the 12-gauge autoloader not far behind. Barrels of thirty inches with full chokes are common and most offerings are equipped with the capability of igniting either 2¾ or three-inch shotshells. Guns in this category are heavier than upland guns, which reduces recoil from the heavier shot charges and loadings. This presents no problem, since the gun usually is carried to the blind and back to the truck; not for miles, as often is the case when pursuing upland game birds.

A compromise between these two firearm styles is the all-purpose shotgun, generally a 12 or 16 gauge. Barrels average twenty-eight inches in length, choked modified, mounted on a pump or autoloading action. Guns of this nature find use both in the blinds or sandhills, and could be the best bet for a one-gun hunter.

For the dedicated claybird shooter, trap and skeet guns are the only ones used. Both can be outlandishly expensive.

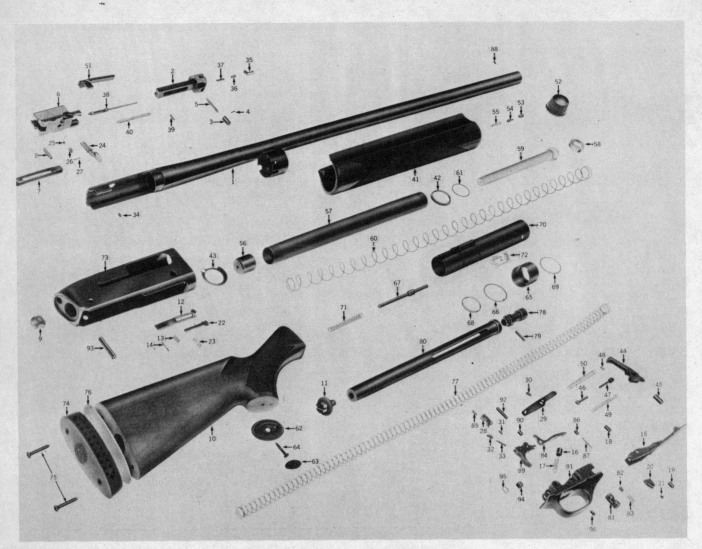

This breakdown of Winchester's new Super X Model 1 autoloading shotgun illustrates the great degree of engineering and the complexity of today's shooting products.

Below: Winchester's Model 12 shotgun had been discontinued from the firm's line, but it proved to continue in popularity to become a collector item for the practicing shooters. As a result, the Connecticut firm has put the pump gun back in production.

Winchester's Model 50, made with full choke only, often was a choice of those who wanted a trapgun that also would double for birds on shore and in marshes.

The solid steel machined receiver is favored by many shooters in spite of introduction of lighter weight alloys.

There have been numerous variable and changeable chokes introduced over the years, including one by Armalite and this Win-Choke made by Winchester. Not all have been commercial successes.

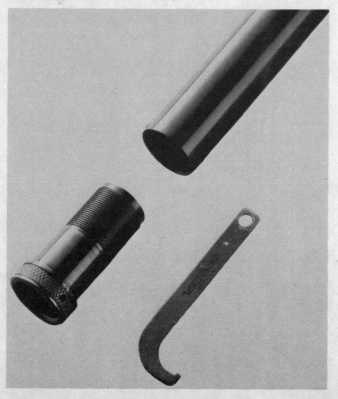

Trap guns, with few exceptions, are of the pump-action or single-shot variety, with thirty or thirty-two-inch tubes choked improved cylinder or modified, although full-choke borings are available. Skeet guns generally have twenty-six or twenty-eight-inch barrels mounted on pump or autoloading actions and are designed to throw the widest pattern possible at twenty-five yards through skeet boring. Both guns have ventilated ribs. A great number of over/under double guns are now seen on the skeet ranges, replacing the side-by-side doubles. Perhaps it is psychological, but many shooters feel more comfortable with the single sight plane than with the side-by-side.

Now, with a short background on uses of various types of shotguns, let's discuss the different types of actions and styles available to the scattergunning fraternity. Essentially, there are six different basic types of shotgun action:

Single-barrel, break-open; side-by-side double-barrel; over/under double-barrel; bolt-action repeater; pump-action repeater; autoloading repeater.

Some of these are offered in six basic bore diameters, reading (from largest to smallest) 10, 12, 16, 20, 28 gauge and .410 bore. Of these, the 10, 12, 20 and .410 are subdivided into standard-length and magnum chamberings.

Beyond that point, the choices branch out into selection of barrel length — somewhere between twenty and forty inches — and the preferred degree of choke for the barrel or barrels. The usual choke designations, in order from open to tightest: cylinder, improved cylinder, modified and full. A fifth choke, termed skeet, is offered on certain guns and

Shooter on left has a side-by-side double, while one on right has single-barrel. The choice of guns is up to the individual as to what suits his needs and his pocketbook.

its capability probably falls between cylinder and improved cylinder, though this will depend somewhat upon the given manufacturer. One further side-road is the option of choosing a variable choke system, of which several are available.

By way of a starting point, let's examine the six basic action categories. The break-open single often is the least expensive of the lot; a no-nonsense, utility type of mechanism to be used as a tool, rather than cherished as an object of art. Farmers and ranchers buy these to keep behind the kitchen door, in the barn, to carry on the tractor or in the pickup truck. It's rough duty and the guns get battered and dinged, perhaps even rusted a bit, but the low original cost helps to ease the pain over such battle damage. Curiously enough, the break-action singles include some of the most expensive shotguns available, these being the more flossy specimens of trap guns and the tab can run to several thousand dollars.

With a few possible exceptions, modern break-action singles are made in standard and magnum length 12 gauge, 16 gauge, and in a choice of standard or magnum chambers for the 20 gauge and .410 bore. Being rather light in comparison to most repeaters, the singles tend to kick a little more vigorously and this pretty well mutes down the public clamor for 10-gauge or 12-gauge magnum versions. There may have been — and perhaps still are — singles in 28 gauge, but they are notable for their rarity.

Most break-action singles have exposed hammers, with some manner of blocking system so that the gun cannot fire when the hammer is in the forward, uncocked position, even though the hammer spur should be struck sharply. Such designs, by virtue of their simplicity, are a good choice as a starting-out point for the beginning shotgunner. For that reason, wide-eyed youngsters are apt to discover them beneath the tree on Christmas morning; an occasion seldom to be forgotten in later decades!

As most break-open single buyers are interested more in function than appearance, arms manufacturers try to shave production costs to the razor edge, often making only pennies on each sale. Consequently, there is virtually no handwork, the major cause of increased costs. Frames are cast, chokes are swaged and stocks are of the cheapest wood available, finished with a spray-on lacquer and sans checkering, all of which saves money.

Previously, it was difficult to determine the amount of choking in a break-open single — no matter what the manufacturer claimed on the box — because swaging leaves something to be desired in terms of exact measurements. More attention has been paid to this area in recent years, which resulted in patterns befitting the choke designation. A wide range of barrel lengths are available, too, even up to the thirty-six-inch Long Tom in some cases. This, I believe, is an outgrowth of the age-old attitude that "the longer the

Custom stocking of shotguns is an art in itself, with long hours of tedious work going into the final project. Measurement of custom stock is treated in another chapter.

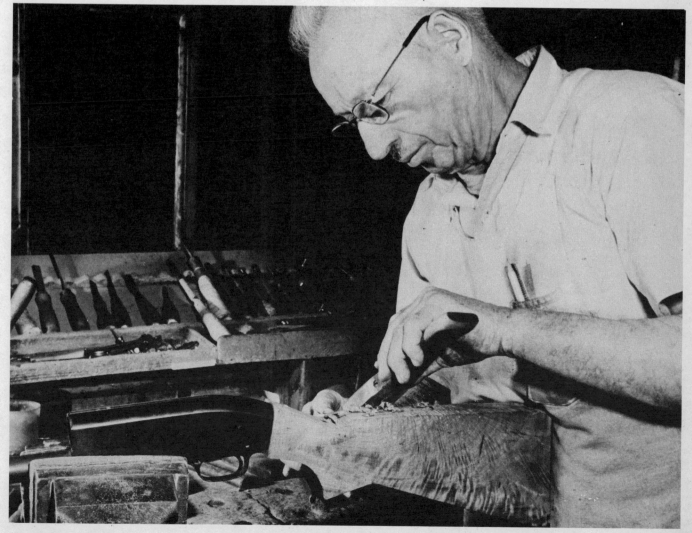

barrel, the harder the gun shoots." Fact or fantasy, guns still are rolling off the assembly lines so outfitted, and perhaps this is another of the psychological advantages I mentioned earlier.

Side-by-side double guns have changed little since the turn of the century, and the few changes that have been made are along the lines of refinements: better metals, springs, etc. Automatic ejectors were perfected in the 1880s and single triggers in the early 1900s. Why then are there so few around, and why are they so expensive?

The problem with side-by-side double-barrels is the cost to manufacture. Before the Second World War there were quite a few American armsmakers producing them, but skyrocketing labor costs following the conflict resulted in virtual extinction domestically. Another reason for their discontinuance was the changing taste of the buying public: Winchester's Model 12 pump and Remington's Model 11 auto sold like hotcakes and were less expensive. Yet

another reason was the retirement of older craftsmen, with no young recruits to fill the vacancies.

Well-made doubles were — and still are — something to behold. Whether they shot where they were pointed is something else again. No matter how carefully the thin-walled barrels are aligned before soldering, something can go wrong, resulting in shot charges that can differ significantly from aiming point to point of impact. I recently heard of a wealthy gentleman who, after a two-year wait, finally received his $2500 side-by-side. Upon testing, he discovered that the barrels did not shoot together. There was a difference in the center of the patterns in relation to the same sight picture of nearly fifteen inches at thirty yards.

Many handmade doubles do shoot together, just as some mass-produced specimens do. A large percentage of the latter types don't, however, so if you can, fire a couple of rounds through it on a pattern board before buying.

It's the contention of most knowledgeable gunners that,

Shooting over decoys can call for fast action and thus a fast-action shotgun such as the autoloader carried by this waterfowl hunter, as he waits at dawn for game.

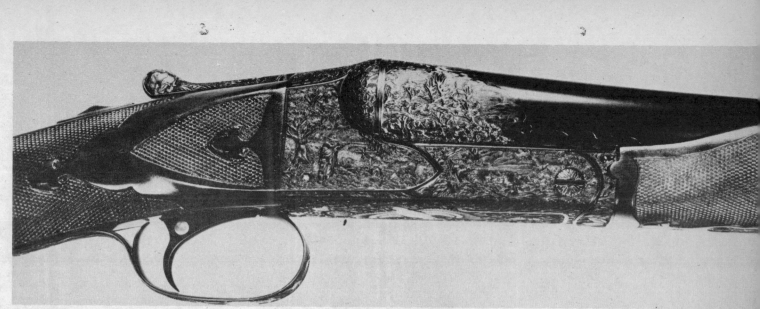

For shooters with whom cost is no object, fine hand-checkering on the wood and the deepest and most intricate engraving come high, but do not make the gun shoot better.

dollar for dollar, you can't get the same quality for doubles that you can for easier to produce shotguns. Consequently, while there are several domestic makers producing relatively low-cost side-by-sides, it might be worth your while to have a hard look at all offered on the market, including foreign models. "Caveat Emptor" — let the buyer beware — certainly fits here.

The over/under shotgun has made significant inroads here in the United States and currently there are more than eighty models, both foreign and domestic, from which to choose. Prices currently range from a low of nearly $250 to upwards of $2000.

The popularity of the over/under, which simply is a double-barrel with the barrels one on top of the other instead of side-by-side, stems in part from that difference: many Americans raised with a pump or single-shot scattergun find sighting easier on the single plane, rather than adjust to the twin aiming points of the side-by-side. Cost and quality for the dollar spent enters the picture, also, most feeling they get more gun for their money than with the side-by-side.

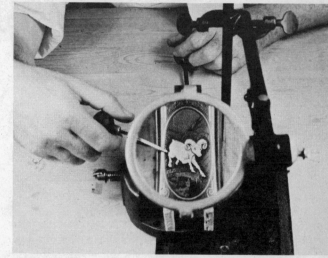

While this engraving and gold inlay is being done for a rifle, it suggests the high art work that is available.

Winchester's Model 21 side-by-side long has been considered a classic and still is made on special order, being completely hand built. This is Grand American grade.

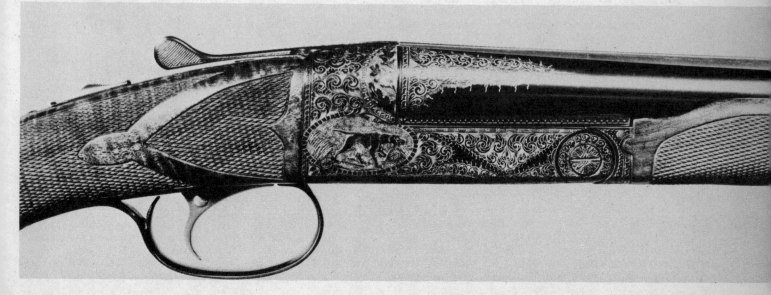

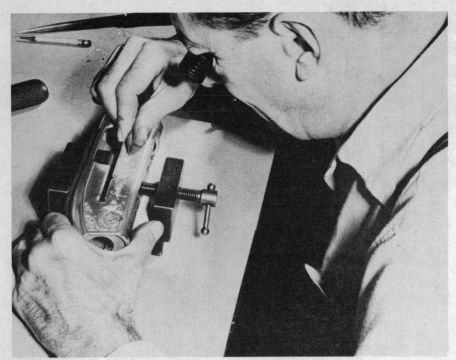

The engraver's art still is practiced in the United States, but many firearms companies have this type work done abroad.

Until just the last few years, Browning's Superposed over/under model, which is made to the company's specifications in Belgium, was the top seller in this country. Other American companies, notably Ithaca and Weatherby, have followed John Moses Browning's lead and are having their O/U guns produced abroad for sale domestically. The plan seems to be working, as Ithaca's prices are substantially lower than for the Superposed and Weatherby's are on a par for their Regency model.

Most over/under scatterguns have shorter barrels than other models and, if well-made, are a joy to shoot through natural balance and "pointability." Virtually all are outfitted with ventilated ribs with either a single or two sight beads, one located at the muzzle and another halfway down the rib for easy sight alignment. Barrel length averages twenty-six inches with the full range of chokes; usually combinations like improved cylinder and modified; modified and full; skeet and skeet; and, occasionally, full and full.

Virtually all are hammerless in design, with the exception of several Savage and Ithaca models which feature a rifled barrel for conventional bullet loadings atop the smoothbore tube, and use a box lock action. Some have double triggers — others a single, selective trigger. Most of the more expensive models have automatic selective ejectors, a Greener-type cross-bolt lock, in addition to top tang safeties. Most have some type of engraving and it's rare to find an O/U without checkering on the pistol grip and forend.

There have been several carloads of bolt-action shotguns sold in this country, their main appeal being low cost and durability. These, like the break-open single-barrel, often are used by farmers and ranchers for drilling predators or zapping the occasional duck off the stock pond.

Filling a limit on quail — or most any game bird, unless they're as thick as apples in an orchard — is virtually out of the question. It is well-nigh impossible for a man to work

In spite of the popularity of over-and-under shotguns, almost all firms still build side-by-sides. This is Model 580 Mauser single-trigger.

the bolt fast enough to jack another shotshell into the chamber from the magazine in time to make a second shot at a rising covey of quail. This, however, needn't be all bad: Its virtual single-shot capability makes it a fine gun for the beginning shooter, and teaches the youngster to make each shot count — he's only going to get one crack at the covey!

Bolt-action shotguns have been made, at one time or another, by Harrington & Richardson, Mossberg, Stevens, Marlin and Western Field, and the latter four still market some model. Perhaps the most famous of the bolt-action

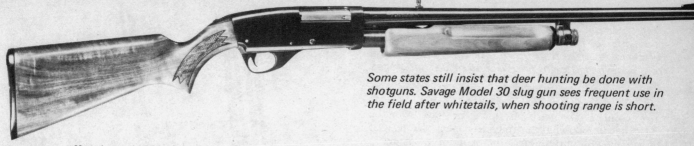

Some states still insist that deer hunting be done with shotguns. Savage Model 30 slug gun sees frequent use in the field after whitetails, when shooting range is short.

repeaters offered is the Marlin Goose Gun, designed to bring down the birds from stratospheric heights. It is in 12 gauge only, using two 2¾ or three-inch magnum shells in its detachable clip at any time. The barrel measures thirty-six inches, choked full and its 7¼-pound weight helps reduce some of the heavy recoil. This definitely is not a learner's gun!

Other bolt-actions are offered in gauges from 12 to .410, with 16 and 28 gauges not present. Most have double locking lugs, thumb safeties, iron sights optional and three-shot magazines. Price, still an attraction, hovers around the $50 mark.

The pump or slide-action repeater, a result of American ingenuity, is the most popular smoothbore with hunters all

Numerous manufacturers build guns today with interchangeable sets of barrels. This Savage 330, imported from Europe, is available with spares and a carrying case.

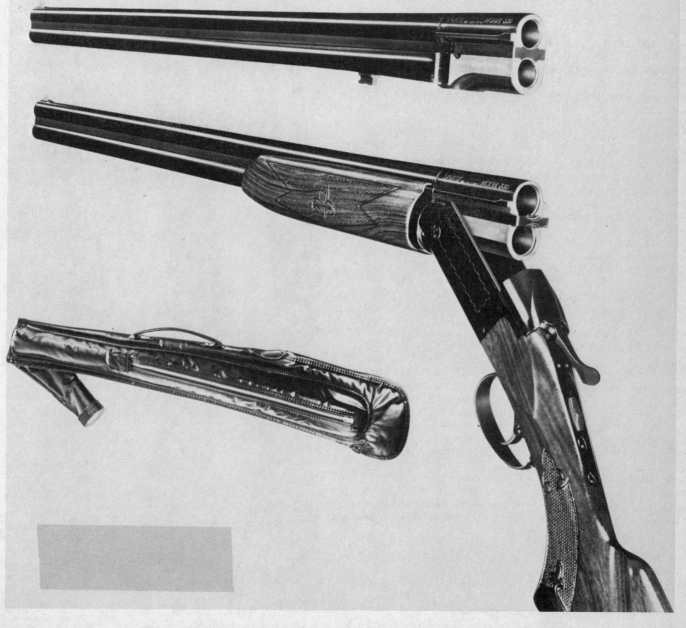

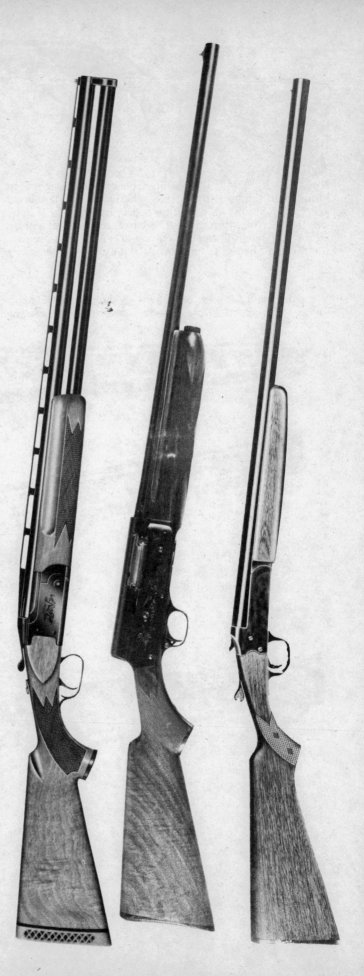

Suggesting the variety of guns available to today's serious shooter are (from left) Remington's new 3200, a recreation of their Model 32; the same manufacturer's Sportsman auto made from 1931 until 1942 under license from Browning; Stevens break-action single-shot model.

over the world. It met with instant acceptance from the gunning fraternity upon its introduction near the turn of the century and still outsells any other action type made.

A pump is rugged, durable and not too demanding in production costs. When first introduced, the trend was for 12 gauges with long barrels and full chokes, which were rather unwieldly. Through advancements in metallurgy, the heavy steel receivers have been replaced with strong yet light alloys, with Duralumin and even fiberglass used in the shorter barrels. All have contributed to making the gun more handy to shoot and lighter to carry.

The all-time favorite pump shotgun was the Model 12, made and marketed by Winchester. The first Model 12 was a 20 gauge with twenty-five-inch barrel, introduced in 1913. This was followed by 12 and 16-gauge models in 1914, and a 28 gauge in 1934. Back in 1964, Winchester discontinued production of the Model 12 but, because of the hand-wringing and loud complaints by gunners, introduced the Model 1200 to take its place. This stilled the din temporarily but, with an eye on tradition and nostalgia, Winchester reintroduced the Model 12 early in the 1970s. It has sold exceptionally well. Another best seller is the Model 870 made by Remington, which has now forged ahead of the Model 12 in all-time sales.

Along with its ruggedness and durability, the pump has a single sighting plane that many shooters find indispensible. Its tubular magazine generally holds three or four shells, which often means the difference between meat on the table or an escaped cripple. It has fast, positive ejection and feeding, a single trigger and a gunner familiar with his pump can bust caps nearly as fast as the autoloader owner.

Despite its tremendous sales volume, the pump-action repeater isn't without its quirks and problems. For example, there is no variation in the choking, as can be had with double-barreled guns. It never will hold a candle appearance-wise to the finely crafted doubles produced both here and abroad, and it takes a degree of familiarity to assure proper working of the pump mechanism upon ejection and feeding.

I have personally had a minor problem with this last category upon occasion, which has cost me a few birds. In most pumps, the slide must be pulled all the way to the rear rapidly, which disengages the extractors from the shotshell case head with a snapping motion and ejects the shell either from a side port or the bottom of the receiver. If the slide isn't pumped sharply enough or isn't pulled back to the full extent, jamming results; the spent shell isn't ejected and you're trying to feed another round into the chamber. So spend a little time with your pump before heading afield.

There is another problem to consider when purchasing a pump action, especially if you're below average in terms of height. Many short men simply cannot handle the pump as it comes from the box and, unless you're willing to whack the stock off to meet your physical dimensions, it would be wiser to look for another style.

Because all patent rights to specific pump designs have expired, it's pretty difficult to distinguish one company's product from another. The action is reliable, so some of the dictating factors to consider are the pocketbook and the degree of finish you would like. Things such as checkering, ventilated ribs, white line spacers at the butt cap or recoil

Grouse shooting usually takes place in wooded areas such as this New Jersey scene.

pad and pistol grip, type of wood and the grain, blueing — in the pump market a man can feel a little more selective and know that it won't cost an arm and a leg!

The last type of common shotgun is the automatic, which really is misnamed. In truth, it's a semi-automatic, because a separate and distinct pull of the trigger is required to detonate each round fed into the chamber. A true automatic will continue to fire by simply holding the trigger depressed.

The autoloading repeater is yet another invention of the inimitable John Moses Browning. His first autoloader operated on the long-recoil principle, described in Chapter 1, whereby the breech block and barrel together moved several inches to the rear upon detonating a shell in the chamber. He first offered the design to Winchester but withdrew the offer over a snarl in the financial arrangements. He then went to Remington but, before negotiations could be completed, Marcellus Hartley, head of the company, died of a sudden heart attack. Browning then took his design to the Fabrique Nationale (FN) in Belgium where an agreement was signed. They produced thousands of the autoloaders,

dubbed the Model 11, which were sold in the United States by Remington Arms.

The Remington Model 11 became to the autoloading scene what Winchester's Model 12 was to the slide-action sect. It was heavy, but this problem was offset by its ruggedness and reliability. This same design is now offered in Browning's Auto-5 series, distinguished by the square-backed receiver. The design has been dropped by Remington, which went instead to the more sleek looks of the Model 1100, another all-time favorite that doesn't use the long-recoil principle, which was fading in popularity following the Second World War.

Unless the long-recoil system was adjusted properly, kick from guns using the system could be quite harsh. However, my experience with the Remington Model 11 Sportsman has been only good. I was All-American for three years with the 12 gauge and won the 20-gauge Nationals using this shotgun.

If set up properly, the original Browning design has less recoil, is cleaner and has less chance of malfunction than the gas-operated autoloader. If you're used to the long-

Actor Lee Marvin uses German-made over/under for hunting doves in California desert.

When Winchester sponsored nation-wide claybirding championships a few years ago, with finals on Grand Bahama Islands, the contestants showed up with a wide variety of shotguns, varying in type and maker. (Below) Film actor John Russell tries out a new skeet gun at Southern California range to find whether it fits his lanky frame.

recoil feel, it is a hard gun to fault. It's not as pretty as some, but it's more rugged or Browning wouldn't still be making the old "square-back."

The short-recoil system, utilizing a sliding chamber within the receiver has less recoil than the first system developed by Browning. The breech block and barrel slamming backwards can add to recoil in the Model 11. The gas-operated system is lower in kick, unless the proper combination of friction ring and collar is made in the Model 11. Expanding gas from burning propellant is allowed to escape into a tube which feeds back to the front of the bolt, pushing it rearward. The rearward progression activates ejection of the spent cartridge and forward movement of the bolt feeds in a fresh shell. The systems are extremely fast but can cause some problems to the uninitiated.

With the gas-operated system, it is imperative that the gas port be free of powder residue for proper function. If left on its own, the gas port eventually would clog completely, resulting in stoppage. Sometimes take-down for cleaning is difficult, and ease of same would be worth investigating prior to purchase.

The short-recoil system suffers the same plight as its long-recoil counterpart, if the system isn't adjusted properly. Aside from that, these two autoloader systems are superior to their early predecessor, developed some seventy years ago.

There truly is a dizzying array of armament awaiting the prospective buyer, but I hope this chapter has afforded some basic idea of the capabilities and uses for the different makes and models, which will aid you in wisely choosing the friend you will carry afield or to the claybird range.

With America's ever-improving technology, even the cheaper grades of shotguns now boast such conveniences as automatic ejectors, as is case with this Fox side-by-side model.

For rough treatment to which one would subject a gun in such areas as Mitchell's Bay, in the Lake Erie district, a good low-cost but good pointing gun serves the need.

Clutching a Winchester Model 12 pump action, Marvin poses with hunting friends, and bag of doves.

Choosing A Shotgun (C)

DYNAMICS OF DOVE DOWNING

Actor/Shooter Lee Marvin Has Some
Definite Likes And Dislikes, With Reasons Why!

AS MENTIONED EARLIER, choosing a gun is a matter of individual preference, but before anyone has been shooting for any length of time, he begins to make his own choices.

For example, I have discussed guns with actor Lee Marvin on a number of occasions, he being one of the most serious game shots still on the Hollywood scene. When I asked what he felt was his greatest hunting thrill, he pondered, then replied: "When I consider the greatest hunting thrill, I think first of downing a grizzly bear.

"The next in line, and probably equally as challenging, is whitewing dove shooting. For even the avid shotgunner, this is one of the most demanding sports to be imagined, at least, in my own experience. In fact, you might say that doves have been the problem of my hunting life."

Marvin owned his first shotgun while he was attending school in Florida. About 14 at the time, he became the proud possessor of a 20-gauge side-by-side that was marketed in those days by Montgomery Ward.

In the Everglades and back country of the Florida swamps, there was plenty of game and the bobwhite quail seemed to be everywhere. This was the chief target for most hunters and the dove went begging for shots, if that's the best way of describing it. As wing shooters didn't pay much attention to them, so Lee was able to shoot more than his share.

In the Florida of that era, the serious deer hunter would load up his shotgun with 00 buckshot — excellent for the heavy brush — and take to the woods in search of the winter's venison supply. "In my own case, the little 20-gauge wouldn't handle the heavy loads, so I would load up with No. 2 buckshot, then attempt to get to within ten feet or so of my quarry before turning loose. This method proved surprisingly effective. I usually came home with a deer," Lee recalls.

"In the years since I discovered dove shooting, I have had plenty of opportunity to test this game species and have been lucky enough to be able to check it out in far corners of the country. It seems that wherever one goes, the dove is just as demanding of a shooter and can make a fool out of any gunner who isn't minding his business."

There was a period, of course, during World War II, when as a Marine rifleman, Lee Marvin was doing an entire-

Right: As he walks desert road, Marvin seems to listen for dove wings. (Below) He awaits arrival of the birds.

ly different type of shooting. Like many a service veteran, I suppose, he went through a post-war period during which shooting held no particular charm. After all, he had spent

Lee Marvin's hunting partner, Al Zapanta, favors Model 870 for which the actor expresses respect as shooter. He dislikes autoloaders for reasons told in the text.

several years virtually married to a rifle and was ready for other things.

Then he got the acting bug and began to concentrate on that. While trying to learn the trade, there was little time

Even after nearly forty years of use, Marvin's German-made still is tight and boasts and excellent shot pattern.

for shooting. When all was added up, he had been away from guns and shooting for nearly twenty years before his interest was renewed.

For some insane reason, motion picture production seems to be tied inevitably to the hunting season; whenever I'm looking forward to a good Fall and Winter of gunning, film offers come along that can't be ignored and there goes another hunting session. Lee Marvin has found himself a victim of similar scheduling.

"When I once again became interested in hunting and found some time for it, I started looking around for a shotgun that would suit my needs best. I tried a lot of them and turned eventually to an over-and-under Gebruder Ademey that I'd had tucked away for a long time. I had found it in New York years before and had purchased it as much for its fine engraving as its shooting qualities. It's hardly the type of shotgun that an arms fancier is going to drag through the mud."

Marvin started shooting ducks along the Mexican border near Mexicali, using this shotgun. It's a real reacher, with thirty-inch fluid steel barrels, that was made in Suhl, now in East Germany, some thirty-five years ago. This firm was in business from 1921 to 1939 and such guns are scarce today. Many of the great guns of that time and place often were made by several families, all of them supplying specific parts to go into certain models. This shotgun is bored full and modified and it'll reach out a lot farther than seems reasonable.

"I like it because it does get far out for ducks and geese, but is equally good for dove and quail, when proper loads are used.

"While I readily admit this old relic is a great gun with its twin barrels, it's not really equal to taking a triple and wing shooting has become my favorite pastime, when I can work out the details of making time and pleasure fit together properly."

In recent years, Marvin has done a good deal of investigation and now contends that the shotguns of modern manufacture far surpass the old classics when it comes to field work.

"In dove shooting, for example, one might worry about carrying an over/under classic such as mine around the brush, scratching the finish or rubbing off the bluing, but you can buy at a reasonable price some of the modern pump-action shotguns, affording you another shot even when the magazine is properly plugged. The Remington 12-gauge Wingmaster, for example, with a ribbed barrel, is fast shooting, and you can buy extra barrels to match a specific type of shooting at a reasonable price.

"The old classics are beautifully built arms; that can't be denied, but there is no getting away from the advantages of modern technology and the fact that today's manufacturers are making a rugged line of shooters that will send shot where you aim it and give you the advantage of more rounds."

As admitted, Lee has done a lot of hunting with the over/under, but in recent years, he has been involved in the type of gunning where one needs the advantages of a fast shooter.

"I've tried any number of automatics and I don't care for them personally. They may be great, properly bored, for trap and skeet, but I had one jam on the second shot when I was face to face with a jaguar in Mexico and I've been somewhat disillusioned ever since," he says. "I prefer the pump or slide action with less dependence upon mechanics for this as well as wing shooting."

The advantages of such a positive action were brought home to him during what might be termed the ideal hunt; this was one of those by-invitation-only soirees held in the Kentucky farm country, literally the land of the gentleman farmer.

"There are literally thousands of doves in the air, diving, swooping and dodging, as the gunners open up. I've heard as many as thirty shotguns go off to sound like a string of Chinese firecrackers, but the birds often are wily enough that they still get through. And it is in situations such as this that one feels undergunned, if he is equipped with only a double. This is where the pump action with its extra load comes in mighty handy," Lee feels.

The shooters in this annual Kentucky outing will hunt only one field, then the following day, will move to another field on another farm.

Personally, I feel a double is plenty of gun. The third shot is only a plus on ducks for cripples. If you plan on doing any European hunting, pump and autoloaders are verboten. As much as I like Lee, I've always found that triples and quadruples are as scarce as five-cent cigars.

Some instructors used to start a shooter with only one shell at a time — when he began hitting regularly, he was allowed to graduate to two shells. But the idea was to teach one to make certain that the first shot counted!

Of course, such experts as Rudy Etchen and Alex Kerr can make quintuple shots, but they are sort of special. And it only takes two seconds to reload a double that has automatic ejectors.

Lee Marvin believes in long barrels for long shots and favors his relic Gebruder Ademey.

BLACK POWDER FOR SHOTGUNNERS

HERE'S A NEARLY FORGOTTEN ART IN BIRD-GETTING THAT BEARS RENEWAL!

Black powder and antique expert Jay Hansen (right) and Bob Stack inspect replica shotgun from Navy Arms Co.

Chapter 3

IN RECENT YEARS, a number of black powder shooting clubs have organized trapshoots that are a throwback of a century or so, but nonetheless provide an interesting outlet.

A couple of years back, at the Grand National Quail Hunt in Oklahoma, the local black powder club sponsored such a shoot, luring some of the assembled Hollywood celebrities into competing. When it was all over, there was black powder all over the ground and the coaches were a bit chagrined that all of those film heros who had shot hundreds of Indians with muzzleloading arms seemed to be all thumbs when it came to loading.

Actually, because of the length of time it took to load, the match was limited to a round of three birds. Actor Dale Robertson walked away with an impressive trophy. He hit two of his three birds, explaining, "That's still more than anyone else hit!"

No one really knows the origin of the shotgun. It seems as though it has always been with us. It was old when George Washington was a boy and some beautiful double-barreled flintlocks hang in Mount Vernon today, favorite sporting arms of our First President.

Even the ancient blunderbuss, erroneously portrayed as the "musket" of the early Pilgrims, was actually a shotgun. This short but lethal firearm was the riot gun of its day and its true uses were in the guarding of English stagecoaches against highwaymen like Dick Turpin or in repelling boarders on the wooden fighting ships. Accepting any firearm fodder from swan drops to gravel to old razor blades, one would still be just as effective today in clearing the bridge of mutineers!

In a later era, percussion shotguns gained a niche in our own frontier history. On the Wells Fargo, Butterfield and other Western stage lines, a man who "rode shotgun" was likely to cause an outlaw to seek a safer stagecoach to hold up.

At historic Yuma Prison, the guards carried shotguns. On the other hand, some Western outlaws also favored the scattergun. One of these was Black Bart, the Poet, who never once had to fire his big double-barrel to enforce the order to "throw down the box!" Years later, he confessed that it never had been loaded, as he had no desire to hurt anyone.

On the day that Curly Bill Brocius ended his career in a desert dry-wash, each member of Wyatt Earp's avenging party had a shotgun hanging by a rawhide loop from his saddlehorn. And of course there was Doc Holliday, the deadly dentist, and his favorite sawed-off.

But after this colorful period, the scattergun was relegated to a position behind the door of a sod shanty, just in case of a chicken hawk. For several decades, it was only another tool, like the hoe, the churn and the kindlin' axe. A man's rifle was a rifle, but a shotgun was very little.

Since I'll be the first to admit I'm a neophyte when it comes to black powder shooting, I took the advice my father once gave me: When you want an expert job done, you get an expert to do it.

I invited Major R.O. Ackerman, a retired Army man and one of the nation's best-known black powder experts, to

In the case of the Navy Arms shotgun discussed in chapter, it comes with extra set of nipples and a steel worm that threads into the reverse end of ramrod that comes with gun.

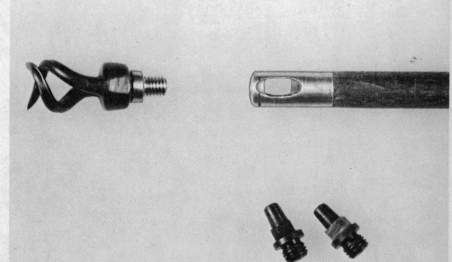

Model 100 shotgun is patterned on a pattern board by R.O. Ackerman for purposes of determining efficiency.

offer some advice on the subject of muzzleloading shotguns. I've included here some of his comments and I suspect those no more experienced in this phase of scattergunning than myself will discover they have learned a good deal by listening to Slim.

"I've seen them used to prop open a hen-house door, in the rain. When I was a kid, every junk shop had a corner full. Going price was three to five bucks tops, only they didn't go. The best original percussion double I ever owned I paid four bucks for, used, by mail, and the advertiser paid the postage," he recalls.

But happily, the venerable two-tube has made a fantastic comeback! Suddenly shooters remember its colorful history and, progressing from there, they are rediscovering the potential of the percussion shotgun as an all-around sporting firearm. From the stiff competition of the quail walk at Friendship, Indiana, to bustin' jacks on the ocotillo flats of Arizona and New Mexico, the bellerin' double has returned to the fold.

"Because of the faster action, I actually get more kick out of this than any other facet of the black powder sports. They all are exciting challenges — big game, small game, competition, you name it. Even plinking at beer cans is twice the fun with a muzzleloader.

"For example, on a recent javelina hunt, my partners were frustrated by the total absence of any recent sign. As I swallowed my disappointment, I loaded up my new Navy Arms' Model 100 percussion 12-gauge double-barrel. Two miles down the valley from our four-wheel drive, I suddenly got into three or four coveys of Gambel's quail. I would fire, they would take off, then sit down sixty to eighty yards away. I would reload, circle around them, flush, fire and they'd fly back to where they had been before. They seemed determined not to leave that particular ravine.

"It was a unique experience and I didn't even wish for a dog — except for retrieving in the catclaw thickets. My hide still smarts.

"This is an example of the sport one may experience in the right place, where a muzzleloader is a challenge, but no particular drawback. I would reload at my leisure, take a fresh chew of Skoal and circle 'em again. Durndest experience I've had in a long time.

"The scattergun I was using is the top shotgun of the Navy Arms Company line and my personal favorite. Their Model 100 is a percussion 12 gauge of the classic English pattern. This means it is on the light side, with a straight stock. The browned barrels are a practical twenty-nine inches long, and are choked-improved cylinder and modified — ideal for most upland game. The pull is a generous

Today's replicas such as Navy Arms' Model 100 have some advantages over originals. It is choke bored and is lightweight by comparative standard.

14¼ inches — great news for us big fellows who feel cramped with the average replica.

"Weight of my gun is five pounds, thirteen ounces, though this will vary with density of the wood. To me, the beauty of the gun is its light weight and beautiful handling qualities. It comes up like a dream and I point instinctively where I mean to hit. I am convinced that Navy Arms has come up with the ideal in compromise measurements. This is not easy to do.

"For me, the drop makes it a natural pointer. It features a matted rib and standard front bead. The walnut stock has a hand-rubbed satin finish and is checkered by hand. Locks are front-action bar locks, engraved in fine English-style scroll and finished in case-hardened colors."

Standard double triggers are provided, and the knurled hammers cock smoothly and easily for a quick shot. As the half-cock safety notches are unusually positive in action, the gun may be carried at half-cock in actual hunting. This cuts cocking time to a minimum.

"They should be this positive on every replica, but unfortunately they are not. Invariably, this is the first thing I check on any new gun, and half-cocks that won't resist a firm pull on the trigger should be repaired by a professional gunsmith before the arm is loaded the first time! I consider this an inexcusable oversight and a completely unnecessary hazard."

As Navy Arms Company does a large portion of their own manufacturing in this country, they have the experienced personnel to properly inspect their imports, also. This is a big point in their favor, compared to distributors with whom a final safety inspection is a pipe dream.

"I have crusaded for safety inspections for many years, with painfully few victories. I hope these brief remarks may shake up a few dealers in cheapies."

Several features of the Model 100 are a great help in cleaning the gun, making this much less of a chore than usual.

For a quick wipe now and then in the field, a detachable gun worm comes with the shotgun, as well as an extra pair of nipples. The worm is a corkscrew-shaped steel accessory with a threaded brass base that fits the reverse end of the ramrod. A copy of a Nineteenth Century tool, this should be in the hunter's pouch or pocket whenever he uses the scattergun.

The handy gadget serves several different purposes for a shotgunner, which is why it deserves this much mention.

Lock mechanisms on today's replica firearms closely follow the design of the originals, but the flat springs, while conventional, are made for hard use.

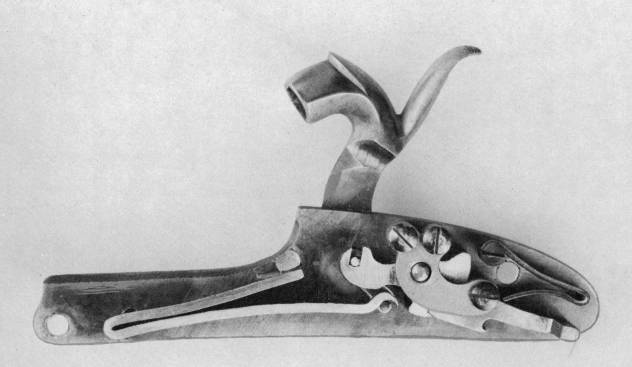

TABLE OF STANDARD LOADS FOR PERCUSSION SHOTGUNS:

	Drams Powder	Oz. Shot	Type Load
12 ga.	4-1/8	1-3/8	Heavy
12 ga.	3-3/4	1-1/4	Medium
12 ga.	3-1/4	1-1/8	Light
16 ga.	3-1/8	1-1/8	Heavy
16 ga.	3	1	Medium
16 ga.	2-1/2	1	Light
20 ga.	2-3/4	1	Heavy
20 ga.	2-3/8	1	Medium
20 ga.	2	3/4	Light

First, it may be used with a flannel cleaning patch for wiping during firing. It also serves for a thorough cleaning job, afterward. Then, if you should be using a jag and you lose a patch down the bore, a twist of the worm will catch it and remove it. Finally, the worm makes it easy to withdraw a load from a shotgun without having to shoot it out. The card wad is the only component that cannot be used next time.

The Model 100's chief aid to easy cleaning is its patent breech or hooked breech. Just tap out the barrel key in the forearm. The barrels will disengage at the hooked breech and may be lifted out. It then is a simple matter to clean the bores by your favorite method.

Solvent or hot water? The controversy will never end among coal-burners. A thorough cleaning with one of the better non-rusting solvents will hold your black powder firearm perfectly well between one hunt and the next. However, it is wise to scrub and flush it out with very hot water before putting it away for the season. A rubber tube from the faucet is a great help here, and most dealers sell such attachments. Otherwise, you might immerse the breech end in a bucket partly filled with hot water and pump this in and out through the nipple seats by a rod, a jag and a snug-fitting patch. If you can hold those barrels without a pad or cloth, the water is not hot enough.

Change water when necessary. When clean, dry as quickly as possible. The heat in the metal will finish the drying, if you move fast. Grease or oil immediately to prevent rust. A preservative such as RIG is advisable.

For long storage, hot water has the advantage of flushing the gunk out of flash channels and breech recesses. A solvent may stop the rusting action of residue, but it is still in there.

The accompanying chart should serve as a general guide for any top grade replica or for an original in very sound condition. For something like a 14 gauge, you can compute between loads given for the 16 and 12. A dram equals 27.34 grains. Thus, 3 drams would be approximately 82 grains. Use black powder only!

For cutting your own wads, order a wadcutter of the desired gauge from Dixie Gun Works or a similar dealer in muzzleloading supplies. The felt wads may be punched with a mallet on the end-grain of a block of wood. Very thick felt may be obtained from weather stripping or from an upholstering shop. Felt wads may be greased by saturating in melted, unsalted shortening, then spread on newspaper to drain until congealed. In loading these over the powder charge, the desired number may be sandwiched between two dry card wads. This will keep fouling soft.

Card wads may be cut from any thin, strong cardboard, but not the corrugated type. They should be just thick enough to retain the shot charge, but not so thick as to disturb the pattern.

An old rule of thumb for the proper shotgun load is that the powder charge should be about equal in depth to the bore diameter. Then the powder charge, the wad column and the shot charge each should be equal in volume. This can be determined in a pill bottle of correct diameter.

For separate loading of shotguns or of big bore rifles, Treso Gun Specialties now offers interchangeable flask spouts in a variety of sizes. These include the larger capacity types that have been so needed. They also have the large fixed powder measures to hang from your horn or your pouch.

Whatever method of loading you adopt, it is wise to try your percussion shotgun on a pattern board. The standard

Note that the locks and furniture on modern replicas often are attractively engraved.

method is to fire at large sheets of paper at forty yards and, after each shot, mark a thirty-inch circle around the densest concentration of shot. Add a black sticker in the center before firing for an aiming point.

This does not simulate field shooting, but it does show you the uniformity of pattern and the centering of it. You can estimate the percentage of the charge inside the circle, and watch for holes in the pattern. These often are correctable by improving your loading technique, an advantage most breechloaders do not enjoy.

Experimentation will teach you much about maximum ranges, effect of different chokes and the most efficient shot sizes.

Also try your load on tin cans. The greatest distance at which you hit consistently and get complete penetration of a can is a guide to your maximum range for a clean kill. Don't keep increasing the load to foolish extremes. You'll do better with standard loads by learning your gun and your own limitations. This holds true for any shotgun.

An appropriate do-it-yourself project would be paper cartridges for the muzzleloading shotgun.

When the birds are coming in fast, cartridges greatly speed up the loading process. They go far toward eliminating the only significant disadvantage of hunting with a percussion shotgun.

Some traditionalists may object to the idea of cartridges in anything but a military musket. Sometimes their zeal is more in evidence than their research.

Our forefathers were practical men who always were looking for the better way to do things. There is constant proof of this in my own collection of original early cartridges. There were many ingenious ways of speeding the loading of sporting muzzleloaders, as well as military ones. As early as 1827, a patent was issued for a manufactured shot cartridge for muzzleloading scatterguns! At that time, even percussion ignition still was in its infancy, but paper cartridges had been around for a long time.

"Several years ago, I described an idea for using the plastic shot cups of the modern reloader as the basis for muzzleloading shot cartridges. That trick now has been copied by a number of writers, but there is one important point which they consistently neglect to mention," Ackerman reports.

This idea was developed for cylinder-bored shotguns, which all of the earlier replicas were. Now that the better grade arms are in a variety of chokes, it is a whole new ball game. With any constriction tighter than an improved cylinder, it is difficult to muzzleload with a plastic shot cup. Hence the need for a different approach in top quality guns.

"The paper cartridges that I make have one distinct advantage. All of the time-consuming work is done at home. In the hunting field, there are no lids to remove, no bottles to salvage. Simply shove a cartridge down each barrel, cap and fire.

Right: The percussion shotguns being produced today offer new, exciting challenges to claybird shooters as well as hunters. (Below) Assortment of flask spouts from Treso Gun Specialties can make loading more simple for all of the black powder fraternity.

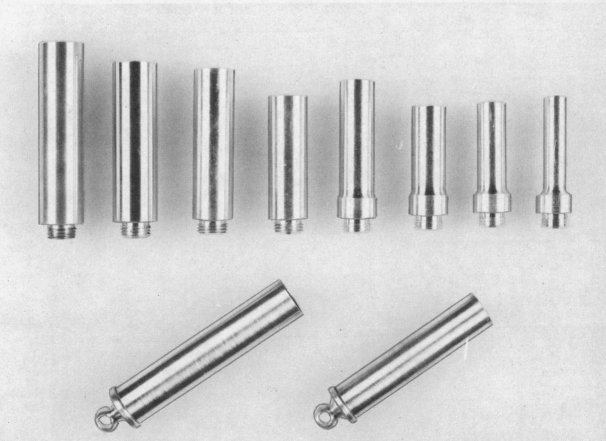

"First, make a cylindrical wooden form. Leave a little extra length and sand it smooth. The diameter should be a few thousandths under bore size of your tightest choked muzzle."

Either a thin bond paper or so-called onion skin paper may be used. Try both; you'll soon develop a preference. You may choose to nitrate this by brief immersion in a saturated solution of potassium nitrate in water, then spread it to dry on newspapers.

Nitrated paper is instantly consumed upon firing — a safety factor — but it has the disadvantage of being somewhat brittle. You may prefer to skip this step.

"Cut a strip of paper that will just fit around the wooden form, with enough overlap for gluing the edge to make a tube. I use Elmer's Glue, sparingly. Slide the tubes off and set aside until the glue dries. Replace each on the form and tie one end closed with strong thread. Snip surplus paper off of this tied end."

Pour a measured charge of FFg black powder into a tube. Gently press the felt wads into place, one by one. These may be compressed for easy insertion, then smoothed out in place.

After the shot charge is poured in, various methods may be used for closing the end with a card wad.

You can insert the card wad and glue the paper's edge down by making the wooden form oversize at this point, so the paper tube will admit a card wad or you can fold the paper over the shot and glue the wad on top. Rubber cement is good at this step. Put it on both surfaces and let it dry for a minute. Align the wad properly because it will adhere immediately upon contact.

Finish by marking the card wad with the gauge, shot size and other desired data. Ackerman uses a waterproof ink felt marker for this.

Each cartridge may be squeezed gently to eliminate any lumpiness and reduce its diameter if necessary for ease of

Paper cartridges for black powder shooting can be made up beforehand. They cut loading time in field or on the trap range. The full directions for making these time-savers is included in the text.

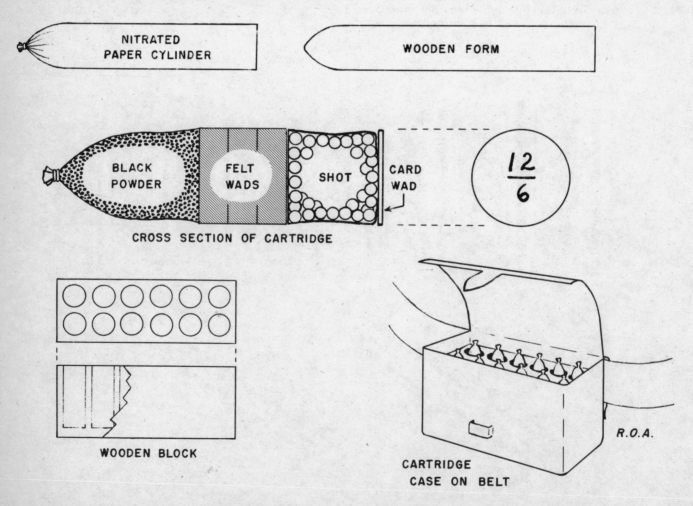

NITRATED PAPER CYLINDER

WOODEN FORM

BLACK POWDER — FELT WADS — SHOT — CARD WAD

CROSS SECTION OF CARTRIDGE

$\frac{12}{6}$

WOODEN BLOCK

CARTRIDGE CASE ON BELT

R.O.A.

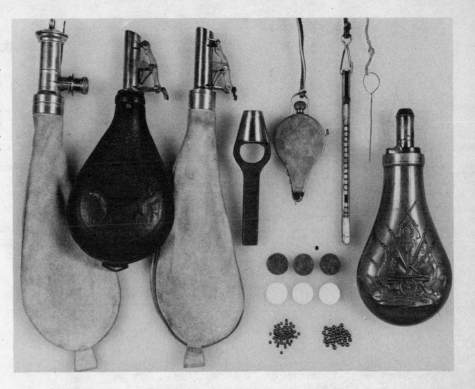

Currently produced accessories for black powder shooters include (from left): Original Remington shot pouch, with two new pouches from the Dixie Gun Works; a wadcutter; two magazine cappers; wire nipple pricker; felt and card wads; No. 6 and 8 shot; Dixon powder flask, which boasts an adjustable charger to aid loading.

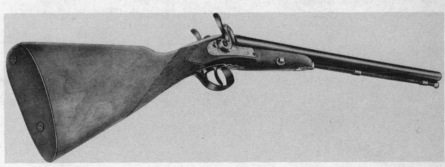

Metal butt plate rather than a pad may frighten the neophyte, but the recoil with black powder is nominal.

loading. It should enter the muzzle with a light push, up to the card wad, centering that wad for a firmer push with the ramrod.

Slim leaves the felt wads ungreased for these cartridges, as grease could ruin both the paper and the powder in time.

As a safety factor, the bottom tip should be torn off of a cartridge before placing in the muzzle. Then the powder will be behind all paper and no smoldering spark will remain in the bore. This takes only a moment and the powder will do its own pouring while you are ramming.

"Let me repeat my standard warning. Please always remove the cap from the unfired nipple if you are reloading only one barrel of a double gun!" Ackerman advises.

Once you've used these super-fast loads, you won't regret the time spent making them. The only other question is carrying them without breakage.

"Each shooter will have his own ideas. I simply borrowed the design of a Revolutionary War cartridge box. Holes drilled in a wooden block hold the cartridges, with the

Dixie Gun Works Model DPS-22 is a Spanish-made single-barrel percussion shotgun of 28 gauge with 33-inch blued barrels.

Connecticut Valley Arms' Frontier 12 gauge is a deluxe shotgun by black powder standards. Patent breech allows for easy take-down and cleaning simply by removing front locking pin.

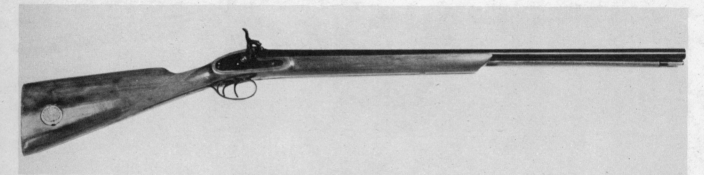

Above: The Connecticut Valley Arms 20-gauge Stagecoach model has few frills, is ideal for hunting use. (Left) CVA guns use a patented breech locking system, threaded plugs for additional strength.

heavy shot end down. A leather flap covers and protects them. End flaps could be added for a damper climate."

Another variation of the Colonial soldier was a longer, slimmer pouch, containing a row of tin tubes for flexibility. A second pouch could carry your gun worm, wiping patches, extra caps, etc.

One final tip: If you have difficulty loading a cartridge into a choked muzzle, sand down your wooden form until the paper tubes will slip easily into the tightest choke you have. If each felt wad is cupped slightly to fit in the tube, no problem. The force of explosion will split the paper and flatten the wads to full diameter, even if ramming did not do it.

With the growing interest in black powder shotgunning, a number of manufacturers and importers have moved into the field, some coming up with replicas of older established models, while others have come up with more modern variations that they feel offer the black powder shooter a better chance at hitting the clay target than was the case with the originals of the last century.

As indicated by Slim Ackerman, though, black powder shotguns seem to come in virtually all grades and it is a good idea to look over a gun firsthand before you start laying out hard-earned loot for the purpose of spraying the sky with lead and burned charcoal.

Dixie Gun Works double-barrel muzzleloading shotgun has brown-finished barrels. (Below) Navy Arms' 1837 Enfield two-band 12-gauge replica has shorter barrel.

Above: Dixie Gun Works single barrel flint fowler is 14 gauge with 37-inch barrels. (Below) 1882 Morse single-barrel 12 gauge is made in USA by Navy Arms Company.

Chapter 4

A MATTER OF FIT

MALCOLM LYELL AND Norman Clarke cut quite a swath through the shooting population of the United States during a trip from England. Their activities in such cities as Portland, San Francisco, Los Angeles, San Antonio, Houston, Dallas, Atlanta and Pittsburgh still are being talked about.

Now in case you never heard of either gentleman, Lyell is the managing director of Holland and Holland, Limited, and Clarke is the firm's senior shooting instructor. I don't know anyone with an interest in shotgunning who hasn't heard of H&H, but for the record, this is the British firm which boasts that it makes the most expensive sporting guns in the world and whose customers include Prince Philip.

Purpose of this swing around the country was to show and demonstrate Holland & Holland's sporting guns and rifles, with Clarke fitting both men and women for new guns, as well as giving shooting instructions. They made a similar tour in the United States a couple of years ago, which must have been relatively successful to bring them back.

Two new H&H models were introduced — one of the chief reasons for the tour. Their Holland-Beretta over/under now is being manufactured by Pietro Beretta, the Italian firm, to the British organization's specifications, then is stocked, engraved and finished by H&H to the cutomer's own wants.

Also introduced was the firm's new single-barrel trap gun, which I have yet to see, but which the two Britishers insisted is of "fine quality especially designed for American trapshooters."

Arrangements were made for gun fitting and coaching to take place at gun clubs outside of all of the cities visited and Clarke was available for instruction — at the rate of $60 per hour incidentally, and such instruction was by appointment only.

Holland and Holland was established in 1835 and remained in the same offices in London's New Bond Street until 1960, when it moved its showrooms and head office to more spacious modern quarters. The London factory is completely self-contained and the guns — excepting the new Beretta model — are made from start to finish in this one building. Special presentation models, customized to individual requirements with gold inlays, can cost as much as $12,000, but I suspect most of us would be more inclined to hire a full-time guard for such a piece and shudder at the thought of shooting such a prize. As one on-looker commented in Los Angeles, with a shake of his head, "That

Here's How The Pros Measure, But You May Be Able To Use The Info For Your Next Buy!

kind of gun's not for shooting; it's just for selling."

Back in 1932, Holland and Holland set up its own shooting school on some sixty acres near London with the idea of providing a high, uniform standard of instruction to live up to the reputation of the firm's guns. To make sure they start the season with eye, swing and footwork coordinated, Lyell says, many of the finest shots in Britain visit the school, where grounds simulate natural conditions.

Holland and Holland, of course, has been producing quality double and single-barrel rifles for more than a century and many of the world's best known big-game rifle cartridges have been introduced by the firm and the belted cartridge case used in most types of magazine rifle cartridges was invented by H&H technicians. However, the firm probably is best known for the Holland Royal shotgun, the most expensive gun in the world.

Lyell, who has been involved with the gun trade for some twenty years, is no desk chair shooter. He has traveled and shot extensively in India, Pakistan, Afghanistan, Iran, East Africa, Ethiopia, Eritrea and Egypt, as well as in Europe.

Norman Clarke, the senior instructor at the H&H shooting school, has been called the finest shooting instructor and coach in the world and he coaches and fits guns for some 1500 people each year at the school.

When he visited the United States in 1966, he coached and fitted about 350 shooters during his seven-week tour.

But these days, one doesn't have to wait for a visiting Englishman to fit him for a custom-built gun. Pedersen Guns, the custom branch of O.F. Mossberg & Sons, Incorporated, is going all-out to see that a man gets the gun he wants and one that fits him at the same time. The firm has set up franchised dealers — all top names in the retail field — across the country and each of these outfits has its own Try-Gun, which is used to fit one exactly for his new gun.

The factors that go into fitting a gun to a shooter, which are incorporated in Pedersen's Try-Gun system, are: height and shape of the comb; length and shape of the stock; the angle or pitch of the stock; and distance of the pistol grip from the trigger. No fitting involves the forend of the shotgun, for this is affected only by stock length.

Standard dimensions from most of the arms manufacturers are:

	Field or Skeet Gun	Trap Gun
Length of pull	14"	14½"
Drop at comb	1½"	1-3/8"
Drop at heel	2½"	1-3/8" & 2"
Pitch (downward)	2" @ 28"	1" @ 30"

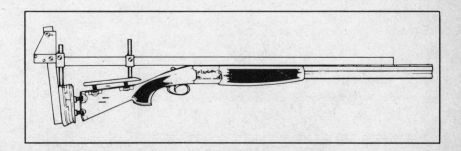

These are the initial settings on Pedersen's Try-Gun when a new shooter comes in for a fitting, since most will deviate but slightly from these measurements. When the gun is set and the dealer has checked that it's safe to handle, it is handed to the shooter for a trial fit.

While the shooter is aiming at a spot slightly higher than head level, the dealer is busy checking the stance, correcting if necessary. The face should be well forward on the comb of the stock, the butt well up on the shoulder. Though inclined slightly forward, the body shouldn't be bent either backwards or forwards at the waist and the leading knee should be bent slightly. In the case of right-handed shooters, the left knee and vice versa for southpaws.

The feet should be spread apart comfortably, with the leading foot pointed at the target and the other angled away from it. The leading foot bears most of the weight, to counteract the effects of recoil when firing the gun in the field.

If the proper stance is assumed, the first measurement taken is the length of pull — the distance from the center of the trigger to the middle of the butt plate. The gun again is held in firing position, well up on the shoulder with the face forward on the comb, and the first joint of the trigger finger wrapping around the trigger. The thumb of the trigger hand encircles the pistol grip and the first area of scrutiny is the distance between the shooter's nose and thumb.

If this distance is an inch and a half or less, recoil might

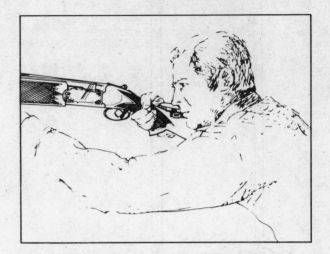

After checking the shooter's stance, the fitter will check the distance between the nose and thumb where the latter overlaps the pistol grip. This distance should be no closer than 1½ inches, nor longer than two inches. This is initial step in determining the length of pull.

The first thing a dealer will do is have the shooter assume the proper stance, as is shown below, aiming slightly above eye level. Stance is critical to fit.

cause the nose to painfully contact the thumb. Conversely, the distance between nose and thumb on the stock shouldn't be much over two inches, as the stock then might be too long and result in snagging on shooting clothes when placing it in the shoulder. This rule doesn't apply for trap guns, however, as they are already in the shoulder when the bird emerges from the trap house. More on fitting trap guns later.

Interestingly, the Pedersen gunfitters have determined that shirtsleeve length often corresponds to proper length of pull. For example, a 33-inch sleeve length probably calls for a stock of 14 inches; 34-inch, 14¼; 35-inch, 14½; 36-inch, 14¾; and big guys around six inches short of seven feet tall might even need a 15-inch length of pull, if they have long arms.

At the other end of the measurement spectrum, men of short, stocky build with short arms may only need a stock of 13¼ or 13½-inch pull, which should fit most ladies of average size, too. Petite women may require a 12½-inch length of pull, but this is determined by the fitter.

The position of the butt plate or recoil pad is the next area scrutinized under the Try-Gun fitting method. Ideally, the gun rests in the hollow between the upper arm and chest, roughly one-quarter to one-half-inch below the top of the shoulder. To be most comfortable, it should repose fully against the shoulder muscle, except for the toe, which isn't allowed to dig in. These factors in mind, the fitter has the shotgunner raise the gun to the shoulder several times, until consistency of placement in the shoulder is apparent, at which time he notes any adjustments that need to be made to bring the gun to the proper height.

Another term for the foregoing is determining the drop at the heel. Once the amount of adjustment is noted, the

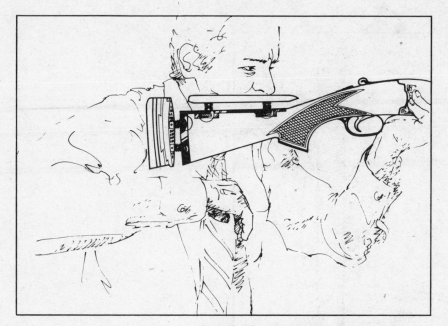

Length of pull established, drop at the heel is calculated. The butt should be nearly level with top of shoulder, but one-fourth or one-half-inch below is okay.

Try-Gun is laid upside-down on a desk or hard, raised surface, the front bead off the edge. A ruler then is employed to measure exactly what the drop at the heel should be.

If the heel — the topmost point of the shotgun butt — is too low and needs raising, this procedure actually decreases the amount of pitch — the angle of the gun's butt — and brings the toe of the butt into closer contact with the shoulder. The shooter raises the gun to the shoulder several more times and, if the fitter is satisfied with the adjustment, the pair move on to the most important stage of all: determining the drop at the comb.

The comb, for anyone not familiar with shotgun terminology, is the area upon which the cheek rests during firing, thereby aligning the aiming eye on the sighting plane. Improper fit at this point could cause many missed shots in the field.

The fitter has the shooter face a window or other light source and assumes a position directly in front of the shooter and between him and that light source, some seven to eight feet away. The fitter then closes one eye and asks the shooter to aim at the open eye. He then holds a forefinger, in a semi-pointing position, just below the front sight and has the shooter hold the point for several seconds before repeating the maneuver. During this procedure, he observes where the shooter's eye is in relation to the sighting plane — in the case of the Try-Gun, a ventilated rib — as well as the shoulder position of the butt and the shooter's stance.

If the stance and buttstock placements are satisfactory, he turns his attention specifically to the pupil of the sighting eye. If he cannot see the pupil of the sighting eye, the comb is too low and should be raised until the pupil is visible over the rib. The entire pupil should be visible and about one-eighth-inch above the sighting plane. If the pupil appears higher than this, the comb must be lowered.

Sometimes the fitter will note a shooter having difficulty aligning his eye directly behind the sighting plane and this condition usually is encountered with individuals having either chubby or thin faces. A gentleman with a thin face often finds his eye over to the right of the sighting plane, as he looks down the barrel. This condition calls for a fuller comb. Conversely, the man with a chubby face will have his eye to the left of the sighting plane as he looks down the barrel and requires a thinner comb than normal.

Thinning the comb generally increases the amount of recoil the shooter feels on his face, which can be uncomfortable at worst or distracting at best. Therefore, much thinning should be avoided.

What the fitter does, if the eye is one-eighth-inch or more off the sighting plane, is cast-off the stock away from the shooter. Cast-off is measured from a prolongation of the centerline of the rib and center of the heel top. Usually, one-quarter-inch of cast-off is enough and seldom is one-half-inch exceeded. Cast-on, or casting the stock toward the shooter, is rarely done and is avoided wherever possible.

As previously noted, the fitter checks the shooter's shotgun behavior for consistency prior to making any changes on the comb height or thickness. It is imperative that he assume exactly the same position with the anatomy on each and every aiming or the readings taken won't necessarily be true.

The pitch or angle of the butt stock, even if fitted with a recoil pad, is one of the last measurements taken. As noted in the chart earlier, the standard pitch on field or skeet guns usually is two inches for a twenty-eight-inch barrel. Trap guns are somewhat straighter, from one to one and one-half inches for a thirty-inch barrel.

67

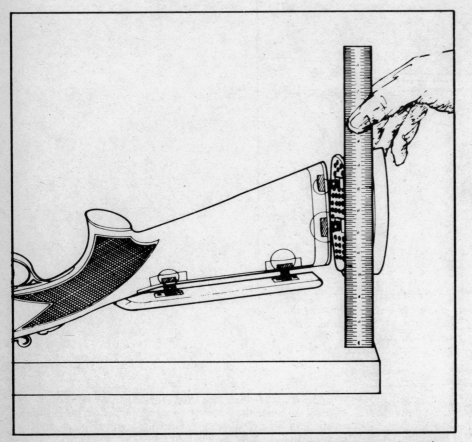

With drop at heel adjustment made on the Try-Gun while on the shoulder, the gun is next removed and placed rib-down on a flat surface. A ruler then measures distance from surface to top of heel in inches.

These measurements are fine for the majority of shooters, but some gunners with heavier or slender frames could require either more or less downward pitch. Heavily built men with barrel chests could require two and one-half to three-inch pitches on a gun with twenty-eight-inch barrels, while a man of slight build might require only one and one-half inches of downward pitch.

The adjustment is calculated while the shooter is cradling the gun in his shoulder. The Try-Gun then is removed, the adjustment made and the gun placed barrel up on the floor, against a wall or other straight surface. After assuring the butt is flatly positioned along its entirety against the floor, the fitter measures the distance from the wall to the top of the sighting plane, which denotes the amount of pitch the shooter requires.

The average distance from the pistol grip to trigger is four inches, which is satisfactory for shooters with average-sized hands. However, for a man with large hands or long fingers, the fitter may determine a measurement of four

and one-quarter inches is better. Likewise, if the shooter's hand is small with short fingers, this distance may be reduced closer than the four-inch average.

Relatively little has been mentioned on using the Try-Gun to fit trapshooters, to avoid confusion since many of the measurements for field and skeet guns differ for trapsters.

Stocks on trap guns are longer than for field firearms, for a multitude of reasons. There is no worry about snagging the butt on clothing when raising it to the shoulder, since the gun already is shouldered when the bird is called for, which means that longer stocks are acceptable. Longer stocks also cut recoil, important when gunners are popping shells by the box for the better part of a day. For these reasons, it's found that most trapshooters prefer their stocks one-half to three-quarters of an inch longer than their field or skeet guns.

Another thing the fitter keeps in mind regarding trap guns is that they're normally held and cheeked more firmly

Probably the most important phase of fitting the shotgun is measuring the drop at comb. The shooter aims at fitter's one open eye, the fitter holding index finger below the barrel. The eye should be directly over the rib on each point, just above it, or some new measuring steps need to be taken.

If a shooter has a thin or chubby face, often the stock must be cast-off away from him, or the dimensions of the comb changed to compensate. Thin faces require fuller combs, while the chubby faces need combs thinner. See text for dangers involved with getting comb too thin.

than field or skeet guns, which means the distance between the nose and thumb on the stock can be increased considerably — even to two and one-quarter or three inches. Most trapshooters also prefer a somewhat higher comb, which raises the eye slightly higher above the rib, so they get a better view of their sighting plane.

On the average, most trapshooters prefer less pitch to

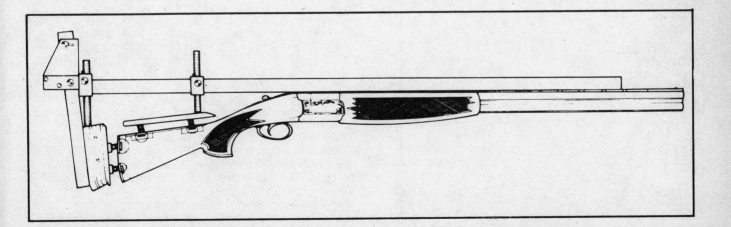

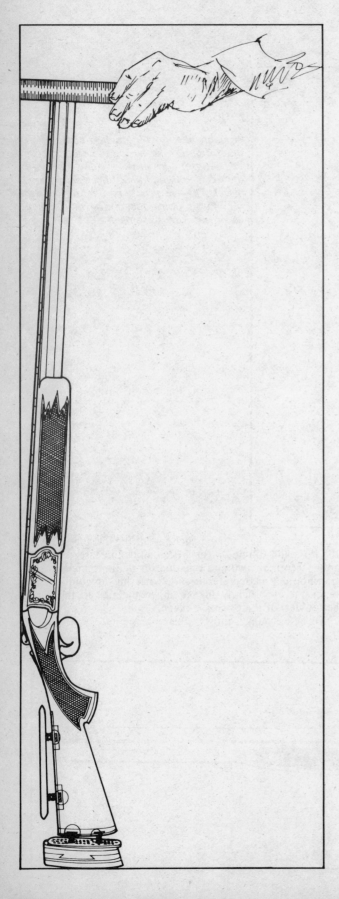

The amount of pitch required by the shooter next is measured, while the shooter is cradling the gun in his shoulder. Some heavy-framed men will require guns with 2½ or three inches of pitch, while slender men require only 1½ or one-inch of pitch. The adjustment made on the gun, it then is removed and stood against a wall or other straight surface, muzzle skyward, butt flat. A ruler then is used to measure the distance between the rib top and the wall, which indicates needed pitch.

their buttstocks than on their field guns, generally one-inch for a gun with a thirty-inch barrel. The toe of the recoil pad is more rounded off than field models, also, and many stocks feature a Monte Carlo design.

The Monte Carlo type stocks often are more of a requirement than a luxury. The combination of high comb, long pull and low heel can make recoil pretty stiff on the cheekbone. But the Monte Carlo comb is straight in relation to the cheek and won't batter the face. The drops at the point and rear of the Monte Carlo comb are generally identical, varying from one and one-quarter to one and three-quarters inches, or even up to two inches, depending upon the individual.

Simply, many trapshooters find the Monte Carlo stock more comfortable to shoot. Also appealing is the lessened effect of recoil from the straight comb and, even if the gun is checked one-half-inch or so from normal, the shooter still is on target.

It would be slightly more than an exaggeration to state that a custom-fitted gun was necessary for optimum accuracy, because this statement is disproved by a big hunk

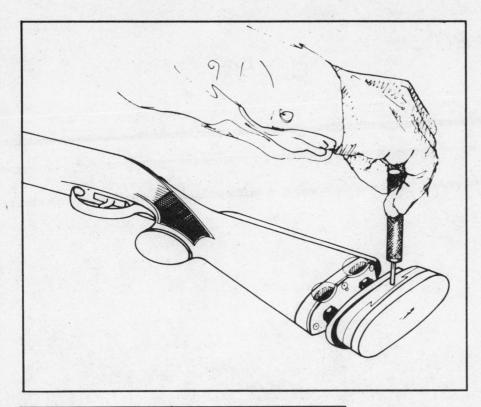

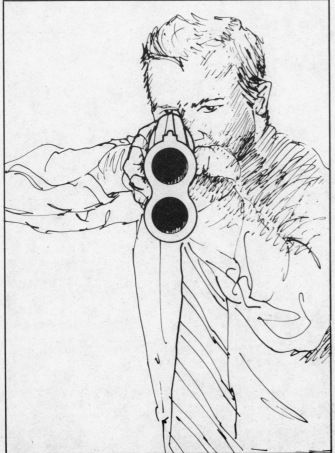

As detailed in the text, casting-on — moving the stock closer to the shooter — is rarely done because recoil is increased. Casting-off rarely measures more than one-quarter inch, in the case of extremely thin-faced men (above). This is how the perfect sight picture should appear (left). Make sure that consistency in placing the gun in the shoulder is present, or all measurements will be untrue. This leads to errant shooting scores.

of the American scattergunning sect every year. Shotguns, depending upon the manufacturer to a slight degree, come off the production lines in pretty much standard dimensions. The reason behind this, naturally, is production cost, which is kept low through this system.

But the standard measurements of factory-produced guns don't fit every hunter, although they can adapt to their smoothbores. In fact, I personally have hunted with some Paul Bunyon-sized gents who literally engulf the shotgun with their huge fists and throw it to their shoulders as if it were no bigger than a cane fishing pole. Others I've seen in blinds have truly had to stretch their short arms to the limit to reach the trigger, often having almost no bend in their elbows!

But these gentlemen have adapted to their firearms and have become consistent meat-takers in the hunting fields. Therein lies the secret of all shooting, whether the gun is custom-fitted or not: consistency. Drawing exactly the same sight alignment each time, calculating the leads, following through, et al.

But the thing that intrigues me is how these gents can tolerate shooting their smoothbores. Shooting, to me, is a form of recreation and relaxation, and I don't want to be fighting my shotgun all the time. Rather than me conforming to its oddities, I'll have it conform to mine.

Chapter 5

Accident-Free Gun Handling Is The Responsibility Of Every Shooter, But Here Are Some Gentle Reminders!

THINK SAFE!

It's better to be safe; taking to the hunting fields these days calls for easily visible clothing such as the blaze orange vests now offered.

THERE'S REALLY NOTHING new to safety, but there are always new shooters and youngsters who don't know the rules and a few others who don't practice them. So, a little repetition can do no harm and hopefully, some good — especially at a time when there is the specter of further gun controls.

Sadly, there are always plenty of stories about hunters shooting people they thought were animals. No one, worthy of the name hunter, ever just thinks before taking the responsibility of releasing a lethal load into the country-side. He makes damn sure first and if there's the slightest shadow of doubt, for any reason whatever, he doesn't shoot. So you lose a bird or a buck and maybe save a life.

This would appear to be the time at which to point out that the nation's anti-gun forces constantly are taking every incident and pushing it for all it is worth. As a result, there are a great number more stories about people being killed accidentally by guns than there are stories about people's lives that have been saved by having a gun — or could have been saved had they had a firearm of some sort. I'm not speaking strictly in terms of crime and law enforcement, either. Instead, I'm thinking of those lost in the wilderness, forced down in aircraft and otherwise find themselves on their own with no way of providing food or signalling for help.

According to one major insurance company which is vitally interested in such statistics, hunting ranks sixteenth in the list of hazardous sports. First on the list is football.

While it may be easy to make mistakes such as the one being illustrated here, think of shotgun safety as common etiquette; consider others as you would have them think of you.

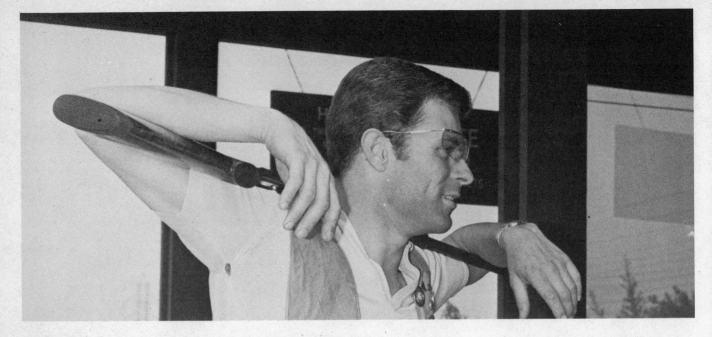

The man who treats his firearm with respect goes far to win the respect of his associates. This shooter's manners may be poor, but he has the good sense to wear shooting glasses.

Left: Never load your gun until on the firing line and ready to shoot. Actions should be kept open with muzzle pointed straight up or down at all other times for safety sake.

Accidents at churches, theaters and concerts rank fifteenth. The full list, in order of danger, is as follows: (1) football; (2) winter sports; (3) baseball; (4) swimming; (5) basketball; (6) skating; (7) accidents in the country or at the beach; (8) bicycling; (9) accidents at parks, picnics and outings; (10) golf; (11) horseback riding; (12) boating and canoeing; (13) gymnastics; (14) fishing; (15) accidents at churches, theaters and concerts; (16) hunting.

Then there are the stories about the people who shoot themselves while cleaning their guns. Ever struck you how difficult it must be to clean the barrel of a loaded gun? But until everyone thinks consciously and deliberately about gun safety and puts it into practical effect at all times,

safety reminders certainly can do no harm and perhaps eliminate some of the sad, unnecessary stories caused by an unthinking minority which make wonderful ammunition for the Anti's to attack the safety-conscious majority.

I've had a number of opportunities in recent years to discuss shotgunning and safety with Derek Partridge, an English shooter with a long list of titles in shotgunning circles in his home country. A perennial Olympic contender for the Great Britain team, he is chairman of the British International Board of Clay Pigeon Shooting Association and is involved in doing public relations for Britain's Shooting Sports Trust, the Gun Trader's Association and the Long Room Committee. The last is a joint body of all

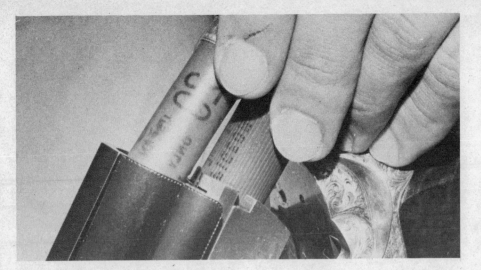

Left: Carelessly loading a 20-gauge shell in a 12-gauge gun, the small shell will drop down the barrel. If a second shell is loaded behind it, your shotgun may possibly blow up.

Gun atop a car roof can fall off at the time the car is started if it is left. Leaning against the bumper, it can be knocked over and could fire.

Gun racks are for holding guns safely. Guns can be knocked down elsewhere, which is dangerous, hard on the gun.

shooting sports bodies against Government legislation on firearms in Great Britain. He also is on the staff of one of the leading European ammunition companies.

As one might suspect, with this background and the means by which he makes his livelihood, Partridge is especially interested in safety in the shooting sports, but he was equally interested during the period several years ago, when he was living in Hollywood, teaching shotgunning to members of the movie industry.

Apart from years of coaching, he has been range safety officer at many clubs and always welcomed new shooters or members with: "I am much less interested in how good or bad a shot you are or will be, than I am to see how safe a shot you are or become."

What his greeting really means (cloaked behind polite British indirectness) is: "If you're safe, welcome among us. If not, learn or beat it."

He always aims to deal politely, but firmly, with anyone committing a breach of gun safety, but in the few cases where someone really asked for it, his character changes rapidly from its usual suave, urbane, cultured self, to sharp, cold, controlled anger.

"Claybusting has a wonderfully accident-free record and I will always do my best to keep it that way. I have been known to brusquely interrupt a competition when a rare emergency situation demanded it. I don't care how many lost targets are blamed on me, if I feel a danger exists. However, whenever possible, I prefer to take the offender aside and quietly explain his misdemeanor — the first time that is," Partridge explains.

"If there's a second, I'll publicly roast him over the loudspeaker system. Harsh words and actions? Maybe. But what price human life and limb? Think too how the perpetrator of such an injury or death would feel, bearing it on his conscience for the rest of his days.

"We all make mistakes sometimes. But a reasonable man

Walking into a gun club with the action closed can get one banned in some of the more safety-conscious establishments. Firearms safety never should be taken for granted.

will accept what you say, apologize and thank you. While others will curse you and leave — good riddance. We don't need that kind of person in the shooting fraternity.

"I am not too impressed by some of the gun handling I have observed at shooting clubs here. Even at the recent Olympic Games Trials, I was horrified to see some of the nation's shooting elite walking round with over/unders un-broken and automatics with their actions closed. There are only two times when a gun should be closed at a club — when ready for firing and immediately before being placed in the gun-rack. At all other times, guns should be broken and automatics, with open breeches, should be pointed away from people. There are no half measures where safety is concerned.

"In the field, it is naturally much harder to control gun handling and safety. The bright, colored clothing worn here by hunters to preserve their lives is unknown in Europe. There they wear sensible, nature-blending colors which won't make game take off for the county line while you're still miles away.

"In Germany, for instance, before they can get either a gun or hunting license, they must pass stiff written and practical exams in gun safety and handling, recognition of which species can and cannot be shot and when, and also basic fieldcraft.

"Even after passing, there is still a long probationary period during which they may only go out with a fully licensed hunter. Tiresome? Perhaps, but how many hunting accidents have you ever heard of in Germany?"

I don't necessarily agree with Partridge on some of his points. I don't believe he ever has done much hunting in the United States, so possibly doesn't understand much of our peculiar problem.

Most hunting in Europe, for example, is closely con-trolled. With the lack of public lands, those who want to hunt usually end up on preserves, where their every move-ment is closely controlled by preserve overseers. In northern Italy, for example, the late King Victor Emmanual's summer palace now sits in the middle of a privately owned game preserve. During the time friends of mine have hunted birds there, each pair of shooters had their own guide and loader; at times there was one game-keeper to each shooter. In such situations, where these gamekeepers know every foot of ground in the preserve and

No matter how empty the chamber may be, there is no excuse for leaning on the muzzle of any firearm. It can cost you an arm or two or your head.

can position a shooter to keep him out of trouble with other hunters, this is a highly controlled situation.

But my feeling is that it verges on becoming a part of the Computer Age. In this type of hunting, there is no such thing as simply taking your gun and your dog, moving out into open fields and hills, or finding a likely looking spot at the edge of a natural duck pond. And in situations where one is on his own, it doesn't hurt to wear bright, alarming colors to let other hunters know you are in the area. In fact, I consider this simple common sense!

There are some basic field safety rules, which you may have read a hundred times before, or never. Whichever the case, think about each and every one. Then, put them into practice for the sake of yourself, your fellow hunters, mem-

bers of the public and for the preservation of your own sport. Apart from the personal suffering caused, each accident not only hurts all of us a bit more, but tarnishes the name we want to be proud to bear — sportsmen.

There are all sorts of rules involving safety; almost every gun club has its own as well as those based upon National Rifle Association recommendations. But here are those Partridge, as a professional instructor, attempts to teach others.

1. Never point your gun at anyone.

2. Never load a gun until it is required for a shot.

3. Never push the safety off until the moment of shooting.

4. Never shoot at anything until you have ascertained,

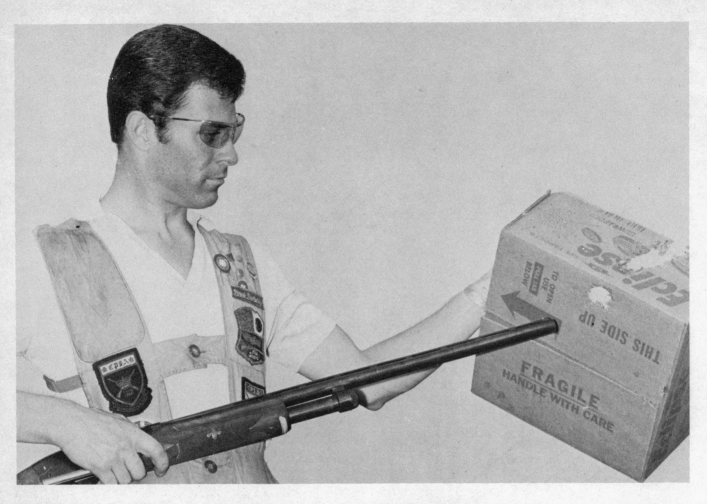

Instructor Derek Partridge uses a cardboard carton, shooting hole in it at close range, during his safety lectures. This illustrates his point. Note he wears shooting glasses.

beyond any doubt, what it is.

5. Never shoot if you can't see, beyond any doubt, that there could be no one in your line of fire.

6. Always make sure you know where all members of your party are — and vice versa.

7. Carry your gun either on your shoulder with the triggers facing upwards or under your arm with the barrels pointing directly at the ground in front of you.

8. Never cross obstacles with a loaded gun.

9. Always unload your gun and leave it open before passing it to anyone.

10. Finally — never shoot — if in any doubt.

11. Check the barrels immediately after assembling to see there is no obstruction.

12. Inspect the barrels again for obstruction before loading.

13. Always inspect a gun to see it is unloaded when taking it from or returning it to its rack or case, or when receiving it from another person.

14. Never load a gun with shells more powerful than those for which the gun is proofed.

15. Never mix 12 and 20-gauge shells. A twenty will drop through the chamber and wedge tight half way down the barrel — allowing the subsequent, inadvertent loading of a 12-gauge shell.

16. Always have guns overhauled annually.

17. Keep guns locked away when not in use.

Until now, most of this discussion has been involved with safety for others, but there is one particular facet that I feel needs mentioning. It can save the individual shooter a good deal of personal grief and, again, comes under the heading of common sense.

In the matter of shotshells mentioned here, there have been instances over the years wherein a shooter has dropped a 20-gauge shell into the bore of a 12-gauge gun, then later shoved another 12 in on top of it, not realizing that the smaller shell has dropped on through into the barrel, past the chamber, to become lodged there. Needless to say, the resulting double explosion is not conducive to personal health and can ruin a shotgun even if one suffers no personal damage.

Federal Cartridge Company, with headquarters in Minneapolis, was the first to pioneer color coding of shotshells. Each of the various gauges was made with a different color paper in the tube. Now that plastic is being used in shotshells, the same colors still are being used to differentiate and serve as an additional reminder to the shooter.

It may not do much for a color-blind shooter, but other companies have taken this lead to start similar color coding plans. The safest method, of course, is not to mix the various gauges in your shell bag, but to keep them separated at all times. Thus, even in the heat of a good bird shoot such as incoming doves at sundown, when there is only a few minutes of fast, frantic shooting, there is no chance of making a mistake that can ruin your shoot, if not your gun or person.

The shotgunner who insists upon wearing shooting glasses may all too often be accused of going Hollywood, bowing to an affectation, but claybird shooting — as well as upland game hunting — is the one area where they are most needed.

I've seen many a shooter who will insist that he can't shoot while wearing glasses; that they get in his way; that he can't get used to them. There is plenty of evidence to show that he should learn to shoot with glasses, even if he doesn't do his best in the beginning.

This brings to mind the case of Henry Joy, one of the early skeet greats in this country. In fact, he was the first shooter to set up a fully automatic skeet field so that the gunner could activate his bird simply by stepping on an electrically controlled button.

Back in the days when he was considered a great shooter, Joy shot without glasses until the day that a pellet ricocheted back and put out his right eye. Much must be said for his tenacity for, instead of giving up the game entirely, he learned to shoot all over again, using his left eye and shooting from the same shoulder. In fact, the next year, he used this method to win the National Skeet Championships. However — and herein lies the moral — he was wearing shooting glasses this time, and shot 250 straight. To the best of my knowledge, he has worn them ever since.

Henry Joy, several times All-American, won every tournament he entered in those days and was 20-gauge Nationals champion the year that I was runner-up. He was undoubtedly the greatest skeet shooter of the early days, to my mind.

Much must be said for his tenacity in learning to shoot all over again after his accident instead of simply giving up the game entirely.

There are those, of course, who will feel that I am particularly prejudiced, but I have worn shooting glasses from the day I first stepped onto a firing line back in my early teens. I probably made mistakes there, too, as I normally wore the darkest shade of sunglasses I could find, then when ready to shoot, switched to something much lighter in color. It made that claybird loom up like a giant condor, but I'm not so sure that it did my eyesight any great amount of good. I'm sure an oculist or optician would have some words of wisdom along this line.

However, over the years, I've had more than one lens of those glasses hit by a rebounding pellet. In fact, I've even seen onlookers at skeet matches suffer similar treatment to their shooting glasses. At eight-post — and that's where Henry Joy got it — or in high wind, this can be a particular hazard, experience has shown.

As indicated, I feel the same about the necessity of shooting glasses in upland game shooting; in any situation where there is a more or less flat trajectory of fire and there are likely to be others in the same area also shooting. It's as important to the shooter's personal safety as not overloading his shells.

In a lifetime of shooting upland game, I suspect that almost everyone has been hit by a stray pellet at one time or another and must realize the importance of wearing eye protection.

I would no sooner allow my wife or children to go to a skeet match without wearing protective glasses than I would allow them to move their seats in front of the firing line.

With the prescription glasses available to everyone today, there is still another advantage, of course. One does not have to simply go and pick up any pair of glasses for protection. He can have his shooting glasses ground to meet his own specific corrective problem — and he'll no doubt find his shooting improved as a result.

I probably have a dozen pair lying around the house and I've found that about the only requirement for being able to shoot with glasses in comfort is to be certain that they fit well enough that they will ride high on the forehead. In this way, one is not looking over the tops of the lenses when his head is down.

All of this no doubt sounds pretty basic to a lot of shooters, but about all one has to do is to go to a skeet match and look around to determine the number of competitors who have not yet gotten the message. Let's hope some of them don't have to lose an eye to learn.

Finally, never fool around with guns — they're lethal weapons, not toys. Remember, kids follow the example of their elders.

To a newcomer, the performance of a gun is almost magical. You pull a trigger, a clay disintegrates, a bird drops out of the sky or an animal drops dead hundreds of yards away.

Partridge, as an instructor, uses the intrigue with firearms to make his safety points.

"A brief practical demonstration, with which I very effectively initiate all my pupils, is to show them a plastic shell with the pellets clearly visible. Then I load the gun and fire it either into a cardboard box or into the ground a few feet in front of you (carefully avoiding the toes — if you go in for long, pointed shoes).

"The gaping, smoking hole should indelibly imprint in their minds a vivid image of a gun's destructive power and insure the proper degree of respect."

Finally, for those interested in seeing the shooting sports continue, simply think of safety as an extension of public relations. As mentioned, the anti-gun forces will use each accident in an attempt to get guns outlawed. They ignore the statistics, including the fact that one can get injured more easily in church than in the hunting fields. So it behooves each of us to do his best to make the statistics even more amazing — in our own favor!

When in transit to or from shooting line, any gun should be carried in the position shown. Note that the trigger guard is up, free of any likelihood of snagging.

In cleaning, solvent, lubricating oil, preservative grease all should be close at hand, with unloaded gun.

These Simple Directions Can Save
A Trauma, When You Stare Down
The Bore Of Your Favorite Shot Shooter!

THE CLEAN SCENE

Chapter 6

HAVE YOU EVER taken your favorite shotgun out of its case to find that it's no longer the pristine beauty it once was? Those once-shiny bores are cloudy in appearance, dark streaks running parallel the length of the bore and, as you check even more closely, you find that around the muzzles, possibly, there's a small ring of red rust. Such sights can ruin the day of even the sturdiest-hearted gun owner.

Even though a firearm is cleaned when we return from a hunting trip, it doesn't mean the gun, itself, is really clean and will withstand several months of being stored in a closet, in the back of a cupboard, or other such customary in-the-home storage places for firearms.

If the gun is to be used again within the next day or so, the customary cleaning that most of us give our gun after a hunt is normally sufficient. However, if the gun is to be put away until next season, then it should be cleaned much more thoroughly and several stronger measures should be taken as concerns lubrication and storage-type coatings.

There are several things to consider, since this type of cleaning is much more extensive, takes more energy, and requires a sturdier workbench than the customary swabbing we normally give a gun.

We'll need a workbench, preferably with some type of a vise with padded jaws. The padding may be lead or copper sheeting, or it could even be pieces of wood. The main thing is that the jaws of the vise, which are normally of steel and often quite rough, must be covered with some type of material which will not scratch the finish off any of the gun parts which are placed within it.

Also on hand must be ample supplies of our favorite powder solvent, gun grease and patches, and we must have a suitable cleaning rod; sturdy enough so that it neither bends nor comes apart at the joints and has threading which will allow the fitting of cleaning attachments in place of the normal jag.

We will need several other items, such as good, heavy bronze or brass-bristled brushes, an old, discarded toothbrush and a Tomlinson cleaner or similar heavy-duty attachment.

If you don't have the latter, you can make do with brass or copper screen material, although it has been my experi-

A vise is better than another pair of hands. But be sure to clamp the barrel at solid points, not on the tubes. Support the other end with block or non-scratching material.

All of these scrubbers can be used, depending upon the condition of the barrel. Do not reverse brass brush inside the barrel, as bristles bend and lose their scrubbing capability.

All vise jaws should be padded. These jaws have been covered with sheet lead to avoid scratching.

Typewriter brushes are handy around the workbench for any number of jobs. In this case, such a brush is being used to clean assembly threads on Model 12.

ence that the Tomlinson cleaner usually is obtained more easily.

Several screwdrivers with the blades ground to fit gun screws also are a welcome addition to any good cleaning kit. One of these should have a long shank and be sturdy enough that you can loosen the through bolt which holds the receiver down into the butt stock of the gun. As a last resort, a small quantity of 4/0 steel wool also should be on hand. Anything more coarse possibly will scratch the steel of the gun upon which you're working.

The next step is to field-strip or dismantle the gun. Some shotguns have what is known as a solid-frame receiver and are not made to be disassembled readily except by a gunsmith. For this particular class of gun, most of the cleaning operations have to be performed from the muzzle instead of the breech end of the barrel. However, if you have any of the breakdown type of guns, such as a double-barreled shotgun, pump gun or automatic, which are of the so-called takedown variety, dismantle them into their major component pieces.

Using whatever material you have on hand with which to pad the jaws of the vise, affix the barrels or barrel or tube into the vise so that it will be held steadily while you conduct your cleaning operation. Do not clamp the hollow tube in the vise. Use a solid portion, such as the lugs on a double gun, etc. The first step is to clean the gun as you do normally; that is, with patches saturated with your favorite brand of nitro or powder solvent, then followed by dry

patches until the barrel is clean and dry. This may take several operations, but it is essential that the barrel be cleaned as well as you can get it, then dried thoroughly.

Even a slight coating of oil or solvent in a gun barrel can mask all types of horrid deficiencies within the inner confines of that tube. It therefore is necessary that, in order to inspect it carefully and thoroughly, the barrel must be clean and dry. One way to dry it more thoroughly and easily is to use enough patches on the drying pass of the cleaning rod to ensure the rod's passage through the barrel is fairly tight. This will clean the barrel and dry it better, more quickly and more easily than if you use the normally loose-fitting patch combination.

Most jags are made small enough to pass down through most full-choke barrels with ease with the use of only one patch. Consequently, if you have a more openly choked tube, an older gun in which the choke may have been opened slightly or the inside diameter of the barrel is a little larger than usual, the use of more patches on the drying pass will make the job go easier and faster.

After the barrel is clean and thoroughly dry — and not before — remove it from the vise and, holding it toward a source of light, such as a not-too-distant lightbulb, move the barrel slowly in a circular motion around the light. Look carefully through the barrel for signs of scratches, dirt patches and dark streaks extending longitudinally from the forcing cone of the barrel or through the choke cone of the barrel.

Any of these marks or dark places in a longitudinal pattern within the barrel denote the fact that the barrel is not clean and has leading or plastic coating. Under these areas, oxidation can form to rust and pit the barrel.

If your bore does betray signs of these disturbing elements, then other, more strigent measures must be taken to clean the barrel. Make several passes through the barrel with the brass or bronze-bristled brush. Reversal of the direction of travel within the barrel itself of this brush will bend the bristles, making the brush smaller in exterior diameter and consequently will impair its cleaning qualities.

When using such brass or bronze-bristled brushes, make full-length, full-stroke passes in one direction at a time through the barrel. All of this scrubbing action should take place, of course, with the barrels reaffixed within the vise.

Check once more against the light source for any dirt or lead streaking within the barrel. If the latter treatment did the job, fine. If not, then even more severe measures must be taken. This necessitates the use of the Tomlinson cleaner, which uses a screen wire mesh held tightly against the barrel by spring action. This same spring action allows it to expand or flex within the barrel as the interior diameter of the barrel changes; consequently, the Tomlinson cleaner gives a tight, cleaning fit against the inside of the tube at all times.

Pass the Tomlinson cleaner through the barrel two or three times. Then, with a clean patch, once again dry the interior of the barrel thoroughly and examine it against the light source. If necessary, repeat the latter step until the barrel is clean. Then, while the barrel or barrels still are held

Above: Double gun tubes always should be clamped into vise at lumps to avoid bends and scratches. (Below) If metal is rusted but not badly pitted, fine steel wool can be used with thin oil in removal of rust.

Some over/under guns have no lumps large enough to hold in vise. Solid portion of tube is blocked by extractors. Here barrels are carefully clamped in.

within the confines of the vise, thoroughly clean the exterior portion of the barrel.

Using the toothbrush, clean the serrations on the ventilated rib and the mounting posts/barrel junctures of the rib and all crevices or other rust-harboring or dirt-harboring areas on the outside of the barrels themselves. If there are any rust spots or places on the exterior of the barrels in which oxidation is taking place, saturate the rusty spot with oil and soak a small piece of the 4/0 steel wool with a good, light oil and apply in long, sweeping strokes until the rust has been carted off. Do not use coarser steel wool and do not use the steel wool in a dry condition — only when it has been well moistened with oil.

At this point, the barrels should be completely clean inside and out. Set the barrels aside and give the same toothbrush/steel wool treatment, if necessary, to the exterior portions of the receiver and the exposed metal of the forend.

In the case of the double-barreled guns or other guns in which there is a separate forend iron inletted into the underside of the wood, be careful to check that particular piece of metal for rust and lubrication.

If your gun is a double-barrel with hand-detachable sidelocks, this is the one time of year the sidelocks may be removed carefully and the locks of the gun oiled and replaced very carefully. If you do not know how to remove the sidelocks of a good double-barreled gun, don't try, but let your local gunsmith or another knowledgeable person remove the locks or plates.

After all metal surfaces are cleaned, if you have the proper screwdrivers and the right equipment, you may remove the butt stock from the receiver of most American-made pump and automatic arms and oil the inside of the receiver carefully. Do not use an excessive amount of oil — only that amount necessary to properly coat all metal surfaces and the working surfaces within the enclosed action. When the gun is placed in an upright position, excess oil will drain downward into the stock area and hasten the rotting of the wood at the juncture of metal and wood. If you can store your guns in any position other than butt down, barrel up, it will contribute to the longevity of the stock wood at its juncture with the receiver.

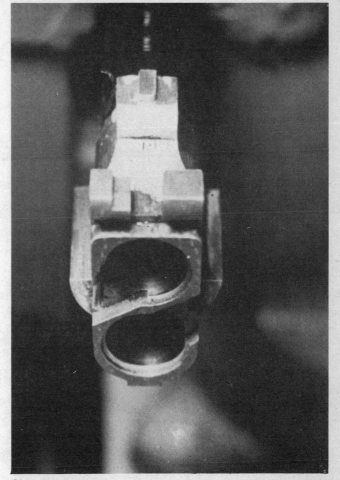

Chamber area, including under-surfaces of the extractors should be cleaned of all old grease and dirt. The area then should be coated with a good preservative.

At this point, all metal surfaces of the gun should be completely free of rust, completely dry, and now are ready for the application of a coat of preservative which will seal the metal against oxidation or rust. For this, do not use your favorite gun oil — or anybody else's favorite — as such oil is light and eventually will evaporate and leave metal surfaces exposed to the oxygen in the air which will cause rust. I favor one of the new patented, metal-adhering lubricant preservative greases. These retain their affinity for metal even when handled by you or persons looking at your guns. Light silicones will evaporate, so if you are inclined to use this type, use a heavy silicone grease and spread it on.

There are other polarized oils with petroleum bases that will do the job as well and better than a silicone grease without the worry of them evaporating before the next season rolls around, leaving your gun unprotected. Some of the aerosol sprays will do this work very well, but care must be used in the application of aerosol products upon firearms. Do not spray the products directly upon the guns themselves, but spray them on a patch, then apply the wetted patch to the exposed surfaces which you wish to protect.

After the gun has been cleaned, dried and preservatives applied, reassemble and keep it in the case or in an area in which you normally store your guns. If you keep your firearms in a fairly air-tight enclosure, the use of a desiccant is a great aid in reducing the moisture content of that area, so that the guns are less apt to rust, even when stored over a long period of time.

With the sharp increase of reloading in recent years, many hunters have been reloading for the field, as well as for claybirds.

THE OLD, THE NEW AND RENEWED OF SHOTSHELLS

Shotshell Development Began More Than Two Centuries Ago, But Reloading Is A Recent Innovation

Chapter 7

THERE ARE PLENTY of shooters who will tell you the only way they have been able to shoot a great deal of trap and skeet is through reloading. There are plenty of budgets these days that just won't stand three or four boxes of shells — or more — a week.

In fact, prior to World War II — and for even a few years after the Late Great Hate — claybirding was considered something of a rich man's sport. Reloading has changed much of that. In fact, it has even gone to the other extreme, putting shooting within the financial reach of almost anyone.

As an example, I repeat the story a friend tells about a visit to a Florida gun shop on the outskirts of Miami. In the middle of the floor was a wheelbarrow filled with empty shotshell cases. A sign stated that they were for sale at five cents per hull.

As this friend was visiting with the owner, an old Negro came in and began pawing through the fired hulls finally selecting three of them for more careful inspection. Finally satisfied, he dug fifteen cents out of an old-fashioned purse and made payment.

"I assume you're going to reload those cases," my friend suggested, "but what are you going to shoot with three shells?"

"Ah'm goin' quail huntin'," was the soft-drawled reply.

"With three shells?"

"I only need three quail," was the self-assured reply.

This potential value of a workable breechloading system was recognized quite early in the development of the shotgun. The appearance of such designs, however, had to await development of the steels and machining technology that could make them practical. Many approaches were tried, with little or no success. Historians mention experimental designs in which loose powder and projectiles were fed into the breech from reservoirs by mechanical arrangements after firing, even the priming charge being dispensed automatically in certain instances.

The big problem, of course, lay in sealing off the high pressure of the gases from the burning powder, to prevent leakage and the obvious hazard to setting off the reserve supply of powder. The principle of the modern shotshell began taking shape early in the Nineteenth Century, but the major stumbling block was the difficulty of setting off the primer and powder charge in a leakproof manner. The modern center-fire primer, with its sealing cup of copper alloy, was the end result of this development.

Early designers of center-fire shotshells included Edward Maynard and F. Draper. This shells were of drawn or machined brass and quite expensive, particularly in view of the limited production techniques of that era. These appeared in the late 1860s and early 1870s. Paper-tube shotshells, not too different from modern patterns, appeared about 1877, being sold empty until about 1886, when the first of the paper-tube, factory-loaded shotshells were marketed.

The early shotshells used black powder as their propel-

Until recent years, black powder shotshells – suitable for use in the antique guns from around the turn of the Century – have been all but unavailable commercially. Recently, Navy Arms Company commenced importing these, made by a German firm.

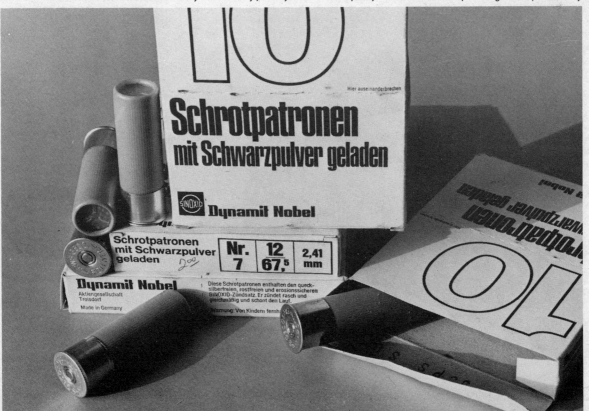

Star crimpers, made by Lyman, are designed to be turned in a drill press or hand drill for making the rolled crimp, as seen on this slug-loaded shell.

lant and, by way of comparison, typical peak pressures may have been in the vicinity of 5000 pounds per square inch. A modern, smokeless powder load, driving the same weight of shot at the same velocity, may average just a bit under 10,000 psi. This is noted to emphasize the folly of firing modern, smokeless loads in antique shotguns. It is noteworthy that shotshells loaded with black powder are being made in Germany by the firm of RWS-Sinoxid, and these are being imported for distribution in the USA by Navy Arms, of Ridgefield, New Jersey.

Some shooters had been reloading shotshells since the introduction of the early breechloaders that supplanted muzzleloading shotguns; some time late in the Nineteenth Century. Many of the early shells were of all-brass construction, having a primer similar to the Berdan system described here in an earlier chapter. You worked the spent primer loose with a prong-type decapper, inserted a fresh one, added a powder charge, an over-powder wad, some shot of the desired size and topped it with an over-shot wad to keep the works in place. Sometimes, they daubed a little sodium silicate solution — water glass — over the mouth of the shell to secure the outer wad against the recoil of a double-barrel shotgun.

The all-brass hulls were rather expensive, particularly so

Another view of the Star crimpers for 20 and 12-gauge shells, other sizes being available from Lyman.

A close look at the rolled crimp, as used with the slug load, compared to a typical folded crimp. Latter is often referred to as a "star-crimp," because of its shape, causing minor confusion, since the Lyman Star crimping head is used to form the rolled crimp. With rolled-crimp shot loads, a thin circle of cardboard goes over the shot charge, being held in place by the crimp.

if you did not reload them, and this brought about the introduction of shells having a short head of thin brass, with cardboard tubing making up the rest of the enclosure. The usual term for these is paper shells. They were usually less costly to manufacture and the little battery cup primer assemblies were introduced, making the depriming and repriming a fairly easy and simple operation.

The mouth of the paper shotshell was roll-crimped back over the over-shot wad, providing a respectably durable shell that would not come apart in your pocket. This is true of the factory load, less true of a reloaded shell with its mouth roll-crimped and progressively less and less true as the given shell was reloaded again and again. The paper tended to get frayed quite rapidly. Ingenious souls invented equipment and techniques for using heat and melted paraffin wax to restore and revitalize the worn mouths of the paper tubes and, while helpful, it was obvious this was not the ideal solution.

Obtaining a good or even acceptable roll-crimp on the mouth of a paper case fairly well required the use of a rotating crimper. One of the more widely used of such devices was made by Ideal and it was called the Star crimper. This can lead to some amount of confusion, since the popular term for the folded mouth closure system used in most of the shotshells today is star-crimp; probably due to the fact that the folds resemble a star. At any rate, we have a befuddling situation in which a Star crimper is used to execute a rolled crimp, while a star-crimp is something else.

Lyman continues to offer the Star crimper which, as noted, is intended for applying the roll-crimp and the modern pattern is designed to be used in a drill press or hand drill. A few factory shotshells still are made up with the roll-crimped mouth, including the less popular items such as 10-gauge. In general, it is difficult to execute a roll-crimp on the mouth of a shell that has been reloaded previously with a folded crimp.

Many materials have been used for the bodies of shot-

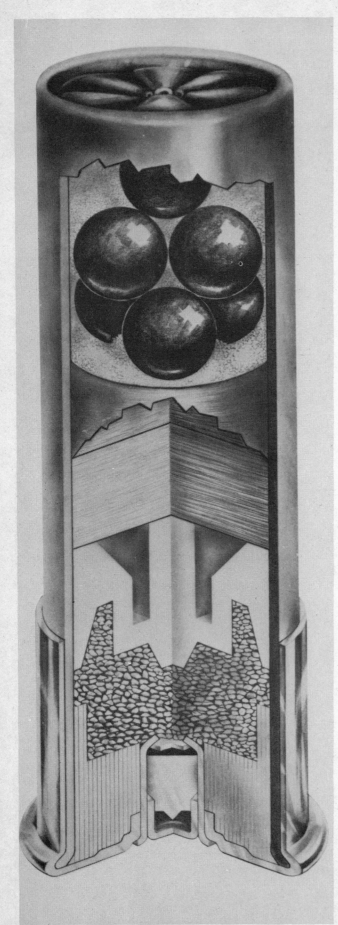

Left, a cutaway drawing of an Alcan shell loaded with buckshot affords illustration of how the pieces fit together in a typical modern shotshell. The tube may be of paper or plastic, the head of drawn brass or steel and, in this example, granulated plastic fills the spaces between the buckshot pellets, preventing deforming.

Below, shotshell design can vary considerably, even between different types from the same maker. Remington RXP, left, is made with tube extruded as a unit while All-American at right has a separate base-wad and thinner walls of tubing.

At one time, the Wanda shotshell was made with integral, moulded one-piece body, as in this 12-gauge example, but its manufacture was discontinued after problems came up.

Examples of the modern, moulded, one-piece wad column assemblies. Two units at left and center are for 12 gauge, varying in length to compensate for variation in internal capacity of shell. Unit at right is for use in the 20 gauge. All feature sealing skirts around the over-powder wad to prevent loss of gas pressure, as well as a protective sleeve between the shot and barrel.

shells, one time or another. Gevelot used to market shells in aluminum cases, with a folded crimp at the mouth and perhaps they continue to do so. Most of the European shot-shells are not reloaded very frequently, as they do not fit the battery cup primers supplied in this country.

Alcan had — and still may have — some all-brass shot-shells designed for use with their Remington size of primers. The brass tube walls are somewhat thinner than the usual paper or plastic tubes, requiring the use of slightly oversized wads. For example, the 12-gauge needs an 11-gauge wad; the .410-bore all-brass case needs a wad made up for the .45 pistol and so on. Alcan used to stock these special wads and they still may have some, though it's not a fast-moving item. Some time about 1959, Alcan offered some shells for reloading, having a tube of thin, seamless zinc and the usual brass heads. These did not prove popular and soon were withdrawn from the line.

The Remington-Peters shotshells came out in 1960 with tubes of linear polyethylene plastic and heads formed of thin steel, with a protective plating of brass. Over the next few years, most if not all of the shotshell manufacturers followed this trend toward plastic instead of paper, many with modifications of their own.

The initial R-P plastic hulls continued to use a paper base wad. This is a short section that fills the space between the primer pocket and the inner wall of the case body.

Above, Alcan's Air Wedge was one of the first of the skirted, sealing, over-powder plastic wads. It was designed to be used with the felt or cork filler wads commonly in use at that time. It features a vent in the center to keep trapped air from pushing it back up out of the shell after seating and the filler wad sealed opening during firing. Left, plated shot, such as these copper-plated No. 4s, was used to control pellet deformation, but the protective plastic sleeves, as shown, made plating unnecessary.

More recently, the trend has been toward forming the side walls and the head in one integral injection-moulding of plastic, thereby dispensing with the base wad.

The different makes of shotshell cases varied somewhat in the height of their base wads, with a resulting variation as to the amount of interior space for the powder, wads and shot. Usually, the different cases were classified as to high base wad or low base wad. These designations confused many reloaders who mistook the base wad height for the height of the brass on the outer rear of the shell.

Customarily, shotshell manufacturers put a somewhat longer brass head on their high powered hunting loads than on the light field and target loads. Perhaps this helps to reassure the purchaser with the belief that a high-brass case is stronger than the low-brass types. In point of fact, there is no significant difference between the strength of the two, all other things being equal.

If the introduction of the folded crimp at the case mouth sparked the modern revolution in shotshell reloading, it was the appearance of the one-piece plastic wad assemblies that added the finishing touches. Prior to the debut of the plastic over-powder wads, the standard nitro card and felt filler wads had not developed notably since the days when the shooter had cut them from fiber board himself for use in the old muzzleloaders.

Considering that typical peak pressures in shotguns run to around 10,000 psi — the term, "LUP," for "lead units of pressure," is about equivalent and is used more commonly today — it is not surprising that a considerable amount of pressure leakage got past the nitro card wads and the ring-waxed felt or cork filler wads of the older wad columns. Not only did this waste some quantity of the latent power in the powder charge, it tended to scramble the resulting shot patterns, as well.

A cutaway of Remington's 20-ga RXP shell illustrated integral moulding of tube body and the portion usually occupied by the base wad, enclosed by metal head.

Above, an adjustable, dipper-type shot measure, as supplied with the Lee Loader kits. It telescopes to marked positions. Left, a 20 gauge, a 4 gauge all-metal (used for industrial processes), an 8 gauge and a 12 gauge, all made by Alcan.

In the days when over-shot wads were used, rather than the folded crimp, the presence of the over-shot wad, ahead of the shot charge, had had a further disrupting effect on closeness and uniformity of the resulting shot patterns.

One final problem came from the rubbing and distortion of the spherical pellets against the inner bore surface. These flattened and deformed pellets tended to veer from the flight path of the remaining, undamaged pellets.

By the early Sixties, several ingenious designs of all-plastic wads had appeared on the market, many of which featured a gas-sealing skirt at the rear of the wad, in contact with the powder, plus a somewhat compressible mid-section and a wall of thin plastic at the front, intended to serve as a protective cushion between the outer pellets and the inner bore surface. The Remington-Peters Power Piston wads are but one example of such designs.

The shot pellets, too, have come in for some share of improvement. Shot is manufactured by pouring molten lead through a screen with holes of appropriate size. This is done at the top of a high tower and the droplets solidify as they fall down through the air. They tend to freeze into fairly perfect spheres, due to surface tension; not into the classic teardrop configuration.

The usual procedure is to let the fresh shot fall into a reservoir of water at the bottom of the tower for final cooling. The shot is scooped out, dried off and trickled slowly down an inclined plane or chute. Here, it picks up forward momentum and, if any given pellet is more or less egg-shaped, rather than spherical, it won't roll quite as fast as the rest. A carefully proportioned gap is set up in the inclined plane, so that the free-rolling, spherical pellets leap across and continue on their way to be screened and sorted as to diameter. The egg-shaped pellets drop through the gap into a container and are hauled back to the top of the tower to be remelted for another try at making the grade.

Various operations are performed on the graded and sorted shot to polish the surface and coat it with graphite. Most of the shot used today is made of lead that has been hardened by the addition of small amounts of antimony and — some say — traces of arsenic. This is known as "chilled" shot and the unhardened variety is called "drop" shot.

Prior to the introduction of the one-piece wad columns with protective sleeves to keep the pellets from being deformed, there had been some amount of demand for plated shot. The pellets were hardened by inclusion of a percentage of antimony and/or other metals and then plated with a suitable metal such as copper, nickel or cadmium. This rais-

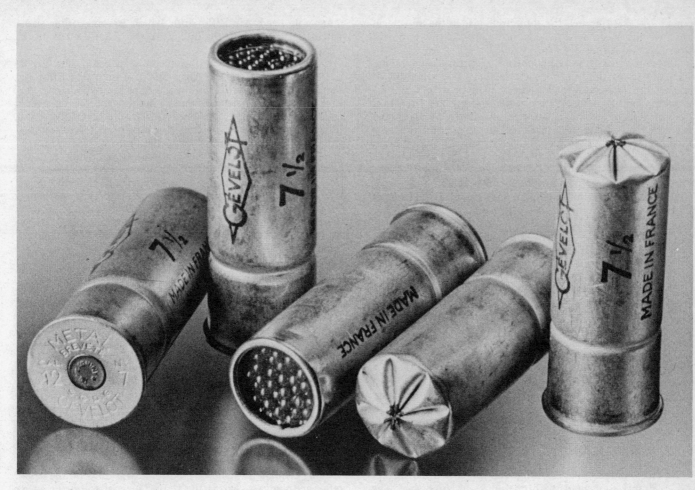

Shotshells from the French maker, Gevelot, show several unusual features, including one-piece design of drawn aluminum, rolled crimp to retain transparent over-shot wad, to show shot size and a version made up with 8-point folded crimp.

ed the cost substantially, but it helped make the pellets less vulnerable to damage during firing and thus filled a manifest need. With the advent of the protective sleeves, plated pellets seem to have been phased out.

Reloading in general and shotshell reloading in particular had a long, steep grade to climb in winning some amount of grudging recognition from the major manufacturers of ammunition as an activity suitable for sane souls to pursue.

Somewhere along the way, it has become inescapably apparent to just about everybody that reloading — far from being a cheapjack and shoddy stratagem to keep from buying new factory loads — is a pursuit that increases the public purchase of not only components, but loaded ammunition (from which to salvage spent cases) and guns, as well.

As we've noted, shotshell reloading has its roots well down into antiquity and this is not an unmixed blessing. It continues to be, if not hamstrung, at least somewhat handicapped by several archaic and outmoded holdovers.

Take the business of gauge designations, as one example. This carries over from the days of muzzleloaders. We all know that a 12-gauge has a larger bore than a 20-gauge, but some may be a little vague as to why this is true. If you were to make up some round balls, out of pure lead, of such a size that each weighed exactly one ounce, it's obvious that sixteen of them would weigh one pound; less obvious is the fact that the diameter of each ball would be the same as the inside diameter of a 16-gauge shotgun barrel.

If you make up the balls a little smaller, so that it takes twenty to weigh a pound, their diameter will be that of a 20-gauge shotgun bore; in the same way, if they weigh one-twelfth of a pound apiece, they're equivalent to the 12-gauge bore diameter and so on. Inevitably, there is an exception: the .410 and, if you wish to be scrupulously correct, you call it a .410-bore rather than a .410 gauge.

In the heyday of muzzleloading shotguns, it did not make a great deal of difference if your barrel was a standard 12-gauge or if it happened to come out as an 11-gauge, 17-gauge or whatever. All you needed was a wad-cutting punch of the corresponding diameter and you were in business. It was not too uncommon to dispense with fancy, pre-cut wads and use wadded-up pieces of newspaper, instead. When the powder went off, everything came out of the muzzle, anyway.

Muzzleloading shotguns were designed for the use of black gunpowder as the propellent and, even with replica shotguns of modern manufacture, one should not attempt to use smokeless or nitro powders in firing any muzzleloader, be it rifle, handgun or shotgun. If there are any exceptions to this rule, you can be sure the manufacturer will include a statement to that effect in his instruction sheet.

It was customary to measure out the charge of black gunpowder for muzzleloading shotguns with an adjustable, bulk-type powder measure and these were graduated in a unit of measure known as the dram. Sometimes, you'll encounter this spelled as "drachm." In the avoirdupois system of weights and measures, a dram is equal to one-sixteenth-ounce, or 27.34 grains. It's something else in the apothecaries' weight system, but let's not confuse the issue by worrying about that.

Shotgunners of the late Nineteenth Century had become accustomed to thinking of their loads — both in muzzle-loaders and the new-fangled breechloaders — in terms of so-many drams of black gunpowder. During the transition to shotshells loaded with smokeless — nitro — powders, the manufacturers adopted a practice of designating the new shells as to a comparative yardstick known as the "dram equivalent."

Thus you might find — and still may find — a 12-gauge shotshell labelled as carrying 1-1/8-ounce of shot at 3 drams equivalent. This — most emphatically — does NOT mean that the shell contains a charge of smokeless powder that weighs (three times 27.34) 82.02 grains. Such a quantity of smokeless shotshell powder would generate enough pressure to demolish the strongest shotgun ever built.

What the designation of "3 drams equivalent" (or whatever) does mean is that the amount of smokeless powder used in the load will develop about as much velocity for the shot charge as would have been produced by 82.02 grains (3 drams) of black gunpowder. It is a thoroughly imprecise and misleading system of evaluation and it has produced much more than its rightful share of confusion and, probably, a few blown-up shotguns in the years since it was adopted.

In more recent times, Browning introduced a line of ammunition under their brand name and their various offering of shotshells are identified by a separate numerical designation. This seems intended to specify the effective range of the given load in yards. For example, the labels on two boxes of 20-gauge Browning shotshells are designated as 35 power and 45 power. The 35 power load is put up in the 2¾-inch (standard) length of hull and it is identified further as 2½ drams equivalent, with one ounce of No. 8 shot. The 45 power loading is in the 3-inch (magnum) cases and, in line with the usual custom, its drams equivalent is designated as "MAX load," rather than some number of drams; it carries 1¼ ounces of No. 4 shot.

It well might be more meaningful and relevant to designate the power potential of factory loaded shotshells in terms of average muzzle velocity. However, when you consider it's not too uncommon to encounter 12-gauge shotguns with barrel lengths varying from the legal minimum of eighteen to as many as thirty-four inches, it's obvious that it could be misleading, too. We may not admire the drams equivalent rating system extravagantly, but it still may be a while before a more acceptable yardstick is in universal use.

When we turn our attention to the matter of a charge of shot, flying through the air, (hopefully) on its way to pepper the intended target, we find that we have opened up a really noteworthy bag of snakes. First and foremost, most shot pellets are more or less spherical in shape. As you might surmise, this does not offer a favorable ballistic coefficient. In fact, about the only contour that might be worse would be a cube. When it comes to bucking the wind, as a direct result of this, shotshell pellets shed their velocity at a truly astounding rate.

Any precise commentary on the exact rate of velocity decay is complicated by the fact that shot is made up in a wide variety of diameters, nominally designated as No. 6, 7, 7½, 8, 8½, 9 and so on down to the smallest, variously known as No. 12 or dust-shot. The different makers may offer charts, specifying the size or diameter, as well as the number of pellets per ounce for each size and there may be a broad variance from one producer to some other. Shot designated as BB size will not fit the average BB gun; for

that, you need Air Rifle shot, which is some other size. When you get up into the buckshot, the situation gets more chaotic, if that's possible.

Nowhere is the situation in shot ballistics illustrated more effectively than on pages 56-57 of the first edition of the Lyman Shotshell Handbook. There are two charts, one each on pellet velocity and energy and on time of flight and trajectory. Shot sizes are covered from No. 2 through No. 9, inclusive, each with a realistic spread of different muzzle velocities. Data are specified at the muzzle, twenty, forty and sixty yards and it makes for some enlightening and educational study.

They specify the diameter and weight of each pellet size, which is most helpful in the event the shot you are using varies from their spec's. The No. 2 pellet (with .15-inch diameter, weighing 4.86 grains), if starting at 1330 fps, is down to but 730 fps at the sixty-yard mark. What is noteworthy is the fact that if it starts at 1220 fps — 110 fps slower — it still is going 695 fps at sixty yards, only 35 fps slower, at that distance.

All of which should make it fairly clear that, if you require a greater amount of power from a shotshell, the most effective approach is to go to a slightly larger size of shot and the second best approach is to increase the weight of the shot charge, provided — and this is most important — you do not exceed the data listed in the manuals as to weight of powder and shot charge. Working through an increase in the powder charge — even though sanctioned by the manuals — is the least productive of the three avenues. This is particularly true as your target progresses to the moderate distances and beyond. It should go without saying, but I'll say it: Under no circumstances should the weight of the powder or shot charge be increased beyond the data given in the manuals.

The Lyman Shotshell Handbook was one of the first reference works to stress the importance of following load data carefully and of refraining from substituting components for those specified. They illustrate the consequences of not following directions by a pair of examples.

Here is a side view of the 4 gauge and 8 gauge shells from previous page, with 12 and 20 gauge samples for comparison.

In the first, all other factors remain the same except for the use of three different makes of primers. Pressures in this series vary from 8500 to 8900 and 10,300 lead units of pressure (abbreviated as LUP, corresponding to the pounds per square inch formerly used).

In the second example, three different wads were tested, with all other components unchanged and, again, the variations were substantial: 7900, 8900 and 10,000 LUP. The corresponding velocities, interestingly enough, were 1110, 1135 and 1140 fps.

The same source goes on to point out that a load which combined the highest-pressure primer and wad would have been well into the area of dangerous pressures, even though the same amount of powder and shot had been used.

One potential problem is more serious than most shotshell reloaders realize and that is moisture. If the loaded shells or the empty hulls are stored in some place such as a damp basement, or in an area subject to condensation, paper tubes are apt to expand and become completely unusable, beyond hope of practical salvage. Even plastic shells and loads can be adversely affected by moisture so that, for example, the primer or powder charge may be deactivated or reduced to sub-standard performance.

Many shotgunners feel there is little need for cleaning the bore of their guns after firing, but this is not necessarily true. It has been found that the plastic wads tend to leave smears of plastic in the barrel, particularly in the area of the choke. It is not only possible but quite likely for moisture to turn up between such smears and the steel of the barrel to cause corrosion damage.

Most of the popular gauges of shotshells have been manufactured in two or more case lengths at one time or another and many still are in production. For example, though it's never taken hold over here, the 12-gauge in nominal lengths as short as two inches is fairly common in Europe, particularly so in Great Britain. Such stubby loads can be made up, if desired, by cutting down standard-length cases and using an over-shot wad and roll-crimp. There is no serious objection to using shells shorter than the length

Close-up of the heads of the all-metal Gevelot shells from a previous page shows the primer which is not interchangeable with the battery-cup primers customarily used with U.S. loads.

stamped on the side of the barrel although, in no case, should shells longer than the specified length be used.

At one time, the 8-gauge was moderately popular, until its use was outlawed for hunting migratory waterfowl. Even more heroic gauges have been used for hunting, particularly in Africa, with solid projectiles for the largest game. Alcan still was handling all-metal, 4-gauge shells as recently as a few years ago, but these were used for industrial applications.

This leaves the standard (2-7/8-inch) and magnum (3½-inch) 10-gauge shells as about the largest to be found in general sporting use, these days. Had this been written a couple of years earlier, it would have been logical to note that the 10-gauge was trending toward obsolescence rapidly. A fresh factor may be changing all that, though. This is the probable restriction on the use of lead shot in specified waterfowl shooting areas. Steel shot, the acceptable substitute, has a lower specific gravity and, as a result, a sharper rate of velocity decay and a curtailed effective range. All of which could bring about a comeback for the 10-gauge.

Ithaca recently introduced a new, gas-operated, autoloading shotgun in 10-gauge magnum. Unlike most magnums, it was conceived and designed from scratch to handle that particular shell, rather than merely representing a beefed-up standard design. They brought out the Mag 10, as it's called, as a notably more effective vehicle for steel shot loads. Surprisingly enough, the recoil — even with magnum loads — is not any more severe than sturdy field loads in a 12-gauge.

It would surprise hardly anyone to hear that the 12-gauge, in its standard (2¾-inch) chambering, today is by far and away the most popular and widely used shotgun; it has been for generations and there is a little basis for assuming it won't continue on for as many more (crossing the fingers, of course, and hopefully assuming the anti-gun crusaders do not succeed in outlawing our hardware altogether!). The 12-gauge magnum (3-inch) has made a fairly comfortable niche for itself and well may be gaining in popularity.

The only outside hope for saving the 16-gauge would be if the skeet shooters were to adopt it as a recognized class for competition. There are skeet classes for the 20, 28 and .410 and this, if nothing else, has transfused new life into the waning 28-gauge.

The 20-gauge cops second place easily, right behind the 12-gauge and, given both a 12 and 20, it's hard to imagine a shotgunning need that couldn't be filled with one or the other in an effective fashion; except for the sub-gauge skeet events, of course. A 20-gauge is the perfect little shotgun for upland bird hunting and, when fed with the milder reloads that can be made up in that size, it is well suited for indoctrinating the beginning shooter, or for use by young boys and delicate ladies; anyone inclined to appreciate a reduction of recoil.

There seems to be a growing inclination toward the magnum 20-gauge, with its 3-inch chamber, in favor of the standard (2¾-inch) version. The magnum chamber will handle standard shells with little or no serious loss in efficiency and the longer loads give performance approaching that of the standard 12-gauge. At least one tireless gunscribe has laid to waste many an acre of pulp timber in essaying to prove the 20-gauge is not only the equal of the 12-gauge, but somewhat superior to it.

The 28-gauge, while a nice little gun, effective when handled with skill, is not enough smaller and lighter than the 20-gauge to offset such intangible considerations as the greater availability of 20-gauge shells in broader variety. The standard 28-gauge has a 2¾-inch case and, if there has been a 28-gauge magnum, I've not heard of it.

HOWS AND WHYS OF SHOTSHELL RELOADING

Wherein Our Author Goes To An Expert For Experienced Advice!

This Ponsness-Warren Model 800B Size-O-Matic is their top-of-the-line progressive shotshell reloader and the accumulation of shells shown here represents no more than a few minutes of working the handle back and forth as the operator feeds empty cases and wads into the works, those being the only manual operations. The shotgun is one of Grennell's particular favorites, a Model 25 Winchester, solid-frame version of the Model 12 and long since discontinued by Winchester for newer pump guns.

AS I ALREADY have said, when one wants an expert job done at anything, he is wise to get an expert. While I have done some reloading of shotshells, I consider myself by no means an expert in that field.

With that in mind, I asked Dean A. Grennell, one of the leading reload experts in the country, to come to my aid in helping to take a long hard look at reloading shotshells. What follows is derived mostly from his expert thinking and experience.

The sectional density of the charge of shot, as contained in the shell and as driven up the barrel, governs the amount of back-pressure against the burning powder and thus it affects the peak pressures developed in firing.

A charge of shot weighing 1¼ ounces will have a substantially higher sectional density if it's confined to the inside diameter of a 20-gauge shell and barrel, as compared to the

The smaller sizes of shot pellets have slightly less air space between them and, as a result, tend to weigh slightly more when measured for a given volume. Scale pans contain No. 6 and No. 9 shot and the latter weighed 14.0 grains more in this test.

same charge in a 12-gauge. As a direct result, you need a fast-burning powder for a light charge of shot in a large bore and a much slower propellant for a magnum load in a 28-gauge or .410-bore, even though the actual charge weight of shot is much less in the smaller bores.

As may be imagined, velocity is much less important in shotshells than in ammunition for rifles or handguns. Even if you succeed in crowding on a few more feet per second at the muzzle, air resistance nullifies most of the advantage

within the first few yards. In shotshells, the more useful gains are made by putting more pellets into motion and/or by increasing the diameter and weight of those pellets. Load data, as given in manuals or handbooks, should be followed with scrupulous care, resisting any temptation toward adding another pinch of either powder or shot beyond the specified amounts of each.

Nearly all equipment for reloading shotshells is designed to measure both powder and shot by volume. This makes

Up to the introduction and wide acceptance of one-piece plastic wad assemblies, most wad columns were made up by putting a nitro card over-powder wad (right) atop the powder, followed by one or more of the felt filler wads, such as this Alcan Feltan Bluestreak, as required to get the right crimp.

the operation simple and convenient, but it introduces a complication. Most shotgun powders are rather fluffy and bulky and, with any unusual amount of jarring and vibration, they tend to settle and pack into a density greater than the average for which the measure or metering bar was designed.

For example, a given charge bar or bushing may be bored to drop 18.0 grains of Hercules Green Dot as a charge during normal operation of the loader. If you were to hold the metering chamber under the powder reservoir and tap or vibrate it for awhile, the chances are that you could pack as much as 21.0 grains into the same cavity.

At the same time, shot size affects the net weight required to fill a given volume in the bushing or charge bar. If you're loading No. 2 shot, there will be a lot more air space between the individual pellets than with No. 12, to cite an

A dependable and accurate powder scale is a highly desirable accessory for checking the actual weights of powder and shot. Ohaus Model 10-10 has auxiliary weight that enables it to weigh as much as 1010 grains at a single weighing.

OUNCES-TO-GRAINS CONVERSION CHART

OUNCES	GRAINS	OUNCES	GRAINS
1/16	27.34375	1-3/16	519.53
1/8	54.69	1-1/4	546.88
3/16	82.03	1-5/16	574.22
1/4	109.38	1-3/8	601.56
5/16	136.72	1-7/16	628.91
3/8	164.06	1-1/2	656.25
7/16	191.41	1-9/16	683.59
1/2	218.75	1-5/8	710.94
9/16	246.09	1-11/16	738.28
5/8	273.44	1-3/4	765.63
11/16	300.78	1-13/16	792.97
3/4	328.13	1-7/8	820.31
13/16	355.47	1-15/16	847.66
7/8	382.81	2	875.00
15/16	410.16	2-1/8	929.69
1	437.50000	2-1/4	984.38
1-1/16	464.84	2-3/8	1039.06
1-1/8	492.19	2-1/2	1093.75

REMINGTON LEAD SHOT

SHOT

NUMBER	DUST	12	11	10	9	8½	8	7½	7	6	5	4	2	AIR RIFLE	BB
DIAM. IN INCHES	.04	.05	.06	.07	.08	.085	.09	.095	.10	.11	.12	.13	.15	.175	.18
APPROX. PELLETS IN 1 OZ.	4565	2385	1380	870	585	500	410	350	290	225	170	135	90	55	50

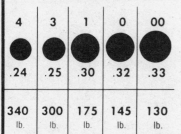

BUCK SHOT

4	3	1	0	00
.24	.25	.30	.32	.33
340 lb.	300 lb.	175 lb.	145 lb.	130 lb.

Remington shot size chart appears here at life size, though it should be noted that shot from others may not correspond precisely.

NUMBER OF SHOT CHARGES PER 25-LBS.*

WEIGHT	NUMBER	WEIGHT	NUMBER
1/2 oz.	800	1-1/4	320
5/8	640	1-3/8	291
3/4	534	1-1/2	266
7/8	457	1-3/4	228
1	400	2	200
1-1/8	355	2-1/4	178
		2-1/2	160

*For 5-lb. bag, divide by 5 or multiply x0.2

extreme example. Most manufacturers of shotshell reloading equipment determine the dimensions of their shot metering chambers by using No. 6 shot and the average weight of the charge can be expected to increase slightly with the smaller diameters (Nos. 8, 9 etc.), decreasing with the larger diameters (Nos. 2, 4 etc.).

These factors are mentioned, not to discourage you from spot-checking the actual weight of the charges of both powder and shot on a reloader's scale to verify that you are within specifications. Compare the actual weights with the nominal weights given by the manufacturer of the measure, charge bar or bushing. Then double-check to make certain neither the powder charge nor the shot charge exceeds the load data given in the manual or handbook.

Make it your standard practice to be skeptical about taking anything for granted. Don't assume you have the shot bushing in place for 1-1/8 ounces without checking to make absolutely certain. An eighth of an ounce of shot

Alcan Kwik-Sert plastic unit was one of the earliest examples of a shot-protective sleeve to prevent distortion of the pellets.

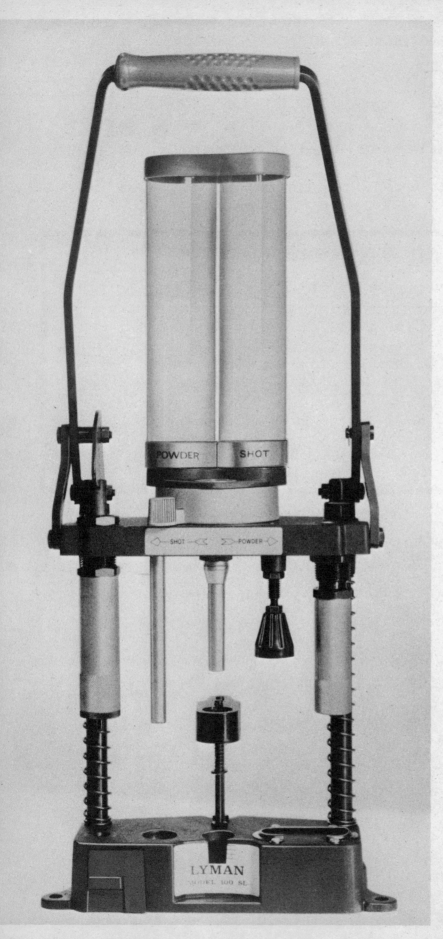

Left, Lyman Model 100 SL loader is comparatively inexpensive and simple in operation, being available for all of the popular shotshells. Below, this Texan press is of the progressive type, with feedplate being rotated automatically as the handle is operates for each shell.

doesn't sound like a lot, but using 1¼ ounces of shot when the recipe calls for 1-1/8 can boost the pressure well into the hazardous levels and one prefers to avoid adventure of that sort.

Verify that you are using the powder that you had in mind. The best way to do this is to pour it out of the can in which the manufacturer packed it, into the reservoir of the measure or into the container from which you plan to dip it. Powder should not be left in the reservoir or in an open container between loading sessions for several good reasons. These include the posing of a significant fire hazard, the risk of incorrect identification, the penchant of double-base powders for attacking most plastics and — according to some opinions — the possibility that prolonged exposure to open air can modify the burning properties.

An accompanying table shows typical shot charge weights in ounces, with the equivalent weight in grains. Should you need the equivalent of a fraction not shown, merely remember that there are sixteen ounces or 7000 grains in one avoirdupois pound. Sixteen into 7000 gives you 437.5 grains per ounce. Convert the fraction into a decimal and multiply ounces times 437.5 to get the equivalent in grains. For example, 1-1/8 is equal to 1.125, so that would be (1.125 times 437.5) 492.1875 grains or round it

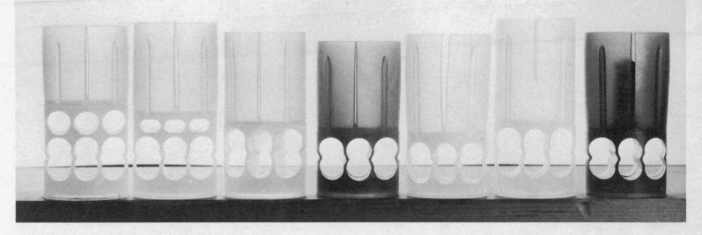

Above, a portion of the wide variety of Remington Power Piston wad column assemblies available for different loadings. The one at right is the Power Post type, with an integral plastic rod in center to help spread the pattern in short-range shooting. Below, three 20 gauge shells, showing variations in the folded crimp at the case mouth. When loading hulls that have 6-point or 8-point crimps, it is necessary to use a crimp-starting head having the corresponding number of points for proper results.

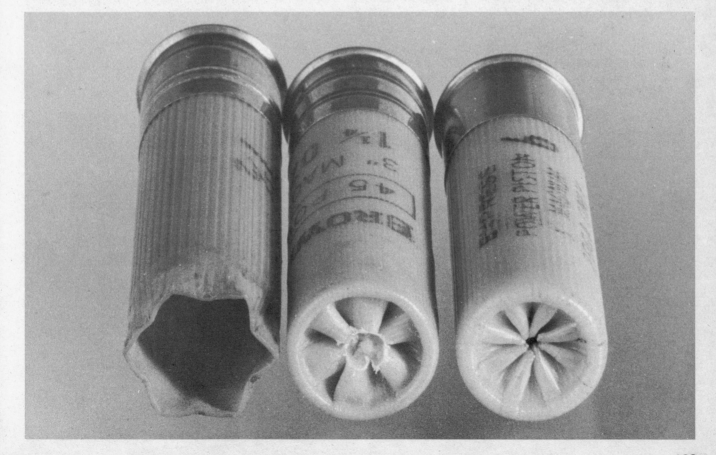

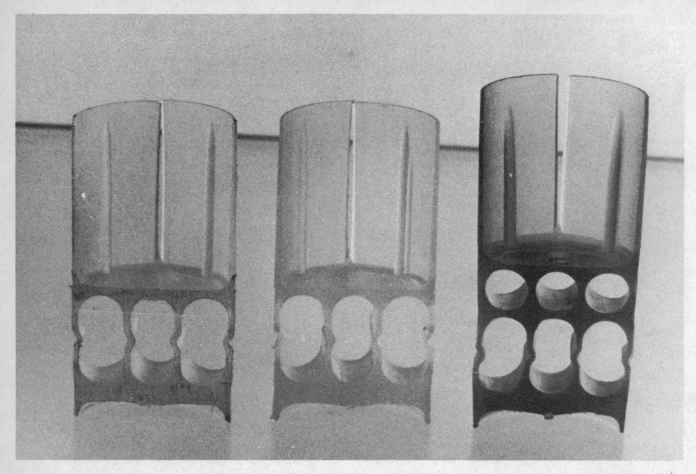

Two halves of the same cross-sectioned Remington Power Piston are at left and center, one lightly inked to show its design. The Remington Power Piston at right is the W29930, with slightly tapered skirt for thicker walls of Remington RXP cases.

off and call it 492.2 grains. One-sixteenth of an ounce is equal to 27.3475 grains and it's not customary to split things finer than that in shotshell reloading.

Do not be surprised if your scale-check of the charge weights of powder and shot gives you slightly less than the manufacturer's nominal figures. Usually, it works out that way, though you cannot and should not count on it without checking. Do not be disturbed at the thought of short-changing your loads by some small amount. The chances are excellent that it will shoot better and pattern more uniformly than if loaded to the absolute maximum limits.

Unless your powder reservoir runs dry, unnoticed, you are not apt to encounter a blooper — sub-power load — when using the skirted plastic wads that have all but taken over. Bloopers were painfully common with reloads in the days when wad columns were made up with nitro card over the powder and one or more felt or cork filler wads on top of that. Some powders seemed more prone to bloop than others. You'd pull the trigger and the sound effects would be a soft, mushy "whoosh," often with a globe of flame at the muzzle and the shot and wads might fall to the ground just in front of the muzzle.

Loading with the card and filler wad columns required strict attention to wad seating pressure. This could amount to as much as 100-110 pounds with some of the slower powders, such as Herco, and making up a batch of hunting loads could involve some strenuous effort; especially if you seated the wads by hand on a bathroom scale.

The general consensus seems to be that no vast amount of seating effort is required with the skirted plastic wads, so long as they are pushed down onto the top of the powder. Some amount of pressure is applied during crimping, anyway, and this is sufficient to assure good, bloopless performance.

If you are going to reload shotshells by the book — an excellent idea — it will involve sorting the empties out as to make and type as a preliminary step. Do not, for example, toss all of the ones with green plastic tubes into one heap and treat them alike. They may all be of Remington ancestry, but some may be RXPs and others All Americans, with perhaps a few Nitro Express for good measure. There is a considerable difference in the height of the inner base wad between RXP and All American, requiring a shorter wad column for the All American for safe and satisfactory reloads. Much the same situation prevails with the different types of hulls made by other manufacturers.

As you sort the cases, watch for obvious defects, such as perforations of the plastic or paper at the top edge of the outer brass, frayed or badly worn mouths, oversized primer pockets — as indicated by loosened primers — and similar defects. Be a little ruthless in rejecting the dubious specimens. Remind yourself you might end up firing it at something you'd rather not miss.

In some instances, you'll encounter shells previously crimped with an eight-point fold as well as six-point crimps. The crimp starter in your press or loading kit will be designed for either six or eight folds and they are not cross-compatible. If you try to start a six-point crimp with an eight-point head — or vice versa — you will end up with a very messy-looking shotshell. After one such mistreatment,

Above, the Remington All American, before and after firing, compared to a pair of Remington RXPs. Note the difference in the pattern of the fold crimp between the two types. RXP types tends to give a better crimp in most shotshell reloader presses. Left, the two types of Remington target cases have been cut away to show difference of head design. A high, separate base wad is used in the All American (left), while the RXP is pressure-moulded in one integral unit, having thicker walls that need the tapered-skirt W29930 wad (on opposite page) to obtain best results.

it is apt to be difficult to get a decent crimp on it again, even with a starter head having the correct number of points.

Most modern shotshell presses resize the case to some extent, simultaneously with the decapping operation. The plastic tubing used in most of today's shells has little tendency to expand with moisture, but the brass head may have expanded slightly in its previous firing. This is not a frequent problem, unless the chamber of the gun is tight, which can cause a malfunction, particularly in autoloaders.

Another source of potential malfunctions is the dished shell head. Few modern shotshell reloading tools seat the primer while supporting the case by the rim, as in the common manner with rifle and handgun reloading. If the primer is seated against rim support, excessive seating pressure may force a concavity in the head, holding the primer away from the firing pin. In shotguns with a weak hammer spring, the firing pin may not strike the primer with sufficient force to ignite the priming mixture. As noted, however, this is not a common problem any more, since most

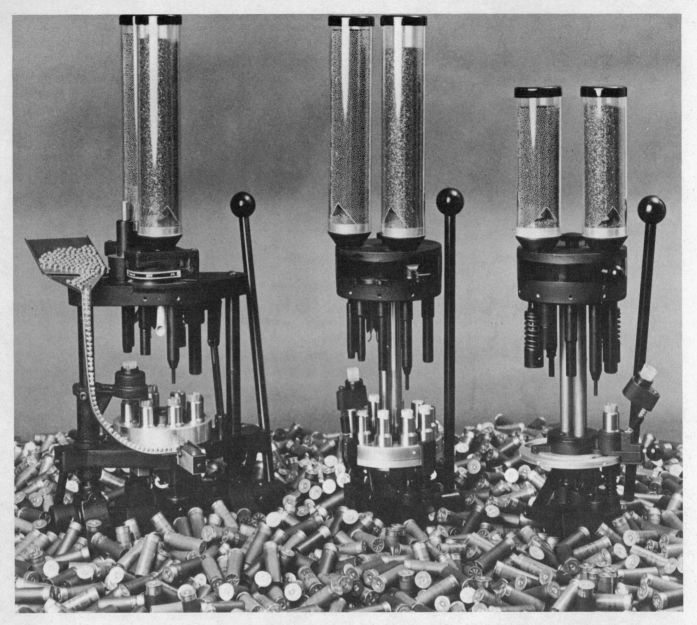

Ponsness-Warren, maker of the three shotshell presses above, likes to qualify that they re-manufacture shotshells, rather than reloading them. From left are the Size-O-Matic, the Du-O-Matic and the Mult-O-Matic each offering specialized advantages.

shotshell reloading equipment is designed so as to apply the seating force from inside the case head and this helps to keep the head flat.

The Lee Loader kits for shotshells are low in price, simple to use and capable of producing good reloads. In terms of output, they are not blindingly fast, but there are shooters who wish to reload with more spare time than investment capital and/or space for paraphernalia. The basic Lee kit required that the wad column be inserted free-hand into the mouth of the case and that was somewhat of a challenge, especially with some of the plastic cases that tended to spring shut slightly. Lee offered a case mouth opening tool — a short section of tapered metal tubing — that could be used for flaring the mouths for easier wad insertion. The tapered tool was helpful, but it has been replaced by a wad starter having thin, flexible fingers. The new starter is positioned over the mouth of the case and the fingers force the edges out of the way as the wad column is seated.

A deluxe model of the Lee Loader was added to the line recently. This has, in addition to the equipment of the standard kit, the accessory wad starter, a crimp starter — in both six and eight-point, if for a gauge supplied in both crimp types — and up to three fixed, dipper-type shot measures. In the example of the 12-gauge, standard length kit, there are three shot measures; these are designated as to volume in cubic inches and the weight of shot: .326 1-1/8; .362 1¼ and .434 1½-ounce. The powder dipper supplied with this kit is the .190-cubic-inch size and it is moulded of red plastic for ease in distinguishing from the shot measures, which are black.

Most plastics used in shotshells having the folded crimp have a trait referred to as "memory." That is, they tend to return to a previous shape or configuration. Once fired, the mouth curves inward, "remembering" its former crimp. Once crimped back, as in reloading, most of the plastics may show an inclination to work their crimps back open. If the reloads are stored for an extended period, some of the crimps may open enough to let the shot pellets leak out.

Above, shells travel around the turret in these steel sleeves as they are carried through Ponsness-Warren presses to keep from being bulged or distorted. Left, inserting wad in Size-O-Matic.

The most effective way of coping with this problem is to provide a crimp that turns inward at the center, to some light degree. This produces a toggle-locking effect, so that no one point can work itself open because all of the other points are in its way. At the same time, the crimped end of the shell should not be so concave or dished-in as to form an opening in the center through which the pellets can leak out in handling.

Getting up into the press-type equipment for reloading shotshells, one of my favorite units is the MEC 600 Jr., which the maker — Mayville Engineering Company — calls their Plastic Master. It is light in weight, compact, extremely simple to operate and respectably fast at refilling fired cases. Unlike loading presses for rifle/handgun ammunition, shotshell presses operate without much expenditure of effort and, as a beneficial direct result, you do not need to anchor them to a massive bench.

When venturing afield for a relaxing session of scatter-gunning — upland bird hunting or perhaps with the hand trap and a few claybirds — it is not uncommon to run out of loaded shells, no matter how lavish the supply seemed when starting out. In such situations, having the trusty MEC 600 Jr., along, with a supply of wads, shot, powder and primers, keeps you in the game until one or more of the components run dry.

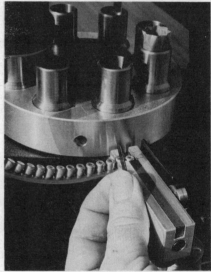

Left, with the handle pushed down on the P-W Size-O-Matic press. the turntable moves up and a fired shell is placed on this post to be fed into the chain of production. Below, a small cutoff gate can be raised to start the flow of primers down to the automatic seater by gravity.

The MEC 600 Jr., can be set up with a No. 12-gauge OH bar, dropping 1-1/8 ounces of shot and about 16.0 grains of Green Dot. The bar is rated, on the MEC charts, at 2¾ drams equivalent, when used with powders such as 700-X or Unique and their No. 12-gauge 0 bar is pegged at 3 drams equivalent with the 18.5 grains of Red or Green Dot that it dispenses. As you might surmise, 16.0 grains of Green Dot makes for a fairly mild load. It's comfortably below the pressure ceiling, extremely pleasant to shoot from a stand-point of noise and recoil, yet surprisingly effective in performance. One can use plastic unit wads — usually the No. W29930 Power Pistons with Remington RXP hulls or the white double-A wads with Winchester double-A hulls.

Such semi-squib loads might be marginal for functioning in some autoloaders, though my Remington M1100 trap gun digests them with total reliability and, of course, the over/under M3200 and the elderly Winchester M25 pump-gun couldn't possibly care less. The main requirement is to crank in just a bit longer lead at the more distant targets.

Several manufacturers offer shotshell loading presses along the general pattern of the MEC 600 Jr., discussed here. The makers of such presses, in addition to Mayville Engineering Company (MEC), include Bair Machine Company, Herter's, Lachmiller Engineering Company, Lyman, Pacific Tool Company, Ruhr-American Corporation and Texan Reloaders. Such presses could be termed multi-station manuals, since the shell being loaded must be moved from station to station by hand as it goes through the various operations of the reloading cycle.

The multi-station manual presses carry price tags in the general neighborhood of $75 — $100, as of the middle Seventies and, with their potential production rate of up to about 250 rounds per hour, are capable of producing excellent reloads in quantities sufficient for the average shotgunner. The next plateau, in terms of production rate, is represented by the progressive shotshell presses. The defining point with these is that they perform more than one operation at each cycle of the operating handle and do so on a series of shells simultaneously. The shells are carried from station to station in a circular turret and this may be advanced automatically by a ratchet and pawl arrangement as the handle is operated or the turret may be advanced man-

ually. The charge bar may be actuated automatically for dispensing the powder and shot charges, or it may be a manual step.

The MEC 650 and super 600 presses are that firm's progressive models. On both models, the turret is advanced manually and is not linked to the operating handle. The 650 has the additional feature of auto-cycle charging, omitted on the super 600. The charge bars of both presses are linked to the operating handle and the auto-cycle assures that the charge bar will not be actuated unless a shell is properly located to receive the powder.

An optional accessory offered by MEC is their hydramec drive unit. This is a small, motor-driven hydraulic pump, located on the floor and actuated by a foot treadle. It frees the hands for positioning cases and wads and, by eliminating variation in vibration from the operating handle, it dispenses more uniform charges of powder and shot. The hydramec unit can be added to the 650 or 600 MEC presses, or either press can be ordered with the hydramec as a package.

The MEC progressive presses have six turret stations, producing a complete shell with each stroke of the handle — once you've gone through the start-up drill and gotten things into production — and, once you've gotten the knack of operation mastered, it is realistic to expect an output of eight shells per minute.

For example, if working with paper hulls that have been through the works several times, you'll want to give a quick inspection of the area at the juncture of the head and tube, watching for blow-holes and perforations. If present, these can cause the head to pull off at the point in the cycle when the completed shell is pulled out of the final-crimp die. This can hang up production for some minutes while you endeavor to extract the upper portion of the case from the die by tugging at the exposed strip of cardboard with a pair of vise-grip pliers.

As you work with one of the progressive machines, you must guard against any small slip-up and these are treacherously easy to commit. You must make certain the supply of powder, shot and primers does not run dry, that the auto primer feed functions in its intended manner, that the wads are introduced at the correct point, every time and so on. The exact details will vary, depending on the given machine being used, but these general observations apply and they are quite important.

Pacific Tool Company's progressive shotshell reloader is their Model DL-366. Its manually advanced turret has eight stations and operation of the charge bar is automatic with each stroke of the handle. Their catalog quotes a production rate of six hundred reloads per hour, but I'd suggest that this figure should be evaluated in terms of the foregoing discussion of all-out production rates.

The Texan progressive shotshell loader has a spade-grip operating handle, with automatic advancement of the turret and automatic actuation of the charging chambers for powder and shot. Primers are fed automatically from a tube reservoir.

The three shotshell reloading presses produced by Ponsness-Warren differ from other makes in that each shell being reloaded is contained within a steel sleeve throughout the entire sequence of operations. After completion of the final crimp, the shell is pushed out of the sleeve by a plunger acting upon the crimped end. Not only does this assure that the stresses of reloading do not cause bulges in the sides of the shell tubing, but it avoids the risk of pulling the head off of a case that has been weakened by repeated firings.

The Du-O-Matic 375 carries the lowest price-tag of the Ponsness-Warren line. The shell, encased in its full-length resizing die, is moved manually to each of the five stations. The upper turret has space for tooling in two different gauges, so that it can be shifted, for example, from 12-

After having passed through the final-crimp station in the Size-O-Matic loader, at the next pull of the handle, a punch pushes it out of the steel sleeve to drop into the sheet metal trough and on to the rear of the press, ready for being packed in carton.

gauge to 20-gauge or back again in a matter of about five minutes. Conversion from standard magnum-length cases takes even less time. Ponsness-Warren rates the Model 375 production capacity at over 250 rounds per hour, putting it on a basis comparable with the other multi-station manual presses.

The Ponsness-Warren Mult-O-Matic 600 loader has a ten-station turret, automatically advanced with operation of the handle. Powder and shot are dispensed automatically, with shut-off controls for use during start-up and shut-down phases. The wad seating guide pivots outward for insertion of the wad column and moves back into position for seating the wad column into the mouth of the case automatically as the handle is actuated. Primers must be seated into the recess at the top of the priming post manually. The Model 600 was designed primarily with the trap or skeet shooter in mind, although it can be used for making up hunting loads by use of the appropriate charge bushings for powder and shot.

Representing the top of the Ponsness-Warren line is the Size-O-Matic 800B. Its eight-station turret advances automatically and, once the controls have been turned on in proper sequence, powder and shot are dispensed automatically with each stroke of the handle. Primers are placed in a slanted tray which delivers them into the feed chute. A good safety feature in the design is that the primers are held by their flanges, rather than front-to-back in a tube. Thus, should a single primer be set off for any reason, it cannot initiate a chain-reaction through the rest of the primers.

In common with most modern-day shotshell reloading presses, the crimp-starting head of the P-W machines is of the free-swivelling type, with a wire guide to locate the crease left from the previous crimp.

So, as we have seen, the mechanical operations of reviving, restoring and resurrecting a fired shotshell can be carried out via many routes, spanning a broad scale of cost and sophistication for the equipment. Once you have the reloads ready for re-chambering, you may feel the need for realistic evaluation of the reload's intrinsic capability. There are obvious considerations to check. For example, it should chamber without undue resistance and it should function through the mechanism of pumps or autoloaders without hanging up and it should send the charge of shot down the barrel when you pull the trigger reliably, without manifestations of excessive pressure.

It's fairly apparent that, in fulfilling its destined role in the gunner's armory, you can't expect a shotgun to deliver groups measuring less than one inch at one hundred yards, as you might hope to do with a rifle. The shotgunner's version of the mystic minute of angle, or MOA, of riflemen is more charitable by a considerable degree. The traditional yardstick for scatterguns involves a circle of thirty inches in

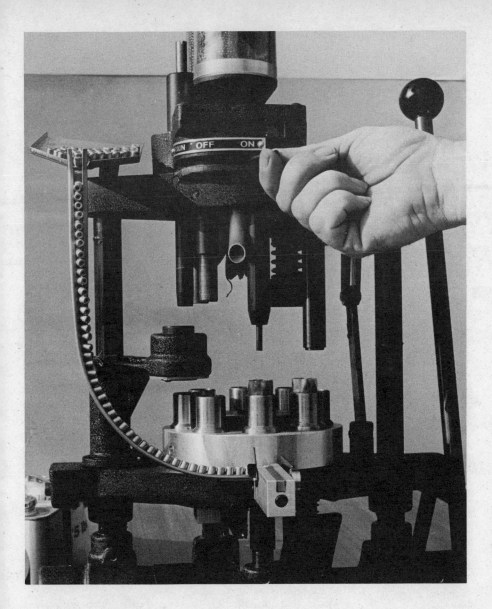

Three-way levers control the powder and shot reservoirs, allowing the operator to turn on each in turn as the proper point in the start-up cycle or turn each off during shutdown. Third position is for draining reservoirs quickly after use.

diameter at a distance of forty yards. The inevitable exception is that, for the .410-bore, it's a thirty-inch circle at thirty yards.

Shotgun performance, traditionally, is evaluated upon a basis of the percentage of the total number of pellets fired that can be enclosed by a thirty-inch circle when shot into a patterning board forty yards from the muzzle. Note well, however, that it is not necessarily the goal to keep every single pellet inside the circle at that distance.

Nearly all modern shotgun barrels incorporate some amount of choke. This is a term for the constriction or reduction of bore diameter for the last inch or three at the muzzle. It is a peculiar trait of shotguns that you accelerate the charge of pellets down the barrel and, by a judicious touch of pinching and squeezing at the very end, you can focus the cone of fire into a tighter beam to the extent that may seem desirable for the application at hand.

For shotgunners, the specter of overkill cannot be ignored; particularly if there is intent to bring home game for the table. It can be pretty disillusioning to convert a regal pheasant rooster into uncookable pheasantburger by a rashly hasty shot, aimed too well and fired several yards too soon. But, on the other hand, it can be immensely satisfying to bring a mighty Canadian honker to bag from the

outer perimeter of shotgun capability. As before, it's a question of matching reload performance to the target you have in mind.

To pattern a shot load with 1-1/8 ounces of No. 7½ shot, it's probable that a table would be consulted, such as the one helpfully supplied by Remington, stipulating the approximate number of pellets per ounce for that size to be 350. A bit of twiddling with the trusty slipstick would round that off at 380 for 1-1/8 ounces — or recourse to scratch paper, if you don't have the slide rule habit, might come up with 383.75 pellets — and we'd be apt to compute the percentage of holes inside the thirty-inch circle with that as a basis.

The usual procedure for checking shotgun patterns involves firing the charge into a sheet of paper somewhat larger than thirty inches in either dimension. Then you scribe a thirty-inch circle, enclosing the greatest possible number of the pellet holes and proceed to count those inside that area. Assume, for example, you started with 384 pellets and kept 275 inside the circle: 275, divided by 384, would be about 71.5% for the effectiveness of the pattern. That, as you'll note, gives you the ability of the shotgun and the given load to cluster its pellets somewhere at the given distance.

With Today's Oil And Paper Shortages, Normal Shotshells Could Become Scarce; Here Is One Man's Answer!

BRASS AIN'T CRASS!

A FEW MONTHS back, I was talking with an old friend, Rex Allen, the singing cowboy who made a batch of films back in the Fifties as a Western hero, then has gone on to do several television series and to narrate a number of the Walt Disney nature-inspired films.

He was wearing one of the wide neckties that seem to be the rage at this writing, although that all may change next season. I admired the tie and Rex grinned at me.

"I never throw that sort of thing away," he was quick to explain. "This is a tie I wore back in the Forties, when wide ties were popular. I just broke it out again, when the new style trend set in."

I pondered the realization that little really is new; I'm certainly not the first with that philosophy, of course, but Allen's point did bring it home.

The same is true of shotshells, I suppose. We went from brass shells to paper and, in more recent years, to the various plastic hulls. Now, with the oil shortage, there is an even more acute shortage of the petroleum-based plastic materials. It could get worse and my thoughts went back to those brass shotshells my father used to keep in the garage.

I looked around for them, but I think they went for needed scrap during World War II. At one time, we had enough of them that, I suspect, they made up into several 155mm artillery cases before the war was ended.

But many of us may become hoarders of old cases, if the shortages of plastic and paper continue and, for one lucky enough to have some of those old brass cases tucked away in the corner of the attic, this becomes a veritable bonanza for the shotgunner who reloads.

I know one individual who learned of a man with a supply of brass shotshells and hotfooted it over to this gent the moment he heard of the plastic shortage. One advantage, I might add, is that brass shotshells have the strength to take just about any load you are likely to stuff into the chamber of your favorite scattergun. They handle No. 9s and buckshot with equal aplomb, if reloaded properly.

"I believe in safe loads and load my shotshells with 18.5 grains of Red Dot, using the overpowder plastic wads or shot cups. This makes a bit more load than you like for a number of rounds of trap, the plastic increases the efficiency of the powder and they might be more comfortable back around 17.0 grains of Red Dot. But with 18.5 grains, I have a load I can use for rabbits or trap; using 1-1/8 ounces of 7½ shot," this reloader explains.

Obtaining the shells proved the easiest of the problems

Setup for reloading brass shells includes Lachmiller press, slightly modified to work with the non-standard hulls, plus special-size wads and Red Dot powder.

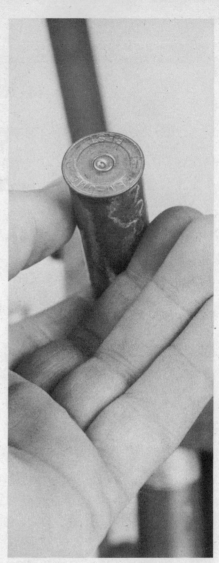

Cases were head-stamped "REM-UMC No. 12 BEST," and were designed for use of standard large rifle primers in place of the usual battery-cup primers employed with modern shotshells.

Left, Lachmiller Super Jet reloader was modified by installation of special depriming punch of larger diameter, with smaller diameter of decapping pin.

Here, the special decapping punch has been run down into the case to knock out the old primer and iron any dents or irregularities out of sides of case.

The thin, soft brass of the hulls returns to a perfect circular cross-section easily, affording easy entrance for the wads.

they presented for reloading. Before this fellow could use his Lachmiller Super Jet shotshell reloader, he needed to make a few modifications. The first was to have a machinist make a new depriming rod and a resizing tool. This goes in the first position on the reloader with the twist of one bolt. The deprimer on the Lachmiller was too large to punch out the rifle-size primer used on the brass shells. This required merely getting it to the right machinist.

To prime the shells, one uses a large rifle primer. This required more modification of the reloader to accommodate the smaller primers and to seat them properly. A letter to the Lachmiller company brought information and they also sent along the last of their roll crimpers for brass hulls. Primer seating was accomplished by making a new unit

for the brass hull to recess in and a smaller pin for seating the primers. It is identical to the unit on the Lachmiller, only in the large, rifle primer size instead of shotshell. These two modifications were all that required any tooling for reloading the brass hulls.

The next problem was to obtain 11-gauge overpowder nitro card and filler wad columns. The brass case walls are somewhat thinner than the usual cardboard or plastic tubes and this requires a larger diameter of wad for a proper gas-sealing fit. It also was planned to use the nitro cards for an overshot wad, since there is no way to crimp the shells and keep the shot in as one does with paper or plastic hulls.

"About the time I had given up finding any nitro cards or wads, I rummaged around my gunsmith's shop and came

Above is the head area of the case, after the spent primer has been removed by modified decapper.

Other modifications to the Lachmiller Super Jet press can be seen in this view. A primer-seating base with a smaller opening was made up and installed for use of the large rifle primers and the wad-seating guide fingers have been removed.

up with some boxes marked: Special Size For 12-Gauge Brass Only," the reloader reports. He was happy to part with these for a reasonable price.

With some five hundred brass hulls, plenty of large rifle primers, along with the 11-gauge nitro card and filler wad columns, he set up his reloading press with modifications for a full brass run.

The depriming punch was replaced with the special unit, the primer seater was replaced with the collar and pin for the large rifle primers and with the removal of the finger guide used for the normal 12-gauge — as the 11-gauge wouldn't pass through the fingers — he was ready to start reloading.

The procedure is the same, with minor variations, that one would use with any shotshell system.

There were some misgivings about the primer punch on the deprimer, since it wasn't hardened. It had been turned from mild tool steel, but there is no pressure except downward, so no problem.

The first step was to deprime all the shells. For this, slip a brass hull over the larger unit, lower the arm of the press and the primer pops out beautifully. When a hull came up that had been stomped or was slightly bent, it was set aside.

The primer unit worked equally well. Placing the large rifle primer in the pocket, he put the hull over the normal rod and lowered the handle. This seated the primers flush with the back of the head. There is no base wad in the brass; it has the primer pocket and the brass base, so some

At left, the primer is being seated, having been placed into the recess, after which the shell is pushed down over holder.

Here, the primed case is being held against the delivery nozzle of the rotary powder measure, as supplied with the press and crank will be turned to dispense powder charge. A corresponding unit dispenses shot charge in the same manner.

adjustments were needed to allow the primer seater to go deep enough to push the primer home. This was done with a few washers under the primer pin on the base of the unit.

After priming, the shells were placed under the powder station and loaded with 18.5 grains of Red Dot.

"I planned to try a few loads on the trap range before going all out on the brass kick I was on. If they worked for the trap loads, they would work for anything else and, by firing the brass on the range, they would be fire-formed for

better fit in the chambers later," recalls this reborn pioneer.

After dropping the powder, the brass hull was placed under the pressure station and the .200 nitro card placed in the mouth of the hull. This was followed by a half-inch Blue-streak filler wad. Both were pushed over the powder with forty pounds of pressure set on the gauge.

There was no problem in the wad pressure station — the finger guides used for the paper and plastic hulls with 12-gauge components had been removed. The larger 11-gauges

117

Special, larger-diameter wads for use with all-brass cases are termed 11 gauge and may be hard to find. The card wad goes over the powder and the felt filler wad goes over that.

Here is another type of all-brass case you may encounter. It was made in Italy and imported by Alcan a few years ago. It accepts the "Remington size" battery-cup primer.

would hang in the upper section and, with removal of this unit, it worked nicely.

A charge of 1-1/8 ounces of No. 8 shot was dropped into the brass tube. This shot was covered by another .200 nitro card for an overshot card. There were available five hundred wad columns and a thousand of the .200-inch nitro cards. Simple math determined all five hundred of the brass hulls could be loaded.

The overshot card was pushed down at the same pressure station used for seating the overpowder card, but pressure was applied only until the gauge rose to the same pressure point.

When the overshot card was in place, there was still about half an inch left between the card and the top of the brass lip.

This confounded my friend, until he measured the overall length of the shell and found it measured 2½ inches. A plastic or paper shell when loaded and crimped will measure two inches to two and a quarter. After the paper shell is fired, the crimp opens and gives the shell the same length the brass now had.

If one wanted to increase the wad column, he could do so, but all he would be doing would be to put more paper into the air with each shot.

One more step was taken with half of the first fifty shells. This was to add a number of drops of a diluted solution of sodium silicate, a material found in any drug store which is used for egg preservation. This is termed a forty percent Baume solution. To this was added two parts distilled water to one part sodium silicate. This solution was

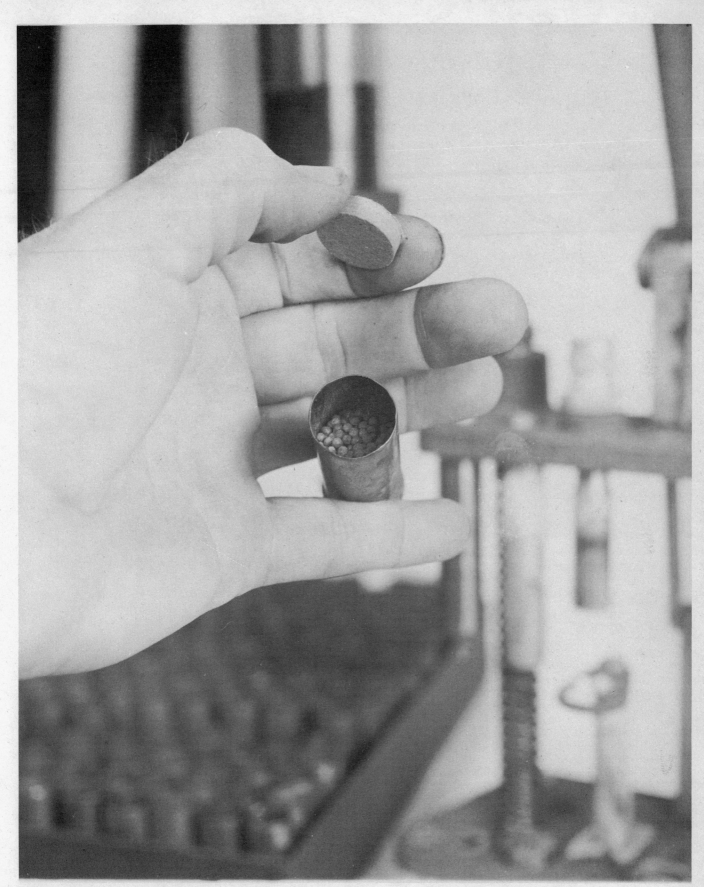

Here, a charge of reclaimed shot from a trap range has been dispensed atop the wad column and one of the card wads, the same as was used for the over-powder wad, is about to be seated in lieu of the usual, thinner, over-shot wad unit.

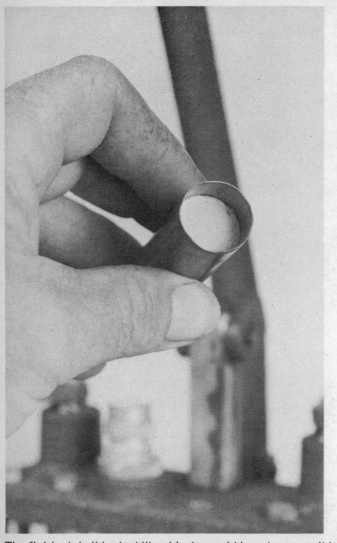

The finished shell looked like this. It would have been possible to increase the wad column to bring the top wad closer to the mouth, but that would have served little purpose. It is notable that the brass cases have room to spare for steel shot, if needed.

Although the loads could be fired in a single-shot with good results at this stage, it is necessary to secure the over-shot wads against the force of recoil if they're fired in a double.

mixed thoroughly, placed in the open mouth of the shells with an eyedropper to keep the amount reasonable, then allowed to dry. It expands the nitro card and is supposed to help keep the card in place over the shot.

Several days later the fifty rounds went on the trap range for a firing test out of a Stevens Model 311A side-by-side 12-gauge with double triggers, full and modified choke.

"It isn't a classic, but it has proved reliable both in the field and on the trap range under various conditions," my friend explains. "Had I owned a pump or auto, I probably wouldn't have bothered with the brass in the first place for fear of feeding problems. Anything you can stick in the tubes of the side-by-side will shoot. At least, they had till now.

"I placed one loaded brass hull in each barrel. I had no intention of shooting doubles and usually shoot all my trap with the full choke left barrel.

"I wanted to find out whether the overpowder shot card would hold up under several rounds being fired in the left

tube. They released the first bird and it was a pure miss. The shell fired all right, but my mind was on the brass and not on the bird. After two stations and ten rounds, I checked the shell in the right tube and the nitro card was still snug over the shot. That proved the sodium silicate helped, at least."

All shells fired with no mishaps, all ejected cleanly and were now fire-formed to the left barrel for easy feed next time around.

These fifty shells were reloaded with fifty more for further tests on the range, still using the 18.5 grains of Red Dot, with overpowder nitro cards and No. 8 shot.

The fire-formed shells were handed to a pump gunner who offered to check the feed of the formed brass through his action. He did find three shells that wouldn't seat all the way, but they ejected when he pulled hard enough.

The other twenty-two shells he fired through his pump fed and ejected with no problems and he stated he wouldn't hesitate to use them on the range or in the field.

Sodium silicate solution, often called water-glass or silicate of soda, can be purchased in most drugstores, being widely used for preservation of eggs and for similar applications.

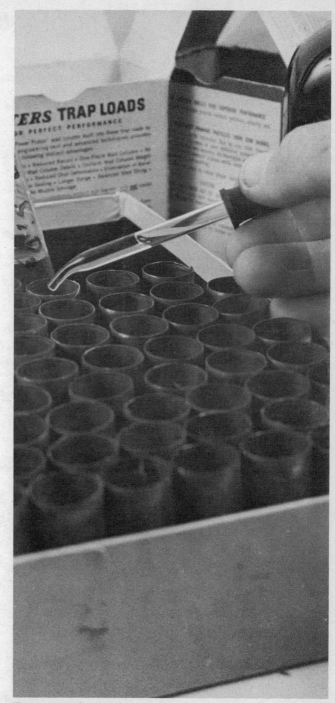

Two parts of water have been mixed with one part of sodium silicate and the solution is applied to the over-shot wads with an eye-dropper. When it dries, it serves to hold the wads down.

"My rounds had two misfires due to primers that were too old. That is the only explanation I could come up with, since the firing pin punched the same depth in the primer, but they just didn't ignite. I could have improved the test by using new primers, instead of cleaning out the reloading bins."

There are now two hundred of the brass shells sitting in boxes ready for any type of shooting that No. 8 shot and the load of Red Dot will allow.

"These will be fired at the claybirds on the range to fire-form them, then they will be reloaded with new rifle primers this time and some test loads for heavier shot."

The basic idea behind obtaining the brass hulls was to load them with the 00 buck or other big loads for varmint backup shells, number 4s for pass shooting at ducks or for pheasant; the list is limitless.

This individual no longer has to worry about high brass, low brass or magnum loads. All he need do is determine the load he wants for the shooting required. There will be a problem obtaining 11-gauge components. A letter to Alcan reveals that they have discontinued making the special brass components but that there still are some sitting in warehouses. Meantime, if this individual decides to phase out the brass shotshells, he can sell them as scrap brass!

Chapter 8
Recoil, Ballistics & Chokes

A Lot Of Ingenuity Has Been Expended Toward The Control Of Shotgun Performance

Here, Stack emphasizes the importance of placement of the butt stock properly against the shoulder so as to minimize recoil effect.

Internal design of the gas-operated autoloading shotguns can be harnessed so as to minimize apparent recoil to a really surprising extent. Midge Dandridge, weighing but 97 pounds, fired field loads in Browning M2000 with very little bother.

A LOT OF attention is devoted to things like the amount of choke machined into a shotgun barrel, the fit of the stock and so on. These things are important and deserve attention. No less important, however, is the balance that should be maintained between a shotgunner's ability to cope with recoil and the load he chooses. If the load is heavy in terms of the amount of powder used, the added recoil experienced by the shooter can quickly cancel any minor advantage that might be realized because of a slight increase in velocity. And while we're on the subject of cancelling advantages, we may as well apply the same general rule to the use of ultra-heavy shot charges.

There seems to be a parallel between the scattergunner and the archer. A beginning bowhunter, enchanted by the glamor of power, is traditionally inclined to choose a heavy bow. He may talk himself into buying a set of limbs with full-working recurve and no less than a sixty-pound pull! A bow of this strength is not for most beginners — in fact, the same fellow probably would do much better with something in the forty-five pound range.

The archer will eventually get stronger or wiser or stay with power he is unable to handle till lousy shooting forces him to give up. The shotgunner, sad to say, is too often inclined to keep right on shooting loads that jolt his dentures for the pure glory of an impressive burst of flame at the muzzle and the dubious security of shooting hot and heavy loads. To illustrate the extremes to which this fascination for power can go, one shotgunner I know customarily totes a pocketful of aspirin when he hunts ducks. This gentleman is sold on the idea that painful recoil is the going

price for the insurance of success he believes he will get with heavy loads!

But the marsh reeds aren't the only things that bend before the awful blast of the magnums. Shooters yield, too — sometimes permanently. Like a hitch in a golf swing, the psychological blocks begin to take form and often snowball into barriers on the road to good shooting that are nearly impossible to overcome. For this reason, it is especially important that young shooters be allowed to cut their teeth on loads that do not produce heavy kick.

This business of balancing a shooter's ability with the load he selects is a two-way stretch. There are a handful of experienced shotgunners who have cultivated the ability to stand behind the extra recoil that goes with magnums. I have seen isolated examples of hunting wherein some advantage came about because of magnum shot charges. The best of it seems to be the fact that a larger shot size can be used without any harmful loss of the number of shot. I remember Alex Kerr and his easy manner with 3½-inch 10-gauge magnum loads holding a full two ounces of No. 2 shot. These relatively large pellets did a convincing job on geese at realistic distances of around sixty-five yards. I don't believe we could have expected these excellent results with lighter loads and certainly not with a shotgunner with less ability.

Sixty-five-yard goose shooting is the exception. Let's face the truth about ourselves and the type of shooting we ordinarily do. Where's the advantage of a few added feet in the speed of your shot cluster if you learn to flinch because of the extra recoil and blast that goes with it? What hap-

Photographed at slow shutter speed, this shows the directions of movement of a shotgun during recoil. The muzzle moves upward in a brief arc and the gun moves rearward simultaneously. Mrs. Dandridge protects her ears with David Clark muffs.

pens to that all-important second shot in the field or when you're shooting doubles at trap or skeet when the recoil of the first shot knocks your head away from the stock? By the time you've blinked and recovered your senses, a speeding target — be it live bird or clay disc — can easily be out of reach. These are the realities that, for most scattergunners, can tarnish the brightest of expectancies.

If you're still in doubt about the virtues of using balanced loads, let's look at the preferences of a few of this country's best shotgunners. Bill Morris, who trap-shot his way to third place in Tokyo's 1964 Olympic competition with a 194 x 200, used a 3¼-dram equivalent powder charge behind a regulation 1¼-ounce shot load. The 3¼-dram load also was used by U.S. Olympian, Frank Little, who racked up a commendable 187 x 200. The beauty of this whole idea doesn't get to you till you take note of the fact that either man could have, according to rules of the International Shooting Union, used loads a full half-dram heavier!

Champion shooter Pete Candy, to mention still another, bases his impressive successes at live pigeon shooting in Mexico upon the use of 3¼-dram powder charges, 1¼-ounce of chilled lead shot and Remington's Power Piston plastic wads. This, despite the fact that thousands of dollars may ride with the taking of a single bird. Again, the less-than-magnum load seems to pay off.

Let's take a fellow who is not primarily a trap shooter and see what might happen with so-called moderate loads. A short time ago, I put together a batch of loads using 18.0 grains of Red Dot, Power Pistons and 1-1/8th ounce of number eight shot. This combination was tucked into

Remington plastic shells. I started shooting from twenty-four yards, using the full-choke barrel of a Browning Superposed. Although I already was sold on the idea of using lighter loads, I'll have to confess some astonishment at what happened. Nineteen of the first twenty birds literally shattered while trying to sail past that cloud of eights! Curious about what would happen from farther back, I retreated to the twenty-seven-yard line and saw the remaining five targets come apart as I shot. I feel it is worth noting that all twenty-four breaks left nothing to doubt and that each bird flew into a burst of tiny pieces with that satisfying puff of black smoke at the center.

An extreme, though meaningful, example of balancing a load and its recoil to the shooter came up a few years ago while I was dove hunting with my brother, Jim. He couldn't score with his 12-gauge, so I offered him the use of a little 28-gauge Parker I had used previously to win the Western Open skeet shoot. Probably because of his greater ability to handle the smaller bore and its light recoil, Jim began making good, clean kills for an eventual bag limit!

Without straying too far away from the point in view, we can say a few words about another aspect of balance in shotgun loads. This deals with the size of the bore and how much shot can be sent through it for best results. Take a pair like the 28-gauge and the .410; the three-inch version of the latter packs a magnumized ¾-ounce of shot. The same weight of shot is standard in the 28. Equal amounts of shot through either bore would lead a lot of shooters to believe that equal results could be expected. However, few veteran shotgunners will argue the fact that the 28 gauge's

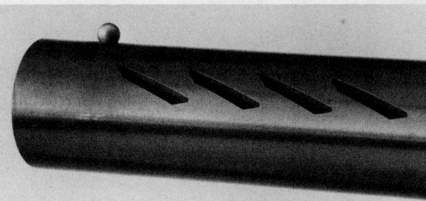

The Cutts compensator is a muzzle attachment capable of reducing apparent recoil by as much as 40 percent. Choke tubes can be interchanged to modify patterns. Right, diagonal slots, such as these, are cut on both sides of the upper barrel surface by EDM device in the Mag-na-porting modification.

shorter, more concentrated shot string will give better results.

Still on the subject of standard 28-gauge versus "magnum" .410, we can recall an event many years ago when skeeter K.C. Miller used ¾-ounce shot charges in his .410 Iver-Johnson to break 100-straight. Miller's feat with this particular load then, as now, can be thought of as a true gilt-edged accomplishment. Meanwhile, 100-straight runs with ¾-ounce loads in the 28-gauge are numerous at virtually every competitive shoot.

My purpose hasn't been to entirely put down the idea of using magnum loads. If you have used them with success — both in your gun and against your shoulder — then by all means stay with what brings you the best shooting.

If, on the other hand, you've gotten a bit starry-eyed about so-called "fast loads," take a long, honest look at

This police shotgun has been given the Mag-na-port treatment, cutting recoil and tendency of muzzle to rise when fired. The shell pouch is by Bacon Holsters, Box 1466, Rosemead, California, holds four. Below, Stack's Perazzi trap gun has four vertical slots on each side of each barrel to cut recoil.

Right, a disassembled 10-gauge magnum shell. When fired, the weight of the powder accounts for part of the recoil.

yourself as a shooter with a particular level of tolerance for being booted by a gunstock. You may find successful shooting doesn't necessarily mean more shot or more velocity when all that's needed is a balanced load and the measure of relaxation that goes with it!

My own contention is that it takes no practice to be miserable, although there are extenuating circumstances to be sure. For example, before I made a safari in Africa, I took out a Winchester .458 magnum rifle and attempted to familiarize myself with it from a benchrest and to zero it in. After the first shot, I felt as though someone had torn my arm off and I commented — meaning it — that I hoped I'd never have to shoot it again.

During the safari, however, this is the rifle that I used in bringing down an elephant, a Cape buffalo and a lion. In the excitement, I noticed no recoil at all, but I only fired the three rounds, each separated, incidentally, by several days.

Sam Lamme was the gunner who taught me about waterfowl shooting. A good many years ago, he was a market hunter, shooting birds for sale. In all of the years that I watched him, I never saw him miss a shot that I can recall. In fact, I've seen him fringe shoot quail so as not to mess up the meat. And he certainly felt no need for big magnum loads. As a result, I don't recall his ever complaining of a sore shoulder, either. In the old days, he would have five dead birds in the air with a five-shot automatic. I've seen him down two crossing birds with the same shot.

Let's take a thoughtful look at this matter of recoil. Essentially, it's a fairly unavoidable by-product of the kinetic energy that is delivered from the muzzle and aimed at the target.

A typical 12-gauge hunting load packs 1¼ ounces of shot, which is equal in weight to about 547 grains. If the shot charge leaves the muzzle at 1330 fps, it would be carrying a muzzle energy of 3.92 foot-pounds (ft-lbs) for each grain of its weight. The would come to approximately 2144 ft-lbs and, in comparison to energies from big-game rifles, that would be fairly mild; about on a par with the .243 Winchester cartridge, for one example.

This poses something of an oddity, since the .243 Winchester cartridge usually is considered to have a fairly modest amount of recoil, yet field loads in a 12-gauge shotgun seem to have an impressive amount of push-back. How do we explain the difference?

Well, for one thing, recoil is proportional but by no means equal to the delivered muzzle energy. It can be worked out by means of a mathematical formula and we insert that here for the benefit of those who find such matters of interest:

$$\frac{1}{2gW}\left(\frac{Bb+Cc}{7000}\right)^2 = \text{Recoil Energy}$$

In which: $g = 32.2$, the gravitational constant
W = total weight of the gun, in pounds
B = weight of the projectile(s), in grains
b = velocity of the projectile(s), in fps
C = weight of the powder charge, in grains
c = the muzzle velocity of the powder
        gases in fps, use 4700

Now, when we consider that the .243 Winchester works up its muzzle energy by driving one 80-grain bullet to a

Below, Browning's M2000 (left), compared to earlier auto of same maker. Though the M2000 is 12 gauge and the other a 20, recoil seemed less with the 12, due to its design features.

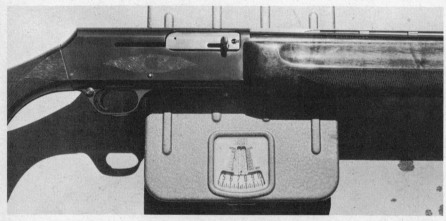

Above, despite light weight of 7¼ pounds, The M2000 Browning's gas-operated system has less apparent recoil than recoil-operated autos. Right, one of several patterns of recoil pads from Pachmayr Gun Works. Such pads help reduce recoil discomfort. Sling swivel is handy when hunting terrain such as steep hillsides; it's also offered by Pachmayr's.

Browning M2000 has loading port on left, chambers shell automatically when the action is locked open, if shell is thumbed into the opening.

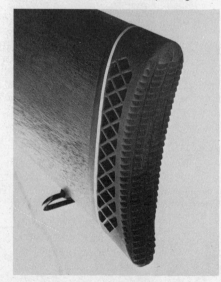

velocity of 3500 fps at the muzzle, probably employing a powder charge that weighs about 40.0 grains, we can work through the formula on the basis of equal weight for both rifle and shotgun — call it eight pounds apiece — and it becomes apparent that the pivotal difference lies in the fact that the charge of pellets from the shotgun is much heavier. The weight of the powder charge for the shotshell can vary anywhere from 19.5 to 40.0 grains, depending upon the type of powder used.

If, for the sake of simplicity and uniformity, we run through the formula twice, assuming that both powder charges weigh 40.0 grains and that both guns weigh just eight pounds, we arrive at a considerable discrepancy: 24.25 ft-lbs of recoil for the eight-pound shotgun, as against a mere 8.69 ft-lbs for the eight-pound rifle. As a matter of fact, delivered muzzle energy for the rifle is just a bit higher: 2180 ft-lbs, against 2144 ft-lbs for the shotgun. And yet the latter kicks nearly three times as hard!

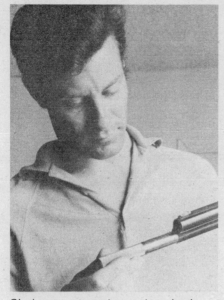

Choke gauges can be used to check barrels. Graduated steps are marked as to diameter, degree of choke.

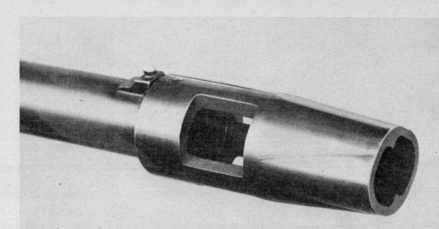

The A&W diverter flattened the shot pattern to a fan-shaped format at a choice of 2:1 or 4:1 ratios, of which this one is the latter. It is installed by means of a collar that is silver-soldered to the muzzle and can be removed, if desired or rotated for vertical spread.

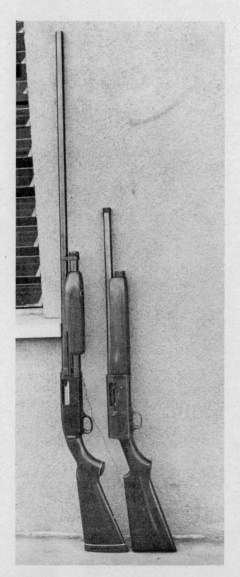

Shades of Mutt & Jeff! Marlin's M120 pump has a 39¾-inch barrel and the elderly Remington M11 carries a 20-inch tube. Various 12-gauge loads were chronographed through each, comparing velocities.

Yes, the shotgunner has problems to surmount, and recoil is not the end of them. If we assume the shell to have been loaded with No. 6 shot, by the time the charge is forty yards from the muzzle the pellets will have been slowed down to an average velocity of about 790 fps apiece. Which means that, even if one target were to be struck by every single pellet, the remaining kinetic energy would have wasted away to 1.38 ft-lbs per grain, or 755 ft-lbs for the entire 547 grains of shot, having lost nearly two-thirds of the steam with which it started out!

Further, each tiny pellet, packing but 2.52 ft-lbs apiece, will have been dispersed across a frontal area hardly less than thirty inches in diameter. There are about 709 square inches of area in a thirty-inch circle and about 282 No. 6 pellets in a 1¼-ounce charge, meaning that we will be driving one pellet, measuring about 0.11-inch in diameter, through each 2.52 square inches of pattern.

In other words, a shotgun — at least, in this example — can deliver about one foot-pound per square inch at forty yards. If we assume that the butt area of an average shotgun

Dean Grennell fired the long and short-barreled test guns through the photo-screen chronograph to measure the actual muzzle velocities obtained with different loads of shotshells.

Here, the 20-inch M11 is caught in full bounce at the instant of firing. A sandbag between stock and shoulder helps to soak up some of the battering-ram backlash of heavy loads.

stock is about six square inches, the net recoil is about four ft-lbs per square inch.

Now, in terms of the striking force of the pellets — especially at the muzzle — a recoil force of 24.25 ft-lbs may not sound impressive, though we're ready to concede it feels impressive. Visualize that another way: Suppose you were lying flat on your back on the ground and someone climbed up a ladder and dropped a one-pound weight from a height of twenty-four feet, three inches, so as to hit you in the shoulder. Without any doubt, it would smart considerably. In this example, the force would be delivered almost instantly and you'd be unable to give with the punch. It is not, by the way, recommended or suggested that you duplicate this experiment, since it would involve a considerable risk of a broken collarbone, even if the weight-dropper was right on-target!

Rather, the illustration was brought up for purposes of examining various means by which the discomfort and punishment of recoil can be minimized or eliminated.

As we observed in the formula for calculating recoil, some of the force is generated by the physical weight of the powder charge being converted into high-pressures gases and blown from the muzzle. It is possible to harness a portion of this gas pressure to neutralize part of the recoil. The Cutts compensator consists of a metal sleeve, with twelve slots cut in its top and twelve more around the lower surface, all at right angles to the axis of the bore.

As the shot charge leaves the muzzle, it uncorks the barrel for the gases to come roaring forth and, as these expand, they exert considerable force against the rear-facing surfaces of the slots in the Cutts sleeve, tending to push it forward and thus setting up a force in direct opposition to the normal recoil. The shot charge makes the free jump of about three inches through the body of the Cutts and then enters one of several choke tubes, which can be interchanged onto the front of the Cutts tube by means of threaded collars. The choke tube may be up to three inches or so in length and the shot charge, in passing through the restriction of the tube, imparts some small additional amount of nullifying effect upon the recoil.

Several other applications of much the same principle are offered currently or have been offered in the past. For example, there is the Mag-na-port modification, in which a series of four diagonal slots are cut into the upper sides of the barrel, near the muzzle. These not only exert a forward counter-pull, to cut down on recoil, but they also help to minimize the normal tendency of the muzzle to climb with recoil, due to the jet effect of diverting the gases upward.

The Mag-na-port slots are cut into the walls of the barrel by means of a device called an electric discharge machine (EDM), which does not leave any burrs on the inner or outer surfaces. As a result, the loss in velocity is negligible; hardly more than fifteen to twenty fps, while the reduction of recoil can be on the order of twenty to thirty percent, depending somewhat upon other related factors, such as the particular shotshell load being fired.

Fortunately, there does not seem to be any appreciable increase in muzzle blast with the Mag-na-port, as compared to firing from a plain barrel of the same length with the same load. In fact, some claim to notice a slight reduction of muzzle blast and there are no restrictions on the use of Mag-na-ported barrels in claybird target sports.

The Italian Perazzi over/unders, distributed in this country by Ithaca Gun Company, can be ordered from the factory, or factory-modified by vertical, gill-like slits in the sides of the barrel, near the muzzle, giving a recoil-reducing effect similar to that of the Mag-na-port modification or the Cutts compensator. The Cutts, by the way, is distributed by Lyman Products for Shooters.

The Hydracoil is a recoil-reducer that is installed in the stock of a shotgun to produce an effect similar to that of an automobile shock absorber. You still get the same amount of recoil, but it is spread over a longer interval of time and thus its effect is reduced to a considerable extent. The Hydracoil still is available as a custom modification from Los Angeles gunsmith Eddie Sowers.

Several recoil-reducers are based upon the principle of having a lead weight or container of mercury free to move within a tubular enclosure installed lengthwise in the stock and concealed. The inertia of the weight, tending to remain motionless as the gun moves rearward, compresses a heavy spring and thereby delays the delivery of part of the recoil for a fraction of a second. Again, it is a matter of a lowered peak of force, spread across a longer interlude.

In recent years, shotgun designers have managed to incorporate some amount of time-stretching effect in the mechanism of the gun, itself. The net gain is a reduction of apparent recoil by substantial amounts. The more notable examples of this approach are gas-operated autoloaders, in which gas is vented from a small port in the barrel a short distance ahead of the chamber and used to drive a metal piston rearward to work the action for ejecting the fired shell and chambering the next round. By blowing the gas piston to the rear, fairly early in the firing cycle, a counter-balancing effect is achieved.

Several modern shotguns of the gas-operated autoloading design are notable in their mildness of apparent recoil and examples include the Model 1100 Remington, Ithaca's XL

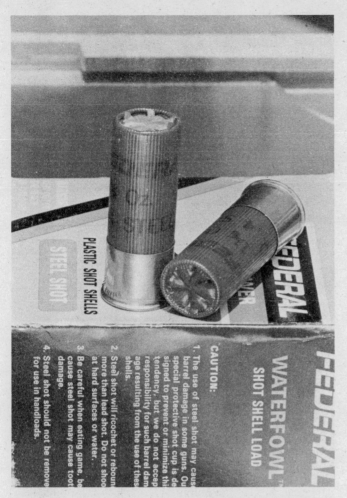

Federal 12-gauge steel shot loads, Index No. W-147, went significantly faster from the long barrel, though other loads were nearly the same and target loads favored short barrel.

series as well as their Mag 10, and Browning's Model 2000. Considering that Ithaca's Mag 10 fires the mammoth 3½-inch, 10-gauge magnum shell, with a full two ounces of shot and, with a gun-weight of eleven pounds, six ounces, its recoil is about the same as 12-gauge field loads when fired in a medium-weight shotgun of that chambering.

The Browning M2000 throttles down recoil to an extent many would find hard to believe unless they tried it against their own shoulder. Weighing less than 7½ pounds, field loads from the M2000 seem to produce less apparent recoil than do light 20-gauge target loads from typical guns of that size.

So, as we've seen, recoil is a definite problem but there are several approaches for bringing it under some useful degree of control. Many find that a good rubber recoil pad offers as much assistance in this respect as they need. The pads from Pachmayr Gun Works enjoy an excellent reputation among the gunsmiths who install them and the shooters who use them. Unlike some of the more radical departures from conventional shotgun designs, a good recoil pad, expertly installed, does not detract from the value of the gun appreciably and may even increase the intrinsic value slightly.

Of the many contributions to the improved design and performance of shoulder arms during the last century, most have been well documented either in the form of patents, or historical recognition of the inventors and innovators.

"But one of the most significant developments, however, is the cloudiest in terms of specific credit." This is the opinion of Dick Dietz of Remington, who adds: "This is the development of choke boring for shotguns. Despite all the other advances that have brought the shotgun to its present degree of sophistication, it would remain an extremely limited sporting arm without the development of the choke." Choke is the constriction near the muzzle that helps determine shot spread.

Early experiments aimed at tightening the patterns thrown by fowling pieces are reported as far back as 1781. No record of any specific success in the matter can be found, however, until the second half of the Nineteenth Century. Then a number of persons, working independently, all began to approach the ultimate solution at about the same time. The result has been more than a little confusion and dispute over who should receive credit for the invention.

An even more interesting aspect of these simultaneous choke-boring experiments is that they occurred in both England and the United States, an ocean apart. Many attribute the invention to an American waterfowler, Fred Kimble, whose initial work in 1866 laid the foundation for future refinements. That same year, though, another American named Roper obtained a patent for a detachable choke device that screwed on to the muzzle of the shotgun barrel. Just six weeks later an Englishman, W.R. Pape, included a method of choke boring in a patent for a breechloading action, but did little at the time to develop the idea further.

Another Englishman, gun designer and maker W.W. Greener achieved public recognition for effective choke boring. For a number of years, public gun trials had been conducted in England to compare the shooting performance of muzzleloaders versus the new, breechloading shotguns. Comparisons were made on the basis of how many pellets a given gun would put within a thirty-inch circle at forty yards — still the standard patterning test today — and how many sheets of paper the pellets would penetrate.

In 1875, a similar public trial was set up to compare performance of the new, so-called choke-bored shotguns. Entries represented such well-known English gunmakers as Greener, Pape, Rigby, Holland and Jeffries. The Greener guns won the trial, but it is significant that all the guns entered produced patterns far denser than those achieved by cylinder bored guns in previous trials. Comparable results soon were being obtained in the United States and the day of the choked shotgun barrel had arrived.

The gunmakers of the day, however, were so fascinated by the new development that, for a number of years, they measured the shooting performance of shotguns only by the denseness of their patterns. This gave the shotgunner a rather curious choice — an older gun for extremely short-range shooting and one of the newer ones for long-range shooting.

Subsequently, the value of a variety of chokes was realized and the shotgun was well on its way to becoming the versatile field piece we have today.

We have noted that muzzle devices and modifications have been used in the control of recoil. They have a further application in the control of the distribution of the pellet pattern.

The shotgunner can improve the effective performance of his gun for the given shooting situation by either increasing the angle of pellet dispersion or focusing it down for a minimum cone of fire. There seems to be a lot of shotgunners who cling tenaciously to the idea that the fullest-possible choke in the longest-available barrel is the only way to

131

fly. While it is true that such guns have their applications, they fall far short of fulfilling the specifications for that somewhat mythical concept, the shotgun for all seasons.

There are a lot of shotgunning applications for which the improved cylinder or modified choke can improve a gunner's shooting capability to a really eye-popping extent, all the way from pheasant down through the smaller species of upland game birds, rabbits and the like. Needless to say, improved cylinder or even straight cylinder is the indicated medicine for quail and for the unpredictable, corkscrew flight path of doves.

Elsewhere in this book, there is a photo showing a series of the Remington Power Piston plastic wad assemblies, including the Post-Wad design, all available for reloading shotshells. The Post-Wad design incorporates an integral plastic post, extending up through the shot charge, producing a spreader effect when used in making up reloads. Other reloaders sometimes make up spreader-loads in which two or three thin card wads of the type used as over-shot wads with rolled crimps, are used to split the shot charge up into two or more sections. This makes for a lot of extra time and bother when making up the reloads, but it tends to increase the pattern spread to a useful extent.

One of the most singular pattern control devices is the A&W diverter. This attaches to the muzzle by means of a threaded adapter that is silver-soldered in place and the diverters are offered in two modifications. In effect, they flatten the pattern into a fan-shaped configuration, at a ratio of two-to-one or four-to-one, depending upon which version is installed. Since most shotgunners tend to be a bit doubtful as to the exact amount of lead to give the target, it's obvious that the A&W diverter is most useful when delivering its dispersion horizontally, rather than vertically. With the 2X diverter, the effective pattern is twice as wide as it is high; thirty inches by fifteen, for example. With the 4X version, it would be forty by ten inches at some given distance from the muzzle.

The 2X version is the one most apt to be favored by hunters, with the 4X type finding most of its application in law enforcement work. With the diverters, it is possible, with a bit of adroit timing, to break skeet doubles with a single shot at Stations 2 and 6 although, of course, virtuoso performances of this nature are not recognized in official scoring.

Exactly how much difference does the length of the shotgun barrel make in muzzle velocity? I've often wondered, so I suggested to Dean Grennell that he check into the matter, some time when he had the chronograph set up for measuring velocities.

"I was able to muster up a pair of test guns," he reports, "with barrel length variations of almost exactly two to one. Measuring from the closed bolt face to the muzzle, the old Model 11 Remington riot gun was exactly twenty inches and the Marlin Model 120 pump, nominally with forty-inch barrel, was 39¾ inches; sufficiently close for Government work, as we say.

"We started off the comparisons with some Federal loads, their code number W-147, with 1-1/8 ounces of No. 4 steel shot at 3¾ drams equivalent, being curious as to the actual performance of this particular load. Three shots apiece came out of the short barrel at 1238, 1272 and 1249 fps; out of the long barrel at 1389-1363 and 1337 fps.

"Recalling that there are goosehunters who favor the 00 buckshot load, we ran three shots apiece of Remington's 3¾-dram loads with nine pellets of that size. The twenty-inch velocities were 1225-1196-1110, with 1220-1178-1203 out of the forty-incher.

"By way of further comparison, we tested some typical target reloads. These had 1-1/8 ounces of No. 7½ shot ahead of 18.5 grains of Hercules Green Dot powder, in Remington RXP shells, with the W29930 Power Piston wad assemblies. Noting that these used a fairly light charge of fast-burning powder, I was not surprised to see the short barrel show a definite edge in velocity with this load: 1087-1091-1084 fps, as contrasted to 910-922-934 fps from the Marlin's forty-inch tube.

"We had some Federal three-inch magnum loads on hand, their code number F129, packing 1-5/8 ounces of No. 6 shot. Obviously, it was impossible to fire these in the old Model 11 Remington, with its 2¾-inch chamber, but we put three through the Marlin M120, which has a three-inch chamber and the velocities were 1337, 1391 and 1378 fps.

"I might note in closing," Grennell concludes, "that firing heavy 12-gauge loads, off the bench and taking care to steer the charges through the small window of the photo-screen chronograph, can prove quite strenuous. The 00 buckshot loads were bad enough, but the three-inch mag-

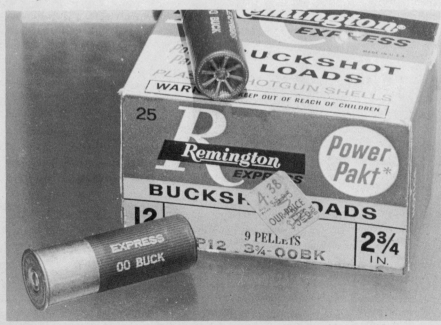

In many shotguns-only hunting areas, deerhunters favor buckshot over slugs, as do some hunters of geese. There was surprisingly little variation of velocity with this load between the long and short barrels.

nums were not the sort of thing you'd benchrest for the gentle relaxation it affords."

All of which tends to bear out that the more extreme barrel lengths do not, by any means, deliver velocity in direct proportion to their length and that the shooter who favors barrels in the 26-28-inch category probably does not handicap himself severely, if at all, for maximum-range shooting. While the forty-inch barrel showed a modest gain with the steel shot and buckshot loads, it's obvious that the last twenty inches of bore did not accomplish a lot of accelerating. With the light target load, it only served to slow the charge down.

Earlier, we touched upon the fact that the Cutts compensator will accept any of six different choke tubes, varying as to length and degree of choke. Lyman rates these for use at 20, 30, 40, 50, 60 and 70 yards, suggesting their use, respectively, for skeet, quail, pheasant, duck, crows and geese. In addition, they offer an adjustable unit that can be varied, by turning the threaded collar, across the entire span of the six fixed choke tubes, with infinite settings at midway points.

Several other muzzle devices are available from the various manufacturers, incorporating either substitution of fixed choke tubes and/or the use of threaded-collar variable chokes. In general, these often prove capable of delivering good patterns, varying the density to the desired degree. Much depends upon the installation, of course, since any slightest amount of angular misalignment of the adapter that is fastened to the barrel can throw the center of the pattern askew in relation to the line of sight.

When working with any shotgun, regardless of barrel length, specified degree of choke or installed muzzle devices, there is absolutely no substitute for firing a few test patterns into a large sheet of paper to verify the type of pattern that the gun actually is putting out. It is a good idea to put a small mark on the pattern paper, using it as an aiming point, to find out if the patterns tend to veer from the aiming point in some predictable direction.

Most of the more dedicated shotgunners feel that a single shot on the pattern paper proves relatively little, the consensus being that you need at least three shots and, preferably, five to strike an average evaluation of performance.

As has been noted elsewhere, the usual test parameters call for measuring the percentage of the total pellet-count that can be enclosed by a thirty-inch circle at a distance of forty yards; thirty yards for the .410-bore guns. Note, too, that the objective is not necessarily to get the highest possible number of pellet holes inside the circle. That might be the case, if working with a gun and loads intended for long-range work on waterfowl, but it would not apply to upland game birds.

As you examine your pattern papers, check for uniformity of pellet dispersion, too. Are there large gaps in the distribution, through which a quail or other small bird could pass without being hit, even though shot is whistling all around it? You may wish to make up life-sized test silhouettes, from colored plastic sheeting, of the intended game species, or perhaps a claybird, as viewed edge-on, so as to be able to slide them about the pattern in checking for loopholes.

As you work with your shotgun, patterning different factory shells or reloads on the paper, you are quite apt to turn up several results that may surprise you, although they can prove valuable when you set out to put next Sunday's dinner in the bag.

For but one example, there is a good chance that changing from one size of shot to another can produce a startling change in pattern percentages. You may, for example, find that the larger pellet sizes, such as No. 2 or 4, give a tighter, more uniform pattern from a modified choke than from a full choke. This is sometimes true, though by no means unfailingly so.

In the end, it gets back to a matter of working with your gun, correcting such detectable shortcomings as it may have and then working upon your own weak points, so that you can function together as an effective team. Only by getting to know its capabilities, as well as your own, can the missed shots and attending frustrations be brought down to the irreducible minimum, and kept there.

A factory-installed adjustable choke device, as supplied on a High Standard pump. Here, it's adjusted for modified. Knurled collar can be turned to any desired degree of choke.

Chapter 9

*Not Many Americans Are Credited With Inventing
A Lasting National Participant Sport,
But This One Is Native-Born!*

THE SKEET FEAT

*The late Clark Gable (left) was one of Robert Stack's
frequent hunting partners and also did his share of
claybird shooting in the early days of the skeet sport.*

I SUPPOSE, DOWN over the years, I have specialized in two types of shotgunning. I've been a skeet shooter since I was in my early teens and, when I got old enough to shoulder a 12 gauge, I learned to shoot ducks on the ponds of a duck club that has been in the family for three generations, including my own son.

It is generally accepted that both skeet and trap were invented as a means of practicing with claybirds for actual game bird shooting. Some of the facts have been lost in time, but perhaps the best accepted version of the beginning of skeet as a game involves one Charles E. Davies, a retired businessman, who owned the Glen Rock Kennels near Andover, Massachusetts. This all took place in the first decade of our century.

Davies, in his retirement years, concentrated on upland game hunting and was constantly attempting to improve his talents with his shotguns. When he missed a target in the field, this became a personal challenge. He would call upon his son and another lad to set up an old Expert trap that was bolted to a plank, then he would take position and angle similar to that at which he had taken his most recent miss on a grouse or other game bird. As the lads would throw targets for him, he would shoot over and over, until he was satisfied that he had cured his temporary problem.

Some time before World War I, Davies and his son, Henry, were discussing how their hit-and-miss correction game might be further developed. After a good deal of discussion, they came up with a circular course with twelve stations. Shooters could compete from all of these stations, with targets thrown from the twelfth position. Such shooting would give each competitor a similar chance at the clay targets.

The course was laid out on the grounds of the kennels with the help of one Bill Foster, Henry Davies' young friend. It was built on a circle that was twenty-five yards in circumference, each of the dozen positions equidistant around the circle.

The trap was positioned so that it would send the targets in a straight line toward the No. 6 position. Actually, the course, as then designed, was laid out almost the same as the face of a clock.

The shooters would start at the 12 o'clock spot, firing two shots from each of the stations. With the single shell left over from the standard box of twenty-five rounds, he then placed himself in the exact center of the circle to shoot the incoming target at close range. The original setup was called "shooting around the clock."

About 1923, the radius of the circle was reduced to twenty yards. This was the result of the discovery that, at the longer range, some of the targets were getting through the shot patterns.

At the shooting ranges originally set up, the patterns became so dispersed that the shot was not concentrated on the flying claybird.

According to legend, half of the circle had to be abandoned when a neighbor began to raise chickens on the boundaries of the shooting club. The stations then were renumbered so that No. 6 became 1, 12 was redesignated as 7, with the midfield station being dubbed as No. 8. Thus the same shooting angles were provided. This is the same setup that is used in today's skeet fields.

Later, I suppose, to give the game more challenge, the Davies clan built the first skeet tower. Instead of it being the type of house from which today's targets are thrown, they simply installed a trap about fifteen feet above the ground, in the limbs of an elm tree. The idea was that one could rig the trap to send a bird downward. Prior to that, all birds had been shot on the rise, since the traps were on

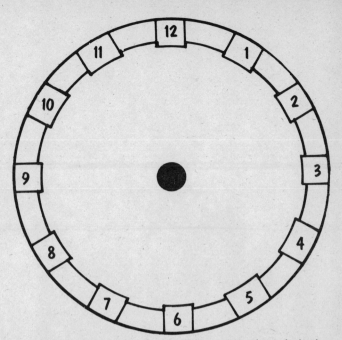

The original layout for skeet was a complete circle that later was cut in half, because a chicken ranch was to be built close to the range. Present layout is semi-circular.

the ground and rigged to throw the birds in a rising pattern.

The same Bill Foster had become editor of the National Sportsman magazine and featured the claybird layout in one of his articles. At the same time, the magazine offered a cash prize of $100 for the best name for this new game. As I recall, a lady named Gertrude Hurlbutt from somewhere in Montana won, with the word "skeet." In her prize-winning entry, she explained that the word was the Scandinavian version of the term, "to shoot."

The American shooter apparently was ready for a practical form of wing shooting with the shotgun that would give him an opportunity to test his skill any month of the year on a series of shots similar to those encountered in hunting and, as evidenced by the popularity of skeet shooting today, it has far exceeded the expectations of its sponsors. Today, for close to 20,000 members of the National Skeet Shooting Association, shattering clay targets is a way of life; exercise for the body, mind and the soul. Through Winter and Summer they shoot at millions of targets — breaking most of them — meet new people and travel across the United States.

As the popularity of the sport grew, the forming of a National Skeet Shooting Association was inevitable. This came about and the first national championship shoot was held Aug. 16-31, 1935, at Cleveland, Ohio. The 12-gauge (then called the all-gauge) entry in that shoot totalled 113 participants. This tournament became an annual fixture, being rotated around the country — St. Louis, Detroit, Tulsa, San Francisco, Syracuse, Indianapolis. The last championship under the original association was held at Syracuse in 1942.

Skeet then became nonexistent during World War II insofar as civilian shooters were concerned. Equipment and ammunition became unavailable. Most of the participants had gone to war. Gun clubs ceased to operate and many disappeared completely. However, the government quickly recognized the value of the sport in gunnery training and all branches of the armed forces relied on skeet to teach servicemen the principle of leading moving targets. Many of the great civilian shooters rushed into the service and most

Sixteen-year-old Bobby Stack was considered one of the hottest shooters on the skeet scene in early national competition, where youth dominated.

of them were used as instructors.

With the end of the world conflict, a dedicated group of skeet enthusiasts officially brought the sport back to the public with organization and incorporation of the present National Skeet Shooting Association in December, 1946. This new association was aided by a substantial, no-interest loan from the National Rifle Association. The national championship shoot was resumed at Indianapolis in 1946 and it has been held annually ever since.

Soon after the new organization was formed, the national headquarters was moved to Dallas, Texas, from Washington, D.C. Dallas also was designated for a time as the permanent home of the association, including the annual national tournament. Due to a number of circumstances, the permanent home policy was abolished in 1952 and since that time the tournament, officially named "World Championships," has been staged at Reno, Nevada; Waterford, Michigan; Lynnhaven, Virginia; St. Janvier, Quebec; Rush, New York; Savannah, Georgia; Bucyrus, Kansas; and San Antonio, Texas. September 1, 1973, the

This rare photo shows Stack and other members of the California skeet team during Western Open at Pacific Rod & Gun Club, San Francisco. Stack won with 100 x 100. He considers the photo excellent example of follow-through.

association headquarters were moved to the site of the National Gun Club in San Antonio.

In addition to the regular skeet shooting program of 12-gauge, 20-gauge, 28-gauge and .410-bore competition, there are the International style and the collegiate divisions, both with specifically designed regulations.

The International style features the previous low-gun position and variable-timing target release, required by NSSA rules up to 1952. Contrasted to the present cheeked gun position, this style is required by the International Shooting Union, a worldwide shooting organization, and the International Olympic Committee, producer of the

Olympic Games, where skeet shooting was first included on the program in 1968.

The National Gun Club is one of the finest shotgun shooting facilities in the world. The club's thirty-two skeet fields certainly make the club the largest skeet facility and, adding trapshooting fields superimposed on nine of the skeet fields and several other shotgun shooting areas makes a complete shotgun shooting facility.

The club is located on 419 acres twenty-five miles northwest of San Antonio in the Hill Country. In addition to the shooting facilities, the club sports a modern clubhouse with bar, short order restaurant, locker room, gun repair shop and pro shop.

During World War II, Stack served as an instructor in skeet and on the .50 caliber machine gun range, teaching gunnery techniques to Navy aviators. As a commissioned officer, he served under command of Alex Kerr, who had been his earlier teammate at skeet.

Headquarters of the National Skeet Association today is located on the grounds of the National Gun Club in San Antonio, Texas, where national championships are held.

The NSSA purchased the National Gun Club, formerly known as the Texas International Gun Club, in March, 1973, and six months later moved its offices there from Dallas.

The NSSA first became associated with the club in 1968 when it joined as a new club affiliate, then again in 1971, when the NSSA World Championships were staged there. Owners built the original club for $800,000 on 214 acres. Estimated value of the property and improvements today runs over $1 million.

Memberships in the club sell for $50 and entitle the member automatically to ten free rounds, use of the club's reloading equipment and other usual privileges usually granted to members of private clubs. Public shooting is also available.

It was back in the mid-thirties that I was involved seriously in competitive skeet shooting. In fact, I shot in the first National Skeet Championships held in Cleveland, Ohio, back in 1935, as a green kid. But I can still recall the color, the comradeship and the sportsmanship that make such events a hallmark of memory even today.

In qualifying, one of the facets which counted in a man's favor was the matter of sportsmanship, which may seem a bit archaic by some of today's standards. But there was more time for social amenities in those days, and competition was more relaxed. At that time, skeet was less than a dozen years old in this country and was a new game. It was

a sport about which most of us actually knew very little and the conditions, the styles and — needless to say — the scores were different than they are today. For example, when I was lucky enough to set the world's long run record of 364 consecutive birds, there were a lot of oohs and aahs. It had never been done before. But by today's standards, if one were to boast about such a score, there would be a lot of raised eyebrows. It wouldn't be considered much of a feat.

The color among competitors was something to behold. Everyone seemed to be trying to outdo his competition as far as oddity of costume was concerned. One shooter who comes to mind wore a pair of shorts and a Boy Scout hat. Lee Greenway, a great shot today and one of Hollywood's leading makeup men, wore an old-fashioned duster of the type favored by early automobile drivers. This was literally covered from shoulder to knee with shooting badges and patches reflecting his prowess as a shotgunner.

And with the newness of skeet in those days, it attracted the Hollywood stars of the era who sought something a little different for entertainment. When I was a redhot fifteen or so, I was doing my shooting at the long defunct Los Angeles-Santa Monica Gun Club. I was in the clubhouse one day when Gary Cooper, one of my early idols, spotted a Parker double of my dad's that I had been shooting.

Coop stood looking down at the gun for all of twenty minutes before he glanced at me to say, in that remembered drawl, "That's a fine looking gun."

A youthful Alex Kerr is considered the all-time great skeet shooter, having won virtually every national title the sport has offered.

Bob Stack pauses with California team coach Harry Fleischman for a bit of advice during the first national skeet tournament in 1935.

The technique used by Robert Stack today (left) in shooting International skeet still resembles closely the style (above), which he used when he was shooting in national competition to place among the sport's top talent.

"Thank you, sir," I half stammered.

"Can I hold it?" he wanted to know.

"Sure. Go ahead and shoot it." The idea of having Gary Cooper shoot my gun — even mine by proxy at that point — was a thrill that made a great story the next week at high school. That gun is still in my collection and one of my favorites.

It was through Gary Cooper that I came to know the other giants of the movie colony of that day. They included Clark Gable, Robert Montgomery, Fred McMurray and a host of others, all of them respected shots in their own right. And I don't deny that getting to be on a first-name basis with them — on the firing line, at least — was something I was mighty proud of.

Today, there are few, if any, skeet shooters among the Hollywood stars. I can't say that I really know the reason for this, but I suspect that it's the matter of specialization that has entered skeet. In the Old Days, when skeet was new to the West Coast, it was no sin to miss a few birds. The kick was in breaking a few.

In my opinion, probably the greatest all-around shotgun pointer today is still Alex Kerr. I started competitive shooting a year before he did, and had never heard of him until I was in Pachmayr's Gun Works one day, and someone mentioned that there was a local shooter who was breaking two hundred or so straight.

It wasn't long before Alex and I were shooting together or against each other. It didn't make much difference, so long as we had fun. We were members of the National Champion five-man team that shot 493 in those days, and we shot together in the National Telegraphic Meet, winning

it in about 1936. But I think the greatest thrill for both of us was beating the Eastern in national competition.

The teams from the East had been introduced to skeet before anyone on the West Coast had started to take it seriously, and I'm afraid they were rather inclined to look down their collective noses at these upstarts from California who dared to think they could shoot in their circle. It was a good feeling to win over them.

Alex, of course, went on to gain world renown as a shotgunner. To my mind, a great shotgun pointer is a man who has a broad base of talent. He's not simply a limited talent in one particular field. Alex Kerr is that kind of man. For example, the first time he shot live pigeons, he killed seventy-five thrown. It surprised everyone, since he was using a duck gun and, frankly, no one expected that kind of a performance, although he was All-American skeet champion at the time.

I've seen him shoot ducks with a 10-gauge magnum — an eleven-pound Parker he favored, using a 3½-inch, two-ounce shell. He'd sit in his blind and wait until everyone at the next club had shot, then he'd shoot at ducks from sixty-five to eighty yards away. He'd fire two shots, wait two seconds, then here would fall two ducks.

When World War II came along, Alex Kerr became a Navy commander and I was eventually commissioned to become a lieutenant. At that time, Alex was teaching aerial free gunnery at the Alameda Naval Air Station near San Francisco. One of the best ways of teaching gunners how to lead is to teach them to handle a shotgun, and I considered it something of an honor when Kerr asked that I be assigned to his outfit. It's a friendship that has continued for nearly thirty years; a friendship that I value.

How And Why Of Skeet

Chapter 10

Everyone Has A Style Of His Own, But Tips From Two Top Champs May Afford The Neophyte A Starting Point

Left: The late D. Lee Braun was considered one of the outstanding skeet instructors of this century, although Stack feels that Alex Kerr was perhaps a better shooter.

WHEN THIS BOOK first came under discussion and we were outlining the concept, I made the flat statement that I didn't feel I should attempt to do a chapter on how to shoot skeet. There have been dozens of books written on the subject, some by shooters far more successful at the sport than I.

However, in discussing skeet shooting with Alex Kerr, one of the all-time great shooters on the skeet field, at trap or in the duck blind, he came up with some thoughts that I certainly feel are worth passing on.

When it comes to talking about leads, everyone has his own ideas. What works in the way of a lead for me may not work exactly the same for someone else. By having someone who is really knowledgeable at the sport stand behind you during a round and tell you what you are doing, then burning up a wheelbarrow or so of shells on each post, one soon will learn precisely where he should be shooting. However, at the price of ammunition these days, that can be the expensive way to learn to break claybirds with consistency.

I consider the late Lee Braun probably the best of all teachers of the shotgun and how to shoot it, but perhaps the greatest theorist of all is Kerr. He revised the radius for the pistol grip of the Remington Model 32 for one thing. He was one of the early guys to over-bore skeet guns at a time when every gun seemed to have a forcing cone that would kick your head off.

Kerr has done considerable instructing himself over the years and has held most of the national titles for all types of shotgunning at one time or another. Luckily, I got a look at the notebook he uses in his instruction and I can't offer advice any better than he does, so I'll quote him directly insofar as skeet shooting is concerned.

His first advice is pretty basic, but nonetheless ignored by most neophytes. "You must shoot ahead of a moving target to hit it," Alex is quick to explain. "The distance ahead is determined by the speed of the target and the distance the target is away.

"The shooter should 'follow through' with the gun after each shot. Stopping the gun will make you miss by shooting behind." We've all suffered this problem from time to time. We may even know what we are doing wrong, but it can quickly become a syndrome that is tough to break. That's also one of the reasons why I favor a gun that is slightly muzzle heavy. It tends to continue to swing in spite of you!

"The shooter should cheek his gun or get his face down on the stock so that you are looking down the barrel and not over the top of it. Looking over the top of the barrel causes you to shoot over the top of the target. And the shooter should face where the target is to be broken," Kerr explains. "Otherwise, the shooter becomes 'wound up'."

That last I consider sound advice and a point that many shooters do not stop to consider. In the game of skeet, they soon come to be familiar with the pattern in which the birds will be thrown. The only thing changing in the pattern of all this is the shooter. By moving from one post to another, he is changing the angle. Therefore, it behooves him to reduce the angle as much as possible and this can be accomplished by choosing the point in the bird's flight on each post at which he can shoot most comfortably, then planning on shooting his bird on that precise point in its flight.

To the beginner, this may sound difficult, but before you have seen many birds fly across your front while at the various posts, the pattern begins to show consistency. The problem then is to become consistent in your own shooting; using the same position and angle of stance on each post. Having to swing about too far, one can become entangled in his own legs. It may sound silly, but I've seen it happen.

Kerr also advises that "the shooter should not drop his gun too far below the line of flight of the target. It is lost motion to bring the gun back up to the shoulder."

He feels, "The gun should be held or started half way between the traphouse and 8 post on all shots except outgoers on 1 and 7 posts and both targets at 8 post.

"Holding the gun too close to the traphouse calls for a fast, inaccurate swing in an attempt to catch up with the target. A gun held too far from the traphouse causes a fast, inaccurate snap shot or a case of riding the target too far.

"In other words, the shooter gets started too late. At 8 post, the gun should be held right off the corner of the traphouse. Above all else, the shooter should be relaxed and not tense. If you are tense, it becomes impossible to swing smoothly."

Okay. You've thought about all that and absorbed it? There is more, which I feel is equally important.

The shooter should lean slightly forward by bending the forward knee slightly. This helps to absorb recoil and also is an aid in keeping the head down on the gunstock. In this

Post 1: Today, because of slower reflexes, Alex Kerr tends to "face the area in which I anticipate breaking the target. Everybody faces the same way for the first shot, but will swing differently on the incoming bird."

Techniques used in skeet were designed originally to duplicate situations one will find in upland shooting.

situation, recoil from the shotgun tends to straighten up the shooter to a normal standing position. However, if the shooter starts at a normal standing position, he cannot retreat farther, so the recoil tends to become excessive. At the same time, the shooter should not squat or stoop as some tend to do. The problem in this type of stance is that one tends to tie up or cramp his swing.

As explained earlier, a modern skeet range is a semicircle, which is marked off at seven different points, roughly resembling half of the dial of a watch. Each point is a numbered post — 1 through 7. Post 8 is midway between 1 and 7 on a straight line between the two.

The high trap is at post 1, ten feet above the ground, while the low trap is at post 7, 3½ feet above ground level. Unless influenced by the wind, skeet targets always follow the same path, the different angles being accomplished by movement of the shooters around the half-circle, from one post to the next.

A bird is thrown from each trap, the high bird first, followed by the low bird, these being shot at each post. When done, this accounts for sixteen shells.

For doubles, the high and low house birds are released at precisely the same moment. These are shot at posts 1, 2, 6 and 7, the practice being to shoot the outgoing bird first, then swinging on the incoming clay target.

The last shell in the box — the twenty-fifth — can be used for any shot the shooter chooses — if he breaks the previous twenty-four targets. If he has missed one or more, the last shotshell is used to repeat the first shot he missed.

International skeet, which will be discussed at length later, is a game similar to our American or so-called regulation skeet — with variations. First, the gun must be held at the waist area, until the target appears. The target is released with variable delays ranging from none to three seconds after the shooter calls for the bird. Also, the target travels more rapidly, covering a distance of sixty-five meters or 71.08 yards. This style of skeet shooting is pretty much the way the game was shot back in the Twenties, when it was originated.

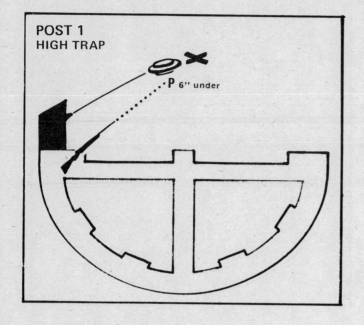

POST 1
HIGH TRAP

P 6" under

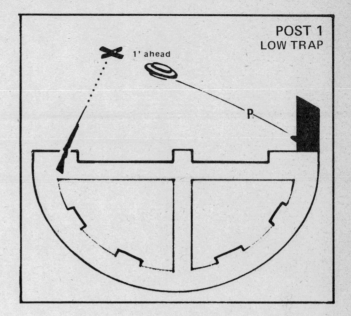

POST 1
LOW TRAP

1' ahead

P

There are all sorts of theories as to how the gun should be held, but I tend to go along with Alex Kerr's advice:

"The hand on the forend," he contends, "should be held as far forward as possible, without stretching the arm uncomfortably. This gives one better control of the gun. At the same time, it prevents flinching with the forward arm.

"The shooter also should hold the hand back on the pistol grip of the gun. This allows the shooter to hold the grip of the stock so that his wrist is in a normal position."

As mentioned, everyone will develop his own ideas on target leads. Much of this has to do with the sight picture of the bird in relationship to your gun as you swing it, how fast you swing and even how you hold the gun. But everyone should have a starting point and Alex Kerr's thoughts afford that. These leads are mathematically correct but will differ with individual timing and reflexes.

On post 1, he suggests shooting six inches under the bird from high trap and leading a foot ahead from the low trap.

Shooting post 2, Kerr shoots a foot ahead when the bird comes out of the high trap and adds another six inches of lead for a low-house bird.

Post 3, Kerr feels, calls for a 1½-foot lead on a high-trap bird, with a three-foot lead from the low house. At post 4, things have sort of leveled out, as he recommends a two-foot lead for birds coming from either house.

At post 5, Kerr allows a three-foot lead on the bird from the high house, cutting his lead to a foot and a half for the low-house clay. At post 6, his high-house bird lead is 1½ feet, reduced to roughly a foot in front of the bird from the low house. At 7 post, he leads the bird by a foot when it flashes out of the high house, but shoots what he estimates to be four inches under the bird. At post 8, he shoots right at the target for both birds.

A lot of years ago, I shot a great deal with the late D. Lee Braun, who had some definite ideas on the proper position and gun elevation for each shot. I have tried the various combinations he suggested and find that this is pretty much the way I shoot, myself, with normal individ-

ualistic differences. After all, I doubt that any two people shoot exactly the same. Each shooter has to find a style and approach he finds comfortable and — assuming it is right from a technical aspect — pursue perfection of this combination.

At 1 post, standing directly in front of the high house, Braun always recommended that one stand with his back to the house, facing post 8, then turning the body about forty-five degrees to the right. In this position, the feet should be angled about forty-five degrees from the face of the traphouse.

While waiting for that initial shot, Braun usually held his mounted gun at an angle of thirty degrees upward, but tended to look another fifteen to twenty degrees above the end of the barrel.

At post 2, Braun recommended the same position, using the path as a guide, since one doesn't have the traphouse to serve as a means of determining the angle of stance. At this post, if the toes were lined up and sighted along, they would provide a line that intersects the path to post 8 at about ninety degrees.

Almost everyone has a cross to bear, but it's not always the same cross. Lee Braun always felt that the three middle posts, 3, 4 and 5, were the most difficult, explaining they "require a longer lead and a more positive follow-through."

As for stance, at post 3 the feet again should be approximately forty-five degrees to the path on which you stand, but one swings from the waist and the ankles — at least, that's the best description I can offer — so that he can get on the bird, gain that lead and swing farther in his follow-through. Shooting this post, one should start with the gun, elevated as before, about two-thirds of the distance between the traphouse and post 8.

For shooting at post 4, if one were sighting across the forward ends of the toes, that line would pass about eight feet in front of the traphouse, while the gun is pointed closer to the traphouse, this time only about a third of the way toward 8 post. That's for the high house.

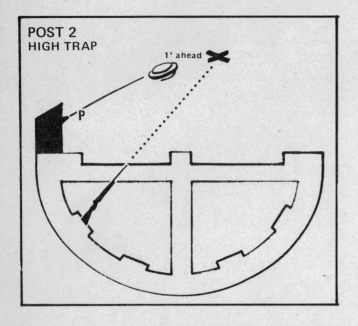

POST 2
HIGH TRAP

1' ahead

P

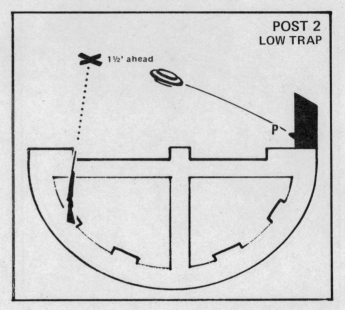

POST 2
LOW TRAP

1½' ahead

P

This shooter appears to be swinging behind his bird, but he scored hit.

For low-house 4, the position of the feet doesn't change, but one should start about two-thirds of the way toward the 8 post for this shot. Again, the position of the feet is much the same for post 5, offering that imaginary line across the toes. Braun recommends one have his gun held about a third of the way out from the traphouse to post 8, when he calls for the bird.

For low-house 5, I guess we all tend to shift position and Lee Braun was no exception. He aligned his feet so that the ends of the toes made a line that would run about a dozen feet to the left of post 8. He started his gun about a third of the distance from the traphouse.

On post 6, Braun recommended that one stand so that his toes line up with 8 post. When shooting the high house, the gun is pointed about a third of the way out from the house, itself. For shooting the low house from this position, he recommended the same position of the feet, with the gun pointed almost straight at the 8 post position — but higher, of course.

Lee Braun always considered the high-house shot from post 7 the easiest shot in the game. At the same time, he warned against over-confidence. The shot is only about ten to twenty percent easier, which isn't much!

For this post, he always recommended standing so that a line extended across the toes would be at a ninety-degree angle with the low house behind the shooter. The gun is pointed about a third of the distance out from the high house to post 8 as a starting point. But the gun should be swung ahead of the target in this instance. As in all shots, the man who waits for the bird, allows it to pass the muzzle, then rushes to catch up is planning on shooting at the air. Usually, his reflexes just aren't that fast and he will shoot behind the bird.

Post 8 — in the middle of the skeet field — is the last station. Flanked on each side by the houses, it looks to the neophyte to be the toughest shot of the game. It is true that the targets from both houses seem to be coming at one with freight train speed, but the shot is relatively simple. It amounts to a form of snap shooting, I suppose, in that you shoot as soon as you have covered the target with the muz-

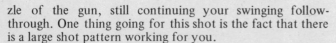

Post 2: "On the high shot, don't look back over your shoulder at the house as some instructors advise" is Kerr's suggestion. "If you look at the house, keep your head on the gun, looking with the eyes only."

zle of the gun, still continuing your swinging follow-through. One thing going for this shot is the fact that there is a large shot pattern working for you.

Those are the bare basics of skeet shooting. Whole books have been written on the subject and I can only assume that a great many more books will see print on the same subject in time to come.

I have quoted D. Lee Braun and Alex Kerr on the subject for the simple reason that, over the years, skeet shooting has become second nature to me. I shoot largely by reflex action, not considering what I am doing or why.

There are any number of other factors that enter into skeet shooting, including the psychological aspects, which are dealt with at greater length elsewhere in this book. However, there are a few general observations I've drawn from my own experience — even problems — that might prove of help.

Keeping one's approach to shooting simple makes the best shots, I have learned, but it is a matter that many shooters never understand. They attempt to complicate their individual styles.

I get into the bad habit myself of moving my head toward the gun, forgetting that you must stand up straight, move the gun to your face, then back it up to your shoulder. One does not put the gun on his shoulder, then move his head down to the gun.

Many of the letters I receive indicate that a skeet shooter is having trouble with shots from posts 2 and 6. He seems to feel he is jinxed, particularly on the latter, and he isn't far from wrong. Even some of the pros consider the six-post shot a psych bird when it's shoved out from the low house.

The initial problem here, of course, is that the closer one is to a crossing target, the faster the relative speed. Actually, 6 post is more difficult than 2 for a right-hand shooter, since one is looking across the gun at the bird. In most cases, the reason for misses at these positions is the fact that the shooter tends to start his gun too close to the house. I know some who will start the muzzle in the house.

If not at first, he will allow the muzzle to creep back toward the house as he continues shooting.

When this happens, the bird becomes a blur for the first few feet and the eyes, nerves and muscles are trying to catch up. As a result, one tends to leap at the bird. As in all shots, the bird is the reference point; one should swing with the bird, then pull ahead to lead it. By starting with the muzzle of the gun away from the trap house, it should be easier to pick up.

Also, as one gets older, the acuity of the eye is not as great as when younger. You don't see things as rapidly and this is another reason that the bird gets ahead of you and you find yourself jumping at it to catch up. Again, starting

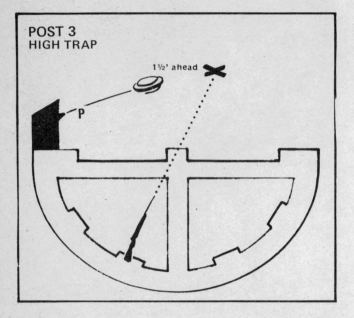

POST 3
HIGH TRAP

1½' ahead

P

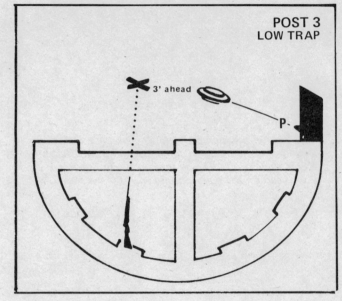

POST 3
LOW TRAP

3' ahead

P

Television comedian Dan Rowan is an avid skeet shooter who makes a highly respectable score showing.

Post 3: The angled strips pointing outward from Alex Kerr's feet mark the limits of the swing he wants to make in taking both of the claybirds.

with the muzzle away from the house is a help.

And the gun barrel should be started at the same elevation as the exit point for the bird. Unlike trapshooting, where one never knows at precisely what angle the bird will appear, one can eliminate many of the unknowns in skeet and this is the thing to do.

Another item, minor though it may seem, is the fact that many beginning skeet shooters pull the trigger with the second joint of the finger. This does not give positive connection and can, of course, cause flinching. If one pulls with the first joint, he has instant contact and can touch off the trigger and not have to yank it.

The latter system, to start with, tightens up all the muscles in the neck and the neck may even be tilted off to the side at times. The head should remain so that the eyes are parallel; otherwise the triangulation principle, your depth perception and judgment of distance and speed tend to go out the window.

This sounds like over-simplification, but it is true. You will find that people who have a lot of trouble — particularly on International skeet — when they move their heads are the ones who usually miss. The great shots are the ones with the simple movement of the gun to the face with no head movement whatsoever. This is because the head is the computer, telling the body what to do, so don't jiggle it around.

By the time you get to skeet shooting, you should have learned which is your master eye, but I've seen shooters who weren't aware of this. There is a system that I learned from Lee Braun, and others: You simply take your hand and put it straight out at arm's length from your nose, then line up your thumb on an object with both eyes open.

If, as you close your left eye, the thumb is on the object, the right eye obviously is your master eye. The reverse is true of your left eye, of course.

As stated, the essential thing about shooting is to find a simple and correct style to begin with, so that it becomes like a game of golf; distinctive and instinctive, the body reacting normally to any kind of shooting.

Again, I use Alex Kerr as the example. He has a simple style that works readily. He is a magnificent shot on ducks and is probably the finest small-bore shot that ever lived. But his style is simple and it's pure, working for every possible kind of shooting. He doesn't have to adjust his style from trap to skeet to bunker to duck shooting.

Most people make an adjustment from one kind of shooting to another, because their basic styles have a flaw. You learn to shoot over the years and you grind in bad habits. You thus learn to compensate and compensation is the destruction of simplicity. In other words, if your style is simple and pure, it is simple for your brain to give the body the message to react.

Keep it simple and clean. You'll do a lot better.

I have referred to Alex Kerr as the outstanding shotgunner of our time. His all-around excellence with a shotgun is constantly evidenced in competitive shoots where he continues to tie down top honors. One Western Open Skeet Shoot, for example, saw Kerr walk away with a flock of laurels that included a .410-bore championship, a first place in the 20-gauge event, another championship in 12 gauge and the coveted high over-all champion award!

What I'm getting at is when a man like this talks, you'd better listen because he's got something important to say...if not by virtue of his ability as a top shotgunner, simply because his experience and personal involvement with shotgunning in general and skeet-gunning in particular carry back to those early days when William Hardin Foster first introduced the game of skeet.

Kerr will reflect with authority upon the late Herb Perk's establishment of the first skeet field in the Southern California area. That was during the late 1920s up in what they call Big Tujunga Wash. Then Perk's extension of Bill Foster's idea for a new game for shotgunners became the famous old Roaring Gulch Skeet Club and things started to happen!

Like basketball, skeet is a game born and developed in America. At the beginning, its purpose was to build field shotgunning skills. Within this concept, the early game call-

Post 4: Kerr recommends a two-foot lead for the bird coming out of the high house. Note that his knees seem bent slightly; he leans into the gun.

During skeet shoot at opening of range at Spring Creek, Nevada, Dan Rowan waits for high house bird, watched by trap champ Dan Orlich, Roy Rogers and Dan Bonillas.

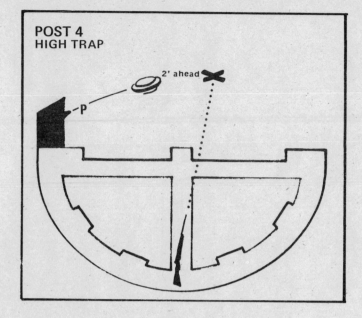

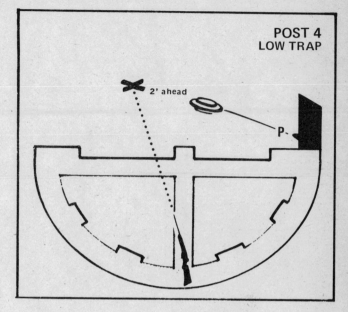

ed for a "low-gun" or belt-level buttstock position and a brief delay — or no delay — on the release of the claybird. The methods were in keeping with the more practical conditions that might be met in the field.

Then, as now, American shotgunners had a right to be proud of their own claybird game and of the way they were able to foster and develop proficient shooters. But as the popularity of skeet became more widespread, organization and guidance were needed. This is where Alex Kerr points to the importance of the National Skeet Shooting Association.

Through the years, the NSSA has continued to grow with skeet shooting which, incidentally, has seen the number of participants double in the past five years! In order to welcome droves of new shooters to the field, new facilities and new events constantly are being planned

With growth and new interest, the nature of skeet shooting changed. For example, many shooters began discovering skeet as a challenge in and of itself; it could be an exciting game, both for the competitively inclined and the shooter who simply wanted to keep his responses from becoming dull, when he hadn't the opportunity to hunt.

Participation in skeet shooting by ever-increasing numbers of sportsminded Americans, along with an awakening to the value of the event as a competitive game, ultimately gave rise to changes in popular practice. The NSSA molded itself to the needs and desires of shotgunners by instituting new rules for a faster, more pliable type of skeet wherein the gun was not held so that the stock was down, as it might be as the shooter walked afield, but posed against the shoulder in a ready position. With this change in ruling came the immediate release of the claybird...instead of the delayed release previously practiced.

In addition to molding itself to the concept of skeet as a competitive game, the new rules system provided an important element: Time! On the average, Kerr says, a five-shooter squad will complete a round of skeet — that is, a total of 125 shots — in about ten minutes' less time than would be required under the other rules. This means that a substantially greater number of shooters can be accommodated at any competitive event or during any day of normal practice shooting at skeet fields throughout the nation.

But what of the average shooter's attitude toward the "low-gun, delayed-bird" brand of International skeet as compared to skeet in its popular contemporary form? Alex Kerr's formidable background of experience and personal contact with skeet and skeet shooters gives us the answer: The average shooter, whether he finds himself involved competitively or casually, prefers to abide by the rules of the "shoulder-ready, no-delay" game, while reserving his interest in the more rigorous International-type game for an occasional change of pace or added challenge.

I've spent a good deal of time in discussing the status of skeet in this country and the fact that, the way it is shot today, we don't show much in the way of competition for the Europeans when it comes to the International matches.

This, I think, was pretty well established at the fortieth World Shooting Championships, which this country hosted in Phoenix several years back. But regardless of whether we have concentrated on International skeet or not, there are some records that are just hard to top and that set by the Russian shooter to win the individual gold medal was one of them. E. Petrov, the 32-year-old Russian shooter, celebrated his birthday in the United States by shooting 200 straight, a perfect score.

In regard to the workings of the Russian system of selecting shooters, I found Petrov of particular interest. He

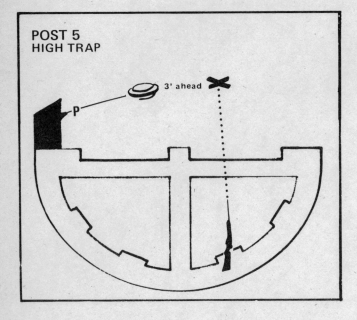

POST 5
HIGH TRAP

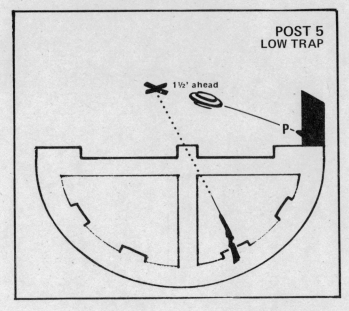

POST 5
LOW TRAP

had, for instance, been shooting skeet since 1957. He took up trap first and shot that for about six months, but switched when he decided that his gun was better suited to skeet. The gun was the MTS Model 8, of Soviet manufacture and he shot AZOT ammunition. The gun measures sixty-eight centimeters and weighs 3½ kilograms.

But the Russian — and then world — champion got into competitive shooting by means of hunting, he says. He belonged to a hunting club in Moscow and had hunted ducks, elk, rabbits, fox and wild boar as a member. According to his explanation, there are many of these clubs in Russia and officials are constantly observing the members. If they seem to have unusual talent in the hunt, they may be offered an opportunity to go in for competition shooting under professional tutelage.

The young Russian had had a long and reasonably successful career, having won the gold medal in the Olympic games in Mexico a couple of years back, also competing in three other world championship outings. And without boasting, but in a most matter of fact fashion, he stated that this was the third time that he has shattered 200 consecutive birds in competitive shooting.

In the matter of training, he said that he shoots only two or three times a week, shooting 100 birds each time. However, because of the severe Moscow winters, he cannot shoot at all from November through February. He does do a good deal of shouldering and pointing of the shotgun in his home during these months, attempting to maintain his style and reflexes.

Actually, Petrov had two shotguns, which are identical and by the same Russian maker, but the one he fired at Phoenix is his favorite. He said that it is a standard gun off the manufacturer's line and that nothing had been done to fit it to his own personal dimensions. In looking over the gun, there is no evidence of custom work, although it is a carefully built arm. He has had this particular gun for fourteen years and says that he has fired more than 160,000 rounds through it. When asked about mechanical trouble, he said that the only problem in that lengthy and explosive

career has been a broken spring and several broken firing pins, all easily replaced.

The gun also was equipped with double triggers. When asked whether it would not be simpler to use a gun with a single trigger, Petrov was doubtful. He prefers two triggers, but admits that he cannot explain the reason for this.

As for his feelings about winning top honors in that world outing, he was frank in stating "Nobody could expect to win. You just come and you hope."

Then, when asked whether he felt he would be honored by his government when he returned to Moscow, this brought another smile.

"I hope," was all he said.

Doesn't it rankle you to reflect that this country of ours, which we like to think of as a nation of shooters, is hard-put to cop the top hardware in international claybird competition? Speaking personally, it bugs the daylights out of me!

It's bad enough, goodness knows, in the example of trap-shooting, but when you stop to think that the game of skeet was invented in this country — Andover, Massachusetts, to be specific — it seems as though we ought to do better: A lot better!

You can pinpoint the core of the problem, quite likely: Both trap and skeet have been watered-down so as to make it easier for the American shooter to run up an impressive score that he can brag about. The rest of the world shoots trap and skeet for grown-ups, while the USA clings to a sort of beginner's version, where the claybirds float out slow and easy. Just to weigh the odds a bit more favorably, the pampered Yankee shooter is allowed to get the butt of the gun all comfortably situated against his shoulder before he calls for the bird.

This, in itself, is nothing short of ridiculous. The entire purpose and motive for claybird shooting in the first place — in case anyone has forgotten — is to train the shooter and sharpen his skill and reflexes for more effective hunting of gamebirds in the field.

Now any hunter in the world can assure you that you

Post 5: Note that, throughout the series, except at post 8, Alex Kerr's feet are angled much the same and that he maintains the same position in the shooter's box.

don't go in quest of wild game with your safety off and the gun in readiness at your shoulder. And you can bawl, "Pull!" till your face turns bright blue without hardly ever having a bird flush from sixteen yards ahead in perfect synchronization for your shot.

Whether or not you agree that art does or should imitate nature, you might be able to go along with this observation: If the sole reason for trap and skeet is to break the highest possible percentage of claybirds, then the obvious, logical, most effective thing that you could do would be to trade your shotgun for a ball-peen hammer.

Lay out twenty-five or more claybirds on the ground, roll up your sleeve and start busting possibles with monotonous regularity. Sound silly? Yes, it sounds silly, but only a little more so than the contemplation of an entire nation that has gotten so obsessed with the importance of impressive scores that it has fudged up the rules until it has turned U.S. skeet and trap into kids' games; until most of the people spoiled on Yankee trap and skeet are cold-turkey setups when they have to shoot under the rules followed by the rest of the world.

Silly and monotonous are words that crop back up as you contemplate the typical claybirding event under the

indulgent rules laid down in this country. Given a match with two hundred birds, you may wind up with as many as twenty or more of the competitors who have broken all two hundred. So then you gather these together and set them to work at the shoot-off. It underlines the too-easy state of affairs when you consider that the eventual winner and his runners-up may go on for another two hundred straight or more before skill, sheer endurance and a bit of help from the fickle Fates produces one lone winner.

It would make just about as much sense if you decided to modify the game of bowling by discarding the conventional ball and replacing it with a gadget resembling a weightlifter's barbells. Proportion it so that one wheel rides in each gutter and it becomes a ducksoup snap to rack up one three-hundred score after another. Grade a golf course properly, with all of the turf clipped short and funneling down toward each flag. Presto! Go around in eighteen, a hole-in-one every time! Why don't bowlers and golfers take these obvious steps toward "improving" their games?

So okay — I'm exaggerating just a little bit here, for purposes of effect and illustration. It's true that every American trap and skeet shooter does not break every bird he shoots at, every time he walks to the line or station. Certainly, it's possible to miss, as I've proved to myself more frustrating times than I really care to dwell upon.

By just how much have we loaded the dice and shaded the odds in our version of trap and skeet? Let's compare both with the way the games are shot in the rest of the world. And let's use the term, "National," for our own pie-easy setup, as contrasted to International trap or skeet.

Let's start by reviewing the genesis and early history of skeet, since that first layout, at Andover, differed widely from the game we know, love and sometimes cuss at.

It first was called shooting around the clock. The field was laid out as a circle, having a radius of twenty-five yards. There were twelve stations, equally spaced, with a marked

At Post 8, Derek Partridge powders both birds as they cross in front of him, a feat few shooters perfect.

153

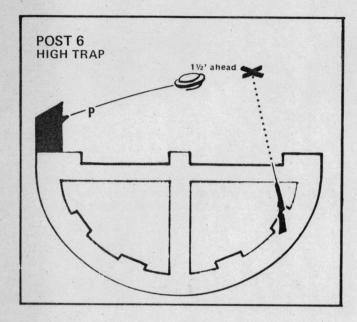

POST 6
HIGH TRAP

1½' ahead

P

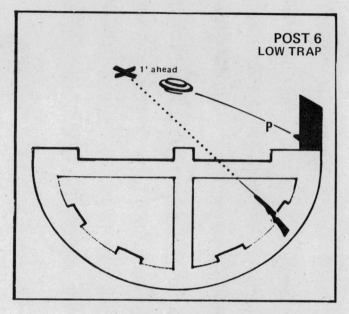

POST 6
LOW TRAP

1' ahead

P

spot in the center of the circle. The single trap was located at the twelve o'clock spot, heaving birds across the circle, straight at the six o'clock point. Shooters fired at two going-away birds from station twelve, then worked their way around the circle in a clockwise direction: Two at one, two at two and so on. The twenty-fifth shot was fired from the center spot at the incoming bird; a shot similar to the present station eight low-house bird.

In 1923, the layout was modified by reducing the circle from a twenty-five-yard radius to one of just twenty yards. In that same fateful year, someone built a chicken house on adjoining property, situated in such a way that it lay in fall-out area of shot pellets from stations seven through eleven. Quite effectively, that put an end to shooting around the clock under its previous ground rules.

Displaying the celebrated virtue of Yankee ingenuity, being hopelessly bitten by what we now know as the skeet virus, the Bay State scattergunners weren't about to chicken out of their beloved pastime with cries of fowl play.

With half of their field wiped out by invading poultry, a second trap was placed in an elevated house at the opposite corner of the surviving semi-circle. Thus, seven stations were equally spaced around the perimeter of a semi-circle, with an eighth in the center. Essentially, the skeet field layout remains unchanged nearly half a century later. The layout that stemmed from a makeshift solution to a purely local problem has spread across the globe.

Yes, the game of skeet is American, born and bred and it accounts for nearly one-third of all the shotgun shells fired in this country in any given year. So, with a lot of shooters and shooting, we should do well in competition with other countries, right? Sad to say, wrong! During the 1968 Olympics, the best that the U.S. skeet shooters could manage was sixteenth and nineteenth.

The game, of course, was International skeet and therein lies the vital difference. In what we'll term National skeet, the shooter puts his gun to the shoulder, makes a swing or two with the sights, gets everything set to his liking and calls for the bird. It is thrown, simultaneously on command, and it's possible to predict its appearance from the trap within a thin fraction of a second. Too, the National bird is traveling at a fairly easy speed, traveling but about fifty yards before reaching the ground.

Contrast this to the International version. Here, you start in a position known as "international ready." The butt of the gun must be touching the shooter's hip and it must remain there, in contact, until the bird comes out of the trap. The bird may appear on call or any time up to three seconds later. The combination of faster birds, the low gun international ready starting position and the variable-delay release all add up to the unique challenge of International skeet.

Similar critical differences exist between our local version of trapshooting and International trap. Instead of a single trap, throwing birds over a moderate and variable horizontal arc — always at the same vertical angle — the International Shooting Union (ISU) or Olympic trench is comprised of fifteen traps, laid out so as to deliver the birds at angles anywhere up to forty-five degrees, as contrasted to the twenty-two-degree arc of National trap.

Too, the International trap bird starts out at a higher speed, traveling an average distance of sixty-five yards, rather than the fifty of the National bird.

It would seem that International trap should have great appeal to people who like to shoot, since it allows two shots to be fired at each bird thrown, with no penalty being attached to firing the second shot and no bonus if you smoke the target with your first shot. It is not only possible, but fairly customary to fire up fifty shots in a single, twenty-five-target round. Many competitive shooters make it a regular practice to fire the second shot, even if the bird was well broken with the first, aiming at the largest piece of clay still flying. Their reason is for the sake of preserving their natural rhythm of aiming and firing, anchoring the instinctive habit of firing twice so that there will be no vital split second lost through hesitation on those birds that are

Post 6: Bob Stack considers this his toughest shot. Alex Kerr says a 1½-foot lead on the high house bird will do, with a foot lead on other.

missed with the first shot.

International trap is a tough game to beat. Not only do the claybirds seem to be rocket-powered in comparison to National targets, but they vary in height, as well. You've no hope of guessing if it will head for the moon or skim along at ground height like a frightened quail.

The National Rifle Association has been working hard to promote both International skeet and trap in this country. All too often, I hear someone remark, "I thought trap and skeet shooting came under the jurisdiction of the Amateur Trapshooting Association and the National Skeet Shooting Association, not the NRA," or something along the same lines.

The NRA has stated it has neither intention nor desire to move in on the two domestic claybird organizations nor to compete with them. The reason why the NRA concerns itself is that the ISU is composed of one associate member organization in each nation that participates in International shooting competition. The NRA is the group representing this country in the ISU and, as a result, must handle all affairs concerning International shooting competition in the USA, whether rifle, handgun or shotgun.

ISU competitions follow a regular four-year cycle and these events include the Olympics, the ISU Moving Target World Championships, the ISU World Championships — such as were held at Phoenix in 1970 — for all guns, and the Pan-American Games.

The first thing I noticed, while firing a round of International skeet with Bob Schuele — a fine, young shooter from Rochelle, Illinois — was the speed of the targets as they were released from the traps; to get the extra fifteen yards of flight, they have to be launched at a much higher velocity.

International skeet is one of those sports in which the fast reactions of youth are a decidedly important asset. Watching Schuele, I couldn't help but notice how cool and calm he appeared as he called for each target, bringing the gun to his shoulder before beginning his swing.

The stance used by the younger shooters may seem unusual to you when first observed; it did to me. I always put some forward lean into my stance when shooting the standard type of skeet, so as to form a better pivot. Instead of leaning, however, Schuele — as well as the majority of other shooters I have observed at Olympic tryouts — stands upright, tilting the gun forward from the hip, with the muzzle just at eye level.

Each shooter in the Olympic tryouts shoots three hundred targets; one hundred per day for three days. Only the two with the least number of misses will go to the Olympics.

Breaking 294x300, Tony Rosetti — an accounting major at the University of Mississippi — was the top gun at the Phoenix elimination, followed closely by Jack Johnson of San Antonio, Texas and the Army's Jim Whitaker, who tied it up with 292x300 apiece. In a twenty-five-bird tie-breaker event, Johnson went twenty-five straight to cinch number two spot on the U.S. Olympic skeet team while Whitaker missed just one heart-breaking bird.

Although both Rosetti and Johnson are civilians at present, both shot with military teams at one time. In fact, Rosetti — then with the Army's skeet team — won the gold medal at the 9th U.S. International Shooting Championships held at Phoenix in 1969. Johnson — more renowned on the International trap circuit — shot with the Air Force team for ten years before retiring.

The paramount reason for the shortage of really top-caliber claybird competitions for the International events lies in the fact that facilities for shooting this type of trap and skeet are few and far between. There were only about one hundred shooters competing at Phoenix for the honor of shooting on our two-man team and this must have represented a large segment of all the International skeet shooters in this country. Since the International version is the only type of skeet that's shot in most of the rest of the world, this means that most of the other countries will be

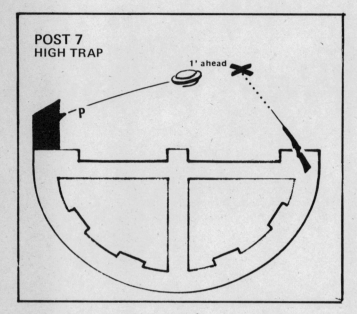

POST 7
HIGH TRAP

1' ahead

P

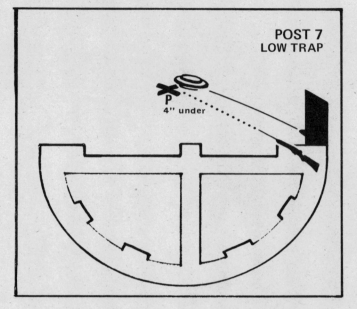

POST 7
LOW TRAP

P
4" under

This type of performance offered by Florida exhibition shooter is not guaranteed to improve your scores, but it might prove interesting in checking your reflexes.

Two claybirds were balanced on the shotgunner's toe before he raised his foot to catapult them into the air. Notice that shotgun already is being brought up.

Post 7: Kerr leads the high house bird by a foot, shooting four inches under it, then shoots directly at the bird passing him from low house.

The shooter already has powdered the first claybird from his foot-powered launch, while the other bird is fair game. Such tricks take practice and coordination.

fielding teams that were winnowed out of several hundred to a few thousand entrants.

It was the consensus among shooters I questioned that there is a severe need for more places equipped to offer practice at the International claybird events. One shooter noted that, for him, practicing meant traveling more than one hundred miles, each way. Actually, he's lucky, since many another would-be shooter would find his distance more on the order of two or three hundred miles!

Setting up facilities for International skeet costs little more than for the common, domestic version of the game. Mostly, it's a matter of adjusting the traps to provide enough starting speed for the required distance. Apart from that, and the delayed tripper, the other points of difference are up to the shooter. There is no valid reason why International skeet facilities cannot be made available, given the number of prospective shooters to make it worth the while of the individual clubs.

It's another matter in the instance of International trap, or it has been, until recently. Setting up the regulation International trench, with its fifteen especially constructed traps, was running the cost into the neighborhood of $20,000 to $30,000 for each layout. Few clubs felt justified in investing such a sum, particularly if there seemed little likelihood that it would draw a high volume of shooters.

There is hope for a solution to that problem, however. Research financed by the NRA has developed a single trap that is capable of almost duplicating the output of the entire fifteen-trap International trench. It may not be sanctioned for use in registered International trap events, but it is capable of providing realistic practice at a small fraction of the going cost of setting up the all-out International trap facility. In fact, typical installations of the NRA's International-type trap are averaging just about one-tenth of the cost of the full-course ISU system.

To make the picture even more attractive, the NRA's new rig can be installed in any trap house that will handle a regulation thrower and, if that doesn't seem within the reach of a club's treasury, then it's possible to modify a

Post 8: Note that the position of Alex Kerr's feet has changed to a degree. On this post, he positions himself to shoot directly at both birds crossing in front of him.

In recent years, the Armed Services have supplied most of the nation's top competition shooters, especially on the International scene. Stack decries seeming lack of interest.

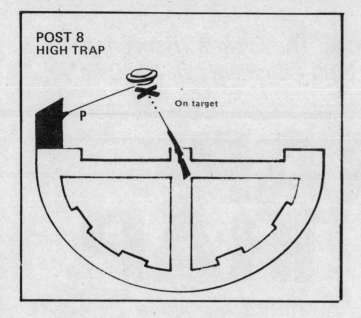

POST 8
HIGH TRAP

On target

P

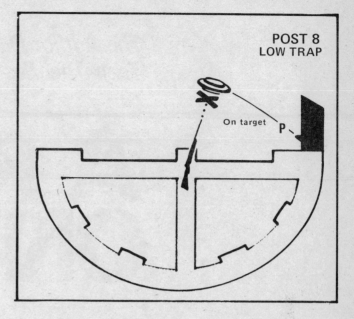

POST 8
LOW TRAP

On target

P

standard trap so that it's capable of throwing birds in the prescribed pattern and specs at a cost of two hundred dollars, or a bit less.

So, it would appear, the cost has been bypassed as the major stumbling block in the way of making suitable practice facilities available on a convenient local level. There is no reason why it should cost substantially more to shoot International skeet than for the standard variety. The club's own investment in the modified International trap layout should not boost the cost of a round by any great percentage. The main added expense in shooting International trap lies in the expenditure of anywhere up to twice as many shells per round and this should not present an insurmountable barrier to the average shooter, particularly not if he reloads.

All of which brings the whole question squarely back to you, the typical American shotgunner. International claybirding is ready for you and for your club; are you ready for it?

Sure, you can expect your cherished average to take a beating when you go up against the tougher International versions of the two games. It might mean snipping that hard-won, hundred-straight brassard off of your shooting jacket...or leaving it on as you fight, fang and claw, toward the day you can add one that says "25-straight, International."

If it's important to impress people, why not try impressing them by the fact that you're not afraid to shift to the kind of grown-up skeet and trap that is shot by all of the other countries? Or does it make more sense to bust a thousand straight with the ball-peen hammer?

These are questions which, given the right answers, will go far toward putting the U.S. of A. on top of the claybirding heap — where I think it belongs.

In Georgia pine forest, the gun is coming up to his cheek as Bob Stack focuses his aim on a bobwhite quail.

*The Author Quotes The Experts, Tempering
Their Theories With Comments Of His Own!*

A RAP
ON TRAP

*The Amateur Trapshooting Association has hosted the Grand American
Trapshooting Championships at Vandalia, Ohio, grounds for fifty years.*

Chapter 11

TRAPSHOOTING may not be quite as old as the concept for the shotgun, but it has to come close. It appears that the origin of the sport is English, as there seem to be no early mentions of it in European sporting records. However, an English publication does refer to trapshooting as early as 1793 and indicates that it was hardly a newly introduced sport at that time.

According to the Eighteenth Century publication, "A shallow box of about a foot long, and eight to ten inches wide, is sunk in the ground, parallel with the surface, and just twenty-one yards from the foot mark, at which each gunner is bound to take his aim. The box has a sliding lid, to which is affixed a string by one appointed to that office, who is placed next to the person going to shoot, from whom he takes the word of command for drawing the string whenever he is ready to take his aim;...The gunner is not permitted to put his gun to his shoulder till the bird is on the wing; and the bird must fall within one hundred yards of the box, or is deemed a lost shot."

That may be the origin of trapshooting, but it is not too far removed from the live pigeon shooting that still is pursued in Mexico, Spain and other Latin countries with great enthusiasms even today.

Dick Baldwin of Remington Arms, who has researched the past and is a great collector of claybird mementos, suggests that there are two possible reasons for such a game being devised in an era when game birds were plentiful.

"Perhaps the sport was invented as a preparation for field shooting, for people living in or near cities," he suggests, "but another interesting prospect presents itself as well.

"In the middle and late Eighteenth Century, contests on driven game were regularly held across the Channel. These matches frequently evoked side bets for large sums of money. So possibly one reason for these early clubs was to sharpen eye and flint for up-coming lucrative events on the Continent."

The first printed mention of trapshooting in America is found in records of the Sportsmen's Club. Headquartered in Cincinnati, this club may well have been the birthplace of trapshooting in America, since that initial mention is found in records of 1831. In that era, passenger pigeons were used in the shoots, although English sparrows also were utilized. By 1840, two trapshooting clubs were in operation near New York City.

As I have mentioned earlier, shooters have become in-

This woodcut illustration from 1793 English magazine shows how live birds were released for the game.

Above: Pigeon shoot illustration was printed in Harper's Weekly in 1881. (Left) Bogardus traps in use were subject of an article in Eighties.

creasingly better as guns and ammunition have improved greatly. This was true even a century ago for, in the 1890s, it was becoming rather commonplace for top shooters to down a hundred live game birds straight. Two of the top shooters of the period were Seth Green and C.W. Bradford, both of whom scored 100 straight with consistency, starting each shot with their guns below their hips until the trap was sprung. This was a rule of the game at the time and was conducted very much like the requirements of today's International claybird games. Bradford, incidentally, was considered the world's trap champion for several years, finally being deposed by one Edward Gilman.

At the turn of the century — not unlike our present era — there was an outcry against live-bird shooting and legislation was pushed through most of the states, banning this phase of the sport. Apparently there had been similar campaigns in England, for her shooters already had come up with a device that hurled glass balls from a position in front of the shooter. This, of course, was the forerunner of the modern target-hurling trap.

This trap, however, would throw the balls only ten yards or so. It was about 1876 that one Adam Bogardus devised a target-throwing device that would hurl one of the glass balls a good thirty-five yards. Bogardus was one of the top exhibition shots of the era and toured the country with his four hard-shooting sons, displaying his prowess with a shotgun.

The early balls were under three inches in diameter and became exceedingly tough targets in that a glancing pellet would not always provide a clean break. As they were clear glass, this made them even more difficult to break.

This problem put the inventors to work and there suddenly were numerous variations. One type was coated with sand to make it seen more easily, while other balls were formed of green or amber glass. One enterprising inventor even came up with a glass target that was filled with feathers. When broken, the plumes exploded in a shower in the air as might a hit live bird. Still another was loaded with chemical fertilizer, which was supposed to automatically improve the soil on the shooting grounds!

Even more spectacular to my mind was a target introduced in 1880, which was made without glass. When penetrated by a shot pellet, this activated a chemical inside, which caused a bright flash and accompanying smoke. This also eliminated the glass problem, as they could be broken in the hand, turning to powder, without injury. And the price was right at $15 per thousand birds.

There were countless other inventions and variations over the years until the development of today's claybird. Incidentally, it has been my experience — and that of

College trap competition has brought the sport to distaffers, who find they can compete on the same level as male shooters. (Right) Collegiate shooter relaxes between rounds.

Checking out Perazzi over/under, Robert Stack illustrates correct method of placing the gun against cheek (above, right) as opposed to the positioning, which allows one to look too high over barrels of the gun.

During opening of trap/skeet club at Spring Creek, Nevada, Bob Stack watches behind the firing line with the club pro, Mike Callagher. On the line are (from left) actor Robert Fuller, Dusty Rogers, Roy Rogers, comedian Dan Rowan. All of these entertainers are outstanding shotgunners.

others — that there still are variations. While shooting in Europe, for example, I have found an inconsistency in the hardness of the birds. Some shatter easily, while others tend to bounce pellets off their tough finishes.

The claybird as such seems to have been designed by one George Ligowski, a shooter of the 1880s. He designed the flat profile, then hired the earlier mentioned Bogardus and W.F. Carver, the latter a member of Buffalo Bill's Wild West troupe, to tour the country introducing the new concept. It was Bogardus, incidentally, who is given credit for laying out the trap field as it is today.

Since that time, claybirds have remained much the same, with a few variations, although I recently saw a new innovation of plastic. Built in two pieces, it is reuseable, since its segments are designed to part, when hit. It then is clamped back together and used again. Just how successful this item may prove is a matter that history will have to decide.

The Interstate Trapshooting Association was formed in 1890 and regulated the sport in the United States until 1922. The first Grand American Handicap shoot was held under its auspices on Long Island in 1900. It was won by one Rolla Heikes of Ohio, who scored 91 x 100 from the twenty-two-yard line. Heikes visited Britain the following year with the American team, demonstrating his feat of

These photos illustrate some of the interest being shown in trap events today by college students. Note the semi-International position at which the gun is held by shooter at left.

breaking a hundred targets in just two seconds under three minutes. For this he used four repeating shotguns, which were being loaded by a staff.

The present-day Amateur Trapshooting Association was organized in 1923 in Vandalia, Ohio, where the Grand American Trapshooting Championships have been held for the past half century.

A few years ago, the ATA boasted some 40,000 members, but publicity releases claim that number since has grown to double that number. Frankly, I can't verify this figure. When Hugh L. McKinley, manager of the Amateur Trapshooting Association, was contacted with a request for

help on this chapter, his reluctance verged on the cool. He even neglected to tell us what the membership amounts to these days and it became necessary to rely upon such experts as Dick Baldwin and another Remington staffer, Dick Dietz, both of whom have been of great help in setting this record straight.

A chapter such as this would be incomplete without mention of the fact that there have been some outstanding women shooters over the decades. Perhaps the first was Annie Oakley. She was best known as a sharpshooter with Buffalo Bill's Wild West Show and has been immortalized as a show business personality more than a shooter by such

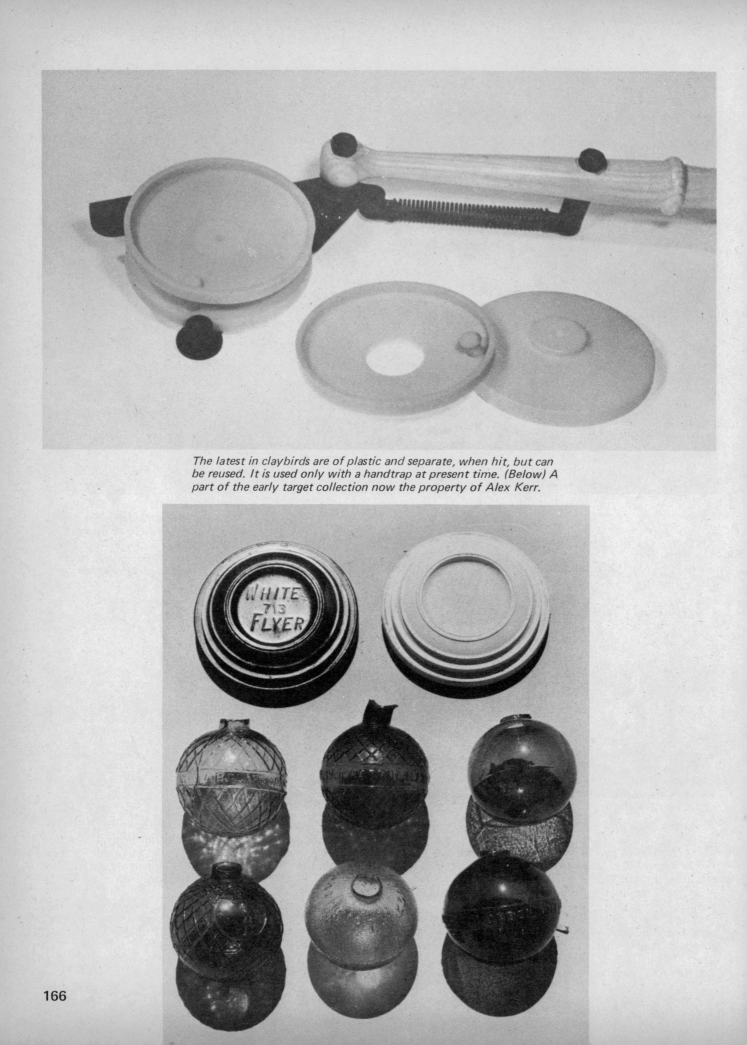

The latest in claybirds are of plastic and separate, when hit, but can be reused. It is used only with a handtrap at present time. (Below) A part of the early target collection now the property of Alex Kerr.

Bob Allen, former trapshooting great (in white shooting coat) and the late actor Van Heflin look over the situation at Grand Bahama Island shooting club during Winchester-sponsored championships.

stage and screen luminaries as Barbara Stanwyck, Judy Garland, Ethel Merman and Betty Hutton. One part of her show act was to leap from a three-foot high table, shooting two glass balls thrown in the air before she landed on the ground.

The Interstate Trapshooting Association voted to allow women to compete as early as 1915 and another star of the traps became Plinky Topperwein, the wife of Ad Topperwein, who was one of the greatest shooters of all time. In fact, it was Annie Oakley who stated that Mrs. Topperwein was the greatest of all women trapshooters.

By today's standards, that title might no longer hold, but Plinky Topperwein is remembered for maintaining an average of ninety-five percent on 8010 targets shot in 1915. The following year she went into semi-retirement — by comparative standards — shooting only 2690 targets, but still maintaining a 94.38 average!

My old shooting partner, the late D. Lee Braun, described trapshooting by saying, "The man has not yet been born who can beat this game and I doubt that he ever will be — which only increases the excitement of the sport."

I don't feel that statement is entirely true these days, for today's trap — starting with the gun at the shoulder — has fallen into the same pattern as skeet. With better shotshells, better shotguns and better shooters, the game threatens to become an endurance contest rather than a game of individual skills. Such top shooters as Elgin Gates not only shoot well, but even train so they will be able to outlast their competitors!

However, for those who never have shot trap, a brief description of the game would appear to be in order.

Quoting Lee Braun again, "The targets leave the trap house at angles unknown to the shooter when he calls for them. I think that there are about seventy-two angles in

Among the top trapshooters of yore participating in the 1967 Grand National were three on right: Hugh Driggs, Hiram Bradley, Joe Fields.

between the extreme left and extreme right angles that the targets can take. Moreover, they are traveling away from the shooter at nearly a mile a minute. Since most trap targets are broken at thirty to thirty-five yards distance, this gives you one short second after calling for your target to estimate its angle of flight, get the lead you will need — if any — take into account such wind conditions as may be present and fire. As you can see, trapshooting is almost like rifle shooting with a shotgun."

I agree on that point with Lee Braun, who spent his last years as a Remington professional shooter. And Lee was not the only great instructor and shooter to make the comparison between rifle shooting and trapshooting.

Skeet shooting is a reaction game, whereas trap requires more precision. On those distant straight-away shots in trap you don't have much of an allowable element of error. Also, in trapshooting, the shooter tends to stabilize himself.

With skeet, you can take a ping pong or tennis player — anyone who is used to working moving objects quickly — and, unless he has an eye deficiency or some other physical shortcoming, you can teach him to be a skeet shooter in no time.

But to add to the comparison between trapshooting and riflery, when I was serving in Hawaii during World War II, the worst time I ever experienced was attempting to teach skeet to a Marine rifle team that held the world's record for 1000-yard shooting. They were taking readings on the wind and everything else. By the time they pulled the trigger, their targets were on the ground. Shotgun shooting has been compared many times to waving a fire hose and this is more true, I feel, of skeet than trap.

At the same time, I cannot help but feel that a skeet shooter can adjust to trapshooting with fair success, while a trap shot has more problems in adjusting to skeet.

Another point I never had bothered to consider was pointed out to me by Alex Kerr: Conformity of the body has a great deal to do with the ease with which one can become a great trapshooter — or for that matter, almost any kind of a shot.

I don't mean to knock anyone's build, but if you have a head that seems to grow out of your shoulders, it is easier to keep your head down. Keeping your face on the gun — or realistically, the gun to your face — is a mandatory part of shotgun shooting; if you have a long neck, you have

One of the consistently best trapshooters in recent amateur history has been Dan Orlich, (shooting.) He is flanked on right by C.E. Barnhart, on left by George Shellenberger during sundown shootoff at Vandalia event.

more of a tendency to peek over the top of the barrel at the target.

Kerr and I once were watching a great trapshooter and Alex commented that he didn't have to worry about keeping his head down, because he didn't have any neck.

In trap, because of the ranges and the speed at which the bird travels, the margin for error is drawn pretty fine. Lee Braun made the point that the margin for error must be minimized for trap. "The gun fit must be exact and the body position must be right. Relaxation is essential and concentration is imperative.

"Each shooter is seeking the quickest and easiest and smoothest movement he can find to break his targets, in accordance with his own timing and coordination and ability. Since no two individuals are the same, the ideal combination for each shooter will be unique. If you ask a hundred different shooters about their techniques for trapshooting, you will end up with a hundred different systems."

I feel that one of the basic problems some beginning shooters experience in trapshooting is the fact that there are only five stations which do not cover too broad an angle of shooting. The traphouse is right there in front of them

and they feel it should be a piece of cake. However, they are failing to take into consideration those seventy-odd angles at which the bird can be thrown. It doesn't take the beginner long to learn that he does well on some angles and needs lots of practice on others.

He was referring to shooting trap doubles, when he offered the advice, but Lee Braun offered an observation that applies to almost all types of shotgunning and especially to trapshooting, I feel.

"Go get a whole bunch of shells and shoot at a whole bunch of targets and you won't have to look far for excuses as to why you missed them. The answer will be obvious.

"The answer, of course, is practice. But with practice, good scores and the thrill of that accomplishment are not beyond the reach of anyone."

In a following chapter, Elgin Gates, one of the all-time greats, offers advice on his own techniques of trapshooting, but one must keep in mind that those are his own systems and may not work for everyone.

As has been suggested several times in this book and probably will be repeated several times more — shotgunning on any level is not something that can be taught; it must be learned. The difference is more broad than one may think at first consideration.

169

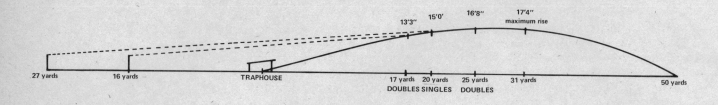

27 yards   16 yards   TRAPHOUSE   13'3"   15'0"   16'8"   17'4" maximum rise

17 yards   20 yards   25 yards   31 yards   50 yards
DOUBLES SINGLES   DOUBLES

16-YARD SINGLES

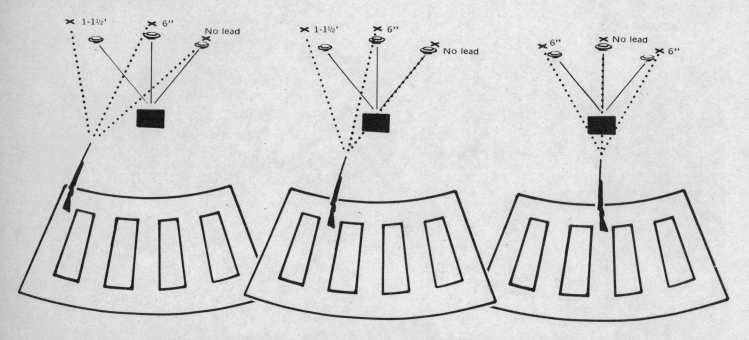

27-YARD HANDICAP

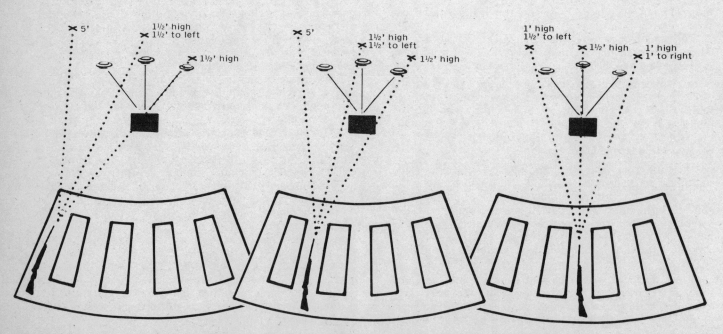

The chart at left indicates the distances at which trap targets are shot. In singles, the claybirds generally are broken about twenty yards from the traphouse — or thirty-five yards from the gunner. The first target in doubles is broken at a shorter range, with the second out twenty-five yards from house. For handicap, you are adding another eleven yards to these figures, leaving little room for error!

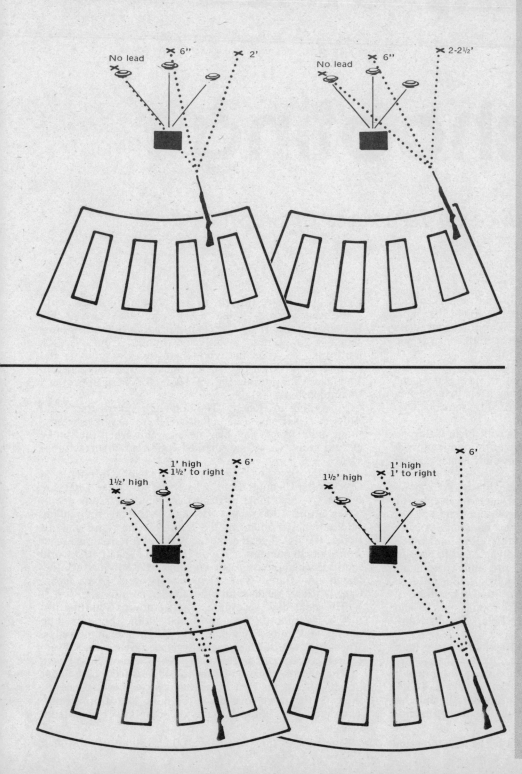

indicates the target, a standard American or European-made claybird.

✕ indicates the point at which the bird should be hit, when proper lead is taken.

◼ designates the trap house from which the birds are thrown in their various patterns.

Each position is shown by the silhouetted shotgun superimposed over the trap layout.

The leads indicated on the accompanying charts will vary from shooter to shooter and these distances are suggested simply as starting points for the individual who never before has shot trap. Individual adjustment of leads will be accomplished through practice.

Only two segments of the trap sequence are shown due to space limitations, with no mention of techniques for shooting doubles. Doubles is a faster game, requiring that the shooter's timing be developed properly. On doubles, the trap is set at prescribed angles and most shooters prefer the straight-away shot first, getting it out of the way.

In 27-yard handicap trap, control and the smoothness with which one handles his gun become important. Wind conditions, the way in which the traps are set and — most important — personal judgment all become factors. But the obvious answer to all of these potential problems is continued practice.

Chapter 12

The Expertise Of Trapshooting

Advice On Techniques Of Crown Seeking!

EVERYONE TENDS TO lump trap and skeet together simply as claybird games, but I've found that most serious shooters are one or the other. I'm not saying there are not shooters who are outstanding at both sports; there are, but they certainly are in the minority.

I shoot an occasional round of trap more as a social gesture than because I'm serious about it; skeet is my game and always has been. For that reason, I felt that the fine points of trapshooting should be discussed by someone who is an expert at it.

In this case, I elected to discuss it with Elgin Gates, an acquaintance of long standing and one of those rare individuals who accomplishes just about everything he has ever set out to do.

Many years ago, he decided he wanted to be a champion speed boat racer, so he became one; later, he decided he wanted to be the world's top big-game hunter and was one of the early winners of the Weatherby Big Game Award, perhaps the most coveted award in trophy hunting circles.

I don't know whether he consciously decided to become wealthy, but he managed that, too, and somewhere along the way became intrigued with becoming a selling outdoor writer. Since that decision, he has sold literally hundreds of articles to the leading outdoor and shooting journals and has authored a best-selling book in the field, "Trophy Hunter In Africa."

Still later, he decided to take up trapshooting and since has become one of the best in the business. In fact, in something like seven years, he managed to go from novice beginner to captain of the All-American trap team. That's an honor that more than 40,000 trapshooters would give their whole gun collections to accomplish and some of them have been trying for decades.

I had known Gates primarily as a big-game hunter and

hadn't given much thought to his shotgunning efforts until I received a note in late 1971 from sports writer Jim Hoben, who reported: "In a fantastic exhibition of shooting skills, Elgin Gates, a big-game hunter from Needles, California, took on the world's greatest trapshooters and mowed them down like sitting ducks." That happened in Vandalia, Ohio, during the 1971 Grand American National Championships.

According to Hoben, "The home grounds of the Grand American National Championships have never seen anything quite like it and may never again. When the smoke cleared away, Gates had smashed 1008 clay targets without a miss.

"In the first major event, the prestigious International Clay Pigeon Championships where Olympic style targets are thrown — much more difficult than standard trap targets — Gates broke 100 straight. He annihilated the top-ranking International shooters of the Navy, Marine Corps and Air Force. He also defeated the crack Army International team from Fort Benning, which won the Gold Medal in the world shooting championships in Phoenix last October. Also defeated by Gates were Olympic shooters from Japan, Canada, Italy, Mexico and other foreign countries."

The next day, according to what now is shooting history, 2242 shooters from every state in the Union lined up on the mile-long firing line for the U.S. championships. When the last shot had been triggered, seven gunners were tied at 200 straight and Elgin Gates was one of those seven.

The shootoffs began at eight o'clock that night under floodlights. In the first extra round of twenty-five targets, three of the seven missed one or more and dropped out. This included all-time champion Dan Orlich of Reno, Nevada.

However, at the end of the 100-bird shootoff, four men

Elgin Gates has developed his own personal technique for mounting his gun to his shoulder, prior to calling for the bird. Here, with action closed and loaded, he's set to start.

Above, with muzzle pointing downward slightly and with finger off the trigger, he beds the butt stock solidly into the socket between chest and shoulder. Below, his cheek is down onto the comb and the muzzle is raised level. "Pull!"

still had shot all of their birds and then the officials of the American Trapshooting Association called a halt at 10 p.m. with the announcement that the contest to determine a champion would be continued the next evening — after another full day of contesting in other events.

The next morning, more than 2700 shooters again toed the line, this time for the Clay Target Championship of America, involving another 200 targets. With ten other shooters, Gates broke them all. He was the only competitor with 200 straight in this and the U.S. championships, which meant that he now was faced with the formidable chore of competing in two shootoffs.

It took another 100 birds that evening for Gates to eliminate his three opponents from the previous day. The last to go down was Bueford Bailey, another all-time champ from Big Springs, Nebraska, who missed his eighty-sixth target.

Gates went on to clean all 100 birds, bringing the crowd to its feet to cheer. He had won the AA Championship of America with 200 straight in the shootoffs.

The man from Needles was advised by officials of the trapshooting association that the rules required an individual shoot only 100 shootoff targets in any one day after a main event. However, Gates volunteered to continue, shooting against the ten reasonably fresh shooters who had tied that same day.

In this shootoff, Gates faced All-American champs such as Frank Little of Endicott, New York, Gene Sears out of Kansas City, Missouri, and Bill Timmonds of Philadelphia. By the time another 100 birds had been thrown under the lights, Gates and Richard Smith, an AA shooter from Dayton, Ohio, were the only ones left. The others had been eliminated.

Again, the shootoffs were halted at the 10 p.m. curfew, but by this time, Gates' score for these two events alone stood at an incredible 700 straight, of which 300 birds had been under pressure and under artificial lighting.

With the kind of shooting that was going on, this became not only a contest of skill, but a contest of stamina as well. It was on his 1009 bird that Gates finally missed. Smith went on to win, with Gates as runnerup, but the winning of two crowns and coming in with a second in this third contest was a new achievement record.

After that came a long list of championships, which I'm certain isn't ended yet. In 1972, he won two national titles for International clay pigeon competition, then went to Australia to take the country's national doubles championship in the same year. In 1973, he became New Zealand's International champion, as well as that country's high gun national champion. In 1974, he won three New Zealand championships, winning the single-barrel title, the high gun crown and the national all-around championship.

He was voted a member of the 1972-73 All-American trapshooting team as well as a member of the All-American International team for the same years. In 1973, he was captain of the All-American International trapshooting team.

Gates set a new world record for doubles in 1973, with a 97.37 average, also winning the Amateur Trapshooting Association's national high average award. So far as I know, he's the only shotgunner to win national titles in three countries, namely the United States, Australia and New Zealand.

Along with his big-game hunting, Gates had the opportunity to do what he terms "a fair amount of bird shooting with what I consider better than average results. Consequently, I never really made any attempt to analyze the finer details of pointing a shotgun. It was enough to know the fundamentals of leading a moving target, a fair eye for

Waiting for his turn to fire, Gates looks relaxed and he is relaxed. Jittery tension wins few if any matches. It should be noted that, in these posed photographs, the action has been closed on an empty chamber. During regular firing, he would not load up until after previous shooter had fired.

Discussed in the accompanying text is the important, but little-known process of "reading" a shotgun barrel by way of learning its individual characteristics. Gates has four barrels for his gun, all but one having been fairly matched.

judging distances and the reflexes to shoulder a gun, swing it smoothly, then pull the trigger at the right instant."

Gates cut his teeth on his father's old 12-gauge Browning squareback semi-automatic, starting to shoot Wyoming sage hens with it when he was about 12. Trapshooting, he grew up to believe, was for people who couldn't hit real birds on the wing. It was a game for kids, women and "old duffers who were over the hill. It was not for men."

Just before World War II, Gates was operating a sporting goods store, guiding duck hunters on the side. Two men with fancy trap guns came out for a weekend hunt. Both were champion trapshooters.

They hunted Friday afternoon and all day Saturday and Sunday, during which time they burned up most of a case of shells. One man bagged six ducks, the other four. Gates limited out easily with a little 20-gauge Model 11 Remington autoloader and gave them his ducks to take home. The episode convinced him that trapshooting must be easy.

In the fall of 1966, a Winchester franchise trap range was opened in Gates' home town and I was invited for the grand opening. The visiting Winchester pro and a couple of men who came with him were the only experienced trapshooters in the crowd.

"When they couldn't break 25 straight of what looked like easy targets, I dashed home to get my old squareback Browning to give the crowd a treat. Fortunately, I didn't voice any of the sarcastic remarks that were in my mind, for after four rounds of 21-17-18-20, a score of 76 X 100, I quietly slunk away when nobody was looking.

"I was hooked, and I don't give up easily. Over the years I had acquired a few more scatterguns, mostly field models. In the weeks that followed I shot at clay targets with all of them. The results were an average of about 80 breaks out of every 100 targets.

"It was maddening to pull up on those insolent clay-birds and shoot, only to see them go sailing blithely on. The madder I got, the harder I tried. The results are unworthy of mention. Finally, I choked down my frustration and began to think. I wasn't doing something right, but what was it?

"I went quail hunting and found that I could still whip the gun up from waist level and knock down speeding birds with satisfying regularity. But with the gun already at my shoulder, knowing the target would appear out of the trap at my call, why was I missing so many claybirds?" Gates wanted to know.

One day he dug out an old Model 25 Winchester, a prize he'd won in a raffle. It had a field stock and a twenty-six-inch, full-choke plain barrel. At the range, weary of the previous routine he had gone through of trying different stances, high elbows, low elbows, holding the gun tight, holding it loose, he brought the Model 25 up without giving any thought to technique and started calling for targets.

"I broke 93 X 100 and danced a little jig. To hell with all the fancy tricks and footwork, the name of this game is to do what comes naturally. There is truth in this, to be sure, but I still had a long way to go. The simple facts were that, while effective in the field, none of my guns were

Here, Gates is demonstrating how a shooter might squash his cheek down onto the comb of the stock if the comb were too high to allow obtaining a proper sight picture. It would create strain and would increase the punishment from recoil.

properly fitted for trapshooting. By accident, the Model 25 was fairly close."

Two weeks later, Elgin Gates went to his first registered trapshoot, sanctioned by the Amateur Trapshooting Association.

Gates broke 99 X 100 in the first 16-yard event to tie with two other shooters. They cleaned his plough in the shootoff but that didn't faze him. He had learned he could hit those damned claybirds!

"Right then I made my first big mistake. If I could break 99 X 100 with this old plain-barreled duck gun, I reasoned, all I had to do now was buy a real trap gun with a ventilated rib and tear 'em up. Fifteen minutes later I peeled off $200 for a Model 12 Winchester trap gun, a fine gun which I still have, and which is still worth $200. But when the next 100 targets had been fired at, my score was 74 X 100."

Disgusted, Gates put this particular gun away without firing it again. "When I pick it up now and look down the barrel I can see three inches of rib between the beads. For me, it shoots four feet high. I could cut the comb down about a quarter-inch, reshape it a little and shoot a perfect

or near-perfect score. But I didn't know the score then and the 'experts' had me thoroughly confused. I remember mentioning that I couldn't line up the sights of the Model 12, but a nearby trap oracle waved my remark off. He said, in a tone that implied everybody ought to know, 'You don't aim at claybirds with the sights, you shoot 'em off the end of the barrel.' I couldn't even hit 'em shooting out of the barrel."

Gates went on, making and compounding every conceivable mistake that can be made, but wouldn't give up. For 1967, his 16-yard average for 2600 registered targets was 86.25. During 1968 it was 89.54 on 3550 targets.

"I tried and discarded a thousand ideas and gimmicks. Trial and error were my forte. I listened to advice, good and bad; I watched the real champions, just like everybody else, trying to ferret out their secrets; and I kept trying. Finally I began to see the light. There aren't any special shells or secret formulas or magic tricks. Most of the ingredients of successful trapshooting are, in truth, simple fundamentals. In short, it was a matter of learning the fundamentals and putting them all together."

In the middle of 1969, Gates began to put it together,

In contrast to the "how-not-to" photo on the previous page, Gates demonstrates the relaxed but ready fit of cheek to comb on a stock that is proportioned correctly. Note that the rollover comb of custom stock tends to distribute contact over a wider area, thereby reducing flinch-causing effect of the recoil.

ending up with a 97.20 average in the Pacific International Trapshooting Association, which put him on the All Star Team for high averages on singles, handicap and doubles. During 1970, due to the press of other affairs, he only had opportunity to shoot at 400 PITA registered targets, but broke 398 of them for a 99.50 average.

So how do you put it all together? How do you go from an 86.25 average to a 99.50 average?

"During the course of learning everything the hard way, I developed a check list of the more important fundamentals and variables. Some are surely well known. Others may not be," Gates says.

Foremost in importance is to have the gun, whatever its make, precisely fitted to the individual. Fitting is almost entirely a matter of stock dimensions, especially the height and shape of the comb. Also important, but to a lesser degree, is the length of the stock and the type of grip. Unless the gun is properly fitted to start with, nearly everything else is going to be a lost cause.

Gun manufacturers mass-produce stocks to fit Mr. Average Man and there aren't too many people who can take a trap gun off of the rack and have a perfect fit. There is wide diversity in the shape of human faces, fat and thin, high or low cheekbones, short or long necks, height and thickness of shoulders, so that a gun out of the box is no more likely to be perfect than a pair of shoes picked off of the shelf at random.

At any trapshoot you can see shooter after shooter contorted into unnatural positions, trying to compensate for guns that don't fit their particular dimensions. This, in turn,

creates a host of other problems, none conducive to good shooting.

One simple test will let you know if any particular shotgun fits properly, so try this test several times with any gun to make sure you are doing it correctly.

Stand in a natural shooting position, holding the gun in both hands at waist level. Then close both eyes and bring the gun up into shooting position solidly against your face (without bringing your cheek down on the stock). Then slide the gun back against your shoulder in what feels like a natural and comfortable position with no undue strain or forcing. Then open your eyes.

If you are looking directly along the barrel at the two beads mounted on the ventilated rib, and they are lined up together and stacked in a figure-eight with the front bead on top of the rear bead, the gun is virtually a perfect fit. What you see is called the sight picture. Almost all factory trap guns have higher stocks or combs than field or skeet guns, so if the front bead is considerably higher than the rear bead in your sight picture, and you can see part of the rib between the beads, you will shoot high, or over the target.

"This is one of the most common faults in trapshooting; and the exact problem I had with the Model 12," Gates recalls. "To compensate for this, most people try to grind the face down hard on the stock or even cant the head sideways trying to get their eye low enough to stack the beads."

This, in turn, opens a Pandora's box of troubles. Recoil

Here is the view from the opposite side for the correct positioning of the head in relation to the stock, as on the facing page. Text discusses procedures for starting with the eyes in proper focus.

begins to bruise their face, which brings on flinching, ad infinitum. The correct remedy is to have the comb cut down to the correct height.

On the other hand, if the beads are buried or blotted out by the receiver when one opens his eyes, then he will shoot low or under the target and the comb must be built up.

"There are several ways to accomplish this," Gates has found. "As a temporary measure, I use layers of moleskin, a thin, soft, adhesive-backed material found at any drugstore, (it is normally used as foot plasters), adding one or more layers until the proper sight picture is achieved."

Many shooters stop right there and, at any shoot, one will see a lot of stocks built up with moleskin. Since trap guns usually are stocked with premium grade wood, it is a shame to hide a beautifully grained stock under moleskin.

Gates feels the same and employs a simple method of building up a stock by forming a plastic clay mould and pouring clear epoxy resin into it. After curing, it can be finished to the exact shape and height desired, yet it is nearly impossible to detect. The original grain of the wood remains clearly visible.

If you open your eyes and find that the front bead is considerably to the left or the right of the rear bead, then the stock needs cast-off or cast-on; meaning it has to be bent to the right or left by a special process or by removing or adding material to the side of the comb so as to bring your face back into alignment with both beads. Again, the clear epoxy resin works fine for this without spoiling the beauty of a fine piece of wood.

Another thing is that most factory trap guns come with a comb that is too sharp on top for many trapshooters. A man whose face is being punished by recoil because of a comb that is too sharp or too high will never enjoy trap-shooting, nor is he likely to join the winner's circle.

Gates favors the roll-over type comb which presents a wider area of contact against the face and provides more support, in addition to dampening recoil. One final effect of a properly fitted stock is to virtually eliminate recoil as a problem; and recoil is a big factor to many shooters.

If you think you have recoil whipped and aren't flinching, try this: On the practice field, have a friend at your side load — or not load — your gun while you are looking away, then hand it to you. Even knowing in advance that the gun may not be loaded, you will be amazed how you will flinch when you call for a target, pull the trigger and there is no shell in the chamber.

There are several devices on the market designed to reduce recoil which are installed in the butt end of the stock. In simple terms, they are spring-loaded lead slugs

Here is Gates' left hand, positioned on the forend, as seen from the left side, comfortably relaxed, but in full control.

Above and below are two different views of the custom stock on Gates' trap gun. The padded butt stock can be adjusted up or down and fastened at the desired setting.

Above, you can see the angular placement of feet in relation to the trap house, as preferred by Gates when firing Station 1. Below, he's ready to call for the bird from Station 2. The text discusses his thoughts on taking a relatively "high gun" stance.

enclosed in a casing. The principle involved is that, when the gun starts to move back in recoil, the heavy lead slug does not attain inertia as rapidly and acts as a shock absorber as the spring compresses against it. There are several opinions regarding their effectiveness. Some claim the added weight of the lead itself tends to reduce recoil. Gates says he uses this type in most of his trap guns for three reasons: (1) He can swing smoother with a heavier gun, (2) he prefers the balance point to be a little farther back than most factory guns come with and, (3) the effectiveness of the reducer, if only of minimal effect, say even five percent, is worth the installation.

A final point on recoil is the selection of shells. Light, 2¾-dram loads are easier on the shoulder than the more powerful 3-dram loads, especially when two hundred or more 16-yard targets are shot in one day. No. 8 shot is preferred by virtually all shooters.

The subject of where and how high to point the gun in relation to the trap house, and from each shooting station, is widely debated. One school, for example, contends that when shooting from station one, the gun should be held on or above the left corner of the traphouse, giving the shooter a "jump" on a hard left angle.

On station five, the procedure is reversed, holding the gun to the right corner of the house for a hard right angle. On stations two and four the distance is split between the center of the traphouse and the corner; and on three, the center station, the gun is held in the center.

"I've worked hard at this," Gates says, "but the advantages of getting the jump on a hard angle target are nullified when a straightaway bird comes out on station one or five and the gun then has to be swung back toward the center. My tendency is to cross over, causing me to miss what should be an easy quarter-angle target. I've settled on hold-

Here, Gates is prepared to call for his bird from Station 1. Accompanying text weighs the pros and cons of aiming toward the center of the trap house or slightly to one side and Gates gives the reasons he heeds.

ing the gun above the center of the traphouse for every shot, and swing a little faster on the hard angle birds.

"For height, I shoot what is called a high gun, meaning I hold about three feet above the house so that, from the side, it appears that my gun is more or less parallel with the ground. This is one of many things I learned from watching the top champions. Virtually all of them shoot high guns. The main reason for a high gun is that less barrel movement is required to get on the target. By aiming down at the roof of the traphouse, as some prefer, the gun must be moved up a greater distance to get on the rising target. In simple terms, the farther the barrel moves, the greater the chance of error."

The opponents of a high gun claim they can't catch the target as quickly as they can with their gun and eyes down on top of the traphouse, but there is one little-known, yet important advantage the high gun shooter has. His eyes are not looking out into space where the barrel is pointed. If they were, he would not see the target until it is well up on its flight path. What he actually does, after raising the gun and verifying that the beads are lined up and stacked properly, is to refocus his eyes out and sort of down and around the barrel to get a sharp image at the roof of the traphouse. He can instantly catch the target coming out, identify its flight path, make a minimum move with his gun and fire. This is sometimes called "punching the shot." If you see a shooter making a wide swing, chasing the bird, you can bet that some of them are going to get away from him.

This matter of focusing the eyes out where the target is

The pre-call position, as corrected for firing from Station 4. The sights are on a level about 3-4 feet above the top of the trap house and just a bit to the right of its center and eyes are alert for the first flicker of moving clay.

going to appear is an important fundamental. The human eye is similar to the iris of a camera. When it is set for close range, objects in the distance are blurred or out of focus. When a shooter brings his gun up and checks the beads, his eyes are focused on the beads. When he calls for the bird, it is a blur or, by the time his eyes have refocused on the speeding target, it is getting out of effective range.

Here is a simple test that will illustrate the point: Hold up a small object about eighteen inches in front of your eyes and focus on it. Hold this focus and you will note that distant objects at, say, fifty feet — the distance to a traphouse — will be blurred. Now, suddenly let your eyes refocus on the distant object. There will be a distinct time interval of about one or two seconds before your eyes are sharply focused on the distant object.

On the matter of guns, Gates has shot perfect 16-yard scores with each of the five makes of trap guns he owns. The one thing they all have in common is a proper fit. For a time, he felt that a different gun was needed for each type of trapshooting, 16 yards, handicap and doubles. Many top shooters use three guns; some use two guns, and I know several of the best that use one gun, a superposed or over-and-under double for all shooting. Gates leans toward the one gun concept, saying, "I believe there is some advantage in getting so thoroughly familiar with a gun that it becomes a part of you; because no two or three different guns, no

matter how carefully the dimensions are matched, ever feel or shoot exactly the same."

While it is a perfectly valid truism that any gun will shoot better than the man using it, there is one factor virtually unknown to the average trapshooter that gave Elgin Gates a great deal of trouble before he solved it; the matter of what we call barrel reading.

"For several months I had been shooting an autoloading model of a well-known make. I like the gun — and still do," Gates reports. "It was properly fitted; I had the feel of it and was shooting some excellent scores. Then the barrel developed a crack near the receiver end, so I ordered a new barrel in the same length and choke. I put it on and suddenly I was missing targets right and left. It had to be me, I thought, as the new barrel was identical to the old one. I went through a terrible period, trying other guns, new techniques; and went from bad to worse.

"Finally, an old gunsmith showed me how to read a barrel. Shotgun barrels are made from thin tubing and, by the time they go through the many operations of manufacture, including the installation of the rib, probably not one in fifty is really true.

"To read a barrel, first, be sure it is clean. Then hold it up so that the receiver or chamber end is about four inches from your eye and point it toward the sky or preferably a light wall; the distance is not important. You will see a

Although these four photos resemble each other closely, they show the sequence of the placement and angle of Gates' feet through the first four firing stations, 1 and 2 above, 3 and 4 below. Weight is divided evenly and knees are straight.

series of concentric rings in the barrel. The first one is the receiver end of the barrel, the second is at the end of the chamber. The next ring will appear to be about halfway down the barrel. Each of these will be progressively smaller in size. In some barrels you may see two or three additional rings. The last or smallest ring will be the muzzle. Now, for the moment, ignore the smallest or muzzle ring and concentrate on moving the barrel so as to center all the other rings inside of each other in the form of a rifle target.

"One can read a barrel quickly by holding it in his hands, with some practice, but for the first few times you may want to do this with the barrel on a table or clamped in a vice. When you have moved the barrel slightly — or your eye — so that the first three or four larger rings are exactly centered inside of each other, then hold this picture and let your eye pick up the smallest or muzzle ring. If it, too, is exactly in the center of the other rings, you are looking down a barrel that is quite true or straight. You

may have to practice this a few times to get the hang of it. If the smallest ring is to the left or the right, high or low in relation to the other rings, your barrel is not true.

"The muzzle ring of my first barrel that was cracked, the one that was shooting well for me, is about a sixteenth-of-an-inch high. The muzzle ring in the replacement barrel was about an eighth-of-an-inch low and a sixteenth to the left. The difference in the impact point of the pattern resulted first in a few lost targets. Then, as I attempted to correct this, things really went to hell.

"After becoming aware of this difference in barrels, I had the first barrel carefully brazed. Having been so badly fouled up in the interval, it took a while to get back in the groove with it. I checked all my other barrels and guns, finding only one really straight barrel.

"One good friend of mine had an expensive gun with which he gradually worked up to AA class shooting, winning several championships. I looked through his barrel one

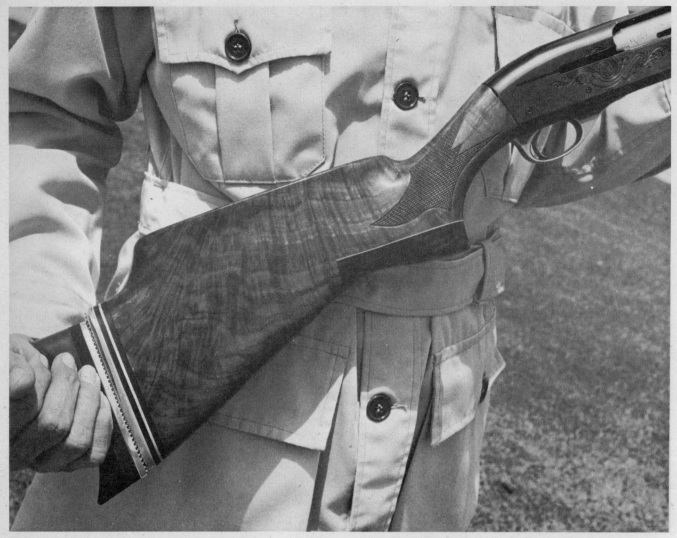

Gates recalls that, although a skilled wing shot on waterfowl and upland birds, his early experiences at shooting trap were anything but encouraging as he tried first one, than another of his several shotguns with sharply limited success. Part of the answer lay in obtaining a properly fitted stock, as shown here. Note the recoil-cutting pitch of the rollover comb.

day, noting that the muzzle ring was low, about the equivalent of a foot at impact distance. Since he was shooting so well, I didn't mention it. Shortly thereafter, returning by air from a distant shoot, the rib of his gun was damaged during baggage handling and he sent the barrel in for repair.

"When I saw him several weeks later, he was on the verge of despair, having shot some horrible scores, going from bad to worse, as I had done. Suspecting the truth after he told me about the repair, I broke the gun open and sure enough, the muzzle ring was almost a quarter-inch high. His original impact point had been changed three or four feet! The heat of silver soldering the rib blocks back had warped the barrel up. He had it straightened to the original impact point and shortly was shooting AA scores again."

The whole point here is that while a man may be shooting up a storm with a gun that has — in his case — a barrel that was shooting about a foot low, let him pick up an identical model with the same dimensions, but with a different — and unknown to him — impact point and he can't hit his hat.

A few professional gunsmiths can realign or straighten barrels. Gates ended up with four barrels for his autoloader, all of which had different impact points. He had them realigned to match the first barrel with the sixteenth-inch-high muzzle ring. Three of them shoot virtually the same. The fourth barrel crawls back out of line during the heat of shooting.

When Gates wants to see exactly where the impact point of a barrel is in relation to the sight picture, he goes to the range with a box of tracer shells. Usually, within five to ten shots at clay targets, he can learn what he wants to know.

Of next importance is a positive mental attitude. Gates admits he used to feel that all sorts of things would affect his shooting: bad weather conditions like wind, rain, heat, cold; the position of the sun in the sky; a different background to shoot against; a bad puller; a trap that was throwing higher or lower birds than another trap; people talking behind the line; or the man next to him whose gun kept misfiring.

"In short, I was harboring all kinds of negative assumptions. When I walked out to the firing line with this kind of thinking, it was inevitable that my shooting would be affected," he says.

"On the other hand, I quickly saw that the real champions, shooting in the same wind, rain, against the same background and under the same conditions, still came in with good scores. They were able to blot out these distractions with simple mental discipline. In other words, they

Above left, a view of the correct position of head, hands and gun. Above right, Protective shooting glasses are important and can be prescription-ground if the eyes require it. Right, engraving on the custom aluminum trigger guard. Below, an illustration of an extreme case of straining and crawling the stock.

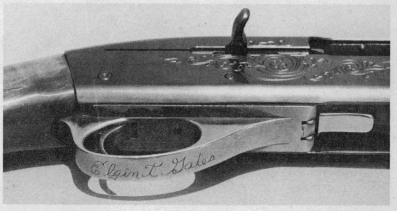

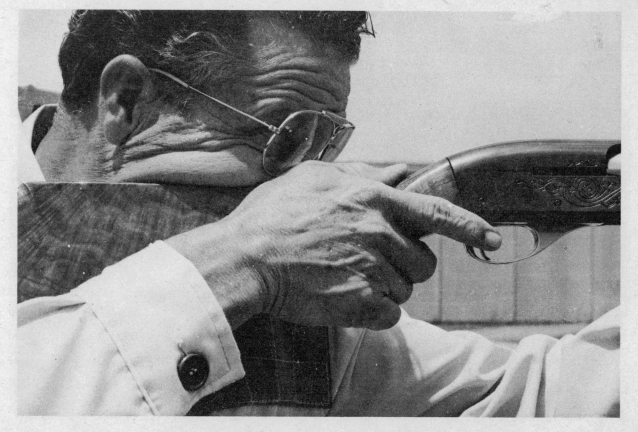

Photos above and below offer a contrast between the pre-call stance for Stations 3 and 5. In the latter, note that toes are almost perfectly in line with the edge of the concrete and muzzle remains fairly well toward the center of the house, so as not to be handicapped by sharp-breaking bird.

had a positive attitude. Now when I go to the firing line during adverse weather conditions, for example, I have the idea that I'm already several targets up on a lot of shooters who are worrying about the wind, the rain or whatever."

Along with a positive mental attitude comes the matter of concentration. The man who is thinking about the one hundred targets he is about to shoot at, or if he forgot to lock the garage at home, or the waitress who gave him poor service, certainly can't give the proper attention to each shot. Targets are shot one at a time.

"All of my mental energy is totally concentrated on breaking the next target, as if it is the winning one and it can very well be," Gates explains. "It is a matter of self-control and, with this kind of concentration, all the other worrisome distractions are blocked out automatically.

"I once shot on a squad with a young fellow from Colorado. Everything went wrong with the other four of us; misfires, delays from gun malfunctions, broken targets coming out of the trap and God knows what else. Our shooting went from bad to worse, trap by trap. Unperturbed, oblivious to our misses and distractions, this young man annihilated all one hundred targets, smoothly and precisely. That's concentration!"

Next is consistency. Gates makes every effort to assume

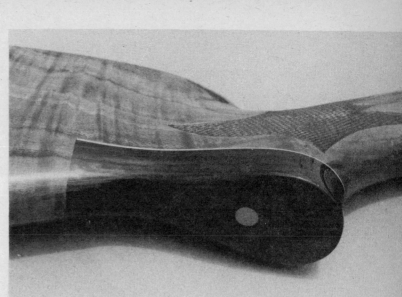

Above, a close look at the inlaid section of the pistol grip, with whiteline spacer. Below, here is the positioning of Gates' left hand and fingers on forend, as seen from right.

Gates, whose rise through the ranks of trapshooting was somewhat meteoric, once he hit his stride and learned what he'd been doing wrong, notes that one ingredient is essential and that is the keen, unshakable determination to win despite obstacles.

the exact same stance for every shot; to raise and hold the gun exactly the same; to instinctively verify that the beads are lined up; to keep both eyes open and to take the same two second's delay to let his eyes refocus out to the trap-house before calling for the target. It is important to maintain the same sight picture and the same firm pressure of cheek against the stock until one sees the target break over the end of the barrel. This means "staying in the gun"; not lifting the head off of the stock at the moment of pulling the trigger, which is a common way of losing targets. All of this goes hand in hand with a positive mental attitude and total concentration.

There are other variables which will affect one man or another, but the idea is to develop and perfect your own style and stick with it.

Finally, there is one thing left: desire. A man may do everything mechanically right, shoot some good scores and enjoy the sport, but he never will be a champion without a deep-rooted competitive desire to win. In short, winning adds up to a positive mental attitude, a well-fitted gun, together with concentration, desire and deliberate, relaxed confidence. This combination, Gates contends, can make a champion trapshooter out of anyone.

Salting away two national trophies in a single year, missing a third by the thinnest of margins and copping honors in other countries as well is not a project for the faint of heart. The shootoffs can be particularly trying but the primary goal is to concentrate on breaking the next bird and keep all other unhelpful distractions from preventing doing that.

THE psyche OF SHOOTING

Mental Attitude And Individual Tricks Of The Trade Have Much To Do With Success!

IT HAS BEEN observed that genius is an infinite capacity for taking care of small details and, deny or accept that definition as you will, it requires more than a touch of genius to become the world champion of International trapshooting...one of the most challenging of all the many forms of firearms competition.

Leon Rossini, who has held that coveted title, also emerged as top civilian gun at the U.S. trapshooting championships in Vandalia, Ohio, in 1969, by way of clinching his shotgunning credentials. Rossini supplied candid answers to a number of questions on the topic of how one goes about climbing to the top of the clay-smashing enthusiasts. Many of his thoughts reflected the psychological conditioning involved.

One secret — which won't be of much help to anyone else — is that you start off with a useful advantage if you can select your personal heredity carefully. Leon's father, Enrico Rossini, was born in 1899 and built his first shotgun at somewhere around the age of 10. It was a muzzleloader, the barrel fashioned from a length of water-pipe and, certainly, a far cry from the handsome 12-gauge Beretta over/under favored by his son. However, Enrico and his brother Eugenio — five years younger — grew up hopelessly, happily smitten by the shotgunning virus and, when an immigrant to America returned to the Rossini hometown of Ancona with glowing tales of the sport of shotgunning at clay pigeons, the Rossini brothers caught his enthusiasm and organized the first clay target contest ever held in Italy. In the years since, both have held Italian championships and Uncle Eugenio fired with the Italian team sent to Berlin in 1939.

But, even if your heredity is no longer yours to select, there are a great many avenues for improving your chances against the rest of the field. Many of these could be summarized by the valid old maxim: "Don't work harder; work smarter!"

Even if International trap is not your game, the basic attitude, the philosophical outlook of Signor Leon Rossini should not prove too hard to adapt to your own needs toward a useful improvement of the odds in your favor.

"I am a keen observer," Rossini confides. "I try to notice every little factor that can have any kind of bearing on breaking the targets. For example, Ancona is located well up the east coast of Italy, high on the calf of the Italian boot, and we shoot toward the sea at our home range. This means that the birds are silhouetted clearly against the sky; easily seen. When I shoot at other ranges,

the backgrounds may be a forest or a mountain slope: quite different as to visibility from the home grounds. So I select a different pair of shooting glasses; a pair of a color and density that is best for the conditions of visibility for that place and those light conditions.

"If you're a photographer, you may have found that the lens of your camera gives you the sharpest image at some one particular lens opening or f-stop. The human eye is not too different from the camera lens in this respect, since the size of the pupil varies in proportion to the intensity of the light which reaches it. If you wear shooting glasses with dark lenses on a day that is gray and overcast, the pupils of your eyes will adapt to the dim light by opening up to a larger diameter — quite possibly at the expense of some sacrifice in sharpness of the image.

"And that brings up the important point: You can't afford any sacrifice of any kind. In International trap, as in most other shooting games, the margin between the winner and the runners-up is thin. Missing one bird that you could have broken can make all the difference. It is simply that you cannot afford to neglect any advantage that can be put to work for you in an ethical manner; not even a little one."

While some might prefer to arrive late and come puffing up the firing line at the last instant, Rossini holds the firm belief that it is necessary to get there early, so as to observe with all possible concentration.

"In Italy, our claybirds are not always like your birds over here. There can be much difference in the hardness and toughness of the Italian clay pigeon. When I get to a match, I always make it a point to inspect the targets. If I can crush a clay pigeon with one hand, it is an easy target to break and I can plan on using the smaller, finer size of shot, with more pellets in each load. But, if I can hold the target a few inches above a table and drop it without breaking, then I know that I will have to use bigger, heavier shot so that I can be sure of breaking it, instead of bouncing the shot off harmlessly.

"Even the weather can have a bearing, quite apart from light conditions. If the air is dry or if it is damp and humid, this can be a factor in the kind of shells that I shoot. In Italy, it is not like the United States, where a few big companies make all the shells for the whole country. Over here, each town has a gunsmith, maybe two or three or more, depending on the size, and these gunsmiths load up the shells for their area.

"If I get a chance to watch other shooters firing before it

Chapter 13

Perennial Olympic contender Leon Rossini passes on some of the techniques of a psychological nature, which he has found useful in consistent wins.

Rossini, shooting a Beretta over-and-under built to his own specifications, leans into gun as he calls for bird.

As he calls for bird, the Italian shooter focuses eyes about ten meters beyond the trench, so that the bird will be sharp when first seen. He admits it requires practice.

comes my turn to shoot, I observe what kind of shells each is using and how they are breaking their birds and, from this, I can get an idea what kind of shells I should use."

Rossini's Beretta has two triggers: "Because I learned to shoot with two triggers and it comes natural to move my finger back for the second shot." The front trigger fires the lower barrel and the rear trigger, the upper one. The rules of International trap permit the firing of a second shot at any given bird without any resulting penalty being deducted from the score of the shooter as a result. Usually, Rossini loads the upper barrel with a slightly larger size of shot, so as to retain more velocity and energy at the longer distance covered by the second shot, should it be needed.

"On the average, I will fire perhaps twelve extra shells in the course of twenty-five targets, perhaps thirty-seven to forty shots for a round. Often, if there are large pieces left after the first shot, I will try to break these up with a second shot."

His number one Beretta is engraved with floral motif in the best Italian high-art traditions and he has been using this gun for most of his shooting over the course of the past ten years or more. When firing at a match, he takes along a second gun, another Beretta tailored as closely as possible to match the fit, weight and balance of the first one. The second gun serves for peace of mind, as a sort of security blanket.

"It's seldom I've ever had to fall back on the second gun — but if I didn't have it along —?" He rolls his eyes upward with an expressive look of consternation in the face of utter disaster. The reserve gun does not enjoy the devotion lavished on his favorite: "Once in a while, some friend will borrow my second gun and shoot well with it and want to buy it. So I sell it to him and make up another one for myself."

As a matter of candid truth, even Old Faithful is not coddled and cherished in quite the manner that you might expect. On the right side of the stock, there is a patch of plastic electrician's tape, bulging in the center with a strip of cardboard that measures roughly five inches long, an inch wide and one-eighth-inch thick. This constitutes Rossini's adjustable stock and is not patented. If he feels the need for a bit more height in the comb, he peels the tape off the side, holds the cardboard in position and smooths the edges of the tape down to hold it in place as a sort of removable Monte Carlo comb.

The lower end of the butt plate has been loosened and a few plies of common cardboard have been wedged into place between the plate and the wood of the stock, with absolutely no slightest concession toward appearance. Rossini claims that this aids in controlling the jump of the muzzle after firing the first shot, enabling him to realign the sights more quickly, by a fraction of a second, should he decide that another shot is necessary. Quite possibly, it works — you can't sneer at success — although it gives the glamorous Beretta the somewhat disreputable appearance of a flawed classic.

In this era of permissive parenthood, we are told that if a child wants to grow up left-handed, any attempt to switch him over to a right-hander is certain to produce dire and traumatic effects on his future development. Leon, in early childhood, was a dedicated southpaw. But Papa Enrico, in a happy world that had not yet heard of Dr. Spock and his singular theories on assorted subjects, gently re-programmed his son to favor his right hand by means of such stratagems as bending the handle of his spoon ninety degrees to one side so that it was impossible to eat with it, unless held in the right hand.

Rossini feels that this, too, has worked to his advantage in the long run. The neural coordination of his left hand

and arm are perhaps a bit better than they might have been had he been born naturally right-handed and this aids the left hand in responding more promptly to data transmitted from the eye and brain, so as to steer the sights onto the target and start tracking in readiness for the shot more quickly and accurately.

One of those fortunate people who retain 20/20 vision into their early forties, Rossini tests his visual acuity by focusing both eyes on a distant point, then semaphores the palm of his hand across first one, then the other, to compare the images transmitted by each. In the matter of hobbies, he is an ardent amateur photographer, but he learned, long ago, to avoid any use of his motion picture camera for a few days to a week before engaging in an important shoot. Holding one eye squinted shut while peering through the view finder of the camera with the other, he finds, is certain to get his eyes out of synchronization with each other. This results in a few claybirds that fly away unscathed, carrying his hopes of victory with them for that particular match. In the same vein, his pre-match training routine includes giving up television watching for about the same length of time and for exactly the same reason.

Although the pet Beretta has consumed upward of 30,000 rounds of 12-gauge ammunition during the decade of the partnership — with no more than rare and minor repairs — Rossini fields the question of practicing by noting that he doesn't practice; he trains.

"One thing about being a trapshooter instead of some other sort of athlete, such as a football player, is that you don't have a trainer to keep you in trim and act as your conscience: You have to do this for yourself. When a match is coming up, the first thing I do is to get a lot of good, relaxed sleep. It tones up the nerves, sharpens the eyes and does more than anything else to get you to your peak of performance. And, of course, I go easy on the vino and pasta; eat small helpings of food that is easy on the digestion, easy on the heart. A man cannot give his best to the contest if he is at war with his own stomach.

"Then, as the match approaches, I shoot a few rounds and these I shoot under the worst possible conditions: when the light is bad, when I am still digesting a meal, early in the morning when I'm no more than partly awake, with white-painted birds in the daytime, when the wind is bad — all of these things with the object of doing my practice under conditions that will be tougher to cope with than the actual match, itself."

The foregoing concept — preparing for the worst and hoping for the best — really paid off at Vandalia. In Italy, if a distraction so petty as a vagrant butterfly flutters into the field of the shooters' vision, shooting is suspended until it goes away. At Vandalia, shooting continued without interruption as jet aircraft took off and landed on nearby air strips: definitely not a place to have brought the pampered nerves of a fair-weather shooter!

One well-meant piece of advice often tendered the tyro trapshooter is to blot out the bird with the muzzle of the gun by way of compensating for the drop of the shot in its trajectory. Rossini disagrees with this theory and demonstrates his idea of the proper sight picture by asking the would-be shooter to place the gun to shoulder and sight down the rib as one would sight down a rifle, with only the front bead showing. At this point, Rossini takes a pair of twenty-five-cent coins, one atop the other, and balances them flatwise across the rear of the rib.

"Now," he says, "move your eye up until you can just see all of the front bead above the quarters; then hold still." He lifts the coins out of the way deftly and says, "There,

Rossini carries a special pad taped to the stock of his gun. It can be removed and placed on the comb where it will do the most good in helping him to adjust his aim.

The stock of shotgun can be changed in measurement by the steps taken. He found that changes in his weight will do much to make difference in how he holds shotgun.

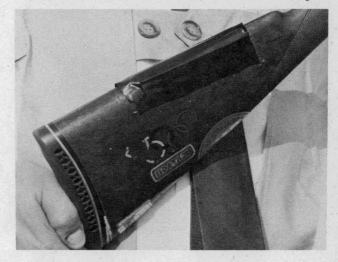

Note that Rossini also has changed angle of the recoil pad by inserting material at the toe of stock. This is another field expedient to help in assurance of a perfect fit.

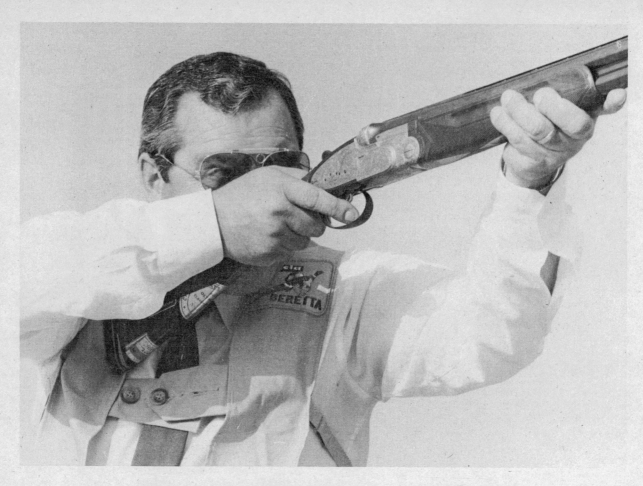

When young, Leon Rossini was left-handed, but was forced to make the switch. Although he shoots right-handed, as trained, he feels that he would shoot better if he had been allowed use of left.

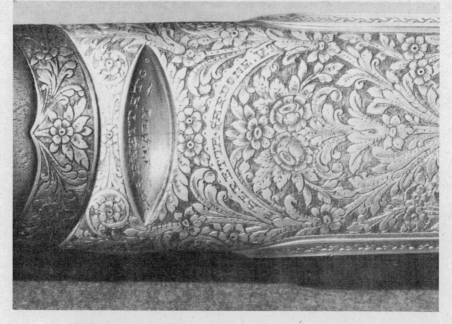

While Rossini takes a matched pair of Berettas to all competitions, he does not feel that heavy engraving or the factor of overall cost are a psychological aid.

Outer third of the rib on both of Rossini's shotguns have been coated with white nail polish, leaving a black, narrow stripe. This gives him different sighting planes for varying backgrounds.

now. That's how it should look when you're ready to shoot."

As a further expedient disfiguration of the long-suffering Beretta, Rossini has painted the two outer thirds of the barrel rib with white nail polish. This leaves a stripe of black down the center, approximately one-eighth-inch in width, the same as the two white tracks on either side of it.

"The reason is simple," he explains. "No matter what the light conditions, no matter what kind of background I'm shooting against, I can either see the black or the white. Usually I can see both, but always I see something!"

Getting back to the all-important matter of vision, Rossini was asked if he closed the left eye or kept both eyes open. He pondered the matter for a moment.

"I start out with both eyes open, while I'm finding the bird and determining its angle and direction and getting my sight picture just the way I want it. Then, just before I squeeze the trigger, I close my left eye nearly all the way.

"But the important thing is where I focus my eyes just before I call for the bird. It is a natural tendency to focus your eyes on the trench, where the bird is coming from. The trouble is, by the time you see the bird and start tracking it with your eyes, it is a good many meters farther away. Now, the eye is like a camera: It has to be precisely focused at a given distance to give you a sharp picture. It takes just a little time to focus the lenses of your eyes to measure the distance and lock onto that flying clay disc. So what I do is to focus on some point about ten meters — call it ten yards — out ahead of the trap. That way, when I first see the bird, I see it clear and sharp. It's just as though you were prefocusing a camera if you wanted to take a picture of it."

On stock fit: "I can't hardly remember the first time I fired a shotgun; when I was 5, maybe younger. It was a 20 gauge and my father would put his hand behind my shoulder to help support me so the recoil wouldn't knock me down. He'd put a clay pigeon out in front of me on the ground, so that I was always shooting at something, not just pulling the trigger to hear the gun go off. And, if I missed, he'd watch to see where it went. He'd keep changing the stock dimensions until I could hit the mark. That is one of the nice things about picking a gunsmith for your father.

"Over the years, I've had to change the cast off of my stocks to match the changes in my weight. When I was in the military, right after the war, I was quite lean in the face

Rossini puts two quarters on barrel and tells Dean Grennell to look over them to pick up gun's sight bead.

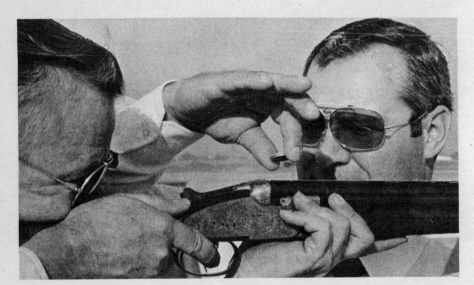

Lifting the coins off the gun, the Italian shooter explains that picture Grennell now sees is how it should be.

and in the body, and I found it best to use a stock that was almost perfectly straight in line with the barrel. In later years, I put on some weight in the chest and my face filled out. I had to move the stock a little to the right, so as to take the force of the recoil with my shoulder instead of with my cheek. The stock still is parallel to the barrel, not at an angle, but there is little offset or dogleg in the area of the pistol grip."

As for the need of regular, intensive practice, Rossini disagrees with Paderewski, the celebrated Polish pianist, who maintained, "If I miss practice for one day, I can tell it, if I miss for two, my wife can tell it and if I go three days without practice, anyone can tell it!"

Rossini does not shoot every day or even, necessarily, every week. Now and then, he fires a round or two in competition with friends and, in such instances, it always is fired with a prize of some sort at stake: a round of cola beverage, the tab for a meal or some similar incentive. The basic bedrock of the Rossini viewpoint is that every single claybird, from the moment it is airborne, must be regarded as vitally important; every concentrated effort must be expended to get it broken and shattered into as many small pieces as possible. It must never be permitted that the mind and the emotions become lax and unconcerned whether this bird or the next bird be broken or missed. For such an outlook would dull the scalpel-sharp competitive edge which has been honed and stropped to the highest attainable pitch of perfection.

In the final essence, the philosophy that carried Leon Rossini to the pinnacle of his chosen field is that you cannot afford to neglect or overlook anything which could have a possible effect upon the final score. Putting it a bit more oddly, success consists of never making the same mistake once. Being a winner means shooting with the feet, the body, the hands, the eyes, the gun, the shells and — far more important than any of these — with the brain, every available cell of it.

Mike Tipa, director of the International and shotgun competitions section of the National Rifle Association, recently sent me a book that would be of value to anyone considering entering such competition. This is the International Moving Target Manual of the United States Army Marksmanship Training Unit. It was written by — and for — shotgunners and the part I find of particular interest is the chapter dealing with mental discipline.

It may seem basic, but the book points out: "Mental

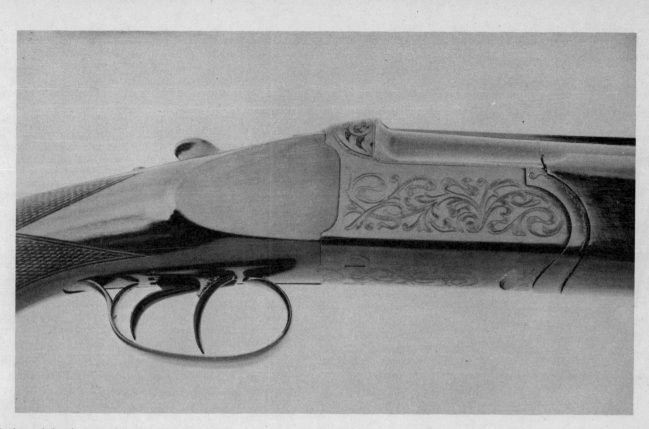

Early training has much to do with how well one shoots. Those trained in using double triggers come to depend upon them.

discipline provides the control you must have of your mental faculties to maintain confidence, positive thinking and sustain the ability to duplicate a successful performance. Mental discipline will help you to avoid over-confidence, pessimism and withstand conditions that may disrupt your mental tranquility."

In this age of continuing pressures, that sounds like something we could use in our everyday living. We verge on a fear of the unknown, I suppose, and this brings to mind some of my own early experiences. In thinking back, I find that the one toughest ordeal of my competitive shooting days involved the national telegraphic meets in which we were shooting against the best in the country. The greatest problem was in not knowing how anyone else was doing, while we were watching our own scores, wondering whether they were good enough to win.

"The continuously repeated, successful execution of a completely planned shot results in the gradual development of mental discipline," the Army shooters contend. "If your mental discipline is functioning correctly, you will be able to control your thoughts and concentration. Your preparations and shooting routine will always be the same.

"Psychologists have discovered that one of the chief reasons for difficulty in the solution of problems is inability to analyze soundly. Pose a clear-cut plan of action in full array. Face the specific difficulty and make a determined effort to break it down. If it can be identified, there is a solution. There are shooters on your team or some other team that are operating without this specific problem putting a brake on their performance. Talk it out. A communal pondering session will break it wide open."

In pondering that particular paragraph, I recall an incident during my Navy days of World War II that would seem to run a parallel. We had a problem, to be sure: Our captain at Barber's Point Naval Air Station in Hawaii virtually ordered us to beat the Navy skeet team from Kaneohe Bay, on the other side of the island.

Recognizing an order as just that, I sat down with my team and we considered the problem and what to do about it. The answer was what I term the "illegal target."

What it amounts to was that we shot black targets against a background of keawe trees, also black. We also worked over the trap until it was throwing birds with such speed that they resembled carbine bullets!

On station 2, for a high house bird, at first exposure you wouldn't even see it, although it made a perfect and legal rise.

With this, our team trained for two weeks before the match against the team from Kaneohe Bay. When it came time for the real shooting, we were geared up for the fast targets — all of which were legitimate — while the opposing team didn't even see some of them!

Oddly enough, with the speeded up shooting, one might think that this would ruin a shooter's rhythm for slower paced contests, but that wasn't the case with our team. We could gear down for them, while other teams found it difficult to move up to the faster targets.

Without meaning to get involved in a show of acute nostalgia, I do feel that this psychological thing, which the Army shooters have discovered can be the difference between winning and not, deserves more thought.

Back in the days when I was a youngster shooting in the Nationals, we had the hottest five-man skeet team in the country and that was no accident. Up to that time, a team was composed of five individuals, all essentially in competition with each other. On the California team, every shooter was doing everything he could to help his teammates break a score. We talked to each other and built a unit spirit.

As a consequence, we not only won the five-man team championship, but I ended up being runner-up in the all-bore and we had shot the fastest round ever recorded.

We had a team captain who was a perfectionist. He reminded us that each bird was the only bird in the world; that as it came out of the house, this was the bird to concentrate upon. Before every match, we would walk through the course, checking out all of its eccentricities. On a race track, the racing car driver checks out the angles of the track, the turns that may give him trouble; Arnold Palmer walks over every golf course he is to play, seeking out any and every potential problem. This is a practice in almost every competitive sport.

The shotgun competitor should check the same way. He should make himself familiar with the prevailing winds at the course site, seek the best lighting conditions. But the things that will separate the champions from the almost-good shooters are two matters, I feel. First is the shooter's state of mind; it's been my own experience that all top competition shotgunners boast what I would term super-selective concentration. The other requirement is a matter of channeled energy.

First, let me offer an idea of what I mean by channeled

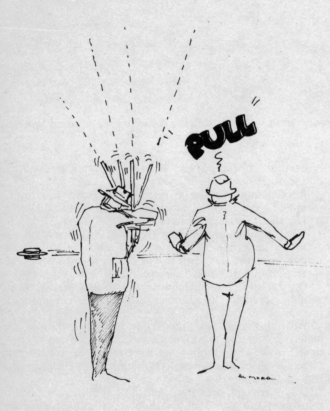

energy. As an example, more birds are missed on high six in skeet when the bird is bucking the wind and looks like a sucker shot than when flying normally or being driven by a heavy wind. The temptation, of course, is to throw your normal timing out the window; ride the bird in and slow or stop the swing — then shoot behind it. Just remember, there are no easy birds.

In this case, the shot is missed because it just looks too easy. In short, the shooter has done nothing more than fallen asleep psychologically. He would find that he does much better by firing a beat faster — channeling his energy — and being less careful!

I feel that many, if not most, targets are missed by a good shot when he calls for a target before he is emotional-

ly geared to break it. He's unfocused; he's shooting blind. When I shot my best, I was charged up on every shot. Then, when the wind blew or any other conditions arose that made shooting difficult, the problems could be used as a challenge to further keep that focus of energy on every bird. In other words, the problems could be used to advantage.

I've watched top shooters fire matches in fog, driving winds and most of the other hazards to scores and they seldom seemed affected, while the same problems literally shattered the competition. But these are the type of men who are able to get a good sight picture in relation to where the bird is going to be before it ever comes out of the house. They know precisely what they are about and, as mentioned earlier, are giving each bird all of their concentration.

At the other extreme, when a man can go 300 straight in practice, then make a poorer showing when the chips are down, this is undoubtedly the result of allowing his mental approach to change. With the pressure on, he is not concentrating upon each bird in the same degree that he did in his practice outing. In my own case, whenever I had a poor practice session, I often came home with the trophies in competition. As explained, I attempted to make my mistakes in practice.

I don't mean to sound like Doctors Freud or Jung, but these Army shooters have spent years in analyzing shooting hangups and, it seems to me, this information can be useful to all of us.

For example, they devote a great deal of time to the dangers of negative thinking and why the individual feels he can't be a winner.

The difficulty in shooting championship scores, they feel, isn't that most of us have not been taught the fundamentals of shooting. Instead, the fault usually lies in that we open our minds to thousands of negative reasons why we can't shoot good scores. Does that seem reasonable?

For example, when the weather is bad, it is simple to say, "It's raining, snowing, the wind is blowing. All my scores are going to be bad." This can become a truth rather than an assumption.

Instead, the Army manual suggests, "Why not think and convince yourself that good scores have been and will be fired under the same bad conditions? Positive application of the fundamentals have produced good results in spite of the numerous difficulties. If your thoughts are directed strongly enough towards planning and executing a controlled performance, you will not have time to worry about the weather."

The Army shooters also advise that we don't play Sunday morning quarterbacks insofar as operation of the range is concerned. "In most instances, all it takes to change an inefficient situation is to have your coach bring the deficiency to the attention of the chief range officer, executive officer or referee. If the condition continues to exist, then convince yourself that 'as long as there is a target to shoot at and I have the proper amount of time to shoot, I will shoot good scores.' "

I'll be the first to admit that, while that advice sounds solid and simple, following it — getting yourself past your own doubts and into the right frame of mind — could almost involve a short course on a psychiatrist's couch.

Have you ever questioned yourself with "why do I have to shoot exceptional scores?" In the case of the armed services, it may be because you've been ordered to and you'd better try, but more realistically, answers to this question certainly should vary with each shooter involved. Basic, though, is the fact that one must be motivated to improve his performance or he should change to something less demanding.

"The most common excuse for not trying your best is lack of incentive, because there is no competition," the Army shooters are told. "A tendency to drift aimlessly through a match becomes a habit. Regardless of the competitive ability present for a particular match, you must employ the fundamentals to the utmost of your ability. You must retain the desire to win and set new records at all times. Failure in this area too often will cause a decline into a habit of treating your shooting as a daily task, instead of a challenging adventure."

There are those who are beaten by allowing themselves to think the cause of a poor performance is poor equipment. Most of us learned a long time ago that a gun usually shoots straighter than we do.

At the opposite end of the pole, if you feel the competition is too tough, it is suggested that you "look at these individuals who now seem to look like supermen. Analyze a few of them and compare their attributes with yours.

"They are built just like you, have approximately the same physical abilities, hands are about the same size. The potential winner is thinking about applying his plan of action and not about how he is going to beat you. He knows that most of the other competitors are beating themselves with their own uncontrolled thoughts. You can be one step ahead of all your competitors by directing your mental effort toward your plan of controlling each shot."

But there is one other facet of self-brainwashing that I feel is of great importance to the serious competitor. There is a first time for a national champion to be beaten just as there is a first time for a shooter to become a national champion. Having been through both of these happenings sometime back in the Dark Ages of my own life saga, I remember both instances well — and the trauma that accompanied them.

Again, the Army shooters have some advice that would parallel my own. They, however, have spent more time thinking about it, so I'll use their words: "The best way is to believe you are as qualified to win as anyone else. Make up your mind that you are going to shoot your next tournament as one big match. Let the individual stages and gun

Initial shoots in the so-called big time environment can be a traumatic experience for neophyte contestant.

aggregates take care of themselves. A good performance on each individual shot is now your aim. Don't let the possibility of winning one little match shatter your composure."

You may find of interest some more of the thoughts and techniques compiled by the Army Marksmanship Training Unit for successful claybird shooting in International competition.

These thoughts come as the result of long experience and consideration and, I feel, involve knowledge of which all of us should be aware, if we are to be serious shooters.

For example, when it comes to reducing tension and attaining relaxation, they look first at the cause rather than the cure, pointing out that the fear of failure to perform up to your known capability gradually will generate increasing tension.

As is explained, "normal tension is a blessing to mankind. Without tension, most problems would not get solved; the world's work would not get done, and championship scores would not be fired.

"Normal tension is the prevailing condition of any organism when mustering its strength to cope with a difficult situation. All animals, including man, tense in situations that involve the security of themselves and their loved ones.

"But there is a kind of tension that is bad for you: pathological tension. This is an exaggeration of normal tension and fairly rare. This type of tension usually requires that the subject be put under the care of a physician."

According to findings, pathological tension is hard to terminate and the whole body over-reacts as if the difficulty confronting it were a life and death matter; the reaction a normal person would have only in a dangerous situation. Blood pressure, heartbeat and pulse go up and stay there.

As for what happens when one faces a challenging situation in shooting, one should become slightly anxious. The reaction is not anxiety in the pathological sense.

In normal tension, the body does undergo certain changes. Adrenalin pours into the bloodstream, while the liver releases sugar to supply energy to the muscles. Your entire nervous system shifts into high gear. There are numerous other changes, too, but normal tension is self-limiting; it does not continue after you need it.

To reduce normal tension, it is suggested that one breathe deeply three times, very slowly, holding the breath for as long as possible at the end of each exhalation. When finished, you should feel more calm and relaxed.

This breaks the tension of your voluntary breathing muscles, causing the involuntary muscles of the lungs, gastro-intestinal tract and the heart to relax as well. For some shooters, this ends tension completely, while others should experience at least emporary relief.

Another method is to sit down and let your head droop forward. In about a minute, raise an arm and drop it in your lap limply, then do the same with the other arm. Let your legs go completely limp, then your stomach muscles, staying in this position for ten minutes. This should relieve tension for several hours.

If you like handwork, pick a kind that is interesting, but not too creative. Finger paintings, woodworking and gardening all are excellent to help one simmer down. "To slow down after stimulation, you require something that is engrossing, but which demands nothing of you intellectually," the researchers say. "Television entertainment and simple handicrafts are ideal."

Another way of dealing with normal tension is simply to take a ten-minute break every hour. This allows one to ease out of working tension more quickly and easily when the day is over.

When we tense to face a situation we tend to exaggerate its importance. Judgment and reason can change this mental state, when it is time to relax.

But one should not become so relaxed that he allows his confidence to slip. Confidence "furnishes the alloy to stiffen the will to win." It is based on a full grasp of the technique of controlling employment of the fundamentals. Confidence — combined with knowledge, skill, physical conditioning and determination to win — provide an edge.

Performing at or beyond your potential will catapult you into the lead. Retain the lead by counting on your competitor's inevitable mistakes and gaps in his knowledge of controlled shooting techniques. You must have confidence that you are capable of a performance exceeding any previous level of personal accomplishment."

I recall some of my own experiences, when the competition — certainly better founded in the basics of psychology — would show up on the shooting line, wearing what we called scare jackets. These are jackets on which are sewn all of the patches and records the individual has won. It can be enough, the first few times, to make one want to hide rather than be shown up by such an expert.

But the Army boys have had some of this same experience and perhaps they have found some answers. They put it quite simply: "The man who has never experienced match pressure has never been in a position to win a match. Where is the difference? Where is the dividing line between champion and plinker? Both may shoot comparable scores in practice, yet one is invariably at the top of the bulletin and the other on the second page in competition."

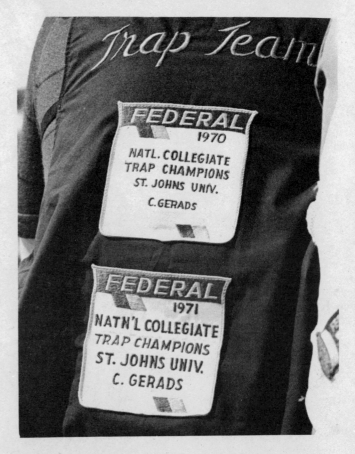

Scare jackets carrying a consistent winner's trophy record have been known to help unnerve the competition.

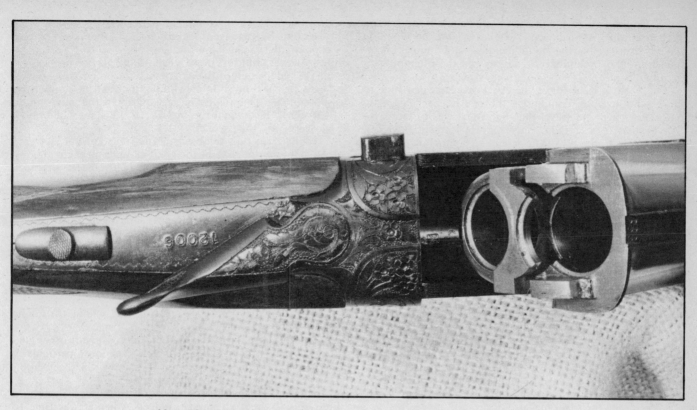

Many shooters prefer over/under or side-by-side shotguns for the tough competition, as they feel there is less room for mechanical difficulty. In fact, many European pros use hammer guns in live pigeon shooting.

That states the problem clearly and the Benning boys feel that the dividing line is equally clear and obvious, simply involving the ability or lack of ability to control one's thinking; in short, mental discipline. I agree with them that some shooters learn to control their emotions and anxieties and go right ahead to perform within their capabilities. Others, even with years of experience, and also with "a wealth of doubts and negative thoughts, pressure themselves out of the competition every time they step up to the firing line."

So what is to be done about it, if anything? The Army has some basic answers to that, too: "First, in our treatment of match pressure, we must find what causes it. Match pressure is the direct result of fear of failure and loss of self-esteem."

When subjected to the mental gymnastics of match pressure, some of us shake, drop our ammunition and our hands perspire. We seem to make unlikely mistakes that normally would not occur. There isn't much in the way of a scientifically oriented cure for this. The main thing that will help is experience and practice in tournament shooting against the best competition.

"The emotional and physical upsets of competitive stress are experienced differently by different persons," according to Colonel Robert F. Bayard, who has commanded the unit. "The condition varies for every shooter, both in its character and its intensity. However, regardless of your experience or your ability to exercise self-discipline, you are to some degree nervous in competition.

"The better you are trained, the more confidence you will have. If you have trained under conditions approximating match conditions and have participated in many tournaments, you will be less nervous."

Looking on the positive side, some of the Army shooters feel there is a definite advantage to match pressure. Many

of the senses become more acute. One sees better and the sense of touch is more exacting. Awareness of the passage of time becomes more vivid. Add these factors together and they should make for a more exacting and consequently a better performance.

In other words, match pressure can be controlled and used to one's advantage. Such shooters as Jimmy Clark, Alex Kerr, Dan Orlich, Ken Jones and many others have learned to control their shooting to the extent that their match and practice scores don't vary to any degree.

"Prior mental determination" — for you can achieve it — "is the most helpful factor. By thinking through the correct procedure for each shot just before you shoot, one can eliminate distractions in the actual execution. If you fail to do this and approach the shot without a preconceived plan of attack, results will be erratic, at best."

The Army shooters try to channel their thinking to the more important fundamentals, reviewing them in their minds. They train so that as many of these fundamentals as possible are executed automatically without tedious effort. "When you do this, you have only the most difficult fundamentals to contend with in the actual firing. This will enable you to direct all of your mental and physical efforts toward keeping your eyes focused on the target and completing your swing-through smoothly."

For example, Tom Garrigus, the 1968 Olympic trapshooting silver medalist, offers some basic advice on winning: "No matter how much natural talent an athlete may have, he has to train himself by practicing constantly so that his reflexes respond quickly. When I was on the Air Force trap team, we used to shoot two or three hours every day. My right shoulder is about three-eighths of an inch larger than my left."

When he entered the Air Force in 1965, he already had received a number of shooting awards. In 1962, he won the junior singles title in the Oregon State Pacific International Trap Shooting Association. Two years later, he won the same title, as well as the Junior handicap and doubles championships, the preliminary handicap and the Champion of Champions race.

But with typical logic, the Air Force assigned him to radio school. Upon completing the course, he had thirty-odd days leave and travel time before he was to report to San Francisco as a radio operator. He learned, however, that the Air Force trap team would be competing in Reno, Nevada, during that time. He went to Reno, entered the Golden West Grand Trap Shoot against the Air Force Shooters. Soon after, he began the remaining 3½ years of his enlistment contract as a member of the team.

Although the young shooter played semi-pro baseball for a season before enlisting, he had decided upon his career. "Trapshooting is where I wanted to concentrate my efforts. The sport is growing tremendously. In this decade and the next, the number of participants will double.

"I'm usually pretty calm in competition," he says, "but while awaiting the shoot in the 1968 Olympics in Mexico City, I was the most nervous I've ever been in my life. Fortunately, the nervousness left me after I started the first round."

Of 200 targets, England's John Braithewaite won the gold medal with 198. Garrigus scored 196, along with a Russian and an East German. In the shoot-off, the East German missed and was out, while Garrigus and the Russian tied 25x25. In the second shoot-off, Garrigus again scored 25x25 to take the silver medal.

His own record for International trapshooting was set in November, 1968, when he won the U.S. Interservice title at Fort Benning, Georgia, scoring 296-300.

A lot of us are inclined to live a bit in the past, and since my father died when I was very young, I still feel that the years of my teens when I was a member of the All-American five-man skeet team helped fill the void for me. Those years allowed me to associate with men older than myself, yet be treated as a man in my own right, one able to carry his own weight on the firing line.

At the other extreme, when I am inclined to start offering advice on shotgunning, I also catch myself — or attempt

to do so — with the reminder that I was a has-been at 19 years old. By that age, I had discovered other interests such as polo, boat racing, ad infinitum.

However, out of those years, I did have some experiences, and learned of the experiences of others which might be of help to the shooter who is interested in competitive shotgunning. One of the biggest bugaboos that any shooter is likely to face when the pressure is on is described rather obviously as "the psyche."

If the term isn't self-explanatory, let me offer an example. Billy Purdue, one of the great all-time skeet champions, as well as one of the country's leading live pigeon shooters, had a little stunt when the heat was on that almost invariably unnerved his opponent on the firing line. He would save the trick until there was a final shoot-off, then he would arrive on the assigned post carrying an entire case of shotgun shells. With great care, he would set this down and start to get ready for the telling contest.

"What are you going to do with all those?" his high-rated opponent would ask, not really wanting an answer.

"Well," Purdue would explain straight-faced, "I don't intend to miss. Do you?"

The idea that Purdue was ready and willing for a long shoot-off was bound to have its effect.

Another approach that was meant to disrupt other gunners usually worked best for a woman shooter, particularly were she shooting against men. It is known in skeet shooting circles simply as "the waiting dodge."

I know of one All-American woman shooter who would use this to great advantage, indeed. When it was time to shoot, all of the other gun pointers would be on their posts, but she would be among the missing. Then word would come out that she was powdering her nose. But before reaching her post, she would have to stop to discuss the situation with the umpire — or anyone else who was available. All this time, of course, the male shooters would be silently cursing the day that women discovered the shotgun. By the time that she picked up her gun and was ready to compete, most of the men would be reduced to a nervous shambles by their own anger.

Then there is the so-called "accident," which is enough to unnerve anyone. I have never tried it and can still hold my head high, but there was a time when I was in an important shoot-off with Harry Fleischman. A friend came up and explained that he had bet some money on me and that he wanted me to win. I promised that I would try.

"You can help," he explained. "When Fleischman is about ready, let one go off a few feet in front of him. That'll shake him up."

As I protested against such thoughts, I fully realized that

One All-American women shooter used the waiting dodge to great advantage in unnerving keyed-up competitors.

Some competitive shooters will use seemingly legitimate delay to break up opponent's rhythm.

having a round of No. 9 shot plowing up the ground in front of one could probably be enough to make you want to find another hobby like bullfighting or swimming waterfalls.

There are other less spectacular approaches that you might also look for. If you recognize that someone is deliberately attempting to spook you, it may help. Then again, it may make things worse. You'll have to figure that part out for yourself.

But in those days, a number of shooters used to wear white hats. These they would use to full advantage by taking them off, wiping their faces, readjusting the hat; anything to disturb the other shooter and break up his rhythm. I've seen the same thing accomplished with an ordinary handkerchief.

Another method, this again aimed at breaking the other shooter's rhythm, is to shout "pull" for your own bird the instant he has broken his. On more than one occasion, I've seen this turn an experienced shooter into a bundle of nerves.

I suppose I have been psyched a number of times and didn't actually realize it. At least, I can always use this as the excuse for the shoots I failed to win. But there actually are two times that I can well recall when I was psyched.

The first time, of course, was in my initial meeting against the late Billy Clayton for the National Junior championship. He was wearing a "scare jacket" that was enough to make a rainbow turn in its colors!

His entire shooting jacket was covered with the multicolored patches representing his wins in various contests and events, and each of those patches meant something. He had so many, or so it seemed to me at the time, that he had them running down his arms, had them sewn under his armpits and, the lesser ones, he had installed as elbow patches to keep from rubbing out his sleeves. In that era, however, this was the fad and I would guess, in retrospect, that none of us were afraid to display our prowess.

The other time that I recall being psyched was in a match in which I was to shoot against a man in a wheelchair. Not only was the crowd with him, but I knew it, and audience reaction can have its effect upon the shooter. It may even have been that in some subconscious way, I wanted him to win, too, but I still gave it all I had. He won, nonetheless, and there is certainly the possibility that he was simply a better shooter that day.

Those are the things to watch for. At the other extreme, if you start using these examples, I'll swear I know nothing about it.

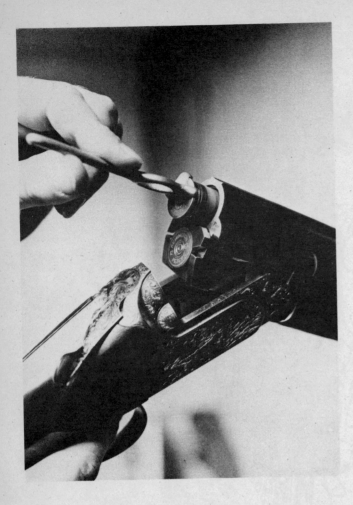

Chapter 14

If a spent hull should become stuck in the chamber, this hand extractor can be the remedy. There is a pry on one end to help loosen a particularly tight-jammed shell.

HAVE YOU EVER met a serious trap or skeet shooter who took his gun out of the factory box and shot it as it was — without altering or customizing anything? Not many.

As a race, claybusters have a passion for endlessly fiddling with our guns, constantly trying to improve them. We are trying to achieve improved performances by adjusting our guns to produce perfect scores.

Derek Partridge, mentioned at length in the chapter on safety, is one of those who is something of a fanatic, always attempting to improve a new gun — or, for that matter, any gun — to offer better performance for the individual.

"Long ago, I realized that if I could get the one behind the gun properly adjusted, only then would I be on the road to those perfect scores. But it wasn't until I began to follow my own advice that halfway decent scores resulted."

In Europe, where many guns are custom-fitted, initially there isn't too much excuse for gun fiddling. The American shooter, relying mainly on mass-produced, standard-dimension guns, has far more legitimate reasons for doing so, because all shooters don't conform to being about five-foot-ten and a slightly overweight fortyish Mr. "Average Man" for whom most factory guns are designed. It is vital that a gun fit a shooter perfectly for potentially perfect results, but it also is important that the shooter believes his gun is right for him. Confidence in one's equipment rates on par with confidence in one's ability in the target-hitting game.

Apart from the gun itself, tools for amateur gunsmithing and minor field repairs, cleaning equipment, clothing and accessories, all play a part in the development of the shooter. Over the last twenty years, Partridge has collected a number of such items — some purchased, some modified and some created. He refers to them as his "survival kit." Even though they may not all be of use to him, he often uses them for other shooters who are still negotiating the tricky path to adjusting behind the gun!

Raising the comb (reducing the drop — making the stock "straighter") is probably the most common of all adjustments. The easiest and most comfortable material to use is the plastic-backed, adhesive rubber tape. It is one-thirty-second-inch thick — an ideal thickness for increasing the height, layer by layer. Secure each layer firmly with strips of Scotch tape. Once the correct height has been reached, you may wish to finish it in a better looking material.

A leather comb can be used, its underside edges neatly chamfered to flow smoothly into the lines of the stock. If your face is getting kicked on recoil, either place a strip of foam rubber under the leather or, if you have a Monte Carlo comb, put a one-sixteenth-inch reverse slope on it. This will take the stock away from your face on recoil and only alters your sighting plane one-thirty-second of an inch.

If your gun feels sluggish and won't go where you want it to in time, odds are that it's muzzle heavy. Remove the recoil pad and fill the recess with some light, bulky padding, like cotton or Kleenex, that is easily removable for subsequent access to the stock-retaining screw. In the very end of the stock, insert old fishing weights or strips of

CLAYBIRDER'S SURVIVAL KIT

The Ability To Make On-The-Range Repairs, As Well As Make Shooting More Comfortable, Can Help You To Win!

bullet lead wire, weighing about an ounce each, until the gun balances on the joint pin and the overall weight feels evenly distributed between your hands.

Make sure the weights are wedged firmly in place by proper packing and covering, so they don't rattle around while you're shooting. The result is that guns often feel a pound lighter, even though they weigh a few ounces more.

Lengthening or shortening stocks is another common adjustment. Temporary and experimental work can be done with a slip-on recoil pad. To increase its length, it can be packed with spacers until the desired length is reached.

"Frank Pachmayr's 550 series recoil pad is the best I have found for trapshooting. It is the first one really contoured to the shape of the body where the gun goes in and, once in place, the saw-teeth make any lateral or vertical slipping absolutely impossible. The 550 series includes a flat-ended model for the skeet shooter," Partridge says.

An adjustable recoil pad allows variance of drop by its up and down movements. In some types, between the hard rubber back and the metal plate, is a layer of sponge rubber: by tightening or loosening the screws at the toe and heel of the pad, the pitch also can be altered.

One Italian-made pad can be angled sideways as well as up and down. This is particularly useful for women shooters, as it allows them to tuck the pad under their armpit and so avoid the discomfort of the toe digging into their breast — while the gun still remains upright and uncanted. Both these pads come with curved or flat ends. Frank

Pachmayr will shortly be producing an American version of the Italian pad.

The standard factory gun usually has a trigger with a flat surface. In order to pull this with maximum ease, the finger would have to be at right angles to it. As one must retain his hold on the grip, this is impossible and the finger pulls at an angle of approximately forty-five degrees.

"To make for a better, more comfortable and easier pull, a little work with a curved file will shape the trigger to the soft forty-five-degree angle of most custom-built guns. To make mine even more comfortable, I also relieved the guard a little."

Some shooters suffer from second-finger bruising. This generally is caused by an incorrect distance from trigger to pistol grip, wrong angle of the pistol grip — or funny-shaped fingers! A rubber finger-protector can be used or it can be duplicated easily, if unobtainable, with a little tape and ingenuity.

Some of the uninitiated don't give a great deal of thought to cleanliness of shotguns. After all, it's only a straight tube, and in this day of chrome-lining, there isn't much that can happen, they feel. But it's not quite that simple.

Corrosion can form in the chambers, especially from the sweating of some plastic hulls. Normal cleaning brushes aren't big enough to clean the chambers. Partridge uses a phosphor-bronze brush that is a refugee from a 20mm cannon cleaning kit, plus a wire spiral meant as a 10-gauge

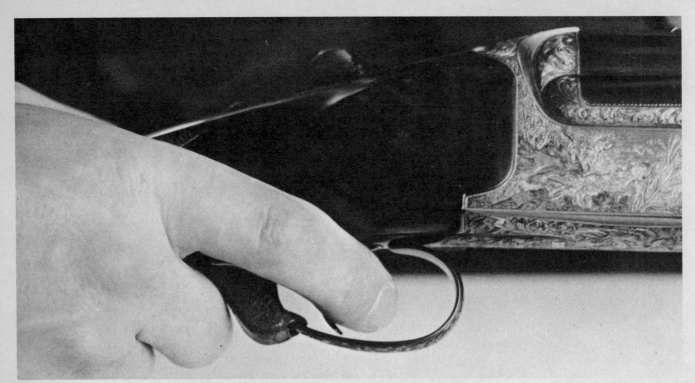

If the trigger guard seems to give one consistent trouble, bruising the second finger, this rubber protector by Parker-Hale of England should solve the injury problem.

Below: One way to raise the comb of a shotgun, yet retain it attractiveness is used by Leonard Mews of Hollywood, California. He builds a simple mould, pours epoxy resin into it, then rubs the comb back to the right height. Note that the coating is transparent.

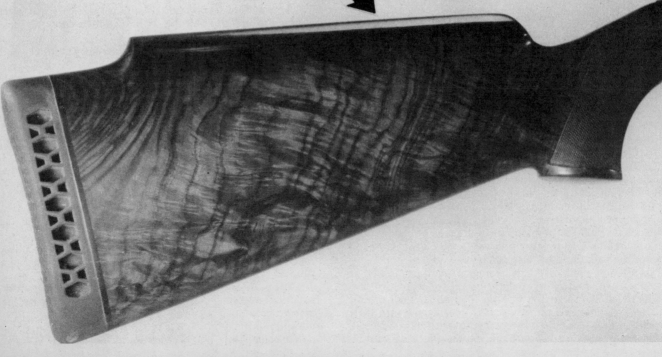

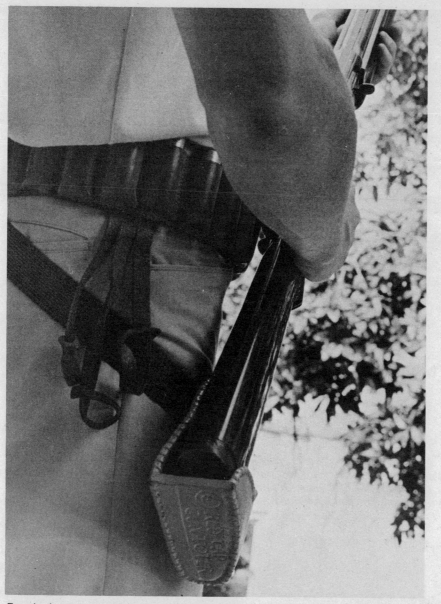

For the hunter, game thongs can be hung from the belt in the rear. This cuts shoulder weight created by birds in a game vest. The Red Cap Gun Toter allows the gun to be carried safely and ready, not tiring the arm.

cleaner for scrubbing out the chambers. Some of the most useful cleaning aids for getting into corners of actions and internal mechanisms are old toothbrushes and typewriter-cleaning brushes.

For those who don't like to be conscious of the sight when actually firing, but shoot off the end of the barrels, some metal bluer will turn a brass sight to a dull, barrel-matching color. Black paint will defeat the purpose, as it would be shiny, and felt-tip pen black wears off quickly.

A steel rule — not cloth, it stretches — is useful for measuring the length of pull. A device for measuring the weight of the trigger pull covers an important factor often ignored by shooters. It can affect the amount of lead given a target, as the harder or heavier trigger generally will require a longer reaction time between brain message and actual pulling.

"To alter the shotgun trigger pull is a highly skilled job best left to professionals. I once ruined four sets of Brown-

ing sears and bents before I began to get the idea!" Partridge cautions.

"I carry an emergency repair kit for all of my guns when competing. With my Remington 1100, occasionally the extractor claw breaks. A punch, turned down to the right diameter and length, pushes out the two pins to drop out the trigger assembly. A small electrical screwdriver, the point especially ground, serves to get behind the broken fragment, then holds the spring depressed, while a new claw is inserted."

In Europe, there is a specific type of costume for shooting, which was mod before the mods got into the act. There is no great point in discussing fashions here, but there are some definite advantages — as your scores will show — in wearing the right kind of clothes and accessories for the firing line. As an example, for those rainy days, why not fit a leather patch to your rainproof jacket? It will allow far better gun-mounting, which is the key to successful shooting.

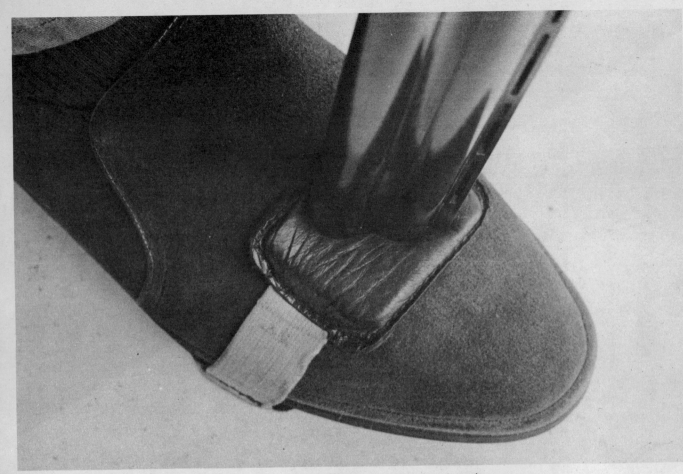

We don't advocate the practice, but many claybird shooters tend to rest the gun barrel on the toe between shots. This pad, a piece of sponge rubber encased in leather, can save on the appearance of your shoes. The pad is held in place by the wide band of elastic.

The average leather shoulder patch is too thin and the rubber pad inserted behind it too flexible. They tend to pinch together when the gun is placed in the shoulder and, if those folds of material include your skin, you're going to have a nasty and painful pinched bruise — apart from the fact that your gun will not always be seated properly.

By using two layers of top quality suede, at least one-sixteenth-inch thick — one outside and one sewn to it as a backing piece inside the jacket — one achieves adequate protection from recoil and a shoulder patch which always retains its flat surface, no matter how much it is used.

The smaller and more numerous the diamonds sewn across the patch, the more rigid it becomes; the larger, the more flexible. Diamonds with sides about an inch long seem a good compromise.

It is important that there is no lateral or vertical movement of your shooting jacket or it will affect the correct placing of your gun. On the normal skeet vest, the weight of shells in the pocket will prevent the important right side of the vest from moving upwards. But what happens towards the end of the round when the shells are almost used up?

"Earl Pellant, inventor of the Stoklokater, gave me a couple of strips of leather and I adapted his idea by fastening the top with an elasticated strip to the bottom of the inside of the shoulder patch. The other end loops around the belt and so holds the patch in position at all times. The adjustment at the belt end is to allow for different thicknesses of belt. Another excellent alternative is to get one of Bill Pleassinger's body-hugging International skeet vests and the problem of vest and patch movement ceases to exist."

If your shooting glasses bear uncomfortably on the bridge of your nose, you can fit Morris sponge-rubber nose pads or soft plastic pads by Danbert of Sierra Madre, California, which fit over the nose pieces and wear better than sponge rubber, as they are not affected by perspiration. A piece of chamois leather is invaluable for insuring maximum cleanliness of the glasses.

So as not to lose your glasses, if there aren't already a couple of slits in the back of the case, cut them so as to fit the case onto your belt. For speedy recognition, mark the color on the outside of the cases. It is important always to wear glasses, even if you do not need them optically. They guard against fatigue induced by excessive brightness,

Above: Putting weights in the stock, if the gun swings poorly, changes the balance point, hopefully for better. (Below) Lengthening or shortening in stocks is common. A slip-on recoil pad (right) can be used, packing it with spacers to determine proper length. Recoil pads such as those shown can be installed to attain the proper length.

against blown back powder particles hitting you in the eye just as you are about to shoot and, if they are toughened lenses, against the remote possibility of a burst barrel.

It is just as important always to wear adequate hearing protection, as being subjected to shotgun reports quite definitely causes hearing loss, which never can be recovered. The product Partridge uses is the Soundown custom-moulded hearing protector by French Laboratories of Sacramento.

So as not to lose them in their small original containers, buy a plastic pill-container, drill or burn two holes in the lid, thread a piece of chain through, attach a clip and you can then keep the ear protectors on your belt.

"I find it comfortable and practical to wear gloves Summer and Winter. In Summer, they prevent the gun slipping in sweaty hands and protect the metal parts from the rusting effects of sweat. In Winter, they keep the hands warm and allow some sensitivity for trigger-pulling. Trueshot gloves by Tarantella of Walsall, England, allow the trigger finger to be exposed. The winter model is silk-lined for greater warmth, the summer model ventilated.

"A good gun deserves good protection. The best is a hard rectangular gun case, but I travel a lot and prefer the convenience of a strong leg-o-mutton case. I replaced the original thin strap, which soon cuts into your shoulders, with a thick, padded golf bag strap. I also replaced the usual sharp-edged handle with one contoured comfortably to fit the hand. Attached to the handle is a label with my name and address and my name also imprinted on the case itself. To the full-length case, which I sometimes carry for local shoots, I added a pouch on the side to hold cleaning rods, cleaning material and some small tools. Also added is a soft shoulder pad fitted to the original thin strap."

International
YOU CAN SHOOT / TRAP & SKEET!

Chapter 15

Here Are The Basics Of The Games,
But Talent And Tenacity Are Up To You!

ONE OF THE problems with International claybird games seems to be that one tends to miss too often and American shooters must see something break, if their interest span is to be maintained. I suspect that only a nation-wide head-shrinking session could cure that facet.

However, the second problem is the feeling that shooting International is an expensive hobby which only the rich can afford. Of course, a few years ago, the general public felt that way about trap and skeet in general; it has been only since World War II that the masses have come to realize these are far less expensive sports than girl-chasing or professional drinking. The International games are not all that much more expensive — if you can find a place to shoot them properly.

International trap, or Olympic trench, as it is known in the rest of the world, consists of fifteen traps laid out in five groups of three traps — or one group for each shooting station. Each of the fifteen throws a different target, but all travel around 100 mph, between 77 and 87 yards, within a ninety-degree angle span and at heights varying from grass-cutters to rockets.

As the shooter moves to the next station after each shot and the whole selection of targets is changed every five shots, it is impossible to know where your target will be going. American trap has one machine throwing targets at a constant elevation, within a forty-four-degree arc between forty-eight and fifty-two yards.

Olympic skeet uses the same layout as the American variety, but throws targets seventy-two yards as opposed to fifty-five. The butt of the gun must be on the hip and cannot be moved till the target appears, which can be immediately or with up to three second's delay. In American skeet, these days the shooter starts with the gun in his shoulder and the target always is released immediately.

As these are the only fields of shotgunning where you can represent your country in the Olympics, World championships, Pan-American Games and all other International championships, they are worth fostering and developing.

Taking International trap first, all you need is a perfectly standard trap gun capable of firing two shots, as you are allowed two shots and sometimes you find yourself wishing for a third! Forget pump guns, as there just isn't time to operate the mechanism and catch up with a 100 mph target.

I have mentioned Derek Partridge several times in this book. As an English shooter, who has contested frequently on the Continent, as well as in his home islands and in the United States, he has had far more to do with International claybird games and styles than I. For that reason, I asked whether he felt there was any special custom-built gun requirement in these contests.

"Although I shot with almost every European, World and Olympic champion over a period of ten years and saw the standard grade guns many of them use, we need go no farther than the fine International shots in this country to prove the point," Partridge says.

The Air Force team almost all use standard Krieghoffs, which have a particular advantage inasmuch as the point of impact of the lower barrel can be altered due to the lack of a separating rib. The Army team seems to prefer the Browning Broadway — again a standard model. Occasionally a Remington 1100 will be seen on International trap ranges. The internationally preferred specifications of these guns are with thirty-inch barrels and a standard ventilated rib, bored to throw 60-65 percent lower and 70-75 percent upper patterns.

"Although the Army team has shot mighty well with the thirty-two-inch muzzle-heavy Broadways, many top International shooters in Europe tried them out, but soon returned to the standard ribbed thirty-inch barrel," Partridge says. "Although it is a matter of opinion, this gun seems better suited to American trapshooting, where a slow, deliberate movement is made to a slow target and the shooting method is that of pointing out a sustained lead. On International, there is no time for this and the only possible method is swinging-through — passing the target at overtaking speed and firing at the moment of passing, the overtaking speed providing the lead. For this you need a gun that shoots exactly where you move it to without the excessive lead given by a muzzle-heavy gun."

International trap targets go low as well as high, so gun must be held low below the middle of the three traps.

If your gun is in this category, it is simple to alter. Remove the heel pad, loosely pack the access hole to the stock-retaining bolt with Kleenex or cotton wool, then put some old fishing weights in the very end of the stock until the gun balances on the joint pin (the large pin just forward of the trigger guard).

This way, the weight of the gun will be distributed evenly between the hands and you won't have to lug a lot of excess weight around in your left hand. Be careful not to make it stock heavy or you then will have muzzle whip. If you want, you can have a lower comb (more drop) than on an American trap gun, as you get low, as well as high targets instead of constantly rising ones.

However, I don't feel it is necessary to start carving down your trap stock, as most International shooters I know use standard trap stocks and many have been successful with even higher combs (less drop).

An alternative employed by Perazzi, who specializes in guns for International championships, is to keep the same drop, but have a centralized point of impact. Most other trap guns are built to throw two-thirds to three-quarters of the pattern above the aiming point at forty yards.

Apart from the Franchi and the Merkel, the only foreign guns which show up in any numbers at International championships are the Beretta — used by Liano Rossini, who placed eleventh in his fifth Olympic Games, having previously placed respectively from 1952: sixth, first, second and tied for second — an outstanding and unique record of both skill and participation in the Olympics. Then there is the Perazzi, designed by Rossini's teammate, Ennio Mattarelli, the 1964 Olympic Gold Medalist. He shot in Mexico with the special Perazzi MX8, imported by the Ithaca Gun Company. Using the original gun built for him by master gunsmith Daniele Perazzi, Mattarelli also achieved the unique feat of winning the Italian, European and World championships.

Other guns quite capable of doing a good job on International are these standard o/u trap models: Ithaca SKB; Winchester 101; Charles Daly and the Remington 1100 auto.

In the 1968 Olympics, Ray Stafford (USA) racked up 293/300 with his standard Browning and Tom Garrigus (USAF) was one bird behind with his standard Krieghoff — excellent scores, which carried these fine young men into the Olympics and twenty-one-year-old Garrigus to the silver medal. Shooting in his first major International Championship, after scoring 196, he went 50 straight in a three-way shoot-off, beating Czekella of East Germany and the experienced Russian Senichev who, in 1964, had beaten America's Bill Morris and former gold medalist Rossini in a shoot-off to win himself the silver in Tokyo. The 1968 Olympic gold medalist for Great Britain was Bob Braithwaite, a 43-year-old veterinarian, who shot a brilliant 198 to equal the Olympic record set by Mattarelli in Tokyo, when Bob came in seventh with 192.

Moving on to skeet, the problem is even easier — it just

The 15 traps in the International bunker are divided into five groups of three, one group in front of each shooting position. Left trap throws target to the right, center trap is straight ahead and trap on right throws its claybird to shooter's left.

isn't a problem. Any standard skeet model automatic or superposed will be perfect. Again the pump is out, as it cannot be operated fast enough for the speedy International skeet doubles. Again, get the gun properly balanced as with the trap gun.

Most International skeet shooters use guns with more drop than American skeet models. As the gun is mounted from the hip, a time saving is effected. The gun is brought up to the face and the lateral swing commenced immediately — without the additional movement of lowering the head far enough to "cheek" the stock. This is done by American skeet shooters prior to calling for the target, when they mount the gun deliberately in the shoulder. Some American International shooters try to copy the same formula, but when mounting from the hip on fast-moving targets there just isn't time. In line with the increased drop and bringing the gun up to the face, most International skeet shooters also adopt a more upright stance than Americans.

The only other change needed will be to cover your rubber heel pad with leather or simply lacquer it to prevent it snagging on clothing as it is mounted from the hip. In my own case, I have used smooth rubber electrician's tape for this purpose.

Turning to loads — the howl goes up that you have to use 3¼-3¾ drams of powder with 1¼ ounces of nickel-plated shot. Although this is the standard load in Europe, it is for a specific reason.

Until the invention of the plastic shot collar, the only way to reduce pellet deformation in the barrel and get really good patterns was to use nickeled shot. This is now obsolete, but as tradition dies hard in Europe and Power-Piston collars are only beginning to be used, there is still widespread use of the more expensive nickel shot. But at layouts like the Bois de Boulogne in Paris and Charleroi in Belgium, where the targets are tougher and often thrown a good one hundred yards, such shooters as Jill Curzon have won gold medals using standard 1-1/8 trap loads in both barrels!

Winchester, Remington and Federal International loads all are excellent. The armed service teams have a preference for the Remington and Winchester, while the Federal is cheaper with a still devastatingly effective pattern. However, it is perfectly feasible to use a standard trap load in the first barrel and only use the heavier shell as a back-up for the occasional second shot. I also have seen shooters put up respectable scores in the 90s using trap loads in both barrels. Favored shot sizes are either No. 8 first and 7½ second or 7½ for both.

People will complain that the use of two shots is going to run up the cost of shooting. The Olympic Games are shot over 200 targets and most other major International championships are over 100 to 200 targets, so you don't have the marathon 500 to 1000 target races, plus shoot-offs.

Shoot-offs are rare in International as perfect scores just don't come that easily. When you do have one, it generally is over after one round of 25, rarely going to 50 targets. So you just aren't going to shoot as much, which means that you will be able to enjoy the sport at less cost than American trap.

Standard skeet loads in either No. 8 or 9 are used universally. Again, major championships are of 100 to 200 targets. The only difference in accessories can be that your skeet jacket can have a shoulder patch running clear down to the pocket to facilitate the mounting of the gun from its position on the hip. International skeet is 12 gauge only.

Both skeet and trap require a greater degree of mental preparation and concentration to hit these fast-moving targets. Timing is the all-important factor and separates the champions from the others. There is not time for the slow pointing-out method. You just haul off and trust your reflexes and instincts. At American trap, you can make an error in pointing and have time to recover, realign and still score a kill. At International style, you have one chance before the target has disappeared over the horizon! On International trap, it's good practice to shoot at bits left from the first shot — it trains you to keep your head glued

to the stock and keep on the target for when you really need that second shot.

Apart from the military layouts at Fort Benning, Georgia, with two trenches; Lackland AFB, Texas; and the Marine Corps base at Quantico, Virginia, the few civilian facilities are as follows:

1. The Texas International Gun Club in San Antonio has a first-class layout with, I believe, trenches conforming to all International standards, including microphone release of targets and a timing mechanism on the skeet ranges. This is possibly the most comprehensive layout in the world (only Bologna in Italy has four trenches) and certainly the only absolutely correct civilian-owned site in the States.

2. International Trap and Skeet Range, El Monte, California, has one trench, which does not conform strictly to International standards and is without microphone release. No skeet timers.

3. Martinez Gun Club, Martinez, California, has one trench that almost never is used, due to lack of interest. No skeet layouts.

Here is a tension-free, simple stance for International trap. Left knee just broken, body inclined forward from the ankles up, head well down on the stock.

4. Renton Gun Club of Renton, Washington. Here there is one trench and no skeet layout.

The Renton layout, however, was built for only $3500, the members contributing their time and labor. Details as to how this was accomplished are available from Merlin Martin of 110 Capri Avenue, Renton, Washington.

With the exception of Texas, all the civilian layouts seem to have been designed from a similar pattern which does not conform to layouts in Belgium, England, France, Italy and Spain. The difference is that here the overall length of the trench is greater and the distance between the traps too far. In Europe, all three targets from each group converge on exit, as nearly as possible, from under the line painted on the trap roof to denote the position of the central trap. With the traps spaced too far apart, this is impossible.

In the absence of sufficient layouts around the country, what can be done to provide worthwhile simulated practice?

ATA modified trap is most certainly no answer at all as evidenced by five excellent trap shooters who qualified for the 1968 Olympic Final tryout with scores averaging in the high 90s over three hundred modified trap targets. They returned averages in the low 70s over the real Olympic trench. They simply were not prepared adequately for what they found and it cannot have been a pleasant experience for them.

The only satisfactory substitute is the ISU (International Shooting Union) Automatic Trap — previously known as the Continental. It is a multi-angling and elevating trap capable of throwing targets full International distances. Winchester-Western's Continental Trap conforms to these specifications and there is also a conversion kit for the regular White Flyer Trap at prices many clubs can afford. The ISU Automatic Trap was pioneered by that champion of International shooting, Mike Tipa of the NRA, who ramrodded its acceptance for the Pan American and Asian games. Layout specifications are available from Tipa at the NRA.

It is also a little sad to note that around Milan, Italy, there are more International layouts than in the whole of the United States. Little wonder the Italians have won medal honors in the last few Olympic Games. This impressive record was contributed to by having Olympic trenches in almost every small town.

But if they can find the money to do this, surely America can.

Here is the International skeet gun-down position prior to target release. Gun may not be moved until target is seen. The delay may be from zero to three seconds after call.

Shooting over the 15-trap bunker at the El Monte, California, International trap and skeet range. Body position shows how far acute right angles go.

GIMMICKS FOR GUNNERS

The Market Is Loaded With Ideas
To Make Your Gun And Shooting Better!

Chapter 16

Clyde Purbaugh, mentioned at length in the text, checks the shot pattern on a target after his gauge-changing tubes have been inserted in the barrels. Note Hydro-coil on his shotgun.

AS MENTIONED AT some length earlier, the more avid shotgunners seem never entirely satisfied with the way their guns shoot. As a result, they constantly are looking for combinations that will improve their shooting, reduce recoil, make them winners or simply perform magic on the range and in the field.

One of the innovations that has created a good deal of interest and seems to be growing in popularity — possibly because of good press — is the release trigger.

If you already own a release trigger or are considering getting one, you should know as much about it as possible, but it is inadvisable to try to work on it yourself, unless you happen to be specifically qualified to undertake such delicate and skilled work. Experts in this highly specialized field do not consider release triggers suitable for home repair work as their structure and tolerances are more intricate, sensitive and critical than standard trigger mechanisms. Basically they agree with Jack Farrar, who is responsible for all the high quality workmanship that comes out of Frank Pachmayr's renowned Los Angeles gun works:

"Personally, I feel there is little a home gunsmith can do toward servicing a release trigger beyond an occasional thorough cleaning of the entire trigger assembly in a good grade solvent, followed by a light oiling."

To some extent, this is because there are parts used in release mechanisms which are finished from investment castings, while others are made from solid tool steel. Some areas of the frames have to be heliarc welded and reshaped to provide stops for the release hooks. The other reason is explained by his closing comment: "All of the final fitting and assembly is a high precision job and must be done by a very competent gunsmith."

Release triggers are enjoying constantly growing popularity and Elgin Gates estimates that ten percent of American trapshooters use them and swear by them. First, we'll examine the reasons for their use and then present some experts' views on their technical requirements. Derek Partridge happens to be one of the few release trigger users in Europe. For this reason, he has been obliged to carry out urgent field repairs and his own maintenance and tuning.

"Although I have learned something from the countless frustrating hours I have had to spend trying to get it to perform at all, then getting it to perform as I wanted it, the experience has undoubtedly added a few gray hairs and has on occasion adversely affected my shooting performance," he admits. "But such is my belief in its advantages that I have stuck to the release trigger despite much European advice to abandon it."

215

Release triggers, discussed in the accompanying text, are an approach favored by some claybird competitors as a means of controlling the tendency to flinch. Type shown here has a single hammer and adjustment screw.

The release trigger was designed originally to overcome the tendency among some American trapshooters to flinch in pulling their triggers. The flinching problem is virtually unknown among International trapshooters in Europe, hence the absence of the release trigger there. It therefore seems logical that flinching is usually in some way peculiar to American trapshooting.

Release trigger specialist Allen Timney of Downey, California, defines the reasons for flinching as "...the combination of recoil, noise of the gun and many times the gun not fitting properly and so kicking the shooter in the face." While I don't disagree totally, it must be pointed out that the European International trapshooter uses the far heavier 3¾-dram, 1¼-ounce load and frequently fires two shots at targets, as opposed to the single shot, 1-1/8-ounce load in America. I agree more when it comes to gun fitting, for most American shooters make do with standard factory guns, while European shooters always have been more inclined to have guns fitted to them.

The only reason left for the difference is that American targets travel at about half the speed of International ones and consequently are generally shot nearly twice as slowly. The International shooter usually gets off his first shot between five-tenths and eight-tenths of a second, whereas his American counterpart takes around nine-tenths to 1-2/10ths. This means that while the fast shooter is firing mostly instinctively, the slower shooter is firing deliberately. The combination of deliberation, conscious aiming and the time taken give the American shooter's mind time to consider that his gun is about to go off, make a lot of noise and possibly thump him in the shoulder and/or face. For the International shooter, it all happens too fast for him to have time to think this way. When such a thought does enter the American shooter's mind, his brain will send a message countermanding the pull-the-trigger instruction, effectively freezing the finger's imminent action: the flinch. At least, that's one theory.

Why does the release trigger resolve this problem? Partridge says, "I am venturing into pure theory and can only suggest possible answers. The pulling action is a muscular contraction which causes a certain degree of tension. The anxiety about the results of the pulling cause further tension of a more powerful nature than the trigger-pull-tension.

"So the greater tension (particularly being caused by fear) outweighs and so stops the lesser. On the other hand, the action of releasing is a muscular relaxation and is executed far more easily than pulling. Such relaxation possibly contains a relief factor, too, thus further facilitating the job of firing the gun through this method. As the releasing action is faster muscularly, this would also make it harder for the brain to countermand a release-the-trigger instruction."

Whatever the reasons for flinching, the use of the release trigger to overcome them can be considered a valid but negative application of a system that has definite, positive

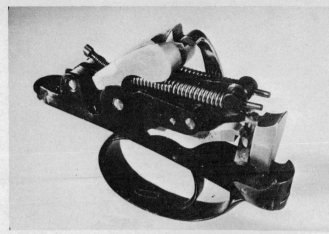

Lockwork for a release trigger, shown with both hammers cocked. As discussed, some install release triggers on doubles to fire first barrel on release, second on the pull.

The same lock as at left, with one of its hammers released. Installation of release triggers is a job for a skilled gunsmith and safety considerations are vital, as discussed.

advantages to almost any shooter. When the American military International trapshooting teams were at their peak, almost all the USAF men shot release triggers and many of the Army team wanted to. At the time, their commanding officer wasn't convinced of the advantages, but today he uses one! These men were top-flight shooters who shot every day, training for International competition shooting. They had access to every available system in the field of shooting and the time and facilities to experiment with them. It is significant that many of these good shooters chose the release trigger and credited it for marked improvements in their performances. In some cases, the release trigger took them into the superstar category. One was Tom Garrigus, who in his first International level competition, won the Silver Medal at the Mexico Olympics with 196/200. Another was Terry Howard who blasted the awesome unofficial world record of 299/300. Ken Jones, who won the world championship in 1966 with the official world record score of 297/300, also subsequently turned to the release. All three were USAF shooters.

"They hadn't turned to release triggers to avoid flinching but believed they were an advantage to good shooting," Partridge recalls. "They made me conduct a simple, but dramatically effective experiment. With an empty shell in my gun, I called for a target and pulled the trigger as if for a normal shot. It was impossible not to notice how the barrels flipped downwards as I jerked the gun on firing — by pulling the trigger. Other people did exactly the same. Then we tried the same operation with a release trigger gun. At the moment of 'firing', by releasing the trigger, the barrels remained perfectly stable and continued their swing through the target without the dip caused by pulling."

It was smoother, because it is difficult to make a sudden muscular contraction without sometimes jerking the object held. Add the undeniable tension of competitive shooting and there's a lot of tension going into that pull. To release the trigger is merely a muscular relaxation. As such, it is an easier function for the body, is faster and involves the use of fewer muscles — the seats of tension. In any game where a ball is struck or thrown, all are releases rather than contractions of muscles. The nearest sport to shooting, archery, also is a release of already contracted muscles; a release of tension, instead of its creation.

It is an aid to concentration at the vital moment of calling for the target. If you're not concentrating, the gun will go off and rudely wake you up! In cold weather, when your frozen finger is insensitive to the feel of the trigger,

the release man has no problem and also can wear warm gloves for comfort. He just pulls back until he hears the setting click and then relaxes the finger muscles to fire.

But if you're going to try a release trigger, it's a good idea to do some dry firing first. This way, you get the feel of it without embarrassing yourself by inadvertently letting off a couple of shots at the club.

That brings us to the consideration of safety. Although a release trigger will occasionally be let off inadvertently, I have seen conventional guns let off unintentionally. Providing shooters follow the most basic safety requirements of always pointing the gun in a safe direction, there is no more problem with a release trigger than with a normal one — with one exception.

On an American trap range, it is possible for an inexperienced trapper to stick his head up from the trap house instead of his red flag. Construction of the International trap bunker tends to preclude this. It is therefore vital on any trap where a release trigger is being used, that the shooter should inform the trapper either personally or through the referee or puller.

The functioning of a release trigger generally is simple. When the trigger is pulled, the sear drops out of the bent in the normal manner, but the hammer is detained by a form of detent hook engaging on a platform cut into the hammer. When pressure on the trigger is released, the detent slides off the hammer, which then strikes the firing pin in the usual way.

On the over/under, most shooters have a release on the bottom barrel and a standard pull on the top, although for doubles some people shoot the double release system — setting the top release trigger during the swing from the first target to the second.

On an automatic or a pump — once converted — the system is release only for either singles or doubles. If your release trigger is set and you don't want to fire — a broken target or slow pull — there is no problem to un-set it. On an over/under or single, keep the pulling (i.e.: setting) pressure on the trigger. Holding the gun back into the shoulder, reach over with your left hand and break open the action. It may seem difficult at first, but it soon becomes second nature. With an automatic you can open the action, but it is easier to have a disconnector fitted. Pump gun users merely open the action with the normal slide release.

The release system is primarily applicable to American and International trap, with a few shooters using the double release system for doubles. They include Tom Garrigus,

Clyde Purbaugh, inventor and gunsmith, poses with some of the numerous trophies he has won on the claybird range. His experience has helped in shotgun developments.

now an Ithaca district sales manager, who won the industry class high-all-around and high-over-all titles at the 1972 Grand American, using release all the way. Some American skeet shooters have adopted it and one International skeet shooter's scores improved greatly after turning to the release, despite the fact that the gun must be brought into the shoulder from the hip! It is neither practical nor safe to use for hunting, in my opinion.

Al Timney adds the following comments: "Many non-flinching, long-yardage shooters favor the release as they say it gives them a faster, smoother swing than a pull trigger. Many shooters are over-concerned with the speed of their release, generally wanting them very fast. The type and speed of release varies with every type of gun. There is an area for adjustment of the release speed, but it takes an experienced release shooter to know what's right for his particular gun and style of shooting."

For many years the release was considered "an old man's system," but more and more shooters, regardless of age, are taking to them. Timney has found women to be unsuited to using the release, but he's not too sure why. In common with other experts in this specialized field, he stresses how important it is for a shooter wanting his gun converted to a release system to be sure to take it to a gunsmith specifically qualified to undertake the delicate work. Some of his models feature release adjustment with an eccentric cam screw and he even has a special one for a Model 12 Winchester which incorporates both pull and release systems, depending which way you push the safety.

B. (Mac) McDaniel of Grosse Pointe Park, Michigan, has been entrusted by the Ithaca Gun Company with the con-

version of all release trigger mechanisms on their imported Perazzi guns. His twenty-nine years of gunsmithing also include experience in tool, die, instrument and even watch-making, along with laboratory research into metallurgy. He feels the release trigger — properly fitted and tuned to gun and shooter — can be of considerable help to the competitive shooter. Like Timney, he has come across many so poorly designed and fitted as to be more hindrance than help. He says all parts should be made from good steels, suitable for heat treatment to be wear resistant and to maintain original dimensions. This allows the shooter to develop his technique, without fear that his release will change from wear or springiness. Also, the trigger should not bind through the raised temperatures of constant firing, as this would give the shooter one more variable with which to contend.

For general use, McDaniel suggests a set of forty to fifty ounces and a release of ten ounces. To slow down the mechanism, he advocates a longer hook engagement with considerably more setting power. He is not in favor of screw adjustments as he feels they are prone to vibrate loose with prolonged firing. He agrees with Timney about the problems of individual tuning, having found that he has tuned a release system to technical perfection, only to find that, due possibly to some peculiarity of the shooter's gun and the way he handles it, the man has been unable to shoot with it satisfactorily.

Different aspects of tuning can be achieved by altering the angle of either the release hook and/or the hammer platform and by using stronger or weaker sear or main springs. A major problem in tuning the release is that, if you don't want one that goes off too fast, the longer hook engagement necessary can tend to hang up and not disengage. If you want one that is fast, the shorter engagement can turn out to be too short, the release operates faster than you intend and you fire before reaching the target. Taken a stage farther, the fast extreme can even cause the gun to go off when you set it, as the engagement, through wear, can become insufficient for the hook to hold the hammer.

"In my experience, release triggers tend to go off too fast, causing the shot to be delivered below the target," Derek Partridge tells me. "This is due to the reduction of the time which usually allows for the continued gun movement or swing — which gives the follow-through necessary to place the shot charge ahead of the target's flight path.

"Frank Pachmayr recently built a release trigger for my detachable Perazzi mechanism which has succeeded in overcoming this problem. The metal parts are properly hardened so that no wear occurs. Apart from the hook/platform angles and relationship, he has slowed it down by increasing the setting pressure. If the setting pressure (equivalent to the pull pressure on a normal trigger) is light — say 2½ pounds — it requires little muscular finger force to hold it and it therefore is released by the most minimal relaxation of the contracted finger muscles and naturally this makes for an ultra-fast release.

"If you double the setting pressure to five pounds, you double the amount of muscular pressure required to set and hold it and this, in turn, doubles the amount of time it takes to release the increased pressure, thus effectively slowing the release time. I have used the Pachmayr release for over a year now and tested both setting and release poundages after each use. They have remained absolutely constant and the performance is equally reliable."

But let's look at one more safety consideration. At any gun club there often are many almost identical, mass-produced guns, with the danger that a shooter can pick up someone else's gun. This may be fitted with a release trig-

COMPANION (FOLDED)

For the man who doesn't want to carry around a long gun case, J.L. Galef & Son, a New York arms import firm, has come up with this single-barrel folding shotgun in numerous specs.

ger. When it fails to fire as the unsuspecting shooter pulls the trigger, the gun is likely to go off as he lowers it from his shoulder to see what went wrong. The gun could give him a nasty kick in his chest, waist or groin. For this reason, it is imperative for all release trigger makers and converters to mark every gun so fitted with a universally agreed, tastefully designed sticker incorporating a red lightning bolt and the words, Release Trigger. To emphasize this point, the situation described above did happen with fatal results.

Whether you decided or decide to try a release because you flinch or simply feel it will be advantageous to your shooting, make sure it is fitted by a proven, highly competent specialist and, unless you are exceptionally skilled yourself, let the same man do any tuning or subsequent alterations to it.

In late 1973, when the Garcia Corporation introduced the Beretta BL-2/S, a new over/under shotgun, they boasted about some unique features.

Their big news about the gun was a new selective trigger. This Beretta selective speed-trigger, as it was called by Garcia, was claimed to be extremely fast in operation, completely selective, easy to use and completely dependable.

The trigger is simple to use. Unlike ordinary single selective triggers, the Beretta Speed-Trigger has a double crescent shape and is pivoted in the middle. In firing the normal bottom barrel/top barrel sequence, the shooter simply pulls the top part of the trigger, lets his finger slide down past the pivot point, and pulls the bottom part of the trigger for his second shot.

There is no separate thumb-activated selector located in the upper tang as with most single selective triggers. Instead, the trigger itself is the selector. But I can't help feeling that, like release triggers, this is going to call for some shooter re-education!

Beretta's BL-2/S over/under shotgun features what they call a speed trigger. On rotating axis, pressure at the top or bottom of trigger determines which barrel fires.

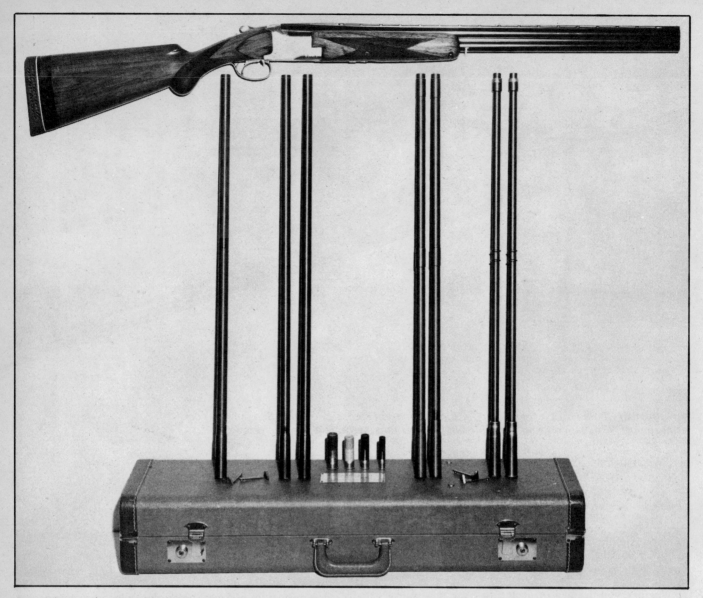

Standard over/under, with these conversion tubes in various chokes and gauges which can be changed with little difficulty, comes close to creating dreamed of all-purpose shotgun.

Now if you were seeking America's premier gunsmith; a man who the USAF in 1966 flew to their Air Force Academy in Colorado Springs to act as technical advisor and official gunsmith during the world championship military skeet matches, you would call on the proprietor of Multi-Gauge Enterprises, in Monrovia, California. Claude Purgaugh, by his own admission, is a lucky guy because after 5 p.m. he is able to combine his vocation and avocation into the same operation. Claude and his right-hand man, Emil Schultz, perform a complete gunsmithing service. They accept any firearm, but their specialty is shotguns and especially the manufacturing and fitting of full length tubes or auxiliary barrels by means of which a shotgun can be converted quickly to another gauge with the use of only a small plastic hammer. Changing the tubes from one gauge to another in no way makes the gun unsuitable for the shotshell it originally was built to handle.

These full length conversion tubes were designed,

perfected and patent applied for by Purbaugh in 1958. His company is the only producer of full length shotgun tubes in this country.

Over 10,000 have been made and sold since he conceived them in 1957, and the backlog of orders keeps piling up. They are now a common sight in the field or at the skeet range.

Purbaugh had been a hunter and clay bird shooter all his life. In 1957 he bought a new gun for dove and quail shooting: a Browning over and under, 12-gauge Pigeon grade with both barrels in open choke. To warm up and get acquainted with this gun, he went to a skeet range. The skeet bug bit him, resulting in the present line of conversion tubes and Claude becoming a nationally known skeet champion.

Before he got a chance to improve his standings he underwent chest surgery for cancer, losing four ribs which left his heart area covered with only skin and muscle.

Of strong will and rugged physique his recovery was

The Purbaugh tubes extend beyond the muzzle of the gun, as is the case on this Browning over/under. With each gun, the tubes must be a tight fit.

fast and he soon was shooting skeet again, but the recoil of a 12-gauge gun was too much for him at this stage of his comeback, so for about a year he shot all four stages of skeet with a Winchester Model 42 in .410 bore, raising his overall average to ninety-four percent. But all the time, he was wishing he could use his beautiful 12-gauge Browning. One day the answer hit him — use an auxiliary chamber or tube, thus permitting the use of all the lighter loads in the one big bore gun. He could find nothing on the market here or abroad that gave the consistent results required for a top skeet shooter.

Being a do-it-yourself guy, he designed and made what has become known as the "full length Purbaugh tube" custom fitted to each gun; at last America's shotgunners could master one gun and fire it for game birds in the field and clay birds on the skeet range.

In 1958, he equipped his Browning with a Hydro-coil stock, keeping recoil to a minimum. By now he was shooting .410, 28 and 20-gauge tubes in his Browning. He got such good results with the 20-gauge load in the all-gauge event that he never has gone back to the 12. Why fool around with a 12 when you can make runs of 100 x 100 with the 20 or 28 gauge?

Using the three sets of tubes in his over and under gun, he fired his first registered four-category skeet match at Fresno in 1959 and was runner-up for the state championship.

By now both the design and production bugs had been worked out of the tubes and their outstanding performance proven both in the game fields and on the skeet range. In 1959 Claude averaged ninety-seven percent on 4,800 birds in the 12-gauge races with the little guns. Alex Kerr, using a pair of 28-gauge tubes during a Canadian duck hunt, outshot his companions. In 1963, Purbaugh won the world's championship at Rochester in the sub-senior division; at the Inter-Americano Torneo De Skeet in 1965 in Puerto Rico,

In fitting the full-length conversion tubes, a good deal of hand work is required for each individual shotgun.

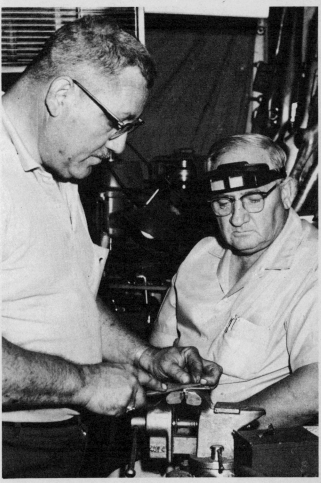

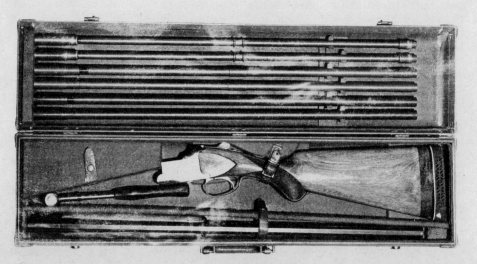

Overall shot of over/under illustrates how tubes fit.

he won the 28-gauge cup with a straight run of 100 x 100, and teaming up with Pepe Freiria of San Juan, he won the two-man 20-gauge event. His trophy collection has grown to over four hundred pieces.

Most skeet shooters are seeking constantly the one ideal, universal gun that will permit them to excel. Purbaugh tubes are a solution to this problem. The action, trigger pull, drop, barrel length, rib, sights and forend remain the same for all events. The weight varies from two to five ounces, depending on the gauge being used. Experienced skeet shooters say the heavier gun permits a smoother swing and follow through for high skeet scores.

A complete skeet outfit using one gun and three sets of *tubes* (.410, 28 and 20-gauge) is less expensive than four separate high grade guns, or one gun and three separate sets of *barrels*.

These tubes are machined from a solid bar of 7075 T6 aluminum especially heat-treated to increase the tensile strength by 10,000 pounds. The bore is made in two passes with a two-step gun drill; choked, then polished to a fine finish. After various other operations and special fitting they are anodized, leaving a hard, long-lasting surface that does not build up with fouling. Each tube is fitted with the proper extractor and both are clearly marked as to gauge, et cetera.

At first the extractors were a three-piece welded and machined assembly; today they are of 4130 chrome-moly alloy steel made in one piece by investment casting. All tubes and extractors are custom fitted to the barrel they are to be used in to assure correct fit and perfect bore alignment and are not interchangeable. Before installing a tube in the 12-gauge or host barrel, it (the barrel) must be carefully and completely cleaned because of the tight, precise fit at the three points where the tube bears: muzzle, midway and near the breech. No further cleaning is necessary when switching from one tube to another.

All guns must be sent to Multi-Gauge not only for tube fitting but, in the case of single triggers, the mechanism must be modified so the light recoil of the .410 sets the trigger for the second shot. Once modified, the unit usually works better than before for all loads.

Any over-and-under, side-by-side, or single-barrel shotgun can be fitted with tubes as well as most automatic and pump guns. The side-by-side shotguns with the beautiful Damascus barrels which were in their heyday half a century ago can be rejuvenated and made safe for today's loads with a set of Purbaugh tubes, in the next smaller gauge, thus being made into a good useful firearm again while still retaining collector value.

The full length tube gives a more consistent pattern quality than the auxiliary chamber or the short tubes. A tube shorter than the host barrel permits the pellets to bounce around more, the burning gases expand, cooling in the process thereby reducing the powder burning rate and reducing the velocity. The jump the charge takes from the shell to the short tube and from the short tube to the barrel builds up heavy powder and metal fouling frequently causing wads to tip and spoil the pattern quality.

The auxiliary chambers and short tubes are less expensive than the full length custom fitted ones and do permit a shooter to start skeet shooting with the minimum cash outlay.

Included with the Purbaugh tubes are all the tools one needs to make the conversion even while in the field.

This line reproduction illustrates the theory used to reduce recoil by Akroeez. The gun is held so that the hook, on a steel shank, goes under armpit for holding.

There is at least one further approach for fighting recoil and an extremely effective one, at that. It has been used to a limited extent on high-powered rifles, but much less on shotguns. This is the hook-type stock and it really is a thoroughly radical innovation. It consists of a wood stock, shorter by several inches than the standard pattern. A steel shank extends rearward from the lower edge of the stock, extending upward into a hook-like projection.

In use, the steel shank goes beneath the shooter's armpit and the hook is pressed forward firmly, bearing against the rear surface of the shooter's shoulder. For a person of average build, strength, it is not at all difficult to apply forty pounds or more of static forward thrust to the gun, between right and left hands and it is this forward thrust that soaks up the force of recoil at the instant of firing.

As of press-time, hook-type stocks — under the brand name of Akroeez, are being sold and/or installed by Conrad H. Campos, a gunsmith in Tonopah, Nevada. The Akroeez unit can be adjusted to suit the shooter's personal preference and dimensions and, for those with a severe physical problem, it well may represent the most effective approach to solving the problem.

Every catalog listing shotguns discusses the type of sights on the gun, yet I find that the average claybirder and even most hunters tend to ignore their sights completely. They can be termed an unnecessary convenience in most cases, since the shooter is looking along the barrel of his gun, but really is gazing far beyond the end of it, concentrating upon his target. In fact, the shooter who tends to look at the sights is going to miss a lot of what he really should be looking at.

But there are special situations in which a sight becomes an aid. With the slug gun, for instance, the only legal firearm for deer hunting in some states, sights become something of a must.

When a one-power scope is mounted on a slug gun, this is what one sees. Photo was actually made through the scope.

The Ithaca Gun Company came up with a configuration on their Model 37 Deerslayer that incorporates iron sights on the rear of the barrel with a front sight of fluorescent pink plastic topping a ramp. The plastic sight — called the Kaybar — is easy and fast to pick up against almost any background. The Model 37 has an interchangeable barrel feature, the Deerslayer barrel is designed so a scope can be mounted on the rear of the barrel atop the integral strip

Ithaca Model 37, with Deerslayer barrel, had receiver tapped to hold the scope mounts. At the distance shown, the proper eye relief was attained. Note the iron sights on the barrel.

that carries the open rear sight. The base is grooved to accept a variety of tip-off mounts.

Dean Grennell tried one of these combinations, using the Bushnell Scopechief IV one-power shotgun scope. This is an unusual looking instrument with a rear eye-piece nearly twice the diameter of the one-inch tube. Therein, Grennell reports, lies most of the secret of the scope's effectiveness under difficult lighting conditions. The rear lens, 1.8 inches in diameter, presents an exit pupil fully 15 millimeters in diameter with six inches of eye relief. That can be a comfort when working with a kicking shotgun.

When you throw a gun topped with this scope to your shoulder, the rear of that sight looks as big as a porthole and you can move your eye over a wide area without losing the image.

In this case, Grennell had the Ithaca receiver drilled and tapped to accept Bushnell's universal mounts. "The recoil of maximum-load 12-gauge shells is considerable and a number were set off in testing and evaluation," Grennell relates. "Throughout the process, the scope remained solidly mounted and unmoved."

By way of checking out the potential of the Ithaca/Bushnell combo, factory slug loads by Federal were fired off the bench at fifty yards. With one three-shot group, the Federal rounds spanned 1.432-inch from center to center — better than Grennell has experienced with some rifle calibers. While the scope involved offers no magnification at all, it does provide cross-hairs for precise aiming, as well as the earlier mentioned light-gathering qualities for bad light shooting.

Following a not-so-similar premise, the R.W. Weaver Company came up with an item called the Qwik-Point. It is similar to a telescopic sight in general appearance and in the manner of mounting, but there similarity ends. Unlike conventional scopes, the Qwik-Point does not magnify and it has no need nor provision for focusing.

The Qwik-Point can be used in firing with one or both eyes open, from any distance behind the eye-piece at which the image remains visible, eye relief thus being unimportant.

Conventional elevation and windage knobs provide adjustment to align the Qwik-Point to the point of impact with any given gun. One click of adjustment with either knob moves the setting by a quarter of an inch at a distance of forty yards; a bit over one-half minute of angle per click. The illuminated red circle, which serves as a reticle for the Qwik-Point, covers an area of about eight inches at forty yards — or twenty minutes of angle.

The red spot does not depend upon batteries or a bulb, but is picked up and redirected through available light upon a short length of slender, red plastic rod enclosed by a transparent dome at the front end of the unit. This is reflected downward by a front-surface mirror at the rear, thus directing the image through a collimating lens so that the point of light remains stationary upon the target, even though the eye is moved slightly. Thus the problems of parallax are minimized or eliminated.

The Qwik-Point is available in two versions: The S-1 is for mounting on pump or autoloading shotguns with the 8A Weaver base. This is attached to the receiver by drilling and tapping. A second version, the R-1, is intended for use on rifles or even handguns.

The Qwik-Point unit is sealed with O-rings and filled with dry nitrogen to assure freedom from fog problems and is recoil-tested to resist stresses equal to 1600 times the force of gravity. The body and lower portion are of black-anodized aluminum alloy. Weight of the S-1 model is 7¾ ounces.

Jack Lewis, who performed one of the earliest tests on this gimmick, recalls that he used birds from a Trius trap during his investigations.

"I held the gun with the butt at my waist," he recalls.

Model 37 Ithaca allows interchange of barrels. Deerslayer turns it into adequate slug gun.

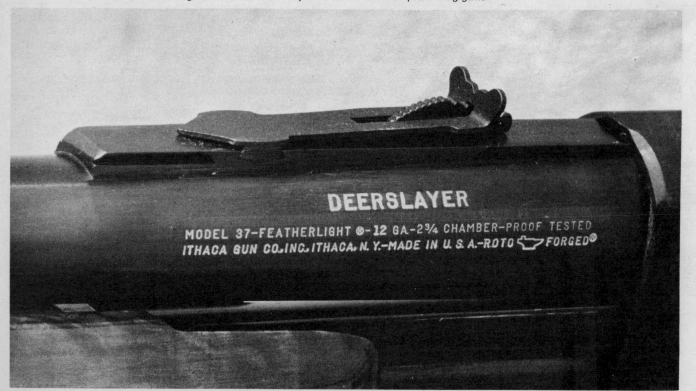

"When the bird appeared on signal, I brought the gun to my shoulder, half seeing the red dot, as I pulled the trigger. The bird shattered at thirty-odd yards and there was a sensation that didn't feel right. Then I realized that I hadn't been watching the dot. I had been concentrating on the bird."

With the next claybird, he made a point of tracking it through the scope-like mechanism, superimposing the red dot over the flying form before pulling the trigger. That bird also shattered into powder.

"When we launched doubles the first time, I missed them both," Lewis says, "but, at least, I knew why. The red dot and the birds were far from together in both instances. In fact, on the second shot, I think I ignored the dot, reverting to type and over-swinging before I triggered.

"In analyzing the sight on a shotgun, I can't say that it made my shooting any better, but it did make it easier. I didn't have to concentrate as much as I do normally to break a bird."

In the matter of game bird shooting, Lewis feels that the sight could afford definite advantages for shots not beyond thirty-five yards. "But in an instance where one would have to visibly lead his game, it could create some problems for me, since I don't possess a computer-like mind," he concludes.

I guess every hunter is looking for a faster and easier way in which to get his shells out of his pocket, shell bag or whatever and into his gun during the height of shooting action. Over the years, I've seen dozens of inventions aimed at doing just that.

A couple of years back, there was a case worn on the belt that had the shells stacked in line, so that they could be pulled out from the bottom one at a time, being held in place by a series of spring clips. I don't know how that item fared, but more recently a vest has been introduced with a similar idea. It's called the Super Vest and is constructed of polyester and cotton fabric. It holds thirty 12-gauge shells.

The idea is that you just grab the shell protruding from the bottom of the vest and pull it down and out. Each time a shell is removed from a dispenser, another shell slips into position. And to prove that a lot of thought went into this item, the designer has included a vinyl game bag, a wallet pocket to hold your hunting license and a pouch for empty shells. Only time will tell, of course, whether this and similar concepts will be accepted by hunters.

The gimmicks I've mentioned are simply some that have caught my fancy, either because they have practical application or because I have something of a Rube Goldberg complex. The list, of course, is endless and there never is likely to be an end to new inventions, more appearing each year, attempting to gain the interest of the target shotgunner and the hunter.

Every year, at such institutions as the National Sporting Goods Association show, new products are introduced. Many are the brainstorms of hunters who have decided the world is waiting for their own personal gimmicks. Some of these items make the grade, while others appear, then disappear just as rapidly when it becomes obvious that they are a bit too out of the ordinary for the average shooter.

A few years ago, I ran across a gent who had devised a simple device which was attached to the muzzle of his gun to give him an idea of how much to lead a duck. Actually, it was little more than a bent coat hanger hung on the muzzle, the ends bent up at an angle. The idea was that when he put the bent end of the wire on the duck, he had the proper lead. As I recall, all of this was based upon the idea that every duck would be flying past at exactly thirty-five yards.

But more recently, I discovered that a similar but more sophisticated device is being marketed by Donald D. Ritter of Canoga Park, California. He calls his device the Duk Hit shotgun sight, which he says is "designed to automatically calculate the required lead for birds at all distances within

The Weaver-designed and produced Qwik-Point is available for rifles as well as shotguns.

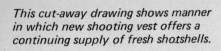

This cut-away drawing shows manner in which new shooting vest offers a continuing supply of fresh shotshells.

PAT. PEND

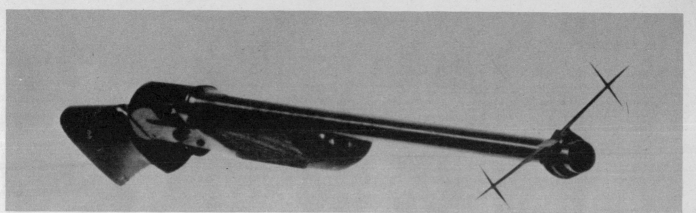

Above: Duk Hit sight is installed on shotgun; it has been designed so as not to damage blue on the barrel. (Right) Illustrates theory used in shooting with Duk Hit.

the effective range of the shotshell. Birds are almost assured, as you pick up your birds faster with this crosshair sight. The natural way to shoot is to look at what you're shooting and this sight allows you to focus your attention directly on the bird."

According to Ritter, the unit slips on the barrel of either 12 or 16-gauge guns in a few seconds and is guaranteed not to mar the blued finish. The unit is made of polypropylene, so weighs less then half an ounce, not making your gun more muzzle-heavy than it is. It also is gun blue in color to match the gun's finish.

I haven't tried this myself, so I can't vouch for it, but it sounds like an improvement on the coat hanger.

Before empty cans became ecologically important, this hurling device was available to launch so-called dead soldiers into the wild blue, affording shooters a cheap target.

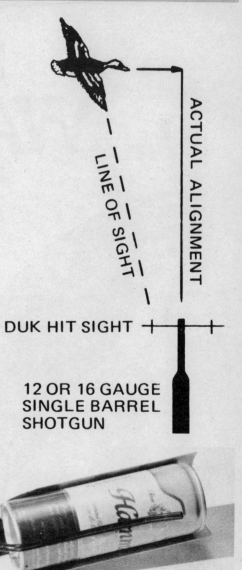

ACTUAL ALIGNMENT

LINE OF SIGHT

DUK HIT SIGHT

12 OR 16 GAUGE SINGLE BARREL SHOTGUN

WINGING IT FOR WATERFOWL

*Techniques For Learning To Shoot Ducks
And Geese Are Acquired Through Trial And
Error, Not Out Of Books — Even This One!*

As I MENTIONED earlier, being able to shoot and being able to tell others how to shoot become two entirely different situations. For example, I've known any number of excellent trap and skeet shots who simply could not shoot waterfowl. Let's face it: this is a different kind of shooting, for this is where one more factor must be introduced to your mental computer and integrated with all of the other things you have come to know about shotgunning.

In rifle or handgun shooting, a beginner can read about marksmanship principles, study positions, trigger squeeze and sight picture. He then can turn in a decent performance with a smallbore gun, moving on to center-fire shooting, when he has gained efficiency and know-how.

But this isn't true of shotgunning, I feel. In spite of the fact that there are literally hundreds of books — past and present, including this one — the definitive book on the shotgun art has not been written yet.

In duck shooting, for example, this is where you get into range estimation and you also have to recognize species. I

With a brace of geese resulting from his calling efforts, Jim Dougherty pauses to look at the evening skies of a barley field in Southern California's Salton Sea area.

took a friend of mine out once, who was about a 98 average skeet shooter, but he never had shot ducks before. He had tough luck, because he couldn't accept the fact that a mallard duck is about three times as large as a skeet target. Needless to say, perhaps, when the duck looks the same size as a claybird, it is at least three times as far away!

To be a good duck shot, one enters a much more sophisticated, even esoteric area. You come to know by the wing beat how far away that bird is flying, then you try to estimate your leads. And if you don't recognize the species, you're not going to have any concept of how far to get ahead, because a mallard at forty yards looks like a balloon. At sixty yards, he still looks to be within range, if you've never seen one before.

This newcomer from the skeet fields shot about ten boxes of shells at mallards and wounded one bird. He was shooting a three-inch magnum and, when I came to his blind, he was sitting in the bottom of it with tears in his eyes. Part of that was caused by mortification and more of it by pain. He had caught the recoil at one point and one of his teeth literally was sticking through his lip.

The best way I know of learning to shoot ducks is to be with someone in a blind, who will tell you when they are in range and what your lead should be. It doesn't guarantee you'll score big, but you won't miss as often.

Alex Kerr is a prime example. I have seen him shoot a 10-gauge using 3½-inch shells with a two-ounce load of 4s in a double barrel Parker. And he shot ducks at eighty yards. I had heard people talk of shooting ducks at that range, but until I saw it, I didn't believe it.

He'd pull the trigger, then we'd wait for a count of about two. Suddenly a duck would drop. But Alex Kerr has a very special kind of a brain. He can compute how far to lead on a target he has never seen before. I can't do that. Unless that picture is familiar to me. I can only make a wild guess.

I once asked Kerr how far he led on shots like that. His instant reply was, "Twenty-two feet."

To shoot like that you have to be fully familiar with a lot of things, including ballistics. Like you have to know what twenty-two feet looks like when you're shooting at a bird eighty yards away. For that kind of arithmetic, I have to pace it off on a floor or use a steel tape!

A gent named Norman Nelson, Jr., has had some interesting experiences along this line and has come up with some answers that might prove helpful to some would-be shooters. At least, I found some of his anecdotes educational after I asked him how his adventures with a shotgun began:

"My long and painful chilled shot odyssey began years ago, when my well-intended father gave me a 20-gauge Iver Johnson single-shot that had been his boyhood gun. It's still in my possession. The little barrel is choked within an inch of its life. Even with small shot sizes, it performs like your garden hose when you screw down the nozzle to let the neighbor's dog have it on the far side of your yard. It's probably the worst kind of beginner's shotgun — lots of

Placement of decoys around a blind is an important part of planning for your duck hunt, with choosing location.

recoil, thanks to its light weight and super-full choking that would tax an expert.

"Worse yet, I had bad luck the first time I fired at flying birds. I knocked down two ducks with one shot There wasn't a happier kid in the world when the two bufflehead plummeted down with dual splashes. But it was years before I could hit anything on the wing again and the letdown was terrific.

"At age 12, I inherited my grandfather's Savage 12-gauge pump, a hammerless model made briefly in the Twenties. This was an improvement. Even with 1¼-ounce loads, the heavier pump wasn't the recoil sadist that the little 20 bore was and perhaps the choke was not as full.

"Then a strange, split personality began to reveal itself in my shooting. We were primarily a family of serious duck hunters, shooting almost always over decoys. I had a terrible time hitting ducks in the air. But when the morning flight was over, I would hike into the nearby forest and hunt ruffed grouse. Here I had some successes. And they baffled me.

"Why could I hit fast, erratic grouse dodging through thick, young aspens and yet fail repeatedly on ducks slowing down to landing speed over decoys and flying reasonably straight?

"It wasn't the gun. I knew enough to realize that my heavy, full-choked pump was not ideal for grouse. The ruffs were frequently badly shot up. But this meant I was making hits despite the handicap of unopened shot charges at close range."

The war intervened, but in 1946 Nelson was a civilian again.

"Rusty from a two-year layoff, I wasn't facing opening day with any confidence as my father and I, in two duck boats, threaded down an old drainage ditch into a big wild rice lake. It was already shooting time. Four strung-out teal suddenly bore down paralleling the ditch. Dad didn't see them, but I dropped my paddle, grabbed the Savage and made a triple for the first time. Shortly, a splashy beating of wings made me twist around, gun in hand, as a bad greenhead erupted out of the rice. He was out a bit, but the shot crumpled him."

Slowly, the first glimmer of a Great Truth began drawing on him. He shot best when surprised. This was why he could nail grouse, though they were obviously tougher targets than ducks in landing patterns over decoys. Both the teal and the mallard had caught him by surprise, yet the result was four consecutive hits. Here was a fascinating theorem to chew on and there were similar incidents in his hunting history to corroborate it.

"At this point, I should have switched to pure jump shooting as long as I insisted on being a hunter of ducks above all else. But I stuck with decoy shooting on the basis that it was easier, more promising shooting for a poor shot as well as more exciting when one saw birds coming in. Thus I missed the point of the great discovery about shooting best when surprised."

The surprise element was only a symptom of the basic problem, which is widespread among shooters. Nelson was too uptight to do good wingshooting. He was trying too hard. By the time ducks completed their preliminary circuit and came in over decoys, he'd be a nervous, dry-mouthed wreck, gripping his gun so tightly that any chance of a smooth, relaxed swing and follow-through was impossible.

"More, I was using the worst possible style of lead calculation for a shooter in my psychological condition. Those two bufflehead years ago had been hit by arbitrarily picking a zone ahead of them and shooting into it."

Anti-aircraft theory calls this barrage fire; a given zone is blanketed with flak through which approaching bombers must fly to target.

With enough batteries firing, it can be effective. However, a shotgunner has only one gun, a limited number of shots, and no sophisticated fire control instruments to help pick the zone. Also, birds can and do often turn or flare, whereas the bombing plane is committed to straight flight to aim its load. Zone shooting with a shotgun usually means missing by shooting behind, although it can be useful in short-range skeet.

Nelson says his psychological condition and mechanical approach compounded each other's felonies; and he continued to miss ducks over decoys or on pass with truly comical consistency. Trap-shooting sessions were of no help. Awaiting the claybird tightened him up just as badly as seeing a flock of scaup whistling down upon him.

Scenes such as this Fall gathering in South Dakota have become less frequent as civilization has encroached upon the nesting grounds of waterfowl, thus reducing their reproduction rate. However, such organizations as Ducks, Unlimited, have done much to aid the habitat problem.

"Meanwhile, I reacted typically by starting the Great Shotgun Search. First, a Polychoke went on the Savage in the hope that broader patterns would make up for the bad shooting. It didn't, probably for the good reason that I was missing by yards rather than feet."

After another season of missed ducks, sorrow, and acid upset stomach, the aged Savage developed shell carrier troubles and Nelson bought a Winchester 24 double.

"This low-priced gun had enough excellent handling qualities to atone for some of my wingshooting sins. For one thing, it helped modify my tendency to shoot rigidly at a point ahead of the bird. The forward heft of the double often made me keep swinging a little whether I planned to or not.

"But in using a double, I mourned the loss of a third shot. If I missed with the first two, there was always the fond — and usually fictitious — hope that the third might connect, if available. If I did hit a duck or two, the third shot was genuinely useful to nail a lively cripple who'd otherwise get away by diving."

Nelson sold the double and bought an Ithaca pump. Its lightness was a willing accomplice to his ingrained tendency to stop his swing to zone-shoot, although he didn't realize it

at the time. Simply adding some lead ballast in place of the normal magazine plug would have eliminated this problem. Meanwhile, ruffed and sharptailed grouse, woodcock or duck who caught him unaware were in some peril, however, since he had no time to think about freezing his swing.

With the Ithaca, too, he tried a variable choke, a Cutts Compensator. Then he stopped hitting even the surprise shots on jumped birds and his despair knew no bounds. It was three years before if dawned on him that the bulk of the big choke device sharply raised the front sight plane. With no correlating increase in comb height, naturally the gun shot low, the worst of all possible sins on sharp-rising grouse or other birds.

"With confidence shattered, I bought a second-hand Model 11 Remington autoloader. To my surprise, I began making a limited number of hits. The muzzle-heaviness of the Browning-action Model 11 was doing its best to prevent me from stopping my swing, just as the double gun had. If this was good, more must be better. I unloaded the well-worn Model 11 and bought a then-new High Standard gas-operated autoloader.

These jobs have a lot of metal and weight out front. Some shooters dislike them for this reason and find them

Left: Hunter swings to catch up with fast-flying duck. Angle makes it look as though he will shoot behind bird. (Below) Sufficient decoys should be put out to convince overhead ducks it is worth dropping into pond for visit.

slow and perhaps clumsy to handle but for a swing-arrester the front end weight of the High Standard was a blessing in disguise. Once again Nelson was accomplishing swing and follow-through by accident of gun weight and balance. The latter is important. The same net gun weight distributed more toward the action and butt probably wouldn't have helped.

"To my astonishment, ducks began to fall over decoys or on the pass. Not fringe-caught cripples but well-riddled, very dead ducks. More amazing, it was generally the bird I was shooting at, not the second or third bird behind which usually had been guilty truth in the past."

Meanwhile, Nelson had a family and other distractions. Duck hunting became a pastime rather than a religion. Also, he moved West where duck and bird hunting was much better than in his native upper Midwest. If he missed a mallard, likely there'd be more right behind him in a few minutes.

In short, he started to relax. And that was even a bigger breakthrough than the mechanistic changes in going to a more ponderous, muzzle-heavy style of shotgun.

Because here is the great alchemy of wingshooting. It must be done well, naturally and easily. To be done well, there must be little or no brain-boggling attempt to second-guess the natural coordination of hand and eye that allows a shooter to swiftly, smoothly and habitually send a lethal pattern of shot on an interception course to a small, fast target. The beginner or problem shooter should be aware of this. Forget trying to work trigonometry in your head or consciously doping target lead in feet.

Try out your gun on a pattern sheet, while wearing hunt-ing clothes, to see where it's actually hitting. If it's placing a shot charge slightly high at thirty to forty yards, you're using a stock that fits reasonably well and a barrel that's straight. This should give you confidence that you're not being sabotaged by your gun.

Second, from pattern board shooting, you'll learn how your gun is really choked. It may be different from the barrel stamp legend. Since World War II, American hunters have gradually outgrown the belief that full choke should be the standard barrel for any right-thinking man. Tight, concentrated patterns are for the experts and even many of them prefer more open chokes for some gunning, at least with 12 gauge.

If your smoothbore is shooting those tight, fire-hose patterns typical of older full choking with modern shotshells, a good gunsmith should be able to ream and polish the choke open to a more practical degree. How much depends on what you hunt and your bore size. A reasonable full choke is still a good bet for a 20 gauge used for all-around water-fowling, for example.

For general use, however, an American hunter is well off with a modified choke 12 bore for ducks over decoys, jump shooting and on most pass situations, plus regular run of upland birds. If he wants to do a lot of forest grouse, wood-cock, or quail gunning, improved cylinder is excellent and still good for ducks over decoys or most pheasant hunting.

Another alternative is a variable choke device. Specify in advance that this will be properly concentric with the barrel to shoot where the gun looks. One advantage of these is that you can experiment with different loads and settings of choke to come up with the best combinations for your

Many hunters feel that suffering through the grayness of overcast, even foggy Fall days offers the best opportunity for taking waterfowl that tend to fly lower in poor weather.

This collection of calls should offer almost any type of enticement for overhead goose, drawing him in for look.

particular kind of game and shooting. You can beat the rap on the higher front sight of a choke by either restocking or adding a rubber cheek piece to prevent shooting low.

But the most important thing is to relax even on anticipated shots and do your gun mounting and snapshooting at the last possible second. The marvelous human faculty for eye-hand-brain coordination will carry you through, if you give it a chance to work by instinct, aided by a few basic habits and a reasonable shotgun fit. Some of the good habits include keeping your head down to avoid over-shooting, carrying some weight balanced on the left foot forward (for right-handers), and swinging from the hips. Drills of

Stubble fields such as this, which still contain grain enough to offer feed, tend to draw geese, but these hunters would be more successful with camouflage gear.

gun mounting in your living room can help instill these habits.

"A combination of relaxation and unstrained snapshooting can be formidable," Nelson contends. "Gunning in a heavy fog, my companion and I had mallards coming in singles and pairs to his excellent calling. They'd materialize out of the abnormally thick mist at about thirty-five yards, seeing us simultaneously. There was no time for agonizing lead calculations — simply poke out and cut loose. We could take six mallards each in that flyway and we had them with almost indecent haste. Only a couple of birds left under their own power. But in a highly similar situation on another occasion, I went through almost a box of shells to take one mallard, simply because I was trying too hard."

The classic example of playing it loose versus being uptight began one afternoon when he quit duck hunting because of bluebird weather. Enroute back across a sedge marsh, his Laborador began to kick up jacksnipe. He had a handful of grouse loads in one pocket. With these ten shells and a casual attitude, he limited with eight jacksnipe. Next day, bubbling, Nelson went back to the same marsh with a companion.

"Trying too hard to uphold my reputation, I burned eighteen shells before guessing a bird, same gun, same ammunition, same targets, same conditions — but radically changed mental or emotional outlook."

The problem is, "relax" is much easier to say than do, but certain things help after the preliminaries of patterning your gun to help establish confidence. First, remember that you're out for fun and relaxation.

Hunting should not be regarded as success-or-failure drama. I've hunted with businessmen who were deadly on clays or crows, but pathetic on game birds. They regarded missing desireable, status targets as "failure," like missing a sale or a delivery schedule. Fearing it, they fell into it. This is an interesting phenomenon. If you put a long, four-inch beam on your floor, you could walk the length of it without a misstep or quiver. But introduce the element of fear by putting a two hundred-foot chasm under that beam and you'd probably fall, as I'm sure I would.

Above all, don't regard successful shotgunning and full bag limits as some manhood rite, carrying a lace pants stigma if not achieved. Avoid this like plague, particularly when coaching a youngster to shoot. Your biggest task will be to keep a boy from taking it too seriously, trying too hard. He'll impose his own performance pressures; don't worry about that.

In shooting ducks, I've found myself wondering why I was getting so many second-shot kills, missing with the first barrel for no apparent reason.

It took a degree of concentration and I found myself ignoring some of my own advice. I contend that one has to bring the comb of the shotgun up to the cheek so that he is staring straight down the barrel. All of this, of course, is pretty basic.

Most of us know that, if one lifts his head as little as a quarter-inch, he isn't looking where the gun is shooting. Not only will you shoot high, but at least in my case, I find myself stopping or slowing my swing down to shoot behind, just as a golf swing goes sour when you pick up your head.

There is a psychological urge, I suppose, to raise one's head to look at a big greenhead mallard coming your way and that's where the trouble comes in. In birds as hard to kill as mallards and sprig, it's important to get as much shot as possible in the bird's front half.

In the flurry of game bird shooting, one knows he misses but does not know why, and in most instances there cer-

In southern Texas, geese flock into Winter plantings, raiding the crops, but usually are careful enough to remain in the center of the field, far out of normal shotgun range.

tainly is no one watching, ready to tell him what he is doing wrong.

In the case of those second barrel kills, I finally doped it out that I was busy watching my bird on the first shot; my head was up. I didn't have the comb of the stock against my cheek until the second shot, the gun properly mounted.

Since, I've had a chance to watch some other shooters making the same mistake, and it seems as though it is almost impossible for the beginning or intermediate shotgunner not to lift his head and take a look at that bird out there just as he shoots. Ironically, the more difficult the conditions, when the birds are hardest to see or are driving downwind, every temptation is to get a better look. This is when the gun really has to be glued to your face.

Another thing I've noticed, too, in duck shooting is that it becomes a pretty impossible task to get that gun up to the shoulder and properly mounted if it is too long in the stock. Cutting the stock off a quarter of an inch on your duck gun can allow for extra clothing that you're sure to be wearing in the blind.

But for the man who doesn't want to reduce this length, there is an alternative that may help. This is simply to pull the left hand back a bit on the forend. Thus, when mounting, the gun is pushed away from the shoulder a fraction of an inch to compensate for the heavy clothing.

Another device that I've found detrimental to my own duck shooting, at least, is a non-slip recoil pad. This pad will invariably catch on the clothing, lousing up the mount when the gun is on the way up. My own cure for this was to get some of the smooth-surfaced plastic tape used by electricians. This can be applied over the non-slip surface and makes it easier to mount the gun without that possibility of the pad snagging.

There has been a good deal said about the matter of shot sizes in hunting ducks, but during a recent five days of constant hunting, I had an opportunity to do a lot of thinking along with my experimental shooting.

There have been people who have hunted my duck club without my knowledge, using 7½ and No. 8 shot on mallards, sprig and other grain-fat birds. As a result, I've found that some of them have crippled as many as fifteen birds and never picked one up.

I'm partial to my double barrel Parker 20-gauge. It has long been my pet and I have shot a lot of ducks with it, using No. 6 shot, alongside of friends with 12 gauges. I got my birds without any trouble, but during this recent outing for those big mallards at forty yards, I had to hit each bird with both barrels, and even then, a few cripples got away.

For the first time in fifteen years, I turned to a 12-gauge Browning over/under, improved modified and full, loaded with high base 4s. There was all the difference in the world. When that size shot slams into a bird, you know it is going to drop. Personally, I would much rather miss a duck or goose altogether than to cripple it, and I've found that No. 4 shot is just the ticket. In using the 12-gauge, it's not a matter of range so far as I'm concerned, but the killing factor that is most important.

At the other extreme, I know those who prefer still lighter gauges, but to me, the idea of shooting at big, beautiful greenheads with a .410 is the height of ego!

Too, I hear a lot of talk about how to lead a duck, but I've become pretty well convinced that this is not really the big problem. Instead, what the shooter must concentrate upon is the consistency of the swing. If he doesn't practice this facet, he'll never know how far to lead. The beginning duck hunter has been told so much about exaggerated leads

In the left photo above, the goose hunters are hidden among their decoys, covered by camouflage netting, which helps break up image. This allows them to observe movement of the overhead waterfowl and to get in position quickly (upper right) for their shots.

that he is liable to poke the gun blindly forty feet ahead, stop the swing and yank the trigger. Any one of these actions will get him a goose egg.

When the gun is properly seated and the shooter is looking down the barrel, at least he is going to be able to shoot where he is looking. Proper mounting and follow-through are all-important. The matter of lead, whether it's two duck lengths, nine lengths or fifty is something that will come only with time and shooting...but one must know how to shoot first!

As you may gather, I have been inclined to look askance at the light gauge shooters when it comes to wildfowl hunting, but I've never been able to forget the advice of an old English shotgunner.

"Pattern your gun to the game you're shooting," he always said. "Use smallbores only where you have controlled shooting." By the latter, he meant where you might find an abundance of game within range or in shooting ducks over decoys.

However, I've run across at least one situation that was seemingly built for the .410 shotgunner. That was sand grouse shooting in Kenya. It was unlike any type of shooting I've ever seen before, and I may never have the opportunity to see anything similar again.

But let me start at the beginning. The shoot took part during the filming of the initial segments of The American Sportsman television series. We had fished for Nile perch on Lake Rudolf, where a gentleman named Poole maintained a camp.

Poole is now dead. He was out in his Land Rover with a Catholic priest when their vehicle was halted by renegades from across the border of Somaliland. They killed both men in order to obtain their firearms, according to the report. Even while I was there, similar dangers apparently existed, for the border of the northern frontier was closed as a safeguard against similar incidents and our white hunters would take us nowhere near the place.

After the fishing expedition was filmed, we were taken by air to an oasis in the desert. Although it was only a forty-five minute flight, there was as much difference in terrain and inhabitants as night and day.

The area edging Lake Rudolf is as close to the surface of the moon as anything possible could be. It is nothing more than a volcanic waste, devoid of any vegetation. The tribe of natives living in the area subsist almost entirely upon a fish diet and, as a result, their bone formations suffer from malnutrition. To a man, when they walk, their knees appear

to be bent at first glance. Instead, it is a case of the bones of their legs and shins being bowed.

But at the end of the forty-five minute flight, one finds himself in an area of sand dunes and desert that could be the Sahara, and here the natives wear the heavy clothing of the Bedouin tribesmen. Camels are the chief mode of transportation, making the picture complete, if you are the romantic type.

The area into which Bill Ryan, one of the veteran professional hunters of Kenya, had brought us was an oasis and it was there that the sand grouse came for water. Apparently, it was the only moisture for miles about and, according to the natives, one could almost set his watch by their early morning arrival and a just as rapid departure. Just where they go after watering is a mystery to which no one I met, at least, seemed to have any answer.

Hunting with me on this particular outing was Joe Foss, who had brought along a Winchester Model 101 over/under. I had settled for my Browning Superposed. Since we had been warned that we would be limited as to the number of guns we would have room for, we both had settled on 12 gauges. The shells we had were high base loads, which proved to be more than we needed for this type of shooting. But let me describe it.

This African sand grouse is about the size of the more familiar white-winged dove, but instead of darting about, it tends to change directions in a swooping type of flight. This still makes for some interesting gunnery. Also, with their rapid arrival and departure, there is only a limited time in which one can shoot. But when they do come, it's like a swarm of bees. In some instances, the sky was literally black with them.

The problem here for the 12-gauge fancier is that the grouse, needing water badly, come in low in flights of ten to twenty. The sport is in picking a shot where you kill only one rather than three or four with a single pull of the trigger. In short, a man with no shooting talent could shoot fifty in a matter of minutes. This type of shooting would prove much more challenging to the .410 shooter than someone armed with a big bore gun, too, giving him a chance to choose his shots and prove his abilities. As I mentioned in the beginning, this parallels the controlled shooting suggested by my English friend.

One other thing about grouse shooting is the fact that the country is completely open so that there is no chance of cripples getting away.

I'd say, too, that this would be ideal shooting for a

One pair of Texas hunters rented stage donkey outfit from costume shop with the idea that it would help them get closer to geese that were feeding amid other livestock.

28-gauge and, under any circumstances, it can be classified among the experiences of a lifetime, but it also is an experience I'd not care to repeat too many times. It's a little like going to Egypt to look at the Pyramids; it's one of those things that everyone should do so long as he's there, but how many times would anyone care to look at the Sphinx?

The thing that would draw me back to Kenya much more quickly would be the opportunity to shoot that country's speckled pigeons. This is similar to our bandtail pigeon shooting here, and standing on a hilltop, trying to get on those pigeons which are bouncing about on a thirty-mile-per-hour tailwind is the most exciting challenge of my life!

Setting up the outer fringe of your decoys no more than forty yards from your blind insures that decoying flocks will be in range and establishes an accurate distance reference for you. On inland ponds and streams, six to a dozen decoys usually are sufficient for dabbling ducks. Over larger, open bodies of water, however, rigs of two dozen or more tend to be more effective on diving species.

Avoid setting up a blind with the wind at your face. Since ducks invariably try to land upwind, your position should permit them to come in from left or right or toward your blind, but not directly over you, going away.

This means that ducks crossing your stool downwind are on an inspection pass, don't intend to drop in and are moving at speeds that make them doubly hard to hit. If they

don't spot any suspicious looking objects or movement, they'll come back into the wind on the next run.

To assure this, remember to camouflage or cover any items of equipment that are shiny or bright in color. Pick up expended shells from ground or water around the immediate area of the blind.

Ducks don't like to set down on a crowded landing strip, so be sure to leave an open space inside a large set of blocks.

Under today's bag limits and point systems, proper identification of species, even by sex, is important. Work on your ability to distinguish one type from another by their most prominent markings at a distance, as well as by individual silhouettes and flight characteristics. It's actually more important to be able to tell one duck from another at forty yards, before you shoot, than when you have them in hand.

Goose shooting is similar to duck shooting only in some respects. Rather than putting my blind on the water, I've had much more success in setting up shop behind a corn shock or even camouflaged in a wheat field surrounded by decoys.

One of the more interesting types of goose hunting is done in the south Texas rice fields around San Antonio. In fact, a gent by the name of Marvin Tyler has made a career of hunting geese with his laundry bag!

It's an old technique, but Tyler, who operates near Eagle

Big problem in original concept described in text was geese hadn't seen donkey climb fence.

Lake, has perfected the method of moving out into a likely looking rice field, which has been harvested, but still furnishes winter feed for the geese from its secondary growth. With dozens of white dishcloths, bath towels, et al., he forms a circle of white, hanging the cotton on stalks and draping them to resemble feeding white geese. Then, with his hunters, he hunkers down under white sheets, a gun lying beside each man, loaded and on safe. They lay there amid this white camouflage and wait for the geese to arrive.

There is a technique to laying out the clothes and positioning the hunters so that the geese will be coming toward them rather than crossing. I guess there also must be a technique to operating a goose call while lying flat on your back beneath a sheet, but Marvin Tyler and his team of guides do all of these things well, for their hunters invariably go home with their limits of big birds.

In many areas near waterfowl preserves, such as the country out of Jet, Oklahoma, goose hunters favor pit blinds of a semi-permanent nature. In fact, I have seen some blinds complete with bottled gas heaters. The hunters remain hidden within the blinds, until signalled by a professional guide that the geese have been called within range. At a given signal, the camouflage coverings are thrown back and the shooting commences.

This can be called hunting in comfort, but there are too many variables. You are stuck in the blind with little opportunity to choose your own ground. If the wind is in the wrong direction, for example, the geese may not come over the blind all day.

My favorite type of goose weather is miserable. When you have blue skies and no clouds, geese tend to rise off their ponds, going straight up a thousand feet or so to level out for wherever they're going. And they seem to use the same routine to return to the pond. After all, an old gander didn't get that way by busting along at treetop level, daring hunters to empty a load of 2s or 4s at him.

But when it is raining or foggy, those big birds come in low and you would think slow, but don't be deceived by the latter. Even at such close ranges, you have to know your gun, your leads, the potential of the size shot you're using — and most of all — you have to know geese.

The Imperial Valley of Southern California has become a favorite goose hunting sector in recent years. In the past three decades or so, what once was barren desert country has been turned into lush farmlands by irrigation. Wheat, rice and barley are among the goose-drawing feeds that are grown there. The famed Salton Sea in the southern part of the valley is a favorite wintering spot for hundreds of thousands of the big birds and they do have to eat.

There amid the barley fields, one technique is to spot a dozen or more decoys, then lie beneath camouflage netting, waiting for the birds to come, as you call them in. The same technique seems to work on Canadian honkers, snow geese and the speckled variety.

Once the donkey-disguised hunters learned to move slowly, imitate animal, they scored well.

Most good goose callers will carry three calls. One will be tuned only for honkers, another of higher pitch for the squealing specks and snows, while the third call is adjustable. They will mix up the calls, since the idea is to sound not like one goose but like a lot of geese. Being able to imitate the sound of the honker is nice, but sounding like the confusion of many geese is what causes a flight to settle in.

Perhaps the best come-on for geese is the feeding call. It is accomplished with light air pressure, the call being blown with a light burr. The gravel-throated sound that results interests all types of geese, but honkers in particular.

In calling geese, it is well to remember that they do not simply honk. They squeal, cluck and run a series of all sorts of high pitched sounds. With the idea being to sound as though every decoy in your set is inviting the geese in, the tone of the call is varied with the hand. By clucking into your call rapidly, while opening and closing your hand, one can achieve the effect of sounding like several geese, all talking simultaneously.

But perhaps the most interesting — even if slightly ridiculous — technique of garnering geese belongs to a couple of Texas men, who came up with what amounts to a moveable blind. Their theory was that, if they couldn't get the geese to come to them, they would go to the geese.

Ben Burch, who operates a chain of restaurants, had been observing the thousands of speckle-bellied geese that feed in the grain fields. But what became obvious was that they chose the center of the field, making it impossible to approach them with shotgun. With a friend, George Austin, he had tried digging pits and putting out decoys, but the geese were wise. They simply chose another field beyond gun range.

So the two would-be goose hunters rented a papier-mache donkey outfit from a costume house after noting that the geese seemed to ignore cattle and horses in their immediate vicinity.

However, on the first run, the two men were overconfident. They drove up to the field in a Cadillac, dismounted, put on the suit and started across the field. The geese fled, never having seen a donkey come out of a Cadillac before. Nor had they ever seen a donkey climb a fence!

The two Texans considered this for a time and concluded they would have to act more like a donkey, wandering about, nipping grass, slowly working their way toward the feeding geese.

They tried this technique and found that it worked. In fact, they insist they were able to work their way right in among the geese before they threw off their disguise and began blazing away. On the first try, they got four geese with five shots. With a little experimentation, they found that they had perfected the technique to the point that they were able to fill out their limits each morning for the next four days!

All of which shows that it takes ingenuity and a bit of daring if you are going to outsmart a wise, old gander.

Chapter 18

UPLAND GAME SHOOTING

*Gauge, Shot Size
And Technique
All Play A Part*

In my own experience, shooting upland game as opposed to waterfowl are about as similar as the temperatures of Brazilia and Little America. For waterfowl, you invariably become involved in a waiting game, while upland bird shooting is a walking situation, best done with a well-trained dog.

The varieties of upland game vary from one geographic area to another. For example, Oklahoma is big on bobwhite quail, but you rarely will see a pheasant. At the other extreme, Oklahomans move north by one state to Kansas and find more than sufficient ringneck pheasants and few quail. There seems to be a weather and cover differential here that is almost as obvious as the Mason-Dixon line. I know of several efforts, for example, in Georgia, where bobwhites are plentiful, to stock pheasants. Even under protected conditions on a game preserve, they simply do not thrive.

At another extreme, the chukar partridge, introduced from Asia in 1893, seems to do well in the high desert country of our American West, favoring arid lands shunned by other upland species. Such birds as the ruffed grouse and woodcock are complete strangers in the West and I know many hunters who would pass up either, because they simply wouldn't recognize them.

Also, species tend to gain geographic names, which can confuse us. In New England, for example, the ruffed grouse often is referred to simply as a partridge. That tends to simplify song writing, I suppose, since a Christmas ditty about a "ruffed grouse in a pear tree" might be a bit tough to handle lyrically.

Most of us, in walking the cornfields and fence rows, do it with friends, so I'd say that some fundamentals in courtesy are not out of place.

The most obvious such rule, of course, is common sense. Add the Golden Rule to this and you can't go too far wrong. These two precepts lead logically to a third which is: don't be a game hog. There's always a temptation to shoot at every bird or animal you see, but a bit of the Alphonse and Gaston routine is in order when you're afield with a friend.

The best way to avoid trouble is to decide on shooting areas and stick to them. If you are walking abreast through a field, agree ahead of time that the shooter on the left takes only birds flushing to this side and the one of the right those on his. Alternate the order for birds coming straight in or going straight away. If there are three of you, let the middle man take the incomers and outgoers, those on the sides taking the ones flushing to the left or right.

If you are hunting with a dog belonging to a friend, let the owner work him. Extra orders from you will only confuse the animal and annoy your companion. Also, remember that a retriever is trained to fetch game to his master, not necessarily the hunter who downed the bird.

If you have filled your limit and your companion hasn't, don't shoot his birds for him. It's against the law and it's poor sportsmanship. In spite of all precautions, there will occasionally be situations where two people shoot at the same bird at almost the same instant and it's hard to say who actually hit it. It's better to concede the shot and keep a friend than risk an argument.

In discussing hunter courtesy with Dick Dietz of Remington Arms Company, he told me that his manners are better in the Fall and, seemingly, so are those of his hunting companions.

"This isn't really too surprising. It's the age-old tradition of field courtesy, the hunting ethic. When we shuck off our dress leather for a pair of battered boots, we seem to lace on a new personality as well. The general courtesy and considerate conduct of the hunting fraternity is one of the most pleasant and rewarding aspects of the sport. The fellow who doesn't know the name of a neighbor three houses down the road will introduce himself to and shake the hand of every stranger he meets at his gun club. The inconsiderate or careless driver on the highway easily reverts to a paragon of safe practice the second he touches a firearm. Consider the hunting camp manners of offering the best bunk, the largest chop, the last cup of coffee to others. Sharing of game with those whose bag is lighter than yours is automatic and accepted as normal by both donor and recipient. Even bird dogs must learn the essential practice of honoring another's point.

"There's ample evidence that field manners are highly contagious," Dietz contends. "A newcomer to the sport takes little time to learn and adhere to the code. Perhaps he learns so quickly, because he finds it such a rewarding experience amongst the universal aura of today's me-first world."

It has long been an axiom in game management circles that wildlife is a product of the edge. And this principle is one that every hunter realizes instinctively, even though he may not have thought of it in these same terms.

When you go hunting for cottontails, you don't put your beagle down in the center of a cornfield or in the middle of a dense woods. Instead, you work the hedgerows, brushpiles and woodland borders. The same thing is true with quail and pheasants. For every one of these birds you find out in the center of a field, you'll find a dozen in the field border, on ditch banks and at the edge of thickets.

The real give-away on where game hangs out is to watch a bird dog with a couple of seasons of savvy behind him. He'll not putter around in the big uniform places. You'll find him skirting the edge of the field, the edge of the plum thickets, the edge of the orchard, and all the other edges where different types of vegetation meet.

It's no mystery why game inhabits these edge situations. That's where they find, in close proximity, all the things necessary for a good life — like at the juncture of woodlands and cropfields. The center of a picked cornfield offers feed aplenty and occasionally the birds will wander out. And the center of a woods will offer protection and, now and again, they will wander in. But the advantages of both habitats can be found at the edge and that's where game will spend most of their time. It's a matter of safety and logistics.

Roughly translating the principle to the affairs of humans, we enjoy the ultimate in edge by having the kitchen, bedroom, bath and nursery all under one roof. It makes for more comfort, better survival and denser numbers than if we had all our kitchens in one part of town and all our bedrooms in another.

In other words, it's not enough simply to have lots of food and cover. Unless they are properly distributed, one in relationship to the other, the amount of wildlife an area will support will be limited well below its real potential. That's why — other things being equal — ten one-acre ponds will produce more ducks than one ten-acre pond. It's a large part of the reason, too, why the small patch farms of the past were more productive of game than the big consolidated farms of today.

In short, stick to the edges and you are certain to find more game.

Perhaps the most underestimated upland game bird is the Chinese ringneck pheasant. He's big, he appears to be — but isn't — slow-flying and that's one reason a lot of them get through each Fall unscathed.

A ringnecked pheasant is beautifully designed to defeat impulsive shotgunners. That long, streaming tail is obvious, so it becomes an aiming point. The average shooter fails to lead, so his shot-string zips harmlessly through the Chinaman's caboose. But there are ways to conquer this curse.

Big, gaudy and loud on take-off, there's no countering the ringneck's nerve warfare other than by iron discipline. Actually, in jump-shooting, or the flush ahead of a pointing dog, time is on the side of the gunner. Slow down. Error lies in panic and there's lots of empty air.

Hens can really move, but a big cock pheasant is no ballistic missile at flush. He makes a lot of noise with battering wings and that shrill whistle of air squeaking through primaries, and he cackles crazily. But he's not an animated helicopter with motor trouble.

When surprised, the pheasant tends to fly straight up, but when it flattens out, gaining top speed, it becomes a challenging target.

The Chinese ringneck pheasant is one game bird variety imported to these shores that has multiplied in great numbers. Photo was taken in Nebraska.

Pheasants usually hold for good dog, if approach is right. Evidence of wide spread of the species is found in fact that this photo was taken on Northern California ranchland.

Most hunters think of New Jersey as a built-up urban area, but it offers excellent grouse hunting in the hinterlands.

cock that has built up a head of steam is another story. Once fully under way, a ringnecked pheasant is faster than a ruffed grouse. Now you'll have to lead and, depending on the angle and range, that lead may be anywhere from four to six feet.

Unlike grouse and woodcock, the pheasant is a glutton for punishment. He must be hit hard and killed seriously dead or you can bet that he'll be running and hiding one split-second after touchdown.

At close range, over a good pointing dog, improved cylinder is enough – but if you plan to make those forty to fifty-yard crossing shots, think about modified at the very least. And make the shells high-based 6s for all-around use. Some shooters use 4s and never apologize.

The 12 gauge is best, I feel. The slowly phasing-out 16 is good, and nobody slurs today's wonderful little 20 and 28 gauges. Some even fool around with the .410, but they're pushing odds. A pheasant is as tough as he is raucous.

Jump-shooting is possible, especially if several gunners work together, quartering a cornfield or a patch of swale. However, a man with a good dog will move ten times the number of ringnecks that can be flushed by a lone brush-beater. A pheasant seems brilliantly colored, but his plumage is perfect camouflage in the shadow and shine of the outdoors. I've even seen a flamboyant cock hide in the close-cropped green of a golf course!

When it's warm and sunny they'll be in the uplands, harvesting seeds, fruits and insects. On a frosty morning or evening, longtails repair to big swale swamps or other heavy cover. They're suckers for cornfields, apple orchards and truck gardens.

Whether it's in palmetto fields in Florida, plum thickets in Oklahoma, the edges of pine woods in Georgia or the scrub oak-covered sand hills of Cape Cod, there is no hunting experience quite as exciting as the flush of a covey of bobwhite quail. Even for expert scattergunners, the explosion of flushing quail offers the supreme test of shotgunning. The old pros know you can't flock shoot – you have to pick one bird at a time or you'll hit none.

The methods of moving around in hunting cover in pursuit of these aristocrats of game birds range from the mule-drawn shooting wagons and horse-mounted dog handlers of a Louisiana plantation to the four-wheel-drive vehicles of an Oklahoma rancher.

Up close, take your time! Forget the burnished flanks and streaming tail feathers. Put the bead an inch ahead of his beak, keep the gun swinging and touch her off! That's a first step in transforming a wild bird into a gourmet's pheasant under glass.

While close-flushed ringnecks are relatively easy, the

Robert Stack swings on fast-moving grouse, during hunting trek in the open countryside of Connecticut. He considers this a difficult target.

The common denominator of all quail hunters is a good bird dog. Without one it's an almost impossible sport.

The esteem with which good dogs are held by quail hunters perhaps is best reflected in a story that comes out of Enid, Oklahoma, the home of each November's Grand National Quail Hunt.

One of the local residents, a self-made millionaire, had a highly favored bird dog that was treated almost as a member of the family — at least by its owner.

After one especially good afternoon hunt, this gentleman came home, had a few after-hunt drinks and suddenly was smitten by the idea that his dog needed to relax, too. A good, warm bath would be just the thing.

He filled the bathtub, plumped the dog into it and was on his knees, washing the dog, when his wife came on the scene.

"You think more of that dog than you do of me," she told him. "Either get him out of my bathtub or I'm leaving!"

The quail-hunting dog washer didn't even look up.

"Pack," was all he said.

This may be an extreme view of the respect an outstanding quail dog can generate from his owner or handler, but there are good reasons for this esteem.

A well-trained pointer or setter can cover the entire range of a covey of quail in a short time. If the scenting conditions are right, and the birds are there, the dog will find them. Then in that classic freeze that is almost as exciting as the flush itself, he will hold his point until the hunter moves in or the birds run out. Even then the body-stiff, tail-straight creep of a pointing dog following running birds gives the signal to the hunter that the covey is moving.

Bobwhite quail, along with other upland game birds, seem to prefer the thickets and heavy cover on the edges of fields for roosting. They move most early in the morning or late in the afternoon as they head into fields to feed and return at night.

Once the birds have flushed and the hunter has tried his skill, the singles will scatter over a wide area. The experienced quail hunter marks the singles as they settle after a flush. If they end up in heavy cover, he might just as well forget about them. If they fly out into more open areas, a good dog can pick up their scent, and flush them one at a time. It's not unusual to pick up one or two birds out of a covey rise, then two or three singles from the scattered birds.

The best shells for quail are field loads with No. 8 or No. 9 shot. Most birds are dropped at ranges of less than thirty yards, so an open cylinder gun is the best bet. Lightweight guns such as Remington's Model 1100 in 20 or 28 gauge are growing in popularity among knowledgeable bobwhite gunners.

There are other varieties of quail across the country, too, of course. In the Southwest is the Gambel's quail, then in the West Coast states, the mountain and valley quail, all of which would seemingly rather run than fly. That, again, illustrates the need for a good dog. When the dog happens on them, they usually will hold until they are flushed. However, if hunters are out by themselves, they can spend days at a time, running after the quail, but never getting close enough to these ground runners for a decent shot.

A species of quail that requires special handling, you might say, is the little known Catalina quail. Somewhat larger than the valley quail, it apparently is a sub-species found only on Santa Catalina Island off the coast of Southern California. The entire island is owned by William Wrigley — with the exception of the only town of Avalon — and the managers allow seasonal hunting at a fee, furnishing guides and transportation.

In spite of the numerous songs about Avalon and the island, itself, its terrain is somewhat less glamorous. It is all hills and canyons. The lower reaches seem to be filled with nothing but scrub oak, wild boar and Spanish goats, while the hills are liberally dotted with mammoth stands of prickly pear.

Because of this cactus variety, it is almost impossible to use a dog for quail hunting. Instead, the guides use quail calls, urging replies from the game, then tracking them down in their haunts.

But when a covey of Catalina quail flushes, you had best be ready for definite shooting. I can think of only rare occasions when one of the birds has fallen in the open, where it can be picked up easily. Instead, no matter how dead, they tend to drop into the very center of a patch of prickly pear, which means one has to go into the cactus to reclaim them.

Sharp-tailed grouse square off for a mock fight in the Sand Hills breeding grounds of eastern Nebraska.

While these hunters are making a wide sweep across an Illinois grain field, more upland game birds usually can be found in cover along edges of fields.

I know hunters who only shoot Catalina quail when wearing heavy bullhide cowboy chaps as protection against the spines of the prickly pear. For simply walking into a patch of this ferocious plant means that you are going to end up with your legs full of spines halfway up the thigh. And, since the spines tend to break off at skin level, there is nothing one can do to remove them. Instead, one simply waits about three days, until they fester, then forces them out!

One has to like quail hunting a great deal for that kind of routine, I'll admit.

In this kind of hunting, where every shot must count for a dead bird, unless you like to suffer a lot, knowing where your shotgun shoots is most important.

No prudent rifleman would think of taking to the field without having previously spent some time on the range to assure that his rifle was putting the bullets exactly where the sights say it should. The sense of this is obvious. A hunter may spend a week in the woods or a season of weekends looking for a fine trophy or even just meat for the freezer. He may have but one chance, perhaps but one shot to accomplish this. He wants that shot to count.

Upland game hunters and waterfowlers usually have more opportunities and larger limits that are renewed daily during the season. But how many come home with half-filled limits because they don't really know where their shotgun shoots for them? They may be shooting above, below or to one side of where they intend.

There are two ways to find out for certain. The first is to zero in your shotgun on a patterning board. If a regular patterning board isn't available, any makeshift backstop of wood or metal at least four feet square will serve. The target can be any piece of paper covering the board with a bullseye drawn in the middle. Back off from the board the distance you expect your game shots to be. Then, bring your gun up quickly as you would in the field, point at the bullseye and fire. Repeat the procedure several times. Resulting patterns should be spread out evenly around the bullseye.

Patterns that are consistently high indicate that you may not be bringing the stock all the way up to your face or the stock may be too long or straight for you. Low patterns indicate you may be crunching your face down too hard on the stock or that it may be too short for you. For most shooters, a correction in gun placement will eliminate the problem, but a very short or tall shooter may require stock alterations. Patterns hitting to the left or right of center mean you are not looking directly down the barrel as you

The larger gauges of shotguns all can be used with adequate results against pheasants, with right choke/shot size.

shoot or that the gun has been knocked out of line and needs a trip to the gunsmith.

Incidentally, this is a good time to examine pattern density to see if you are using the proper choke for the distance you expect to shoot. Patterns that are too thin will merely cripple, but won't down game. Patterns that are too dense will cause misses or spoil the game for the table.

The second practice — mentioned earlier — that can pay off in increased game dividends is to sharpen up your eye on clay targets before the season begins. There's an old adage that says many good field shots are also good clay target shooters, but virtually all good clay target shooters are crack field shots. This is generally true.

Two of the most challenging upland game birds are ruffed grouse and woodcock of the Northeast. Often found in the same general areas, they both favor heavy cover and have an uncanny knack of putting large tree trunks or bushes between hunters and themselves the minute they flush. With grouse in particular, hunters often hear birds as they break cover but may only get a fleeting glimpse of them as they disappear.

The most likely spots for woodcock are alder thickets, young birch and poplar runs and brushy sections. In partic-ular, they favor places where the ground is fairly soft and damp where there are plenty of earthworms — their favorite diet. One good indication that they are around are the white droppings they leave and holes bored by their long bills as they probe for food.

Woodcock are migratory and early in the season, you are likely to find natives that have spent the Spring and Summer in an area. Later on, flight birds will stop off on their way South.

Woodcock will hold well for dogs, but when they flush, they tend to fly in a corkscrew pattern and often seem to go straight up in the air.

Ruffed grouse like the same kinds of terrain but will move off into drier sections rather than sticking to swampy, low-lying areas. If you flush a grouse and fail to get off a shot before he disappears, don't despair. They seldom fly far and if you work along the line you think he took, you may well find him again. Of course, as is true in all upland hunting, a good bird dog is a vital asset.

Any discussion of grouse hunting techniques becomes automatically contradictory. The grouse often is one of the most difficult upland birds for dogs to hunt. And when you do find or develop a crack grouse dog, he's frequently

One of the big problems in hunting areas near population centers is the fact that available ground, cover draw more hunters than game as in this opening day scene in New Jersey.

mediocre on, or disinterested in, other game birds. It seems almost as if such a dog becomes even more addicted to this one quarry than the hunter himself. Yet the ruffed grouse is also one of the few upland birds you can actually hunt with any success without a dog.

Perhaps this is because it isn't too hard to learn and recognize the kind of cover he favors within his normal range. It is also the result of his tendency to hold tight and not be spooked by the noises you make plowing through the brush. In fact, one of the most successful ways of walking up grouse is to move along at a steady pace, then stop dead periodically. It's the sudden silence that often disturbs him into exploding out of his cover with a racket that would unnerve Nimrod himself.

"Fast shooting is a prerequisite for successful grouse hunting. If you don't get on him quick, he'll unfailingly put the biggest tree in the territory between you and him in nothing flat. Consequently, a light, fast-handling shotgun, open bored, and small-sized shot is the most appropriate equipment," according to Remington's Dick Dietz, who favors this game bird.

"Look for grouse in thicket pockets or draws on the sides of hills, in groves of nuts, fruits or berries, on abandoned farms or the edges of apple orchards. Find a hemlock or pine stand in the midst of hardwoods and you're likely to find grouse around the fringe. Chances are you'll have to find the good cover yourself, though. Hunters who will give you their last dime gladly become amazingly evasive when you bring up the subject of grouse cover. They tell the story of the fellow who borrowed his best friend's grouse dog one Saturday and kept the dog blindfolded during both ends of the trip. It isn't true, of course. He merely kept the dog's head below window level of the wagon."

While doves cannot rightly be considered upland game as such, this book would be incomplete without mention of them. The whitewing doves of the Southwest are a demanding target, but perhaps no more so than the mourning dove. which is much more widespread in availability to the hunter.

The mourning dove nests in forty-eight out of our fifty states, is the most sought-after game bird in the thirty states in which it may be hunted legally, is famed as the symbol of peace — even though it is aggressive by nature — and is known as a rain crow by many a self-styled weather prophet. Aerodynamically, it possesses all of the qualities

Hunter has raised his head from gun to admire fast-flying bird and probably will miss it.

of a good fighter plane in that it has remarkable maneuverability and swiftness of wing.

Harold S. Peters of the National Audubon Society describes the mourning dove as follows:

"It has the longest breeding season of any North American bird. It adapts easily to any terrain, temperature and feeding condition. It nests around homes in towns, as well as in rural areas. It shows peculiar adaptability to man-made habitat. In early days, the clearing of forests and westward spread of agriculture favored the dove. It increased in numbers rapidly and now is much more abundant than in colonial days. Diversified agriculture has provided increased feeding facilities."

And finally, Peters says: "Man has been good for the mourning dove — and the dove has been good for man."

Because of the importance of the mourning dove, the Southeastern Association of Game and Fish Commissioners started a research project to study their habits way back in 1949. Ten states were involved originally. The major result of this project was a call-count technique that can be used to determine breeding populations.

Today a call-count survey is conducted annually by Federal, state and independent observers on more than eight hundred prescribed routes. Each of these routes is on a back road with twenty three-minute listening stations spaced at one-mile intervals. Between May 20 and June 10, an observer drives the twenty mile back road early each morning and stops at each station and records the number of dove calls he hears.

The dove, like the Canada goose, generally mates for life. Their flimsy nests are built by both males and females. The male gathers the material and the female does the actual building. The dove lays five or six clutches of eggs each year. About half will be successful with four or five young making it to flight stage. The female normally lays two white eggs and then incubation begins. The female sits on the nest from about 5 in the afternoon until about 9 the next morning. The male takes over from 9 a.m. to 5 p.m.

After hatching, the young are rather helpless for the first few days. The adult birds regurgitate pigeon milk, partially digested food on which the young feed. Later they are introduced to insects, worms and seeds.

If each pair of adults raises four or five young to flight stage, then why aren't we overrun with these birds? The

Not being migratory in nature, ringneck pheasants winter where feed, cover are available.

Gunner (above) has his gun low on his shoulder and is not looking along the barrel; it's good technique for a miss. Shooter below is aiming correctly. Note that gun still moves in follow-through as shell ejects, bird crumples.

answer is that Nature is often very hard on certain species. It generally works out that those that have the highest reproductive potential also have the highest death rate. For example, some fish must lay literally hundreds of thousands of eggs in order to insure survival of a small percentage of their young.

In the case of doves, approximately seventy percent die before they are one year old. Yet, every year, new hatches produce vast numbers of young birds that are destined to follow the same cycle. It is thus apparent that this surplus that is destined to die anyway can be harvested by hunters. By regulating the bag limit and the length of the season, the hunters can take their limits without harming the resource.

Doves may be very seclusive during certain periods, but by early September they are quite gregarious and feed in large flocks. Some of their favorite feeding areas are wheat fields, silage corn after cutting, harvested field corn and millet fields planted specifically to attract them. Feeding areas — or dove fields, as they are called — may contain a few birds or hundreds.

There are lots of theories about the best type of guns and shells to use for doves, but the best advice is to shoot what works best for you. One wildlife management expert of my acquaintance likes a 20 gauge with improved cylinder barrel early in the season and later switches to a modified barrel. In addition, he favors No. 7½ shot. Others need the spread of a big 12 gauge. Most of us could buy a lot of

Even if the hunting is not up to expectations, there is little more satisfying than a long day in the field with good friends and the companionship that goes with the sport.

milk-fed veal for what we spend on trying to bag a pound of doves.

Everyone knows that there are scattergunners who swing a piece without consciously aiming, place a shot string in precisely the right place, and bring down a fast-flying game bird. They are called snap-shooters, and they are as traditional as apple pie and ice cream.

But, unless definitions have been altered, there is no such thing as a snap-shooter who never leads a speeding target, moves like lightning — and yet never fails to center a bird. There is an aura of mythology about it that we tend to foster. However, there are precisely two ways to hit flying birds. One is the calculated sustained lead espoused by such greats as the late D. Lee Braun; the other is the rapid swing-through in which a trigger is pressed as a gun's muzzle is moved past the target.

Practically all so-called snap-shooters use the latter method — because there isn't time to do anything else. Many of the best performers actually believe that they never lead, but they do. Simple physics proves as much.

Snap-shooting is nothing more than a vastly accelerated version of sustained lead. You swing from behind the bird, overtake it and press a trigger as the muzzle reaches a spot that seems entirely right. Lead is always there, whether it be a foot or four feet in front of a hurtling target.

Aborigines may think they are right on a speeding mark, but human time-lag — the instant it takes for the brain to direct an impulse to the trigger finger — insures that the gun will swing on through and insure lead.

Lead is always there on anything but the straightaway shot — and straightaway shots are not very plentiful in the boondocks. You hose them fast! It takes a lot of practice and that's why the best performers are flat-bellied oldtimers with a lot of time logged in the uplands.

If there's any instruction of value, other than years of belting at rapidly disappearing targets, it is an injunction to keep that gun swinging! The greatest sin of the snap-shooter is a tendency to stop the gun. He has to follow through. More pellets trail a bird than precede it.

It isn't enough to anticipate a target and hope that there'll be enough time to mount a piece. Carry the gun at a modified port arms so that it can be shouldered quickly, the safety catch snapped off as it comes up. Be slick, be quick, swing and follow through. Snap-shooting may be spectacular, but it's just a speeded-up version of something very basic — proper lead and shot placement.

251

Chapter 19

PRESERVE SHOOTING

As Hunting Acreage Declines, This May

Become A Way Of Life In America As It Has In Europe

WHEN SOMEONE BRINGS up the term, "preserve shooting," the dyed-in-the-wool outdoorsman often is inclined to elevate his nose and mutter something about this type of hunting being for armchair shooters.

But the fact that shooting preserves are growing in number may be evidence of things to come. With the continuing encroachments of civilization upon our wilderness, the population explosion which is gobbling up the wastelands for housing, the day is not far off when this may be the only type of live bird shooting available.

Half a century ago, it was possible to shoot ducks by the dozens, even hundreds, each day, but any hunter would be hard put to find that kind of shooting today on the North American continent.

What the next half a century brings may be more frightening.

But let's assume that we don't care — for ourselves, at least — what hunting is going to be like several decades hence. What about today? Where does this thing called preserve shooting fit into the present pattern?

Charles Dickey, while with the National Shooting Sports Foundation, probably came up with the best answer to date: "Few American hunters will admit they are getting enough hunting."

Shooting preserves are privately owned commercial operations or are run on a club basis. Pen-raised game is released for hunting, the shooters paying a fee. In most instances, there is an extended season longer than the state-regulated seasons; there is no bag limit on released game; and the area is licensed or sanctioned by the state game commission.

For the doubter, who revolts at the idea of shooting pen-raised birds, one should remember that roughly the same thing is taking place in what we generally refer to as our Great Outdoors. In this instance, game birds are raised or purchased by the various Fish and Game Departments of the states, then released. They may be protected for a period of time, allowing them time to multiply on their own before an active shooting season is opened; yet the area has been stocked initially by other than natural means.

There is more time involved and the shooter is paying taxes for the manning of the public lands, paying for the raising and releasing of the game birds on these lands.

More important to the man who feels he doesn't get enough active shooting during the regular game bird season, most of the game preserves in the country have seasons that extend from either September or October through March and even April. At least two states — Alabama and Oklahoma — have no closed season at all on released game. Here one can shoot 365 days a year.

Today, it is legal to operate shooting preserves in forty-five states and, at my last count, there were such installations in forty-two thus far, as well as five Canadian provinces. At last count, there were more than six hundred operating shooting preserves spread across the United States, plus twenty-two more in Canada.

Recent studies show that shooting preserves gain most of their customers from cities with populations of over 50,000. In checking the current listings, I found this to be true: The preserves are concentrated in the areas most heavily populated. For example, New York State leads with a total of seventy-two commercially operated preserves; Illinois is second with forty-five; and California has forty-four.

This matter of correlation between population centers and the number of such live-bird shooting installations is certainly an indication: It is conservatively estimated that, within the next sixty years, the population of this country will double!

This opus is not meant to serve as a pitch for birth control, but one can hardly ignore the fact that we have been romancing ourselves out of a place to hunt!

In recent months, I, with some of the editorial staff of this book, have had an opportunity to check out the facilities of several of these commercially operated game preserves, including three in Southern California and one in Georgia.

The Riverview Plantation at Camilla, Georgia, specializes in bobwhite quail hunting and is without a doubt one of the nation's leading preserves. The operators actually farm

In the photo sequence above, cock pheasant takes off as shooter and guide spot it. In center photo, the bird has been hit, while in the final picture, it is being picked up by well trained spaniel. Most shooting preserves such as this, California's Las Flores, furnish dogs.

Proper cover and feed are planted in most commercially operated shooting preserves. This helps to assure birds will remain in area and multiply.

some of the ground, not putting all of their quail in one covey, so to speak. They also raise quail, hatching them for similar preserves and for the state of Georgia's release program. Located on the banks of the picturesque Flint River

Game preserves are operated under the rules laid down by the states.

and framed against a background of Spanish moss, this operation comes under the heading of luxurious living. There is a huge lodge with individual two-man cabins that are built in rustic but comfortable design. The going charge, the last I knew, was something like $75 per day, but for this fee, you are allowed to take a dozen quail, you eat like a king, sleep on a thick mattress and there may even be a bit of Jack Daniels-inspired revelry in the evenings.

In the field, each party hunts from a fully equipped jeep with an experienced guide — familiar with the ground and the game — handling a pair of pointers or setters selected from the forty-odd dogs housed in the kennels. If you're a little rusty, there is a practice trap that hurls claybirds out across the river, giving you an opportunity to sharpen your eye before departing for the tall pines.

In this area, the pen-raised birds are interspersed with the native bobwhite quail, but both make for demanding shooting. The birds are thick enough to spoil one for life.

Needless to say, an operation such as this doesn't run itself. Each year, from October 1 to March 31, the operators, C.B. Cox and Don Hays, have their hands full. They must combine the mismatched attributes of a hotel entrepreneur with the rustic knowledge of the dedicated outdoorsman.

In Southern California, we had an opportunity to use the facilities of the Etiwanda Game Association, which is located on some 1500 acres in the foothills of the San Gabriel Mountains, forty-odd miles from downtown Los Angeles.

This is an entirely different type of operation, conducted on the club principle. There is an annual membership fee of some $150, or an associate membership priced at a third that, and for each bird you bring down, you pay a per-bird fee. The pheasant season runs for some six months, with a limit of six birds per day, while the chukar season is restricted to two months with a four-bird limit. There is a year-round season on guinea fowl, plus normal seasons on wild dove, rabbit and other game.

To fill out the outdoor activities here, the association

Inasmuch as they are raised for sport shooting, hens and cocks are equally fair game on most preserves.

even conducts extensive prize-shooting programs, including turkey shoots, scatterboard and trap. There is even a trout pond for those who indulge in angling. The association is chartered by the State of California and the fields are planted according to plan to provide natural food and cover for the game that is stocked within its perimeter.

Operating on a private club principle, membership at Etiwanda is limited to two hundred. Dog-training facilities are available and tournament field trials are sponsored here by local dog clubs. There are clubhouse facilities, including a snack bar, lounge and the necessary supplies for the hunt are available there.

These are only two examples of the type of installations that offer extended pay-as-you-shoot seasons, but they do have parallel problems to which all game preserves find themselves subject.

For example, game birds that are pen-raised for release must be constantly conditioned. Reason for this is the fact that the hunter who is paying for the privilege expects his birds to fly in the fashion of the native game. Therefore,

there is a need for large exercise pens and both humans and dogs must be kept away from the birds as much as possible.

A pioneer in U.S. shooting preserve development, Charles Dickey, points out, "A constant breeding of better and wilder strains is practiced by smart preserve operators. Perhaps in the future, game breeders will be able to develop wilder strains by careful breeding. It is perhaps the greatest challenge facing the game breeders today."

A recent survey shows that charges range from $3 to $12 per bird for the hunter, with the average running at about $5. For that sum, he expects service. Not only does he expect to work with adequate birds, dogs and guides, but he expects a bit more. Chances are, the first birds he shoots will be taken home undressed so that his wife can admire his prowess with the shotgun. Chances are equal that thereafter, he will want the birds to be dressed and ready for the oven when he takes leave of the place. Wives have a habit of running out of patience in this department. As a result, nearly all preserves have a setup for cleaning your game.

Operators have found that dogs are important in the

Hunters can kick up game birds on
their own, as is being done in
this case, but preserve operators
find it economically advantageous
to use dogs in helping point birds.

On commercially operated preserves,
game limits often are controlled
by the operators, although in some
states, game department sets limit.

Hunting areas on public lands are becoming more regulated or are disappearing entirely. In Europe, privately owned hunting grounds have been a way of life for decades and such may be the future in U.S.

matter of time. Statistics show that, if an operator does not provide dogs, he is using only five percent of his business potential. Without dogs, a party may trample over the terrain for half or a full day to get their birds. With dogs, a two-hour hunt usually will do the trick. Also, dogs are important for the operator in the matter of recovering cripples that otherwise would escape the shooter. In fact, most preserves also supply dog-training services and even boarding facilities for hunters who want to work their own.

Few of these operations are begun on a shoestring and the shooter who wants to hunt past the normal season by taking advantage of such installations must realize that his host is out to make a profit on his investment and headaches.

However, there are additional benefits to all shooters. For example, in checking with Carl Mills of the Mills Shooting Preserve at Bakersfield, California, he reported that some twenty-one percent of the pheasant, quail and chukar which he stocks eventually escape to surrounding lands. This means that they become fair game either for the "for-free" type hunter, or have an opportunity to reproduce more young. The Etiwanda Game Association reports a loss of about twenty-five percent of their pheasants, while a loss on chukars has not been tabulated. Since the latter seem to prefer high rocky slopes, chances are that more of these

birds head for such heights which tower over the game preserve but are beyond the boundaries. Most other preserves report similar population declines.

An example of how preserve shooting can benefit all hunters is illustrated in an incident which took place on one preserve where I observed the hunting. The field we were shooting over was on the extreme edge of the tract and when we flushed a pheasant and didn't get a shot at it, the bird barreled across the fence and onto adjoining land. There, a non-paying hunter was waiting and downed him with ease. Once the pheasant was over the boundary line, it was anybody's bird.

Species released on preserves include pheasant, quail, chukar partridge, turkey and mallard ducks. Well-trained dogs are generally available. Some preserves charge for birds bagged while others charge for those released. In some states, hunting licenses are required while in others they are not.

Full information, including names, telephone numbers and locations of preserves, along with types of hunting and lengths of seasons, are contained in the North American Shooting Preserve Directory available from the National Shooting Sports Foundation, 1075 Post Road, Riverside, Connecticut 06878. Single copies are available for twenty-five cents.

OF DRILLINGS, COMBOS & SLUGS

Chapter 20

*Wherein We Investigate Some Of
The Less Scattered Aspects Of Shotgunning*

Hollenbeck drilling with 16-gauge tubes was utilized in hunting New England woodcock with gratifying results. Following day, Glad Zwirz used .30-30 barrel to take a deer.

No BOOK ON shotguns would be complete without some mention of combination guns and drillings. This has been the more or less traditional hunting tool of many European sportsmen with its origin seeming to have been in Germany and Austria.

While shotgunners have sought to come up with the all-purpose shotgun for a couple of centuries, the methodical Teutons had gone a few steps beyond, seeking the all-purpose gun. The result, usually with three barrels, incorporated the better features of a shotgun with a rifle.

Variations in such firearms are limited by the caliber, gauge and number of each one desires. There have been any number of side-by-side 12-gauge guns with a center-fire rifle barrel slung beneath. There were guns that boasted rifle barrels in two different calibers, with a single shotgun barrel completing the combo and I have even seen at least one drilling that had a big bore rifle barrel, combined with shotguns in two different gauges! Just how practical this last conglomerate might be is open to serious question in my mind.

In the hunting fields of this country, one is not likely to find many drillings. The European influence has not yet caught on to that great a degree and another reason involves the fact that such guns cannot be considered cheap.

The combination's popularity in Europe involves the fact that hunting, in most instances, is not all that great. If one is going afield, it is with the idea of coming back with something. The fact has carried over into some sections of the United States, too, but it is more a matter of our having a spread or overlapping of game. For example, in the Northeastern states, where deer, bear and smaller game are found among the alder marshes and along wooded streams, these same areas often are rife with woodcock and partridge.

My occasional shooting partner, Bob Zwirz, tells with great relish the adventures of one of his friends. It seems this individual, armed with a shotgun, was crawling through a thick patch of alders that edged a stream, seeking woodcock sign, when he came literally face to face with a 260-pound bear running toward him. Whether a matter of wind direction or some other reason, the bear had not detected the hunter's presence until the last moment. The hunter, however, did have time to eject a 16-gauge shell loaded with No. 7½ shot and replace it with a rifled slug. That day, he walked out of the woods with five woodcock, one partridge — and the black bear.

However, had he been armed with a drilling, there would have been considerably less wear and tear on his nerves as he hunkered there in the shrubbery, trying to change shells.

The fact that drillings never have gained great popularity in the United States perhaps is reflected in the fact that there are few importers of such combo guns; this probably relates to the fact that the price is not ultra-conservative as mentioned.

In fact, as of this writing, the only two organizations to import drillings are Colt, which has brought in a few of the guns made in Germany by Sauer, and an outfit in Nashville, Tennessee, which is handling the Krieghoff Trumpf drilling. In both cases, these guns start at somewhere in the vicinity of $1500.

A year or so ago, when Colt first brought in the Sauer-made drilling with a pair of side-by-side 12-gauge barrels centered above a .30/06 rifled barrel, they invited my editor, Jack Lewis, to try it out in New Mexico on a somewhat unlikely combination. The idea was that they would try to shoot a coyote with the rifle in the morning, then hunt mourning doves in the late afternoon. All of this took place in an area called Mescalero Sands and sounds like something of a comedy of errors, as Lewis reports the happenings. He was there with Colt's Duane Small, who had brought the first gun imported by the Hartford firm, and John Goodwin of the New Mexico Fish and Game Commission.

The area, a few hundred thousand acres of rolling sand dunes only loosely held in place by growths of mesquite, had the look of good hunting country, as Small handed one of the three-barrel firearms to Lewis, indicating that this worthy would have the initial honors.

"But I've never fired the thing!" Lewis protested. Small shook his head, while John Goodwin of the New Mexico Fish and Game Commission watched thoughtfully. The latter was putting together the Johnny Stewart electronic game call.

"I haven't fired it either," Small stated, "but think of the challenge. You'll prove before the day's over that this gun is that so-called all-around piece. You shoot a coyote now, then later we'll go shoot a limit of doves!"

"Just like that?"

"Just like that!" Small thumbed at Goodwin, who was making like an electronic technician. "He says there are lots of doves around."

Both of them cast an eye through the growing light that

Configuration of the Krieghoff drilling is shown, with the 7X57 rifle barrel centered beneath the side-by-side.

revealed several hundred miles of New Mexico terrain below the butte on which they stood. Nothing was flying.

"The coyote first," Goodwin suggested, moving out into the mesquite flanking the deserted ranch road.

Ten minutes later, Goodwin had set up shop on a low knoll, using mesquite for cover. The Johnny Stewart tape had been inserted into the electronic call and an injured rabbit was wailing his hurt. Lewis, loads of 00 buckshot in the twin shotgun barrels and a .30/06 cartridge in the rifle barrel, was stretched out on his belly, attempting to find a field of fire through the growth. On the opposite side flanking Goodwin were Small and Jack Pratt, Colt's firearms production ramrod. Somewhere farther down the road, another gun writer, Hal Swiggett, Bill Montoya of the Fish and Game Commission and Dick Brown, vice-president of engineering for Colt, were undergoing similar experiences.

"Shoot him!" Goodwin whispered hoarsely. Lewis settled in, flicked the button that raised the rear sight and actuated the rifle trigger. But there was no coyote. Then he saw it. The dog — no more than three-quarters grown — was headed away, cutting through the mesquite, having been hidden beneath the roll of the knoll before.

At seventy yards or so, the coyote halted and looked back over his shoulder. Notching the front sight in the dim light, Lewis held his breath, then squeezed. The firearm bucked against his shoulder, the bullet kicked up dust beneath the coyote's belly and he disappeared amid the proverbial hail of lead from the others who were shooting a variety of varmint calibers.

"I should have used the shotgun barrels," Lewis alibied, "but that didn't seem too sporting."

"You were most sporting," agreed Small, as he rose. Lewis also rose, glancing down to discover that he had picked the greatest crop of sand burrs in the entire Southwest in which to make his stand. Out came a variety of pocket knives which were used to scrape the burrs from his person.

"We might as well try another stand down the road," Goodwin suggested, picking up the electronic caller and hiking for the vehicle. "That one for sure isn't coming back."

Several miles down the trail, the electronic device was set up once more, but Goodwin was checking the growing wind, shaking his head. "Wind's not going to help," was his prophecy.

At left: Hollenbeck has 16-gauge barrels over .30-30 rifle. Other gun is an old Charles Daly model with exposed hammers. Note the rear sight.

Bob Zwirz carries drilling out of the North Woods, as well as a deer taken with combo.

Again, while the game warden worked with the caller, the others took up likely looking positions. This time, Lewis made a quick check of the ground, then picked a bare spot in which no burrs could possibly be present. As he lay on his belly, eyes sweeping the approaches, seeking any sign of movement, he experienced a twinge. Then another. At first, he tended to blame this upon the fact that he was not used to lying on the cold ground this early in the morning. But he soon realized there had to be more to it than that. Gritting his teeth, he tried not to feel the pain, watching for the coyote that never came.

Finally, Goodwin shut off the tape player and rose. "Too much wind," he announced, but Lewis was already on his feet, tossing the German-made combination gun at him. As Goodwin caught the piece, the shooter was beating savagely at his legs and thighs.

"Red ants!" he exclaimed, waving at the hill from which the tiny denizens marched now in an unending stream. Others gathered about, offering sympathy, slapping at the offenders that seemed bent on vengeance against this mountain of flesh that had invaded their domain.

"We could dunk you in a river," Goodwin suggested. "That always gets rid of them. Only problem is, it's twenty miles to the Pecos River and it's got little water, when we get there."

Instead, battle had to be against the individual warrior ants. Finally, it appeared they had been bested and Goodwin suggested it was time to look for doves. A quick survey showed that a few birds, mostly mourning doves, were flitting about. Lewis pointed to a meadowlark, telling Duane Small, "In Italy, they shoot those and eat them. There, it's called a quail."

"In New Mexico, it's called a citation," Goodwin put in, his tone now professionally severe. Back in the car, the guns unloaded and the Colt-Sauer drilling held between his knees, Lewis had an opportunity to take a closer look at the firearm that had been issued to him less than an hour before.

The two shotgun barrels — the right one bored modified choke, the left one, full choke — were side-by-side, the rifle barrel slung beneath and between in a triangular effect. A thumb safety activates a plunger device on the tang. This raises or lowers the rear sight, at the same time activating the firing pin for the rifle barrel, working off the front trigger.

When the sight is lowered, the same front trigger actuates the firing pin for the modified barrel. On the left side of the stock, within easy reach of the same thumb that activates the plunger and slide on the tang, is the safety.

261

The Savage Model 24 combination rifle/shotgun comes in several styles, has a long history.

When it is pushed down, a red dot denoting firing position is revealed.

The barrels, measuring 24-7/8 inches, are of Krupp barrel steel, with an engraved rib that cuts down glare and a gold bead front sight. The gun is built with a self-cocking action; double cross-bolt locks; a separate cartridge extractor.

Bob Zwirz uses Krieghoff drilling in 20-gauge to bring inconvenience to a fast-flying New England woodcock.

Overall weight was right at eight pounds. The stock on the gun Lewis was shooting featured a Monte Carlo roll. Radius between the front sight and the pop-up rear sight was 16½ inches and the barrels themselves, removed from the stock and forearm, weighed four pounds. Checkering on the stock and forearm, incidentally, measured twenty lines per inch — as nearly as the two typewriter technicians could determine with their failing eyesight.

Goodwin brought the vehicle to a halt somewhere on the far edge of nowhere, pointing to a windmill and water tank.

"There ought to be doves in here," he suggested. Moments later, the twin barrels stuffed with No. 8 shot, Lewis was flanking the game warden as they set out through the mesquite, the idea being to flush the birds out of the cover they had taken due to the winds.

The pair had gone no more than thirty feet when there was a suspicious rattling sound. Lewis lowered the barrel of the shotgun and decapitated with one round the huge rattlesnake that boasted ten rattles and a button as evidence of his state of health.

"Oh, yeah," Goodwin muttered. "I neglected to mention that the whistle worms are out pretty good."

"Many thanks," Lewis returned, as he sliced the rattles from the still writhing remains. "But I'll now spend the rest of the day watching the ground rather than looking for birds."

During the heat of the day, there were no birds to watch and there was conjecture that they had headed South, keeping ahead of an expected cold front. The cadre set up shop on the edge of a mesa and began to work out Lewis' earlier claim that he had missed the coyote because the gun shot low. Before it was over, after bouncing bullets off of six-inch rocks at three hundred yards or so across the canyon, he was willing to admit that the firearm "shoots where you point it."

"But I'm beginning to feel a little foolish," Duane Small put in. "I invited you all this way to shoot coyotes and doves. So far, we've seen one coyote."

As the afternoon sun dropped, the group — Lewis and Swiggett each carrying the Colt-Sauer drilling — was back at the water tank. At first, there was nothing. Then, suddenly the sky darkened, flitting wings shapes coming in cloud-like formations.

All along the line shotguns began to boom, birds to fall. In all, there was less than thirty minutes of fast action, but when it was over, the twelve-bird limits had been filled out with one or two exceptions.

While it was agreed that the drilling probably was never meant to be a dove gun, one could catch up with elusive targets after once learning how to swing the rather centralized weight.

According to Small, who since has moved on to another

branch of Colt Industries, the firm sold all of the drillings they could obtain from Sauer during the first year, but he feels that many of them were sold to collectors who had to have one to hang on the wall.

The earlier mentioned Kreighoff import is available with side-by-side 12-gauge barrels, while the rifled barrel is in .30/06. Or if you fancy the three-inch 20-gauge chambers, you can have that combined with a .243 Winchester under-barrel.

Closely akin to the drillings and also of European origin is the combo rifle, which usually utilizes a boxlock action with over/under barrels, one a shotgun tube, the other a rifled barrel. Again, Kreighoff has such a gun that handles 12, 16 and 20-gauge shells in the top barrel, while the lower barrel is chambered for almost all U.S. and metric cartridges, rimless and rimmed. In fact, it is set up to handle scope mounts and one of the more interesting features to the rifleman is that the rifle barrels can be interchanged to handle .22 Hornet, .222 Remington and .222 Remington magnum. Price on this one starts at upward of $1200.

Flaig's has been importing the Ferlach combination turkey rifle and shotgun from Austria. This features a boxlock action of Anson & Deeley design with barrels of twenty-two or twenty-four inches. It is available in 12, 16 and 20 gauge with the rifle barrel in calibers ranging from .22 Remington through .30/06.

The only firm that has had any success with an American-made combination gun has been Savage Arms Company, whose Model 24 in various configurations has been a standard in the line for years. With these guns, however, the shooter is limited to 20 gauge and .410 on the underslung shotgun barrel and on all but one model, .22

rimfire is the fodder for the rifle. The Model 24V, limited to 20 gauge, also will handle either .222 Remington or even .30-30 rifle cartridges, depending upon ordering instructions. This model, incidentally, is tapped for a scope, while one is limited to iron sight use with the others.

Slug guns have been mentioned in passing in earlier chapters, but this might be the appropriate area in which to offer some remarks on the potential of this shotgun type.

Ed Andrews, one of those perennial experimenters with a practical scientific bent, has made some investigations into this facet of shooting.

The big, clean-cut holes that a rifled slug leaves in a paper target gives some indication of the punch-press power involved, but what are the chances of that slug hitting the mark intended?

The tests were conducted with several Ithaca Model 66 single-barrel shotguns, which still are in production and open by means of a frontierish-looking underlever. Two of these guns were factory-equipped with V-notch rear sights with fluorescent front sights. The twenty-eight-inch full-choke versions were equipped with the one-sixteenth-inch silver bead sight at the front, while commercially made rifled slugs were from Remington and Winchester.

The tests proved one thing for sure: whether Remington or Winchester, we never could determine any appreciable difference in accuracy or performance between either make of slug.

The method used for sighting in the M-66s with only the front bead is as follows: For windage, a linear mark with a ball point pen was inscribed at the highest, visible point of the shotgun's action and as close to the center as possible. While firing sighting shots, the mark was moved in the

The Voere combo, made in Europe, features 20-gauge magnum and .222 Remington configuration.

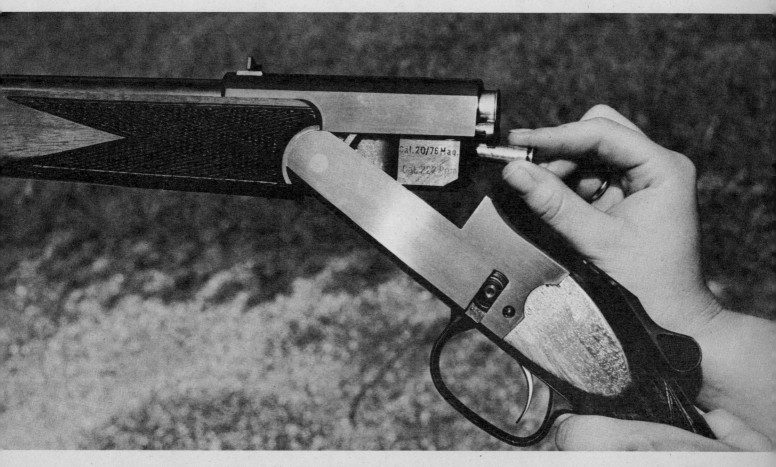

Ithaca slide-action slug gun was used to down this wild pig in Argentine wilds. Note the peep sight that has been installed, as well as convenient sling for easy carrying.

direction we wanted to move the point of impact, until the slugs were hitting the center of the target. Andrews then used the sharp edge of a file to remove a small amount of blue where the last ball point pen mark was made. By holding dead on the bullseye, the groups were about three inches high at fifty yards.

Only three-shot groups were fired and were measured center-to-center of the widest spread. The best group at fifty yards was from one of the twenty-eight-inch full choke models, a fantastic 1-5/8-inch group. The best group either of the special slug models could account for was 3½ inches, center-to-center. Ten three-shot groups were fired with the twenty-inch slug barrel and the same number with the twenty-eight-inch full choke models. Overall average for

the latter was 2.4275 inches and 3.8875 inches for the slug barrel with sights. Remington's record was 2.650 inches for the full choke barrel and 3.900 inches for the slug version. Winchester racked up the best overall score with a slug barrel average of 3.875 and 2.205 for the long tom. Winchester's ten-group average was 3.040 inches, while Remington scored 3.275 inches. All of these figures are for fifty-yard groups only.

All the shooting up to now was from a solid benchrest where Andrews could line up the silver bead and the bright file mark. He tried a couple of groups standing on the hind legs, offhand.

"The twenty-inch slug barrels continued to produce groups only slightly larger than those from the benchrest,

One can reload his shotshells with slugs such as the Benco-Vitt, with minimum equipment. The Lyman roll crimper was inserted in the drill and used to put roll crimp over slug.

but the no-sights, full choke tubes went up to over a six-inch average. I think, with sights equal in quality to those on the shorter barrel, the twenty-eight-incher would have continued to produce good groups," Andrews reports.

Rifled slugs are loaded in all five of our standard gauges. However, muzzle energy drops off fast and the .410 slug has only 345 foot-pounds of energy left at fifty yards, 200 less than the .357 magnum pistol cartridge puts out at the same distance. The 28 gauge's one-half-ounce of lead manages 670 foot-pounds of energy at fifty yards, still only about 130 pounds more than the .357.

When we step up to the 20 gauge with a slug weight of 5/8 ounce ahead of 2¾ drams of powder, performance gets into the .44 magnum class. Projected killing power of the 16-gauge slug would be roughly equal to the old favorite .30-30 and the 12 gauge could be compared with the seventy-year-old .30-40 Krag. Past a hundred yards, velocity drops fast and the big slugs are more aptly compared with a stone from David's slingshot; great for Goliath's eye, but not too effective on a tough old buck.

"Sighted in three inches high at fifty yards, your bird and bunny buster should manage a crack-down on any delinquent deer out to about a hundred yards. The local gun peddler tells me that ninety percent of his rifled slug sales are in quantities of three to ten rounds, certainly not enough ammo to sight in a smoothbore, sights or no. My humble advice is buy a box and blast off enough slugs to predict where they will hit."

Only the individual presently loading shotshells should consider the possibility of loading rifled slugs. However, to the reloader, the challenge of devising an accurate load will add the olive to the martini.

Here on the West Coast, the likelihood of choosing a smoothbore for buck blasting is remote, since ranges are

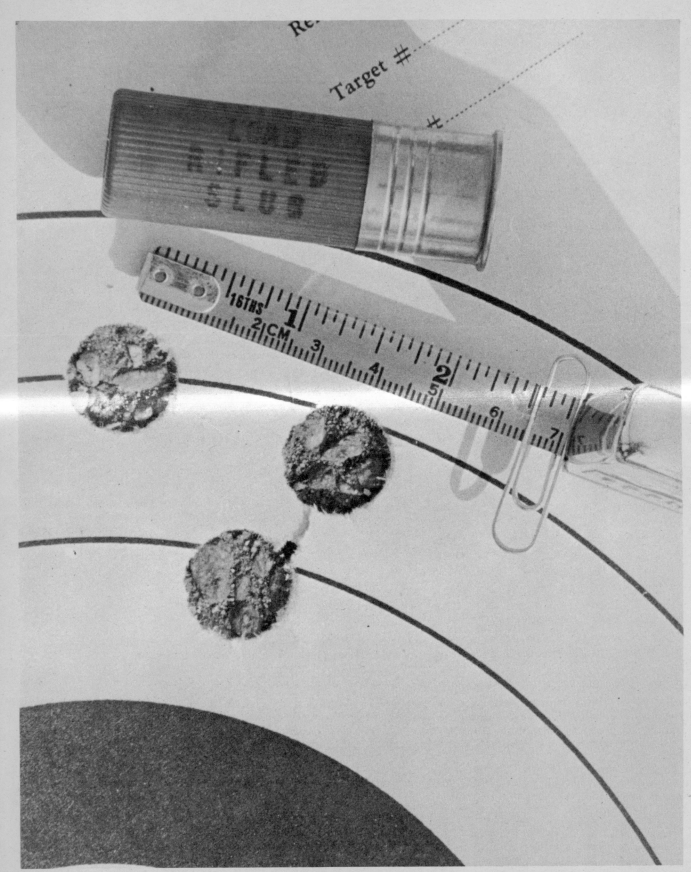

Firing with a scope-topped Ithaca Deerslayer, Dean Grennell was able to achieve this three-shot group, measuring roughly 1½ inches, center-to-center from 50-yard rest.

generally extreme. The exception, of course, is where quail, pheasant or small-game seasons coincide with deer season, as they do in California.

In the East, where the choice is made for you and leaves you only the pleasure of selecting make, gauge and sights, you'll find this is no little chore. Make, of course, is a matter of personality, for every make has its own idiosyncrasies.

A 20, 16 or 12? Any one would be a good choice for deer-size game. The rule of thumb on sights is get the best you can afford. Sights are your best insurance and, like an insurance company, they have to be reliable.

Getting back to what Ithaca calls its bird, boar or bear buster, the Super Single, the ones we used to check performance of the rifled slugs all were chambered for the 20 gauge three-inch magnum. However, the shells used were 2¾-inch. There are individual guns, too, that are inherently more accurate than others of the same make, model or gauge.

A review of the results would indicate that you can expect groups averaging four inches at fifty yards. Maximum effective range can be predicted to exceed one hundred yards – slightly.

"As to the oddball that produced exceptional groups, all I can do is appreciate it like a good bottle of wine or a beautiful woman. For the economy-minded hunter the shotgun with sights would appear to be the all-around, all-purpose gun, be it a single-shot or a pump, semi-auto or over/under double," says Ed Andrews.

Single-shot firearm, the action of which is opened by the lever, was used in conducting some of the tests with slugs. The barrels are interchangeable for other types of shooting.

Above: Robert Stack pauses in Northern California river to ponder the future of today's shotgun and how it will be affected by call for steel shot. (Right) Steel shot already is being made by several firms for purposes of experimentation in game management.

IS STEEL FOR REAL?

Substitutes For Lead Shot In
Waterfowling Are Being Demanded,
But It's Not All That Simple.

AT THE MOMENT, a controversy of long standing is going on within the firearms industry — in the shooting sports, in general — but we seem to be no closer to a solution than we were several years ago.

The controversy has to do with poisoning of ducks from lead shot and what to do about it. There are those who claim — and not without foundation for their opinions — that if steel shot is substituted, more ducks will fly away to die as cripples than are killed by ingestion of lead shot with their food.

As background, the National Wildlife Federation points out that "waterfowl hunters scatter an estimated 6000 tons of lead shot across American wetlands each year. Feeding waterfowl pick up some of this shot, which fouls up their digestive systems and they literally die of starvation, even though their crops may be full of food."

Studies conducted in the Fifties estimated that nearly twenty-five percent of the North American mallard population eats lead shot and that four percent of the entire mallard population dies from lead poisoning.

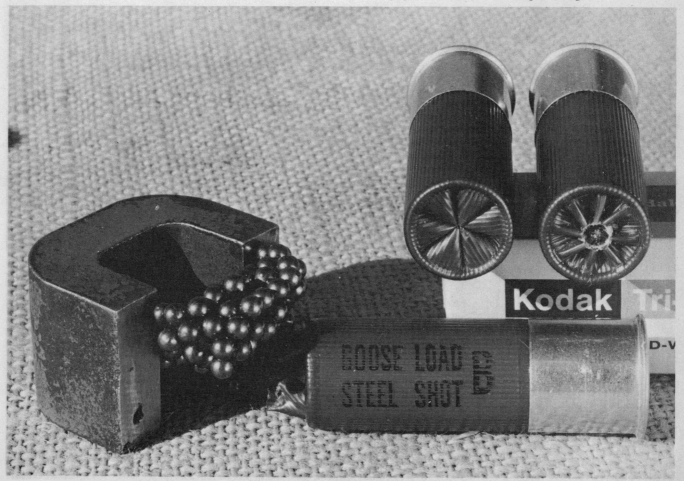

The federation contends that "the ammunition industry has tried unsuccessfully to come up with a modified lead pellet that wouldn't poison ducks. After a good deal of research by industry and government, shot of soft iron appeared the answer. In fact, in 1971, John Gottschalk, director of the U.S. Bureau of Sport Fisheries and Wildlife, estimated that hunters would be using iron shot within eighteen months. The following month, the International Association of Game, Fish and Conservation Commissioners adopted a resolution calling for a non-toxic waterfowl shot-shell by 1973.

The ammo industry, however said 1973 was too soon. The Sporting Arms and Ammunition Manufacturers' Institure — SAAMI — reported technolgocial snags; iron shot used in earlier tests had hardened with age and tended to chew up shotgun barrels and chokes. Also, they had not located a reliable source of soft iron for additional testing.

The federation began researching the problem and came up with what they term "additional information that was both frightening and confusing."

"The frightening part was recent studies by Dr. Lars Karstad of the University of Guelph in Ontario, Canada. His work indicates lead poisoning causes heart damage in ducks, in addition to fouling up their digestive systems.

"The confusing part came, when federation researchers started turning up manufacturers who were unmistakably optimistic about getting soft iron shot into waterfowl hunters' hands in the near future."

Superior Steel Ball in New Britain, Connecticut — the backyard of the firearms and ammo industry — is making a soft iron shot now that they say will not harden with age. A spokesman for the firm says: "Given a time-table by industry, in ten to twenty weeks, we can be producing up to 20,000 pounds of non-toxic shot a day."

Apparently U.S. Steel also is making a soft iron wire that federation investigators felt would meet shotshell specifications and the MPB Corporation in Keene, New Hampshire, claims "excellent potential" in the iron shot market.

Going a bit beyond and into the realm of shooting, representatives of Poly Choke in East Hartford, Connecticut, are reported to have said "the possibility of getting iron shot on sporting goods shelves is definitely realistic" and would not damage its chokes.

"As far as my position goes, I understand both sides and I recognize the shortcomings of steel shot," Richard C. Wolff, vice-president of the Garcia Corporation, says. The corporation is one of the leading importers of quality Italian shotguns and, of course, has an interest in the proceedings, even though they are not in the shotshell business.

"However, I question why we should impose the steel shot law in deep water areas where lead is not a problem," Wolff continues. "I think a test area should be established in the Atlantic flyway and the results studied through questionnaires supplied to shooters. I cannot justify in my mind the mandatory use of a less effective load without knowing all there is to know about it and without undertaking an educational program to prevent the shooters from shooting at game beyond the effective range of the gun."

His opinion not withstanding, Garcia has been subjecting one of its shotguns, the Beretta BL-2/S, an over/under shotgun introduced early in 1974, to steel shot damage tests. At the last report I had, more than 2000 rounds had been fired through one of these guns at headquarters of the Federal Cartridge Company in Minnesota. At that time, there was no visible damage to the barrel from the steel shot, I'm told.

And, as might be expected, the shot problem has become a political crusade in some quarters.

Early in 1974, Idaho's Senator James A. McClure introduced a bill to place a freeze on any decision to ban lead shot for hunting "until the Congress has an opportunity to hear the evidence and take legislative action on the issue.

"The Interior Department is very close to issuing an order that could ultimately end the use of lead shot for waterfowl hunting across the nation," the senator said at the time, "and nowhere in the process of making these new regulations have there been either public hearings or consultations with the Congress.

"In this case, the Bureau of Sport Fisheries and Wildlife is locked to an idea without sufficient scientific evidence or expert opinion on all sides of the issue to warrant a fair decision. Certainly there is evidence of waterfowl kills from lead poisoning through shot ingested in feeding, but there is ample evidence that a ban of lead shot without a suitable alternative is no answer at all," the senator stated.

"In fact, there is much scientific weight to show that the alternative steel or iron shot that will be ordered as a replacement will bring about more needless waterfowl mortality than any now attributed to lead poisoning."

Senator McClure said that, under his bill, the Secretary of Interior would be prohibited from issuing any order banning or replacing lead shot, until the proper committees of the Congress can weigh both the practical and scientific arguments on all sides and for all alternatives.

Idaho, of course, is a lead-producing state.

Not only has the Bureau of Sport Fisheries and Wildlife conducted exhaustive tests relative to the practicality of substitutes for lead shot, but some of the firearms firms have carried out equally exhaustive and expensive programs. Among those conducting their own investigations have been Winchester-Western, Remington-Peters and Federal Cartridge Company.

Dr. Ed Kozicky of Winchester-Western's conservation department, headquartered in East Alton, Illinois, has been one of those most involved in continuing research.

"Waterfowl represent a priceless resource that we are striving to maintain on a constantly shrinking habitat base. Because of that dwindling habitat, all loss factors of waterfowl have taken on new importance in recent years, and waterfowl lead poisoning has become a matter of deep concern," Kozicky says.

As a possible alternative to toxic lead shot pellets, the testing of steel shot began as early as 1949 when Frank Bellrose of the Illinois Natural History Survey and Winchester-Western technicians worked together on the problem. Out of this grew Bellrose's classic lead poisoning study of the 1950s, again in cooperation with Winchester-Western.

The next steel shot study was at Nilo Farms, W-W's demonstration and experimental shooting preserve near Alton, Illinois. That 1964 test was conducted by members of the Mississippi Flyway Council with free-flying mallards. Shooting was done by gunners of varying ability from four different blinds and range estimates were made by observers. Not only were the range estimates subject to error, but in many cases shooters in different blinds were responsible for hitting the duck.

In 1968, the Bureau of Sport Fisheries and Wildlife at Maryland's Patuxent Wildlife Research Center conducted a steel shot study that was carefully designed, monitored and controlled. They used 1¼-ounce, No. 4 and No. 6 lead loads and a one-ounce steel load.

Early in 1972, Winchester-Western began planning a similar test at Nilo Farms, and for good reasons: The Patuxent results had held some ballistic surprises — such as "the performance of soft iron shot was close to that obtain-

Left: Surprinted is Beretta over/under mentioned in text, which is being used by Federal Cartridge Co., in steel shot tests. (Above) Dean Grennell holds sandhill crane taken with Ithaca 10-gauge, which is being developed with the idea of shooting steel shot.

In spite of photos such as this, today's duck population has been decreasing, but it has been more the destruction of Canadian breeding grounds than the threat of lead shot many insist. Ducks Unlimited has purchased and developed many new nesting grounds for ducks.

ed with commercial lead loads" between thirty and sixty-five yards.

"Although we knew that the number of pellets striking a duck is important, we were surprised to learn that, according to the Patuxent definition for 'bagging' ducks, 6 lead shot out-performed 4 lead shot at sixty-five yards," Kozicky says. "Maybe there was a difference in measurable ballistic energy of a shotshell in the lab and its actual efficiency in bagging ducks."

In addition, new shotshells had been developed in the four years since the Patuxent work. The Nilo study would use a No. 4 steel load with 1-1/8 ounces of shot, instead of the one-ounce loads fired at Patuxent. Because the No. 6 lead load had performed so well in the federal study — reflecting the efficiency of dense patterns and large numbers of small shot pellets — bureau technicians who participated in planning the Nilo test wished to see a 1-1/8-ounce load of 6 steel shot used in the Nilo work.

Winchester technicians also wanted to study a 1-1/8-ounce load of pure No. 4 copper shot. Pure copper's specific gravity lies about one-third of the way between iron and lead and it has a lower modulus of elasticity than iron. Being more malleable and less elastic than steel, copper probably would do less damage to shotgun barrels.

So Nilo used three non-lead shotshell loads that had not been examined anywhere else: a 1-1/8-ounce, No. 6 steel load, a 1-1/8-ounce No. 4 steel load, and a 1-1/8-ounce load of pure copper 4s. The interstices between the shot pellets were filled with grains of high-density polyethylene in an effort to flow the shot charges more easily through the gun barrel and choke.

These three non-lead loads were compared to No. 4 lead shot in the Super-X, Mark 5 XX Magnum, which carries 1½ ounces of shot as well as the polyethylene grains. Decision to compare non-lead loads with the XX Magnum was based on four points: that this load (as were the copper and steel loads) was the best they could make; that the pellet count in the XX Magnum was similar to that of the No. 4 steel load; they needed verification of the relationship of measurable ballistic energy to efficiency in bagging ducks; and if such a relationship existed, they would have a spread of ballistic energy reference points to develop a mathematical lethality model for ducks.

All of the ammunition was manufactured and on hand before the start of the experiment, and was stored in an unheated area throughout the test.

It was decided to schedule the Nilo test during the Fall and Winter under conditions similar to those of the hunting season, since air temperature does affect shotshell efficiency. The University of Wisconsin would make fluoroscopic studies of broken bones and embedded shot pellets. In addition, copper toxicity tests on wild mallards were initiated with the Illinois Natural History Survey and a barrel damage test was begun by W-W ballisticians.

The Nilo duck transport device was a cable-driven trolley running on a one hundred-foot track. Controlled by rheostat, the trolley could run down the track at a consistent 18 mph, with an electronic timer measuring the top speed of each run to a thousandth of a second. Prior to the Patuxent test, Bureau technicians determined that a duck had to be traveling about 20 mph to stimulate the bird to use its wings.

Shooting was done at wind velocities less than 10 mph and shooting was postponed or halted when gusting winds could cause a drift of more than fifteen inches to No. 6 steel shot at any given yardage — that shot being the most susceptible to deflection by wind. Shooting was halted when there was rain or when the temperature was less than 8F.

Firing was done from ranges of 30, 40, 50, 60, 70 and 80 yards. A Winchester Model 1200 pump gun, with a full choke, twenty-eight-inch barrel, was rigidly mounted in a machine rest and triggered by a solenoid that was activated by a limit switch on the track.

The barrel of the shotgun was checked at the end of each six hundred birds for choke deformation and pattern levels to assure consistency of patterns.

Pattern tests were made before and after each group of five birds to assure the center of pattern being on target.

There were only eight sets of five birds discarded during the test for various reasons — wind, rain, electronic problems, or pattern shifts. The centers of shot patterns were obvious on the four-foot square patterning board through fifty yards, but at sixty through eighty yards the patterns grew so large and diffuse that it was necessary to draw a thirty-inch circle and count the pellets within it to determine the pattern center. All variables — with the exception of individual shotshell performance, temperature conditions, and non-uniform distribution of vital areas on a duck's body — were controlled within specific limits. The Nilo study involved firing at 2400 experimental mallards.

In the earlier Patuxent test, all birds dead within five minutes or birds with broken wing bones were considered "bagged." However, Frank Bellrose expressed reservations about assuming that any mallard with a broken wing bone constituted a bagged duck. His field experience indicated there was about a fifty-fifty chance of a bird with a broken wing bone being bagged or lost.

The Patuxent test classified all birds without a broken wing bone that died between five minutes and ten days after shooting as "lost cripples." "Survivors" were those birds in apparent good health at the end of ten days. "Survivors" in the Nilo test had to pass an objective flying test. Whether or not such birds would be considered bagged, crippled or survivors in the wild is another question. Birds in the wild that are shot but not bagged do not have ten days, with free-choice food and water and protection from predators, in which to recover.

Before the Nilo test, there was a theory that steel shot would bag ducks efficiently at forty yards and fifty yards,

In the era of twenty-odd years ago, when Robert Stack, Clark Gable and other shooters hunted ducks in prime marshlands, there was a higher limit and no one ever had heard of the threat of lead shot. Today, this has become a major problem of the ecology.

Some authorities question whether introduction of steel shot is necessary on a nation-wide basis, as not all hunting areas have the same type of waters where duck can ingest poisonous lead shot. In areas with bottoms of silt, the lead quickly is buried beneath it.

do a minimum of crippling within a limited yardage, then become harmless. This did not prove to be the case. Even though 6 steel was as efficient as No. 4 lead at thirty yards, it crippled eleven percent of the birds at forty yards, reached a high of twenty-nine percent at sixty yards and fell to a low of ten percent at eighty yards.

The drop in efficiency of the four shotshell loads is apparent. The No. 6 steel loads started to lose effectiveness at forty yards; No. 4 steel loads at fifty yards; No. 4 copper loads between fifty and sixty yards; and No. 4 lead between sixty and seventy yards.

"It isn't until we reach eighty yards that the No. 4 lead load cripples more birds than the other three loads; however, in crippling twenty-three of the one hundred birds, No. 4 lead also bagged sixteen birds," Kozicky notes.

"One of the common misconceptions in comparing lead and steel shotshells is the use of separate statistical analyses of 'bagged' and 'crippled' birds, especially the latter," Kozicky contends. "What must be evaluated is the number of birds bagged per bird crippled at a given yardage. This is the only true measure of shotshell efficiency as it relates to field conditions.

"Only ducks brought to bag constitute part of a daily limit. Hence, the efficiency of a shotshell in hunting ducks is best determined by the ratio of ducks bagged per cripple. The hunter always shoots to bag a duck and not to cripple. If your shot charge does not have enough energy to bag the duck, it will cripple the duck. Cripples are a lost resource and a blight on the day afield. Every hunter hopes for clean kills."

In terms of bagged birds, the four shotshells were comparable only at thirty yards. The No. 4 lead load proved superior to the other three from forty through eighty yards. The No. 4 lead did less crippling than the other three loads until it reached seventy yards, when No. 4 copper and 6 steel did less. At eighty yards, the other three shotshell loads crippled less than No. 4 lead, but the lead also bagged sixteen percent of the birds.

"In summarizing the Nilo test data, we verified the direct relationship of measurable ballistic energy and shotshell efficiency in bagging waterfowl. We can only conclude that the use of steel shot in the 2¾-inch, 12-gauge shotshell for waterfowl hunting will significantly increase crippling loss," Kozicky contends.

He feels that use of steel shot will result in a trade-off: a

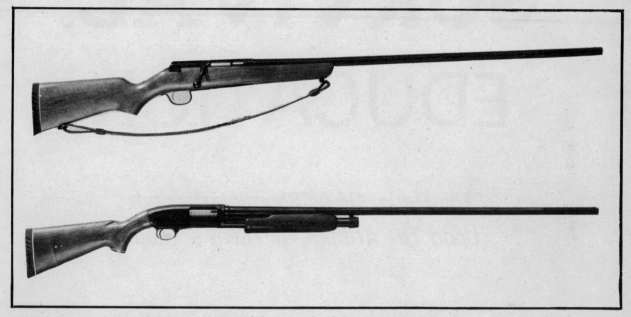

Marlin Firearms is one of those producers of shotguns that have decided that longer barrels will be of some aid in making lighter weight steel shot more deadly at the extended ranges. Their bolt-action goose gun (top) and pump gun have been revamped.

gradual decrease in lead poisoning losses for an annual increment in crippling loss of waterfowl. And to us, a less efficient shotshell load, with its attendant increase in crippling of birds, will reduce the quality experience of waterfowl hunting as we know it today.

"Hence, the Bureau of Sport Fisheries and Wildlife needs to validate current lead poisoning losses by flyway prior to a final decision on the use of steel shot."

Personally, I view the controversy with mixed feelings. I don't like seeing ducks crippled, nor does any other hunter. This sort of thing serves as grist for the mill of the anti-hunting forces, as well as insulting the integrity of the serious sportsman. On the other hand, neither do I like to think of ducks dying of lead poisoning.

I do have to agree with Garcia's Dick Wolff on one facet, however. I don't see the value of introducing steel shot — if that is the ultimate answer — on a nationwide basis. Where one is shooting over deep water, ducks are not likely to pick up lead shot. Here in California, similar studies have been made and fish and game personnel feel that, in our type of terrain and soil conditions, the shot is buried almost immediately in the silt, thus poses no threat.

Meantime, those firearms companies not actively engaged in the production of shotshells seem to be looking ahead, accepting the fact that there will be changes. The Ithaca Gun Company, for example, recently introduced an automatic 10-gauge magnum. The theory is that the larger shell will pump out more lead — or steel — to improve the lethality factor. Other companies such as Marlin Firearms and Harrington and Richardson are turning out shotguns with forty-inch barrels. As I understand it, the theory here is that, while they don't shoot any harder, they should tend to hold a tighter pattern at extended ranges, thus providing greater impact upon the waterfowl.

In the matter of copper, initially researchers found this of interest, because copper has several properties not found in iron and steel. Copper, as mentioned, is heavier that steel, which affords a ballistic advantage. It also is more ductile with what the experts called a lower "modulus of elasticity than steel." Since copper is deformed more easily than soft steel, it may flow more readily through a shotgun barrel with less deformation of the gun's choke.

According to Bill Talley of Winchester-Western, a friend since my youth, the solid copper pellets are formed by the same process by which steel shot pellets are made. The shot is not dropped in the molten state as is the case with lead. Instead, it is cut from wire and rolled between steel plates to obtain the necessary spherical shape.

Newer research, however, shows that ducks that have been feeding on corn find copper toxic, when ingested, so it appears that avenue has been shot down.

However, I have faith that any nation that can hit the moon with a rocket can devise a means of efficiently shooting ducks without the unpleasant alternatives outlined. And development of the proper load shouldn't cost nearly as much as a moon shot!

For Shooters' SURVIVAL: EDUCATION

The Future Of All Shooting Depends Upon The Attitude Of Today's Youth!

WE ARE IN an age in which anti-gun forces, often misguided and unknowledgeable concerning any phase of the shooting sports, seek to ban ownership of firearms. Over the past two decades, they have used numerous ploys as a means of chipping at our freedom to own and use firearms. It was Winston Churchill who once expressed the thought that any freedom lost never is regained. And, a bit at a time, ownership of even sporting arms is becoming increasingly more restricted.

In recent years, the anti-gun faction has found that sportsmen tend to band together when threatened. As a result, these forces seem to have abandoned the effort to get all firearms banned immediately. Instead, they have begun to nibble at the edges of the sport, mouthing mistruths, distorting fact and ignoring the obvious as a means of propagandizing their effort. The target of such a campaign is the non-shooting citizen who never has handled firearms; with his lack of actual knowledge, he becomes easier to convince of the dangers of any and all firearms in the hands of their fellow citizens. Several years ago, these forces were able to get mail-order guns banned. Many of us were in favor of such a law and saw the wisdom of such a move, but we also realized it was just the beginning of a continuing program of taking a piece here, taking a piece there, until nothing is left.

In recent seasons, there has been an effort to ban handguns known as "Saturday Night Specials," yet there is no real definition as to what constitutes that particular category of gun.

In the event a law is passed banning specific handguns, that will be another victory for the anti-gun forces and they undoubtedly will set up another immediate objective aimed at bringing them one step closer to banishment of private ownership of all firearms.

With my own background in the shooting sports, I can't help but be concerned for all types of target shooting and hunting. This has been a way of life in America for centuries and I was brought up on the value of individual rights — which includes keeping firearms in accord with Constitutional guarantees.

Roy G. Jinks of Smith & Wesson, one of the nation's oldest firearms companies, has made an extended study of the problem. He says, "There is no doubt that the present situation requires urgent action with individuals writing to their legislators to express their views that firearms are no different than the tools of every other sport and that new legislation will not serve to limit those with criminal intent.

"However," adds Jinks, "this method is short-term and is the type of fight that, in the long run, will prove fruitless, because human endurance to fight off legislation year after year causes individuals to feel locked to a hopeless situation and interest drops to the point of asking what good does it do to write year after year, when new bills are continually introduced."

Age and sex are not handicaps in the shooting sports. In 1968 Winchester claybird finals, 15-year-old Jim McNeal and 58-year-old John Kuslich were on opposing teams. (Below) In first intercollegiate claybird tournament, student Ruth Johnson was one of three girls in finals. She was the lone lady on an otherwise all male team.

I have to agree with Jinks and others that education is the key to survival of the shooting sports, whether trap and skeet, handgun targetry or big-game hunting. There are those who will say that we already have educational programs, but such courses as hunter safety, homegun safety, et al., seem to be aimed at those already interested in shooting. In short, we end up talking to ourselves.

Instead, we need to reach the public which never has had much to do with shooting; that segment that is influenced easily by the propaganda of the anti-gun cults. The future of firearms obviously lies with the young people of our country.

The first question is how to develop shooting sports programs in schools and colleges. The basic problem is staff to provide instruction in shooting-oriented programs. There is some of this being done on a minor scale already, of course.

Roy Jinks instructs a teen-ager in the techniques of shooting in the field. In this case, a break-top single-shot was used because of simplicity and as a safety factor.

Take, for example, the community of Osage, Iowa. The town and its school officials, aware that theirs is a hunting area, think enough of the gunning future of their juniors that they hired a qualified instructor to teach hunting and gun safety to students.

Teaching gun safety in the Osage school system actually is not new. For the past dozen years, gun safety assemblies have been included at least once each year — usually before hunting seasons — on the schedules. Then about six years ago, gun safety classes were incorporated as a regular part of the curriculum. During these years, the classes were taught by members of the school staff.

A.O. Swenson, then Osage's high school principal, is credited with being the original instigator of the plan for firearms training, which began in the senior high school program. Beginning with the senior classes, each succeeding class was given gun safety instruction until the seventh grade level was reached. At this point, Keith Duncan, principal of the junior high school, inherited the course and it still is maintained as a part of the seventh grade curriculum listed under required social studies courses.

In view of new developments in the field of sporting arms, it was decided to hire an outsider well qualified in gun handling. Dave Dunlop of Osage was hired to spend a full week on the program. He is active in programs of the National Rifle Association and is a hunter safety instuctor certified by the Iowa State Conservation Commission.

Dunlop cooperated with Alan Roemig, the locally based conservation officer, to present a course of instruction backed up with slides, charts, graphs, movies — and actual guns used as practical props and models.

In the first day of the reorganized course, Roemig presented the legal aspects of the hunting-guns picture, then

From left: Dick Waide, founder of the University of Iowa shooting program; Jeff Wambacher, then president of the gun club that offered support, and Don Schoote, who was installation manager.

In the first intercollegiate claybird finals, students from twenty colleges and universities invaded the Iowa campus to take part. Since that time, in 1968, more than 200 institutions of higher learning have adopted the shooting program as part of their recreation programs.

three days of intensive instruction were climaxed by the final day of tests.

The examination papers were sent to the state capitol at Des Moines, where Charles Olofson, hunter safety officer for the conservation commission, checked all results and issued certificates of competency to the students involved.

The certificates were awarded in a classroom ceremony, with the qualified student shooters being issued patches to be worn on their hunting jackets. Boys and girls alike were given the course.

According to Swenson, who started the whole thing, the little time out of the school year that is devoted to the specialized training is well received by teachers, students and parents. It also is building a safety sense concerning guns and hunting within the community that should result in a safer, better trained citizenry. It is a program that other schools across the nation might well look into.

At one college in Pennsylvania, the state that supposedly has the nation's largest deer population, there is a course in deer hunting with success in the course dependent upon whether one gets his deer. The course is taught by qualified instructors from the state's fish and game department, as well as by practicing local guides.

On a more commercial note, Daisy, who has been mak-ing BB guns for more generations than most of us care to remember, has sponsored the National BB Gun Championships with a big, final three-day contest around the Fourth of July. This is aimed at youngsters and, I feel, has done much to interest many in shooting.

Roy Jinks, however, suggests workshops for those who already are teaching physical education in the schools.

"These people already have been trained in the techniques of teaching and need only to experience the basic shooting sports skills, receiving information as well as practical experience concerning common faults and teaching corrections, as well as information necessary to establish a program."

Such a workshop was conducted in late 1973 at the Cispus Environmental Center in Randle, Washington. According to Jinks, "Participants left not only with a high degree of interest and enthusiasm, but with real skills and practical knowledge needed to initiate a shooting sports program at their home institutions."

Jinks suggests clinics or workshops can be sponsored by an educational institution or jointly by the institutions, the firearms industry and organizations such as the National Shooting Sports Foundation and National Rifle Association.

Members of the Air Force Academy trap and skeet teams have been among those showing great interest in college claybird programs; some colleges allow credits for shooting.

Winchester-Western has been one of the biggest supporters of the college shooting programs, even furnishing the ammunition for national tournaments.

"In any clinic, the staff should be skilled not only in teaching a skill to students, but in helping those students to become effective teachers of the sport," Roy Jinks adds. "Time must be devoted to coaching techniques, teaching progressions, organization and safety. This is the type of intensive experience teachers want and need."

At Arnold College, University of Bridgeport, in Connecticut, students majoring in physical education can elect a course in the shooting sports on an independent study basis. The course includes teaching-coaching experience, care and maintenance of equipment and safety, as well as learning the shooting skills. Needless to say, personnel of

Remington Arms, headquartered in Bridgeport, offer support in this program.

For the most part, however, these programs all are on the advanced level and there aren't many of them. What does the individual father do, if he wants his son to learn to shoot?

My own teen-age son got off to a poor beginning in his shooting career. I had been pondering when I should introduce him to skeet shooting and had been doing some work with him with a little .410. But when he was about 6 years old, he was out with me when someone urged him to try a 20-gauge gun, promising him there was nothing to it.

Sharon Lang, top girl shooter of the initial claybird intercollegiate tournament, displays the form she used in firing on equal terms against her male opponents.

The recoil shock and surprise from that single round discouraged him considerably. I think most fathers who have a love for shooting want their sons to feel that same love, and I'm just as certain that any son who fails to take the same interest in guns that is felt by his old man may be creating some sort of secret sorrow for his dad. It could even be a little selfish on my part to look at it this way, but the fact remains that I have wanted my son to be a shooter almost from the day he was brought home from the hospital.

The relationship between a boy and his gun should be one of confidence. It should be a new experience, an exciting one. Fear has no place in it.

I've wanted him to forget that incident dealing with the discovery of recoil. Finally that day arrived and he asked if he could go shooting with me and learn something about skeet technique. That was one of the happier days of my life.

I spent some time in telling him of the fun of shooting, explaining that it was just a game; that whether you won wasn't as important as simply having fun.

I was nearly twice as old as my son when I started serious shooting, but I made some friends during that period that I've kept all my life. I want that same opportunity, those same friendships, for my son.

In getting a boy started, the first thing, of course, is selection of the shotgun. I chose a Stevens .410 single-barrel hammer gun and the lightest loads I could lay hands on. This was to impress upon him that the recoil from this gun doesn't hurt.

In choosing this model, I also was selecting the smallest gun I could find. In my youth, the shotgun I used was a 20-gauge L.C. Smith double. It had thirty-inch barrels, but these were cut off to twenty-six, thus having no choke. I'm not convinced, though, that this is the answer and I really believe that manufacturers are missing the market by not building more youth guns; shotguns and rifles that are tailored literally to the smaller measurements and stature of a boy.

Charlie and I already had spent a good deal of time on gun safety and I'm sure he understands the requirements. One of the reasons for choosing the .410 hammer gun was the visual factors. If the hammer is back, one knows it is

From left: Sharon Lang, Jim Dee of Winchester-Western's shooting program staff, are present as she is awarded trophy from Bob Froeschle, who represented University of Iowa.

Qualified shooters are selected at college level shoots to do the official scoring, handle administrative chores.

dangerous, and he has to break the gun to tell whether there is a round in the chamber.

In my own case, I was extremely careful with guns when I started shooting, but I had to be, since I was shooting with men much older than myself and I wanted to be accepted by them. I have attempted to instill some of this feeling of responsibility in my own son and to show him the reasons why he must be responsible.

In teaching kids to shoot, I think it's most important that they be able to see the results of their shooting. In short, there has to be some excitement to it; they have to be able to see something break. Even to most adults, knocking over birds in a shooting gallery is more exciting than simply punching holes in paper. So, if the lad can see the bird break when his shot hits it, he knows he is accomplishing something and his interest doesn't wane. If he finds he's doing nothing but shooting holes in the blue, it won't be long before another potential shooter has found other interests.

At the range, I started young Charlie at low house one, shooting at in-comers, obviously the easiest shot. It took him a few rounds to learn what he was doing, then I worked him up until he broke five out of ten birds from low house six. It requires a lead of only a yard and a half or so, and he picked this up in a matter of minutes. If you can instill lead and follow, the rest becomes only a matter of degree.

At the other extreme, had I started him at four post, he'd probably have shot up a case of shells before he hit one. At this early age, I'm sure a boy's concentration is somewhat scattered and chances are that his interest would not have lasted until he hit a bird.

The .410 shotgun with the short shell, of course, is the most difficult arm known to man when it comes to shooting skeet, so it is important to keep in mind that with so light a gun, one should only plan on giving his son the feel of the game, hoping that he will hit an occasional target. If he starts to lose interest, it's not difficult to tell. Either he'll be wandering around picking up empty cases, or you won't be able to find him when it's time to shoot.

This is the time to take him out of the game and return to some practical plinking such as shooting at a target against a hill or cans tossed in the air.

Throughout this early training with my own son, I did my best to give him the impression that he was not being pushed. At the other extreme, I've seen experienced shoot-

ers who took their sons and attempted to make them into instant competitors. They made the entire job of shooting seem like homework and I felt certain, after observing the relationships, that here were boys who would not stick with shooting. Each would find other pursuits where there was less fatherly enthusiasm.

And I think that every father, regardless of his technique, is thinking secretly of the day when he can share with his son the fun of occupying the same duck blind. This is the only way in which an adult can recapture the thrill of the sound of wings in the fog. For him, the thrill long since has diminished and he is attempting to regain it through his son the first time the boy hears a flight of geese coming in through the mists. The real fulfillment is in re-experiencing such a feeling. Perhaps, as I suggested in the beginning, there's even something selfish about it; trying to relive your own youth through the eyes and mind of a son. But there also must be a feeling of giving in sharing with your son the same things that afforded you pleasure when you were his age.

Insofar as the claybird sports are concerned, perhaps the greatest educational force to date is Association of College Unions International, which has sponsored the national Intercollegiate Trap and Skeet Championships since 1969. In the first such tournament held on the University of Iowa campus at Iowa City, Dale Reiter of North Iowa Community College was presented a Winchester shotgun and a trophy, being named the individual trapshooting champion of that first national intercollegiate tournament.

But the event was more significant that simply providing this shooter with a trophy. It provided a breakthrough in the field of collegiate competition.

In past decades, we have looked to colleges and universities for nearly all of our Olympic athletes — with the exception of the shooting sports. This facet of international competition has been dominated almost exclusively by the military, which has had the time, manpower and facilities for training top marksmen in all categories. However, this could change in due time, with the help of the students, themselves.

The recreation committee of the Association of College Unions International authorized development of pilot programs in a number of outdoor areas. Area X, which covers the Midwest colleges and universities, surveyed interests in thirty-one recreational activities. Surprisingly to some, trap and skeet showed the highest percentage of interest.

R.E. Waide, then associate director of the Iowa Memori-

Air Force Academy shooters take competition seriously, displaying form that is taught them at Colorado Springs campus by experts.

Students at Connecticut's Arnold College receive excellent instruction at gun club operated by Remington.

al Union at the University of Iowa, says that "we asked the recreation committee to sponsor intercollegiate competition in trap and skeet. These sports were chosen because of the Olympic competition potential; there was no organized intercollegiate competition; both men and women could participate; and because claybirding was one of the most rapidly growing recreational activities. At the time, we found that the number of participants had quadrupled in five years."

Waide also presented the committee with the fact that claybird shooting was listed by the National Safety Council as one of the ten most safe forms of recreation, as there never has been a disabling or fatal accident in organized competition. Also cost of facilities would be comparatively low and industry support was available. Also, Waide found, at that time, seventeen colleges and universities offered academic credit for trap and skeet as a part of their physical education programs.

"Winchester-Western offered to provide financial support for the pilot program," Waide recalls. "They were selected, because their shooting sports development arm is not a function of the marketing division. It also was agreed that the marketing division would not become involved in the program.

"Winchester-Western provided $1800 to cover a part of the cost of the pilot program, the funds being used for travel, telephones, mailings, as well as targets and ammunition for introductory meets."

Initial competition between colleges was a pair of postal matches to determine interest. The first was held with twenty-seven Midwestern colleges participating. The second postal match had eighteen teams participating, but the drop in seeming interest was due largely to the fact that the match was held during some of the worst winter months in Midwestern history. On the basis of such interest, it was decided that the first head-to-head competition should be on a national basis rather than simply a regional affair.

The first national college tournament was held at the University Gun Club, a privately financed range on the outskirts of Iowa City. That first year, eighty-five students, representing twenty colleges and universities — including three girls — arrived on the University of Iowa campus for the competitions. While geographic distribution was centered primarily in the Midwest, there were exceptions, such as the Air Force Academy team from Colorado and one lone student from the University of Connecticut. There also was one three-member team — two boys and a girl — from Edinboro State College in Pennsylvania.

Oddly enough, when it came to International skeet, none of the fifteen competitors ever had shot the event before. In more recent meets, they have not been quite so naive, I might add.

While hunting is a way of life in the Midwest and students can be expected to show interest in shooting, the Ivy League schools also have begun to show interest. Yale, as an example, has taken the old engineering school with several hundred acres of woodlands and is incorporating an entire outdoor complex in this area. Included in the overall plan will be shooting, fishing and camping facilities.

In 1974, when the intercollegiate championships were held for the sixth time — the site the Cleveland-Chardon Winchester Gun Club in Chardon, Ohio — there were 238 shooters from forty-two colleges and universities, representing twenty-three states. Actually more than two hundred colleges are involved in the overall program.

But perhaps most important of all is the fact that some of the future leaders of our nation are becoming interested in the shooting sports. Among the college shooters are future lawyers, administrators, teachers, doctors — even politicians — all of whom will be able to lend voices in their individual communities.

I have no doubt that education of the public is our greatest problem; getting youngsters to listen to the truth about the shooting sports. And as I close this book, I ask all of you to give this facet of education serious thought and to determine what you can do in your own communities to see that an American way of life does not become doomed.

Directory Of Manufacturers & Importers

AMMUNITION (Commercial)

Alcan Shells, (See: Smith & Wesson Ammunition Co.)
DWM (See RWS)
Dynamit Nobel of America, Inc., 105 Stonehurst Ct., Northvale, NJ 07647 (DWM, RWS)
Federal Cartridge Co., 2700 Foshay Tower, Minneapolis, Minn. 55402
RWS (See Dynamit Nobel)
Remington Arms Co., Bridgeport, Conn. 06602
Service Armament, 689 Bergen Blvd., Ridgefield, N.J. 07657
Smith & Wesson Ammunition Co., 3640 Seminary Rd., Alton, IL 62002
Winchester-Western, East Alton, Ill. 62024

AMMUNITION (Custom)

Collectors Shotshell Arsenal, 365 S. Moore, Lakewood, CO 80226
Man-Tol Shells, Box 134, Bunnell, Fla. 32010
Numrich Arms Corp., 203 Broadway, W. Hurley, N.Y. 12491
Robert Pomeroy, Morrison Ave., East Corinth, ME 04427 (custom shells)
A.F. Sailer, 707 W. 3d St., Owen, WI 54460
Whitney Cartridge Co., P.O. Box 608, Cortez, CO 81321 (shotshells)

AMMUNITION (Foreign)

Abercrombie & Fitch., Madison at 45th St., New York, N.Y. 10017
Canadian Ind. Ltd. (C.I.L.), Box 10, Montreal, Que., Canada
C-I-L Ammunition Inc., P.O. Box 831, Plattsburgh, N.Y. 12901
Dynamit Nobel of America, Inc., 105 Stonehurst Court, Northvale, NJ 07647 (RWS)
Gevelot of Canada, Box 1593, Saskatoon, Sask., Canada
Stoeger Arms Corp., 55 Ruta Ct., So. Hackensack, N.J. 07606

AMMUNITION COMPONENTS — BULLETS, POWDER, PRIMERS

Alcan, (See: Smith & Wesson Ammunition Co.)
Ballistic Research Industries, See: Smith & Wesson (12 ga. Sabot bullets)
Division Lead, 7742 W. 61 Pl., Summit, Ill. 60502
DuPont, Explosives Dept., Wilmington, Del. 19898
Farmer Bros. Mfg. Co., 1102 Washington St., Eldora, IA 50627
Hercules Powder Co., 910 Market St., Wilmington, Del. 19899
Herter's Inc., Waseca, Minn. 56093
B.E. Hodgdon, Inc., 7710 W. 50th Hwy., Shawnee Mission, Kans. 66202
Kush Plastics, P.O. Box 366, Palatine, IL 60067 (shotshell wads)
Lyman Products for Shooters, Route 147, Middlefield, CT 06455
Meyer Bros. Mfgrs., Wabasha, Minn. 55981 (shotgun slugs)
Michael's Antiques, Box 233, Copiague, L.I., NY 11726 (Balle Blondeau)
Norma-Precision, So. Lansing, N.Y. 14882 (powder)
Omark-CCI, Box 856, Lewiston, Idaho 83501 (primers)
Pattern Perfect, P.O. Box 366, Palatine, IL 60067 (shotshell wads)
Red Diamond Distributing Co., 1304 Snowdon Dr., Knoxville, TN 37912 (black powder)
Remco, 1404 Whitesboro St., Utica, NY 13502 (shot capsules)
Remington-Peters, Bridgeport, Conn. 06602
Smith & Wesson Ammunition Co., 3640 Seminary Rd., Alton, IL 62002
Speer Products Inc., Box 896, Lewiston, Ida 83501
Thompson/Center Arms, Rt. 2, Box 7E, Rochester, NH 03867 (Hot Shot capsules)
Winchester-Western, New Haven, Conn. 06504

CHOKE DEVICES & RECOIL ABSORBERS

Arms Ingenuity Co., Box 1, Weatogue, Conn. 06089 (Jet-Away)
Contra-Jet, 7920 49th Ave. So., Seattle, Wash. 98118
Dahl's Gun Shop, Rt. 2, Billings, Mont. 59101
Diverter Arms, Inc., 6520 Rampart St., Houston, TX 77036 (A&W shotgun diverter)
Edwards Recoil Reducer, 269 Herbert St., Alton, Ill. 62002
Emsco Chokes, 101 Second Ave., S.E., Waseca, Minn. 56093
Herter's Inc., Waseca, Minn. 56093 (Vari-Choke)
Lyman Gun Sight Products, Middlefield, Conn. 60455 (Cutts Comp.)
Mag-na-port Arms, Inc., 16746 14 Mile Road, Fraser, MI 48026 (muzzle-brake system)
Pendleton Dekickers, 1210 S.W. Hailey Ave., Pendleton, Ore. 97801
Poly-Choke Co., Inc., Box 296, Hartford, Conn. 06101
St. Louis Precision Products, 902 Michigan Ave., St. Louis, Mich. 48880 (Gun-Tamer)
Williams Gunsmithing, 1706 Rosslynn, Fullerton, CA 92631

CHRONOGRAPHS AND PRESSURE TOOLS

Avtron, 10409 Meech Ave., Cleveland, Ohio 44105
B-Square Co., Box 11281, Ft. Worth, Tex. 76110
Chronograph Specialists, P.O. Box 5005, Santa Ana, Calif. 92704
Display Electronics, Box 1044, Littleton, CO 80120
Diverter Arms, Inc., 6520 Rampart St., Houston, TX 77036 (press. tool)
Herter's, Waseca, Minn. 56093
Micro-Sight Co., 242 Harbor Blvd., Belmont, Calif. 94002
Oehler Research, P.O. Box 9135, Austin, Tex. 78756
Sundtek Co., P.O. Box 744, Springfield, Ore. 97477
Telepacific Electronics Co., Inc., 3335 W. Orange Ave., Anaheim, CA 92804
M. York, 19381 Keymar Way, Gaithersburg, MD 20760 (press. tool)

CLEANING & REFINISHING SUPPLIES

ADSCO, Box 191, Ft. Kent, Me 04743 (stock finish)
Allied Products Co., 734 N. Leavitt, Chicago, Ill. 60612
Armite Labs., 1845 Randolph St., Los Angeles, CA 90001
Armoloy, 206 E. Daggett St., Ft Worth, TX 76104
Backus Co., 411 W. Water St., Smethport, Pa. 16749
Ber Big Enterprises, P.O. Box 291, Huntington, CA 90255
Birchwood-Casey Chem. Co., 7900 Fuller Rd., Eden Prairie, Minn. 55343
Bisonite Co., Inc., 2250 Military Rd., Tonawanda, NY 14150
Jim Brobst, 299 Poplar St., Hamburg, Pa 19526
Geo. Brothers, Great Barrington, Mass. 01230
Browning Arms, Rt. 4, Box 624-B, Arnold, Mo. 63010
J.M. Bucheimer Co., Airport Rd., Frederick, MD 21701
Bullet Pouch, Box 4285, Long Beach, Cal. 90804
Burnishine Prod. Co., 8140 N. Ridgeway, Skokie, Ill. 60076
C & R Distr. Corp., 449 E. 21st So., Salt Lake City, Utah 84115
Cherry Corners Mfg. Co., 11136 Congress Rd., Lodi, Ohio 44254
Chopie Mfg. Inc., 531 Copeland, La Crosse, Wis. 54601
Clenzoil Co., Box 1226, Sta. C, Canton, O. 44708
Dex-Kleen, Box 509, Des Moines, Ia. 50302 (gun wipers)
Dri-Slide, Inc., Industrial Park, Fremont, Mich. 49412
Forty-Five Ranch Enterpr., 119 S. Main St., Miami, Okla. 74354
Garcia Sptg. Arms Corp., 329 Alfred Ave., Teaneck, N.J. 07666
Gun-All Products, Box 244, Dowagiac, Mich. 49047
Percy Harms Corp., 7349 N. Hamlin, Skokie, Ill. 60076
Frank C. Hoppe Div., P.O. Box 97, Parkesburg, Pa 19365
Jet-Aer Corp., 100 Sixth Ave., Paterson, N.J. 07524 (blues & oils)

Knox Laboratories, 2335 S. Michigan Ave., Chicago, Ill. 60616
LPS Res. Labs. Inc., 2050 Cotner Ave., Los Angeles, Calif. 90025
Carl Lampert Co., 2639 So. 31st St., Milwaukee, Wis. 53215 (gun bags)
Liquid Wrench, Box 10628, Charlotte, N.C. 28201
Marble Arms Co., 420 Industrial Pk., Gladstone, Mich. 49837
Micro Sight Co., 242 Harbor Blvd., Belmont, Ca. 94002
Mill Run Prod., 1360 W. 9th, Cleveland, O. 44113
Mistic Metal Mover, Inc., R.R. 2, P.O. Box 336, Princeton, Ill 61356
Mitchell Chemical Co., Wampus Lane, Milford, CT 06460
New Method Mfg. Co., Box 175, Bradford, Pa. 16701
Northern Instruments, Inc., 4643 No. Chatsworth St., St. Paul, MN 55112
Numrich Arms Co., West Hurley, N.Y. 12491
Nutec, Box 1187, Wilmington, Del. 19899 (Dry-Lube)
Outers Laboratories, Box 37, Onalaska, Wis. 54650
Reardon Prod., 323 N. Main St., Roanoke, Ill. 61561
Reese Arms Co., R.R. 1, Colona, IL 61241
Rice Dry Film Gun Coatings, 1521-43rd St., West Palm Beach, FL 33407
Riel & Fuller, 423 Woodrow Ave., Dunkirk, N.Y. 14048
Rig Products Co., Box 279, Oregon, Ill. 61061
Rocket Chemical Co., Inc., 5390 Napa St., San Diego, Calif. 92110
Rusteprufe Labs., 605 Wolcott St., Sparta, Wis. 54656
Service Armament, 689 Bergen Blvd., Ridgefield, N.J. 07657
Sheldon's Inc., Box 508, Antigo, Wis. 54409
Silicote Corp., Box 359, Oshkosh, Wis. 54901
Silver Dollar Guns, P.O. Box 489, Franklin, NH 03235
A.D. Soucy, Box 191, Ft. Kent, Me. 04743
Southeastern Coatings, Bldg. 132, P.B.I. Airport, W. Palm Beach, Fla. 33406
Sportsmen's Labs., Inc., Box 732, Anoka, Minn. 55303 (Gun Life lube)
Surcon, Inc., P.O. Box 277, Zieglerville, Pa 19492
Testing Systems, Inc., 2832 Mt. Carmel, Glenside, PA 19038
Texas Platers Supply Co., 2453 W. Five Mile Parkway, Dallas, TX 75233
C.S. Van Gorden, 120 Tenth Ave., Eau Claire, Wis. 54701
WD-40 Co., 1061 Cudahy Pl., San Diego, Ca. 92110
W&W Mfg. Co., Box 365, Belton, Mo. 64012
Williams Gun Sight, 7389 Lapeer Rd., Davison, Mich. 48423

DECOYS

Carry-Lite, Inc., 3000 W. Clarke, Milwaukee, WI 53245
Deeks, Inc., P.O. Box 2309, Salt Lake City, UT 84114
G & H Decoy Mfg. Co., P.O. Box 937, Henryetta, OK 74437
Tex Wirtz Ent., Inc., 1925 Hubbard St., Chicago, IL 60622
Woodstream Corp., P.O. Box 327, Lititz, PA 17543

GUNS (Foreign)

Abercrombie & Fitch, Madison at 45th, New York, N.Y. 10017
American Import Co., 1167 Mission St., San Francisco, Calif 94103
Armoury Inc., Rte. 25, New Preston, Ct. 06777
Atlas Arms, Inc., 7952 Waukegan Rd., Niles, Ill 60648
Blumenfeld Co., 80 W. Virginia Ave., Memphis, Tenn. 38100
Browning, Rt. 4, Box 624-B, Arnold, Mo. 63010
Century Arms Co., 3-5 Federal St., St. Albans, Vt. 05478
Champlin Firearms, Inc., Box 3191, Enid, OK 73701 (Gebruder Merkel)
Connecticut Valley Arms Co., Candlewood Hill Rd., Higganum, CT 06441 (CVA)
Continental Arms Corp., 697 Fifth Ave., New York, N.Y. 10022
Daiwa, 14011 Normandie Ave., Gardena, CA 90247

Charles Daly, Inc., 10 South St., Ridgefield, Conn. 06877
Davidson Firearms Co., 2703 High Pt. Rd., Greensboro, N.C. 27403
Davis Gun Shop, 7213 Lee Highway, Falls Church, VA 22046 (Fanzoj, Ferlach; Spanish guns)
Dixie Gun Works, Inc., Hwy 51, South, Union City, Tenn. 38261
Firearms Center Inc. (FCI), 113 Spokane, Victoria, TX 77901
Firearms Imp. & Exp. Co., 2470 N.W. 21st St., Miami, Fla. 33142
Firearms International Corp., 515 Kerby Hill Rd., Washington, DC 20022
Flaig's Lodge, Millvale, Pa. 15209
J.L. Galef & Son, Inc., 85 Chambers, New York, N.Y. 10007
Garcia Sptg. Arms Corp., 329 Alfred Ave., Teaneck, N.J. 07666
Gevelot of Can. Ltd., Box 1593, Saskatoon, Sask., Canada
Hawes Firearms Co., 8224 Sunset Blvd., Los Angeles, Calif. 90046
A.D. Heller, Inc., Box 268, Grand Ave., Baldwin, NY 11510
Herter's, Waseca, Minn. 56093
Interarms Ltd., 10 Prince St., Alexandria, Va. 22313
Intercontinental Arms, 2222 Barry Ave., Los Angeles, Calif. 90064
International Firearms Co., Ltd., Montreal 1, Que., Canada
Ithaca Gun Co., Terrace Hill, Ithaca, N.Y. 14850
J-K Imports, Box 403, Novato, Cal. 94947 (Italian)
J.J. Jenkins, 462 Stanford Pl., Santa Barbara, CA 93105
Guy T. Jones Import Co., 905 Gervais St., Columbia, S. Car. 29201
Kassnar Imports, P.O. Box 3895, Harrisburg, PA 17105
Kleinguenther's, P.O. Box 1261, Seguin, TX 78155
Krieghoff Gun Co., P.O. Box 48-1367, Miami, FL 33148
L.A. Distributors, 4 Centre Market Pl., New York, N.Y. 10013
Marietta Replica Arms Co., 706½ Mongomery St., Marietta, OH 45750
Marketing Unlimited, Inc., 1 Ranch Rite Rd., Yakima, WN 98901
Marubeni America Corp., 200 Park Ave., New York, NY 10017
Mauser-Bauer Inc., 34577 Commerce Rd., Fraser, MI 48026
Musgrave Firearms, J.J. Sherban & Co., 2655 Harrison Ave., S.W., Canton, OH 44706
Navy Arms Co., 689 Bergen Blvd., Ridgefield, N.J. 07657
Pachmayr Gun Works, 1220 S. Grand Ave., Los Angeles, Calif 90015
Pacific Intl. Merch. Corp., 2215 "J" St., Sacramento, Ca 95816
Palmetto Imp., Inc., P.O. Box 4008, Columbia, SC 29204
Ed Paul Sptg. Goods, 172 Flatbush Ave., Brooklyn, N.Y. 11217
Premier Shotguns, 172 Flatbush Ave., Brooklyn, N.Y. 11217
Richland Arms Co., 321 W. Adrian St., Blissfield, Mich. 49228
Sanderson's, 724 W. Edgewater, Portage, Wis 53901
Savage Arms Corp., Westfield, Mass 01085
Service Armament, 689 Bergen Blvd., Ridgefield, N.J. 07657
Simmons Spec., Inc., 700 Rogers Rd., Olathe, Kans. 66061
Sloan's Sprtg. Goods, Inc., 10 South St., Ridgefield, Conn. 06877
Stoeger Arms Co., 55 Ruta Ct., S. Hackensack, N.J. 07606
Tradewinds, Inc., P.O. Box 1191, Tacoma, Wash. 98401
Twin City Sptg. Gds., 217 Ehrman Ave., Cincinnati, OH 45220
Universal Firearms Corp., 3746 E. 10th Ct., Hialeah, Fla. 33013
Universal Ordnance Co., Inc., P.O. Box 15723, Nashville, TN 37215 (Krieghoff combination guns)
Weatherby's, 2781 Firestone Blvd., So. Gate, Calif. 90280

GUNS & GUN PARTS, REPLICA AND ANTIQUE

Antique Gun Parts, Inc., 569 So. Braddock Ave., Pittsburgh, Pa. 15221 (ML)
Armoury Inc., Rte. 25, New Preston, Conn. 06777
Artistic Arms, Inc., Box 23, Hoagland, IN 46745
Bannerman, F., Box 126, Blue Point, Long Island, N.Y. 11715
Shelley Braverman, Athens, N.Y. 12015 (obsolete parts)
Carter Gun Works, 2211 Jefferson Pk. Ave., Charlottesville, Va 22903

Cornwall Bridge Gun Shop, P.O. Box 67, Cornwall Bridge, CT 06754 (parts)
R. MacDonald Champlin, P.O. Box 74, Stanyan Hill, Wentworth, N.H. 03282
Dixie Gun Works, Inc., Hwy 51, South, Union City, Tenn. 38261
Kindig's Log Cabin Sport Shop, R.D. 1, P.O. Box 275, Lodi, Ohio 44254
Lyman Gun Sight Products, Middlefield, CT 06455
Numrich Arms Co., West Hurley, N.Y. 12491
Replica Models, Inc., 610 Franklin St., Alexandria, VA 22314
S&S Firearms, 88-21 Aubrey Ave., Glendale, N.Y. 11227
C.H. Weisz, Box 311, Arlington, Va 22210

GUN PARTS, U.S. AND FOREIGN

Badger Shooter's Supply, Owen, Wisc. 54460
Shelley Braverman, Athens, N.Y. 12015
Philip R. Crouthamel, 817 E. Baltimore, E. Lansdowne, Pa 19050
Charles E. Duffy, Williams Lane, West Hurley, N.Y. 12491
Greeley Arms Co., Inc., 223 Little Falls Rd., Fairfield, N.J. 07006
Hunter's Haven, Zero Prince St., Alexandria, Va. 22314
Numrich Arms Co., West Hurley, N.Y. 12491
Pacific Intl. Merch. Corp., 2215 "J" St., Sacramento, Ca 95816
Reed & Co., Shokan, N.Y. 12481
Ruvel & Co., 3037 N. Clark, Chicago, IL 60614
Sarco, Inc., 192 Central, Stirling, N.J. 07980
Simms, 2801 J St., Sacramento, CA 95816
Triple-K Mfg. Co., 568-6th Ave., San Diego, CA 92101

GUNS, U.S.-made

Cumberland Arms, 1222 Oak Dr., Manchester, Tenn. 37355
Esopus Gun Works, Port Ewen, NY 12466
Firearms Imp. & Exp. Co., 2470 N.W. 21st. St., Miami, Fl 33142
Golden Age Arms Co., 657 High St., Worthington, O. 43085
Harrington & Richardson, Park Ave., Worcester, Mass. 01610
High Standard Mfg. Co., 1817 Dixwell Ave., Hamden, Conn. 06514
Intercontinental Arms, Inc., 2222 Barry Ave., Los Angeles, Ca 90064
Ithaca Gun Co., Ithaca, N.Y. 14850
Iver Johnson Arms & Cycle Works, Fitchburg, Mass. 01420
Ljutic Ind., Inc., P.O. Box 2117, Yakima, WA 98902
Marlin Firearms Co., 100 Kenna Dr., New Haven, Conn. 06473
O.F. Mossberg & Sons, Inc., 7 Grasso St., No. Haven, Conn 06473
W.L. Mowrey Gun Works, Inc., Box 28, Iowa Park, TX 76367
Navy Arms Co., 689 Bergen Blvd., Ridgefield, N.J. 07657
Numrich Arms Corp., W. Hurley, N.Y. 12491
Pedersen Custom Guns, Div. of O.F. Mossberg & Sons, Inc., 7 Grasso Ave., North Haven, CT 06473
Potomac Arms Corp., P.O. Box 35, Alexandria, Va 22313
Savage Arms Corp., Westfield, Mass. 01085
Sears, Roebuck & Co., 825 S. St. Louis, Chicago, Ill. 60607
Sturm, Ruger & Co., Southport, Conn. 06490
Tingle, 1125 Smithland Pike, Shelbyville, Ind. 46176
Universal Firearms Corp., 3746 E. 10th Ct., Hialeah, Fla. 33013
Ward's, 619 W. Chicago, Chicago, Ill. 60607
Weatherby's, 2781 E. Firestone Blvd., South Gate, Calif. 90280
Winchester Repeating Arms Co., New Haven, Conn. 06504

GUNSMITHS, CUSTOM

Abe Van Horn, 5124 Huntington Dr., Los Angeles, CA 90032
P.O. Ackley, 2235 Arbor Lane, Salt Lake City, UT 84117
Ahlman Cust. Gun Shop, R.R. 1, Box 20, Morristown, Minn. 55052
R.E. Anderson, 706 S. 23rd St., Laramie, Wyo. 82070
R.J. Anton, 1016 Riehl St., Waterloo, Ia. 50703
Bacon Creek Gun Shop, Cumberland Falls Rd., Corbin, Ky. 40701
Joe J. Balickie, 6108 Deerwood Pl., Raleigh, N.C. 27607
Barta's, Rte. 1, Box 129-A, Cato, Wis. 54206
Bayer's Gun Shop, 213 S. 2nd, Walla Walla, Wash. 99362
Bennett Gun Works, 561 Delaware Ave., Delmar, N.Y. 12054
Irvin L. Benson, Saganaga Lake, Pine Island Camp, Ontario, Canada
Gordon Bess, 708 River St., Canon City, Colo. 81212
Bruce Betts Gunsmith Co., 26 Rolla Gardens Dr., Rolla, Mo. 65401
John Bivins, Jr., 446 So. Main St., Winston-Salem, N.C. 27101
Edwin T. Blackburn, Jr., 474 E. McKinley, Sunnyvale, CA 94086
Boone Mountain Trading Post, Averyville Rd., St. Marys, Pa 15857
T.H. Boughton, 410 Stone Rd., Rochester, N.Y. 14616
Kay H. Bowles, Pinedale, Wyo. 82941
Breckheimers, Parish, NY 13131
L.H. Brown, Rte. 2, Airport Rd., Kalispell, Mont. 59901
George Bunch, 7735 Garrison Rd., Hyattsville, Md. 20784
Leo Bustani, P.O. Box 8125, W. Palm Beach, Fla. 33407
Gus Butterowe, 10121 Shoreview Rd., Dallas, Tex. 75238

Cameron's Guns, 16690 W. 11th Ave., Golden, Colo. 80401
Carpenter's Gun Works, Gunshop Rd., Box C, Plattekill, N.Y. 12568
Carter Gun Works, 2211 Jefferson Pk. Ave., Charlotteville, Va 22903
Cassell Gun Shop, 403 West Lane, Worland, Wyo. 82401
Ray Chalmers, 18 White Clay Dr., Newark, Del. 19711
N.C. Christakos, 2832 N. Austin, Chicago, IL 60634
Kenneth E. Clark, 18738 Highway 99, Madera, Calif. 93637
Cloward's Gun Shop, 4023 Aurora Ave., Seattle, WA 98102
Philip R. Crouthamel, 817 E. Baltimore, E. Lansdowne, Pa 19050
Jim Cuthbert, 715 S. 5th St., Coos Bay, Ore. 97420
Dahl's Gunshop, Rt. 2, Billings, Mont. 59101
Dave's Gun Shop, 3994 Potters Rd. West, Ionia, Mich 48846
Dee Davis, 5658 So. Mayfield, Chicago, Ill. 60638
Joe E. Dillen, 1206 Juanita S.W., Massillon, Ohio 44646
Dominic DiStefano, 4303 Friar Lane, Colorado Springs, CO 80907
Drumbore Gun Shop, 119 Center St. Lehighton, PA 18235
Charles Duffy, Williams Lane, W. Hurley, N.Y. 12491
Gerald D. Eisenhauer, Rte. 3, Twin Falls, Ida. 83301
Bill English, 4411 S.W. 100th, Seattle, Wash. 98146
Ken Eyster, 6441 Bishop Rd., Centerburg, O. 43011
N.B. Fashingbauer, Box 366, Lac Du Flambeau, Wis. 54538
The Fergusons, Temple Rd., New Ipswich, NH 03071
H.J. and L.A. Finn, 12565 Gratiot Ave., Detroit, MI 48205
Loxley Firth Firearms, 8563 Oswego Rd., R.D. 4, Baldwinsville, N.Y. 13027
Marshall F. Fish, Westport, N.Y. 12993
Jerry Fisher, 1244-4th Ave. West, Kalispell, Mont. 59901
Frazier's Custom Guns, Box 3, Tyler, WA 99035
Fred's Gun Shop, Box 725, Juneau, Alaska 99801
Frederick Gun Shop, 10 Elson Drive, Riverside, R.I. 02915
Fuller Gunshop, Copper Landing, Alaska 99572
Georgia Gun & Smith, 5170 Thistle Rd., Smyrna, GA 30080
Ed Gillman, 116 Upper High Crest Dr., R.F.D. 1, Butler, N.J. 07405
Dale Goens, Box 224, Cedar Crest, NM 87008
A.R. Goode, R.D. 1, Box 84, Thurmont, MD 21788
Griffin & Howe, 589-8th Ave., New York, N.Y. 10017
H & R Custom Gun Serv., 68 Passaic Dr., Hewitt, N.J. 07421
Paul Haberly, 2364 N. Neva, Chicago, IL 60635
Chas. E. Hammans, Box 788, Stuttgart, AR 72160
Harkrader's, 111 No. Franklin St., Christiansburg, VA 24073
Elden Harsh, Rt. 4, London, O. 43140
Rob't W. Hart & Son, 401 Montegomery St., Nescopeck, Pa. 18635
Hal Hartley, Box 147, Blairs Fork Rd., Lenoir, N.C. 28654
Hubert J. Hecht, 55 Rose Mead Circle, Sacramento, CA 95831
Edw. O. Hefti, 300 Fairview, College Sta., Tex. 77840
Iver Henriksen, 1211 So. 2nd, Missoula, Mont. 59801
Wm. Hobaugh, Box 657, Philipsburg, Mont. 59858
Richard Hodgson, 9081 Tahoe Lane, Boulder, Colo. 80301
Hoenig-Rodman, 853 So. Curtis Rd., Boise, ID 83705
Hollis Gun Shop, 917 Rex St., Carlsbad, N.M. 88220
Hurt's Specialty Gunsmithing, Box 1033, Muskogee, Okla. 74401
Independent Machine & Gun Shop, 1416 N. Hayes, Pocatello, Ida. 83201
Jackson's, Box 416, Selman City, TX 75689
Paul Jaeger, 211 Leedom, Jenkintown, Pa. 19046
J.J. Jenkins, 462 Stanford Pl., Santa Barbara, CA 93105
Jerry's Gun Shop, 9220 Ogden Ave., Brookfield, Ill. 60513
Jerry's Gun Shop, 1527 N. Graceland Ave., Appleton, Wis. 54911
Johnson's Gun Shop, 1316 N. Blackstone, Fresno, Calif. 93703
Kennedy Gun Shop, Rt. 6, Clarksville, Tenn. 37040
Monte Kennedy, P.O. Box 214, Kalispell, Mont. 59901
Kerr Sport Shop, Inc., 9584 Wilshire Blvd., Beverly Hills, Calif. 90212
Kess Arms Co., 12515 W. Lisbon Rd., Brookfield, Wis. 53005
Kesselring Gun Shop, 400 Pacific Hiway 99 No., Burlington, Wash. 98233
Knights Gun Store, Inc., 103 So. Jennings, Ft. Worth, Tex. 76104
Ward Koozer, Box 18, Walterville, Ore. 97489
R. Krieger & Sons, 34923 Gartiot, Mt. Clemens, Mich. 48043
Lacy's Gun Service, 1518A West Blvd., Charlotte, N.C. 28208
Sam Lair, 520 E. Beaver, Jenks, OK 74037
LanDav Custom Guns, 7213 Lee Highway, Falls Church, VA 22046
Harry Lawson Co., 3328 N. Richey Blvd., Tucson, Ariz. 85716
John G. Lawson, 1802 E. Columbia, Tacoma, Wa. 98404
Gene Lechner, 636 Jane N.E., Albuquerque, NM 87123
LeDel, Inc., Main and Commerce Sts., Cheswold, Del. 19936
Art LeFeuvre, 1003 Hazel Ave., Deerfield, Ill. 60015
LeFever Arms Co., R.D. 1, Lee Center, N.Y. 13363
Max J. Lindauer, R.R. 1, Box 114, Washington, Mo. 63090
Ljutic Ind., Box 2117, Yakima, WA 98902
Llanerch Gun Shop, 2800 Township Line, Upper Darby, Pa. 19083
Bill McGuire, Inc., 7749 15th Ave., N.W., Seattle, WA 98117

Pat B. McMillan, 1828 E. Campo Bello Dr., Phoenix, Ariz. 85022
R.J. Maberry, 511 So. K, Midland, Tex. 79701
Harold E. MacFarland, Star Route, Box 84, Cottonwood, Ariz. 86326
E.H. Martin, 937 S. Sheridan Blvd., Denver, CO 80226
Maryland Gun Exchange, R.D. 5, Rt. 40 W., Frederick, Md. 21701
Mashburn Arms Co., 1020 N.W. 6th St., Oklahoma City, OK 73102
Mathews & Son, 10224 S. Paramount Blvd., Downey, Calif. 90241
Middaugh's Nodak, 318 2nd St., Bismarck, N.D. 58501
C.D. Miller Guns, St. Onge, SD 57779
Earl Milliron, 1249 N.E. 166th Ave., Portland, Ore. 97230
Mills Custom Stocks, 401 N. Ellsworth, San Mateo, Calif. 94401
Mitchell's Gun Repair, Rt. 1, Perryville, Ark. 72126
Newman Gunshop, 119 Miller Rd., Agency, Ia. 52530
Nu-Line Guns, Inc., 3727 Jennings Rd., St. Louis, Mo. 63121
Oak Lawn Gun Shop, Inc., 9618 Southwest Hwy., Oak Lawn, Ill. 60453
Pachmayr Gun Works, 1220 S. Grand Ave., Los Angeles, Calif. 90015
Harry Pagett Gun Shop, 125 Water St., Milford, Ohio 45150
Charles J. Parkinson, 116 Wharncliffe Rd. So., London, Ont., Canada
Pendleton Gunshop, 1210 S.W. Haley Ave., Pendleton, Ore. 97801
C.R. Pedersen & Son, Ludington, Mich. 49431
Al Petersen, Box 8, Riverhurst, Sask., Canada SOH3P0
Gene Phipps, 10 Wood's Gap Rd., Floyd, Va. 24091
Purcell's Gunshop, 915 Main St., Boise, Idaho 83702
Ready Eddie's Gun Shop, 501 Van Spanje Ave., Michigan City, IN 46360
Marion Reed Gun Shop, 1522 Colorado, Bartlesville, Okla. 74003
Ridge Guncraft, Inc., 234 N. Tulane, Oak Ridge, Tenn. 37830
Carl Roth, P.O. Box 2593, Cheyenne, Wy 82001
Royal Arms, Inc., 10064 Bert Acosta, Santee, Calif. 92071
Murray F. Ruffino, Rt. 2, Milford, ME 04461
Sam's Gun Shop, 25 Squam Rd., Rockport, Mass. 01966
Sanders Custom Gun Serv., 2358 Tyler Lane, Louisville, Ky 40205
Sandy's Custom Gunshop, Rockport, Ill. 62370
Saratoga Arms Co., R.D. 3, Box 387, Pottstown, Pa 19464
Roy V. Schaefer, 965 W. Hilliard Lane, Eugene, Ore 97402
George Schielke, Washington Crossing, Titusville, N.J. 08560
N.H. Schiffman Cust. Gun Serv., 963 Malibu, Pocatello, ID 83201
Schumaker's Gun Shop, 208 W. 5th Ave., Colville, Wash 99114
Schwab Gun Shop, 1103 E. Bigelow, Findlay, O. 45840
Schwartz Custom Guns, 9621 Coleman Rd., Haslett, Mich. 48840
Schwartz's Gun Shop, 41-15th St., Wellsburg, W. Va. 26070
Jim Scott, Hiway 2-East, Leon, IA 50144
Scotty's Gun Shop, Second and Rancier, Killeen, TX 76541
Joseph M. Seliner, 1010 Stelton Rd., Piscataway, N.J. 08854
Shaw's, 1655 S. Euclid Ave., Anaheim, Calif. 92802
Harold H. Shockley, Box 355, Hanna City, Ill. 65126 (hot bluing & plating)
Walter Shultz, R.D. 3, Pottstown, Pa 19464
Simmons Gun Spec., 700 Rogers Rd., Olathe, Kans. 66061
Simms Hardward Co., 2801 J St., Sacramento, Calif. 95816
Skinner's Gun Shop, Box 30, Juneau, Alaska 98801
Markus Skosples, 40 Ziffren Sptg. Gda., 124 E. Third St., Davenport, IA 52801
Jerome F. Slezak, 1290 Marlowe, Lakewood (Cleveland), OH 44107
John Smith, 912 Lincoln, Carpentersville, Ill. 60110
K.E. Smith, 8766 Los Choches Rd., Lakeside, Calif. 92040
Smitty's Gunshop, 308 S. Washington, Lake City, Minn. 55041
Snapp's Gunshop, 6911 E. Washington Rd., Clare, Mich. 48617
Eddie Sowers, 8331 De Celis, Sepulveda, CA 91343
Sportsman's Den, 1010 Stelton Rd., Piscataway, N.J. 08854
Sportsmens Equip. Co., 915 W. Washington, San Diego, Calif. 92103
Jess L. Stark, 12051 Stroud, Houston, TX 77072
Ikey Starks, 1058 Grand Ave., So. San Francisco, Calif 94080
Keith Stegall, Box 696, Gunnison, Colo. 81230
W.C. Strutz, Rte. 1, Eagle River, WI 54521
Suter's House of Guns, 332 N. Tejon, Colorado Springs, Colo 80902
Swanson Custom Firearms, 1051 Broadway, Denver, Colo. 80203
T-P Shop, 212 E. Houghton, West Branch, Mich. 48661
Talmage Ent., 1309 W. 12th St., Long Beach, Calif. 90813
Taylor & Robbins, Box 164, Rixford Pa. 16745
Daniel Titus, 119 Morlyn Ave., Bryn Mawr. PA 19010
Tom's Gunshop, 600 Albert Pike, Hot Springs, Ark. 71901
Dave Trevallion, 3442 S. Post Rd., Indianapolis, IN 46239
Trinko's Gun Serv., 1406 E. Main, Watertown, Wis. 53094
C. Hunt Turner, 618 S. Grove, Webster Groves, Mo. 63119
Upper Missouri Trading Co., Inc., Box 181, Crofton, MO 68730
Roy Vail, R. 1, Box 8, Warwick, N.Y. 10990
J.W. Van Patten, Box 145, Foster Hill, Milford, Pa 18337
Herman Waldron, Box 475, Pomeroy, WN 99437 (metalsmithing)

Walker Arms Co., R.2, Box 38, Selma, Ala. 36701
Harold Waller, 1288 Camillo Way, El Cajon, CA 99347
R.A. Wardrop, Box 245, Mechanicsburg, Pa. 17055
Weatherby's, 2781 Firestone Blvd., South Gate, Calif. 90280
Wells Sport Store, 110 N. Summit St., Prescott, Ariz. 86301
R.A. Wells, 3452 N. 1st, Racine, Wis. 53402
Robert G. West, 6626 S. Lincoln, Littleton, Colo. 80120
Western Stocks & Guns, 2206 E. 11th, Bremerton, Wash. 98310
M.C. Wiest, 234 N. Tulane Ave., Oak Ridge, Tenn. 37830
W.C. Wilber, 400 Lucerne Dr., Spartanburg, SC 29302
Williams Gun Sight Co., 7389 Lapeer Rd., Davison, Mich. 48423
Lou Williamson, 129 Stonegate Ct., Bedford, TX 76021
Wilson Gun Store Inc., R.D. 1, Rte. 225, Dauphin, Pa 17018
Robert M. Winter, Box 484, Menno, SD 57045
Lester Womack, Box 17210, Tucson, AZ 85710
W.H. Womack, 2124 Meriwether Rd., Shreveport, La 71108
York County Gun Works, RR 4, Tottenham, Ont. Canada
Russ Zeeryp, 1601 Foard Dr., Lynn Ross Manor, Morristown, TN 37814
R.E. Zelimer, W180 N8996 Leona Ln. Menomonee Falls, WI 53051

HEARING PROTECTORS

American Optical Corp., Mechanic St., Southbridge, Mass. 01550 (ear valve)
Bausch & Lomb, 635 St. Paul St., Rochester, N.Y. 14602
David Clark Co., 360 Franklin St., Worcester, Mass. 01604
Curtis Safety Prod. Co., Box 61, Webster Sq. Sta., Worcester, Mass. 01603 (ear valve)
Hodgdon, 7710 W. 50 Hiway, Shawnee Mission, Kans. 66202
Sigma Eng. Co., 11320 Burbank Blvd., No. Hollywood, Ca 91601 (Lee-Sonic ear valve)
Sellstrom Mfg. Co., Sellstrom Industrial Park, Palatine, IL 60067
Smith & Wesson, 2100 Roosevelt Ave., Springfield, MA 01101
Vector Scientific, P.O. Box 21106, Ft. Lauderdale, FL 33315
Wilson Prods. Div., P.O. Box 622, Reading, Pa 19603 (Ray-O-Vac)

RELOADING TOOLS AND ACCESSORIES

Alcan, (See: Smith & Wesson Arms Co.)
Anchor Alloys, Inc., 966 Meeker Ave., Brooklyn, N.Y. 11222 (chilled shot)
Anderson Mfg. Co., Royal, Ia. 51357 (shotshell trimmers)
Bair Machine Co., Box 4407, Lincoln, Neb. 68504
Belding & Mull, P.O. Box 428, Phillipsburg, Pa 16866
Bonanza Sports, Inc., 412 Western Ave., Faribault, Minn 55021
Cascade Cartridge, Inc., (See: Omark)
Division Lead Co., 7742 W. 61st Pl., Summit, Ill 60502
Farmer Bros. Mfg. Co., 1102 Washington St., Eldora, IA 50627
Flambeau Plastics, 801 Lynn, Baraboo, Wis. 53913
Forster-Appelt Mfg. Co., Inc., 82 E. Lanark Ave., Lanark, Ill. 61046
Gopher Shooter's Supply, Box 246, Faribault, Minn. 55021
Ed Hart, U.S. Rte. 15 No., Bath, NY 14810 (Meyer shotgun slugs)
Herter's Inc., RR1, Waseca, Minn. 56093
B.E. Hodgdon, Inc., 7710 W. 50 Hiway, Shawnee Mission, Kans. 66202
Hollywood Reloading, See: Whitney Sales, Inc.
Hunter Bradlee Co., 2800 Routh St., Dallas, TX 75201 (powder measure)
JASCO, Box 49751, Los Angeles, Calif 90049
Kush Plastics, P.O. Box 366, Palatine, IL 60067 (shotshell wads)
Lachmiller Eng. Co., 11273 Goss St., Sun Valley, CA 91352
Lage universal shotshell wad, See: Farmer Bros.
Lee Custom Engineering, 21 E. Wisconsin St., Hartford, WI 53027 (Lee Loader kits)
Ljutic Industries, 918 N. 5th Ave., Yakima, Wash. 98902
Lyman Products For Shooters, Route 147, Middlefield, Conn. 06455
MTM Molded Prod., 5680 Webster St., Dayton, OH 45414
Mayville Eng. Co., 715 South St., Mayville, Wis 53050 (MEC shotshell loader)
Murdock Lead Co., Box 5298, Dallas, Tex. 75222
National Lead Co., Box 831, Perth Amboy, N.J. 08861
Normington Co., Box 6, Rathdrum, Ida 83858 (powder baffles)
Ohaus Scale Corp., 29 Hanover Rd., Florham Park, N.J. 07932
Omark-CCI, Inc., Box 856, Lewiston, Ida. 83501
Pacific Tool Co., P.O. Drawer 2048, Ordnance Plant Rd., Grand Island, NB 68801
Pattern Perfect, P.O. Box 366, Palatine, IL 60067 (shotshell wads)
Personal Firearms Record Book, Box 201, Park Ridge, Ill. 60068
Ponsness-Warren, Inc., P.O. Box 861, Eugene, OR 97401

RCBS, Inc., Box 1919, Oroville, Calif 95965
Redding-Hunter, Inc., 114 Starr Rd., Cortland, N.Y. 13045
Remco, 1404 Witesboro St., Utica, N.Y. 13502 (shot caps)
Ruhr-American Corp., So. East Hwy. 55, Glenwood, Minn. 56334
SAECO Rel. Inc., P.O. Box 778, Carpinteria, Calif. 93013
Smith & Wesson Ammunition Co., Inc., 3640 Seminary Rd., Alton, IL 62002
J.A. Somers Co., P.O. Box 49751, Los Angeles, CA 90049 (Jasco)
Texan Reloaders, Inc., P.O. Box 5355, Dallas, Tex 75222
Webster Scale Mfg. Co., Box 188, Sebring, Fla. 33870
Whitney Cartridge Co., P.O. Box 608, Cortez, CO 81321 (shotshells)
Whitney Sales, Inc., Box 875, Reseda, CA 91335 (Hollywood)
Xelex, Ltd., Hawksbury, Ont., Canada (powder)

STOCKS (Commercial and Custom)

Abe-Van Horn, 5124 Huntington Dr., Los Angeles, CA 90032
Adams Custom Gun Stocks, 13461 Quito Rd., Saratoga, CA 95070
Ahlman's Inc., R.R. 1, Box 20, Morristown, MN 55052
Akro-Eez Gunstocks, Box 687, Tonopah, NV 89049
R.E. Anderson, 706 So. 23rd St., Laramie, Wyo. 82070
Dale P. Andrews, 3572 E. Davies, Littleton, Colo. 80122
R.J. Anton, 1016 Riehl St., Waterloo, Ia. 50703
Austrian Gunworks Reg'd., P.O. Box 136, Eastman, Que., Canada
Jim Baiar, Rt. 1-B, Box 352, Columbia Falls, Mont. 59912
Joe J. Balickie, Custom Stocks, 6108 Deerwood Pl., Raleigh, N.C. 27607
Bartas, Rte. 1, Box 129-A, Cato, Wis. 54206
Al Biesen, West 2039 Sinto Ave., Spokane, Wash. 99201
E.C. Bishop & Son Inc., Box 7, Warsaw, Mo. 65355
Nate Bishop, Box 334, Minturn, CO 81645
Kay H. Bowles, Pinedale, Wyo. 82941
Brown Precision Co., 5869 Indian Ave., San Jose, CA 95123
Lenard M. Brownell, Box 25, Wyarno, WY 82845
Calico Hardwoods, Inc., 1648 Airport Blvd., Windsor, Calif 95492
Dick Campbell, 1445 So. Meade, Denver, Colo. 80219
Cloward's Gun Shop, 4023 Aurora Ave., Seattle, WA 98102
Mike Conner, Box 208, Tijeras, NM 87059
Crane Creek Gun Stock Co., 25 Shephard Terr., Madison, WI 53705
Charles De Veto, 1087 Irene Rd., Lyndhurst, O. 44124
Custom Gunstocks, 1445 So. Meade, Denver, Colo. 80219
Reinhart Fajen, Box 338, Warsaw, Mo. 65355
N.B. Fashingbauer, Box 366, Lac Du Flambeau, Wis. 54538
Ted Fellowes, Beaver Lodge, 9245 16th Ave. S.W., Seattle, Wash. 98106
Clyde E. Fisher, Rt. 1, Box 170-M, Victoria, Tex 77901
Jerry Fisher, 1244-4th Ave. W., Kalispell, MT 59901
Flaig's Lodge, Millvale, Pa. 15209
Horace M. Frantz, Box 128, Farmingdale, N.J. 07727
Aaron T. Gates, 3229 Felton St., San Diego, Calif. 92104
Dale Goens, Box 224, Cedar Crest, N.M. 87008
Gould's Myrtlewood, 1692 N. Dogwood, Coquille, Ore. 97423 (gun blanks)
Rolf R. Gruning, 315 Busby Dr., San Antonio, Tex. 78209
Gunstocks-Rarewoods, Haleiwa, Hawaii 97612
Hank's Stock Shop, 1078 Alice Ave., Ukiah, Calif. 95482
Harper's Custom Stocks, 928 Lombrano St., San Antonio, Tex. 78207
Harris Gun Stocks, Inc., 12 Lake St., Richfield Springs, N.Y. 13439
Elden Harsh, Rt. 4, London, O. 43140
Hal Hartley, Box 147, Blairsfork Rd., Lenoir, N.C. 28654
Hayes Gunstock Service Co., 914 E. Turner St., Clearwater, Fla. 33516
Hubert J. Hecht, 55 Rose Mead Circle, Sacramento, CA 95831
Edward O. Hefti, 300 Fairview, College Sta., Tex. 77840
Herter's Inc., Waseca, Minn. 56093

Klaus Hiptmayer, P.O. Box 136, Eastman, Que., Canada
Richard Hodgson, 9081 Tahoe Lane, Boulder, CO 80301
Hollis Gun Shop, 917 Rex St., Carlsbad, N.M. 88220
Jack's Walnut Woods, 10333 San Fernando Rd., Pacoima, CA 91331
I.D. Johnson, Rt. 1, Strawberry Point, Ia. 52076 (blanks)
Johnson's Gun Shop, 1316 N. Blackstone, Fresno, CA 93703
Monte Kennedy, P.O. Box 214, Kalispell, Mont. 59901
Leer's Gun Barn, Rt. 3, Sycamore Hills, Elwood, Ind. 46036
LeFever Arms Co., Inc., R.D. 1, Lee Center, N.Y. 13363
Bill McGuire, Inc., 7749-15th Ave. N.W., Seattle, WA 98117
Maryland Gun Exchange, R.D. 5, Rt. 40 W., Frederick, Md. 21701
Maurer Arms, 2366 Frederick Dr., Cuyahoga Falls, O. 44221
Leonard Mews, R.2, Box 242, Hortonville, WI 54944
Robt. U. Milhoan & Son, Rt. 3, Elizabeth, W. Va. 26143
C.D. Miller Guns, St. Onge, S.D. 57779
Mills (D.H.) Custom Stocks, 401 N. Ellsworth Ave., San Mateo, Calif. 94401
Nelsen's Gun Shop, 501 S. Wilson, Olympia, Wash. 98501
Oakley and Merkley, Box 2446, Sacramento, Calif. 95811 (blanks)
Ernest O. Paulsen, Rte. 71, Box 11, Chinook, Mont. 59523 (blanks)
Peterson Mach. Carving, Box 1065, Sun Valley, Calif. 91352
Andrew Redmond, Inc., No. Anson, Me 04958 (birchwood blanks)
Richards Micro-Fit Stocks, P.O. Box 1066, Sun Valley, CA 91352
Roberts Wood Prod., 1400 Melody Rd., Marysville, Calif 95901
Carl Roth, Jr., P.O. Box 2593, Cheyenne, Wy. 82001
Royal Arms, Inc., 10064 Bert Acosta Ct., Santee, Calif. 92071
Sanders Cust. Gun Serv., 2358 Tyler Lane, Louisville, Ky. 40205 (blanks)
Saratoga Arms Co., R.D. 3, Box 387, Pottstown, Pa. 19464
Roy Schaefer, 965 W. Hilliard Lane, Eugene, Ore. 97402 (blanks)
Shaw's, 1655 S. Euclid Ave., Anaheim, Calif. 92802
Walter Shultz, R.D. 3, Pottstown, Pa 19464
Sile Dist., 7 Centre Market Pl., New York, N.Y. 10013
Ed Sowers, 8331 DeCelis Pl., Sepulveda, Calif. 91343
Keith Stegall, Box 696, Gunnison, Colo. 81230
Swanson Cust. Firearms, 1051 Broadway, Denver, Colo. 80203
Talmage Enterpr., 1309 W. 12 St., Long Beach, Ca 90813
D.W. Thomas, Box 184, Vineland, N.J. 08360
Trevallion Gunstocks, 3442 S. Post Rd., Indianapolis, IN 46239
Brent L. Umberger, R.R. 4, Cambridge, OH 43725
Roy Vail, Rt. 1, Box 8, Warwick, N.Y. 10990
Harold Waller, 1288 Camillo Way, El Cajon, CA 92021
Weatherby's, 2781 Firestone, South Gate, Calif. 90280
Western Stocks & Guns, Inc., 2206 E. 11th, Bremerton, Wash. 98311
Joe White, Box 8505, New Brighton, Christchurch, N.Z. (blanks)
Williams Gunsmithing, 1706 Rocklynn, Fullerton, CA 92631
Lou Williamson, 129 Stonegate Ct., Bedford, TX 76021
Robert M. Winter, Box 484, Menno, S.D. 57045
Fred Wranic, 6919 Santa Fe, Huntington Park, Calif. 90255 (mesquite)
Paul Wright, 4504 W. Washington Blvd., Los Angeles, Calif. 90016

TRAP & SKEET SHOOTERS EQUIP.

Creed Enterprises, P.O. Box 3029, Arcadia, CA 91006
Filmat Ent., Inc., 200 Market St., East Paterson, NJ 07407
The I and I Co., 709 12th St., Altoona, PA 16601
Old Mill Trap & Skeet, 300 Mill Ridge Rd., Secaucus, NJ 07094
Outers Laboratories, Inc., P.O. Box 37, Onalaska, WI 54650
Remington Arms Co., Bridgeport, CT 06602
Safe-T-Shell, Inc., 4361 Woodhall Rd., Columbus, OH 43221
Trius Products, Box 25, Cleves, OH 45002
Daniel Titus, 119 Morlyn Ave., Bryn Mawr, PA 19010
Winchester-Western, New Haven, CT 06504